The Music of Sp

The Music of Space

Scoring the Cosmos in Film and Television

CHRIS CARBERRY

Foreword by Nami Melumad

McFarland & Company, Inc., Publishers

Jefferson, North Carolina

LIBRARY OF CONGRESS CATALOGUING-IN-PUBLICATION DATA

Names: Carberry, Chris, 1968– author. | Melumad, Nami, 1988– writer of foreword.
Title: The music of space : scoring the cosmos in film and television / Chris Carberry ;
    foreword by Nami Melumad.
Description: Jefferson : McFarland & Company, Inc., Publishers, 2024. |
    Includes bibliographical references and index.
Identifiers: LCCN 2024003157 | ISBN 9781476688978 (paperback : acid free paper) ∞
    ISBN 9781476651460 (ebook)
Subjects: LCSH: Motion picture music—History and criticism. | Science fiction films—
    History and criticism. | Science fiction television programs—History and criticism. |
    Star Trek television programs. | Star Trek films. | Star Wars films. | Space flights
    in motion pictures. | Outer space in motion pictures. | BISAC: MUSIC / General |
    PERFORMING ARTS / Television / History & Criticism
Classification: LCC ML2075 .C358 2024 | DDC 781.5/42—dc23/eng/20240122
LC record available at https://lccn.loc.gov/2024003157

BRITISH LIBRARY CATALOGUING DATA ARE AVAILABLE

ISBN (print) 978-1-4766-8897-8
ISBN (ebook) 978-1-4766-5146-0

Front cover: Key art of the Mothership from the 1977 film
Close Encounters of the Third Kind (Columbia Pictures/Photofest)

Printed in the United States of America

McFarland & Company, Inc., Publishers
Box 611, Jefferson, North Carolina 28640
www.mcfarlandpub.com

For Heather, Maddy and Lucie

Table of Contents

Acknowledgments

This book was an extraordinary journey that progressed during one of the most challenging periods in history, as humanity contended with the COVID-19 pandemic. I would like to thank the extraordinary medical professionals, first responders, scientists and other "essential personnel" who often risked their lives to guide us through this ongoing crisis.

The pandemic also heightened my appreciation for the film and television industry. While movie theaters were closed for many months, movies and television were an essential ingredient in maintaining our collective sanity through months of isolation from the workplace and ordinary human interaction.

This book would not have been possible without the help and support of dozens of individuals and organizations. First, I would like to thank my wife Heather Carberry for her extraordinary editing of this book. I would also like to thank Amy Imhoff for her expertise in proofreading the manuscript, and my daughter Maddy Carberry for her expert citation preparation. Thank you to Ron Sparkman for his assistance collecting imagery.

I would also like to thank my employer, the remarkable space exploration non-profit Explore Mars, Inc., for giving me the flexibility to research and write this volume.

I had the pleasure of conducting interviews with, and receiving valuable feedback from, the following composers, producers, directors, journalists and other experts: Paul Apelgren, David Arnold, Emilio Audissino, Rick Berman, Howard Blake, Jeff Bond, Bruce Broughton, Sam Burbank, Jon Burlingame, Jay Chattaway, Cady Coleman, Emil de Cou, Ann Druyan, Greg Edmonson, Cliff Eidelman, Jonathan Frakes, Justin Freer, Michael Giacchino, David Green, Harry Gregson-Williams, Tim Greiving, Chris Hadfield, Marc Hartzman, Natalie Holt, Ron Jones, Kevin Kiner, Peter Lauritson, Dennis McCarthy, Bear McCreary, Jim McGrath,

Joel McNeely, Nami Melumad, Nicholas Meyer, Glen Morgan, David Newman, Robert Picardo, Stu Phillips, Sian Proctor, Jeff Russo, Craig Safan, Felipe Pérez Santiago, Clinton Shorter, Siu-Lan Tan, Neil deGrasse Tyson, Bert Ulrich and Tim Welch. Lastly, I would like to thank Charlie Perdue and the staff of McFarland.

Foreword
by Nami Melumad

"I've learned that people will forget what you said, people will forget what you did, but people will never forget how you made them feel."—Maya Angelou

As a film and television composer, you're tasked with making people feel and relate to the drama on screen. You'll create sonic soundscapes that support the story and memorable melodies that (you hope) will enhance the viewer's emotional connection with the characters. You'll shape each and every scene, as well as the overall story arc. You'll build emotional climaxes, set up jokes, make breakups even more heartbreaking, make chase scenes and fight scenes more exciting, and help the audience experience the same fear and hope that the characters experience. Sometimes you'll add a sense of danger, or hint at story elements that aren't being told visually. In the sci-fi genre, you'll also transport the audience to other dimensions, distant planets and alternative realities. This book will help you better understand the role of music in sci-fi storytelling, and also tell you how we do it.

On a personal note, stories about space fascinated me from a very young age. I was about 12 when I encountered a documentary about the race to the moon, and I remember being absolutely taken with it: the bravery, the stakes, the determination and the will to know what's out there. I started taking an interest in astronomy. On our first date, a boyfriend invited me to watch *Star Wars: Attack of the Clones*. I had no idea that this movie would make such a big impact on me, but I was absolutely wowed by John Williams' score that echoed in the theater long after the credits rolled. It was there and then that I became a sci-fi fan. Twenty-two years later, I still feel transformed when I hear this music.

Space has been an inclusive place for nerds like me: Between the alien planets and the different species living on them, the misfit crews and the tireless rebels, I felt right at home. It allowed me to hope, and to believe that small actions can make a difference. In the sheer vastness of it all, space stories have a way of capturing one's imagination, a way of inspiring us to dream big. They show us grit and determination and the promise of a better future. They show us the courage to dare, to ask questions about the universe and about our own human nature, too. You can say that music plays a huge part in making these stories so impactful on the viewer.

Space: the final frontier. It stands for endless possibilities not just for humankind, but also for storytelling and music. Those two come together like a package deal, as music in sci-fi has played a key role in bringing the mysteries and wonders of the cosmos to life. Some of the most iconic scores of our time have been written for sci-fi works. In space, we can explore strange new textures, seek out new instruments (or new uses for traditional ones), and go where music has never gone before. For example, Hans Zimmer's captivating compositions for *Interstellar,* featuring an organ. (Fun fact: This score has found its way to the temp tracks of many projects I've worked on.)

These scores have not only shaped new melodies, new harmonies and new instrumentation, they also shaped an entire generation of thinkers who dare to imagine: engineers, biologists, astrophysicists, mathematicians, teachers, filmmakers and storytellers. All share the same passion and curiosity inspired by the sci-fi stories we love.

Writing is hard, even for authors who do it all the time. I know this first-hand from my experience writing music for film and television: finding the right tone, being creative with a deadline in mind, and overcoming self-doubts. Writing is a challenge that starts on a blank page, no matter how many times you've done it. That's why I'm so proud of my friend Chris Carberry, whose tireless work made this exceptional book possible. Chris has been involved as a leader in the space community for a long time now. He is the co-founder and CEO of Explore Mars, Inc., a non-profit created to advance the goal of sending humans to Mars, and also to instill a desire to pursue space exploration for future generations via STEM curriculum. Chris is also an accomplished writer who has authored over 100 articles and op-ed pieces concerning space policy and politics. He contributed positioning work for the Republican Party's National Platform in 2000 and even testified before Congress two times. Chris' fascination with sci-fi music has led him to write this unique book that brings sci-fi music to the forefront, and I'm very grateful for his knowledge, effort and appreciation of the subject.

This book delves into the creation and impact of musical scores in science fiction, showcasing the creativity and innovation of composers and the role of music in shaping our perceptions of the iconic works we all admire. It features a large variety of interviews with some of today's leading composers, whose works I personally find inspiring. The conversations delve not only into the composition process and creative approach of each composer but also provide a unique look into the technical prowess behind these musical scores, storytelling decisions and fun anecdotes from behind the screen (or ... behind the scoring stage!). The insights presented are simply invaluable, as readers will gain a deeper understanding of the artistry behind these scores.

I hope that this book inspires a new generation of composers, storytellers and sci-fi fans to explore the possibilities of their respective fields and push the boundaries of what is possible. As you delve into this book, I encourage you to listen to your favorite sci-fi scores and allow yourself to be transported to a galaxy far far away...

Whether you are an aspiring musician, an experienced composer, a sci-fi fanatic or just someone who gets inspired staring up at the stars and considering all the endless possibilities: May this book ignite your imagination and inspire you to boldly go where no one has gone before.

Nami Melumad is an award-winning composer of music for Star Trek: Strange New Worlds; Star Trek: Prodigy; Thor: Love and Thunder; *and numerous other films, television shows and videogames.*

Introduction

"Music is the magic dust of movies!"—George Lucas[1]

Since the early days of motion picture production, film scores have helped define our emotional and aesthetic perception of stories of innumerable genres. For example, just a few notes from the score for *The Good, the Bad and the Ugly* conjures images of cowboys and the American "wild west" in the minds of people around the world, even if they do not know the origin of the music.

This phenomenon is particularly true with space-related films and television. The music from such productions as *The Day the Earth Stood Still*, *2001: A Space Odyssey*, *Star Wars*, *Star Trek*, *Interstellar* and *Battlestar Galactica* have helped define the public's enthusiasm about space almost as much as the films themselves. In some cases, they have redefined the norms of film music. *Star Wars* not only revived the popularity of orchestral film scores but also helped stimulate public interest in classical orchestral music.

The musical score plays a substantial role in filmmaking. Imagine for a moment that you are sitting in a movie theater (or on your couch) and *Star Wars* or *2001: A Space Odyssey* begins. Instead of the rousing musical pieces that are synonymous with these films, there is just silence or the sound of special effects as the opening title sequence appears upon the screen. These sequences would be greatly diminished or seem sterile and flat. However, it is not just the opening burst of energy that relies on the magic of music to elevate a motion picture. Musical scores direct our emotions, can serve as a surrogate for things that are not seen on screen, or even compensate for shortcomings in the film. Anyone who has watched *Jaws*, *Star Trek: The Motion Picture* or *Star Wars* with the sound turned down knows how vital the music is to those films. Without their engaging musical scores, each of these films would be greatly diminished; or in some cases might have failed. In *Jaws*, the music literally serves as a

4

surrogate for the shark during a substantial portion of the film. Without the music, the movie does not work.

Film production and music have had a symbiotic relationship. Film scores help define characters and emotions as well as driving the narrative rhythm of a movie. According to music psychologist Dr. Siu-Lan Tan, "Music plays a key role in the power of a film to hold us in its grip: to absorb, to transport, to intensify emotion and accent action, to direct attention, to frame scenes and set our expectations, and to shape our impressions of the characters and storyline, often without our conscious awareness."[2]

Whether a film is space-related, an Earth-based drama or another genre, music plays a critical role, often equal to the actors, plots and sets, in creating the "magic" of filmmaking. The role of film scoring is distinct from any other genre or medium of music. The primary role of film music is *not* to stand alone. It is not composed for its own sake. According to musicologist Maurizio Caschetto, "Film-music is 'applied art' first and foremost, a discipline that must serve a greater purpose. At its most successful and well-executed, film-music fulfills all the needs of storytelling, while also functioning as an emotional trigger for the audience."[3]

Film music is often most effective when it is only heard on the subconscious level, as it helps manipulate the emotions of audience members, provides clues regarding the plot, or creates a sense of mood or nostalgia, a sense of closure, or even a lack of closure. According to film historian Leonard Maltin, "Music has the ability to shape, and in some cases, alter or even subvert what the filmmaker is communicating."[4]

In many regards, film music is the most mysterious part of filmmaking, particularly when that art form is done well. In trying to explain the role, impact and mystery of his *Star Wars* scores, John Williams stated, "I wish I could explain that. But maybe the combination of the audio and the visual hitting people in that way—that it [speaks] to some collective memory ... that we don't quite understand. Some memory of Buck Rogers or King Arthur or something earlier in the cultural salts of our brains...."[5]

Psychologists and neurologists have studied the question of how music is interpreted by the brain, and also how it is applied in films. Specifically, it is how the musical additions to film or television helps to convey emotions and often trick or coax the brain into believing something good or bad that is inevitable. Imagine a scene where a young woman is walking through a meadow of flowers. The scene is inherently pleasant—and can be amplified by uplifting music. However, if foreboding or creepy music is applied to the same scene, the audience will instantly assume that the young woman is in danger.

Music can also have a physical impact on the body. It stimulates parts of the brain associated with pleasure and excitement. "We are having some sort of a physiological response, that the body is showing, and the goosebumps is actually just a sign of what's happening inside your body," said Dr. Tan. "It's interesting because the same kinds of pleasurable feelings we get from chocolate, dopamine release, we could see some of the same kinds of activations in the brain to music."[6] Even though a musical soundtrack is not present in real life, the lack of music in a film or TV series can often make them sound and feel unnatural, as though they lacked emotion and momentum. Noted film composer Lawrence Rosenthal echoed this: "Total silence is an unnatural vacuum in a film. The ear seems to insist on filling it—whether with a few harp notes, the rustle of clothing, or human voice."[7]

Influences

Film music has been inspired by styles of music from around the world. In addition to western classical music, as motion picture production progressed, films have utilized such music genres as jazz, folk, rock, country, avant-garde, swing, non-western and pop. Alex Ross of *The New Yorker* notes that film scores have "gone through several phases, which might be called the Romantic, the jazz-modern, the pop-avant, the neo-Romantic, and the pop-synthetic," but the consistent staple of the art form has been Romantic and late Romantic orchestral music. "The heyday of the Romantic period [in film music] was the nineteen-thirties, when émigré composers such as Steiner and Erich Wolfgang Korngold specialized in post–Wagnerian opulence."[8]

There can be little argument that classical composers of the Romantic period played a more significant role in influencing film scoring than any other genre of music. Composers Richard Wagner, Gustav Holst, Richard Strauss, Antonín Dvořák and many others established the musical model embraced by such early film composers as Korngold, Max Steiner and Alfred Newman. Many of the norms of film composition are still firmly in place today.

More recent classical orchestral composers have also played a significant role. Musical references to the modernistic Russian composer Igor Stravinsky can be heard in many musical scores of the past century, including *Star Wars*. Avant-garde composer György Ligeti became influential in film music starting in the 1960s, with his pieces utilized in *2001: A Space Odyssey* and references to his works in *Close Encounters of the Third Kind*.

Scoring Space

Countless volumes have been written about the motion picture industry as well as the music and composers which have symbiotically partnered with that industry. However, this will be the first book specifically examining the history and impact of music in space-related film and television; and how that music influenced our perspective of "the sound of space."

The purpose of this book is not to provide a detailed analysis of *every* film and television score produced since the early 1900s. Even within this very specific genre of film and television music, a detailed analysis of even a small number of space scores could fill many volumes. This book provides some musical analysis of a select number of scores written over the past century, but the book's primary focus is to tell the stories of the composers, individuals, influences and backstories that shaped the sound of space-related film and television scores, and follow trends in film composition. The book will serve as a primer for those interested in how and why the musical sounds that we associate with space have changed over the past century.

Finally, this book will document how the sound of space is not only being defined by motion pictures and television: The final chapter examines music in "real" space. It tells the stories of astronauts who have performed in space, the role of music for space explorers, and how music has been used to reach out to potential intelligent life in the universe.

Absolute silence may reign in the vacuum of space, but music is and will continue to be an essential ingredient in our understanding, appreciation and awe of this "final frontier." Whether composers are finding new ways of conveying our wonder and emotions in film and television, or if astronauts and future explorers are expressing their experiences through composition and performance, music is how humanity will fill the silence of space.

1

The First 50 Years of Space Films

From Silence to Sound

The turn of the twentieth century saw one of the most significant technological and social transitions in human history. Humanity was entering the modern age. In just a few decades, automobiles, telephones, electric lightbulbs, phonographs, subways and escalators had become ubiquitous in urban areas. Orville and Wilbur Wright conducted the first controlled, powered flight of an airplane in Kitty Hawk, North Carolina. As University of California historian Edward Ross Dickinson wrote, the transformation of society was "unprecedented in its speed and in its scope—in the number of different sciences and technologies involved, and in the rapid translation of scientific advances into technological innovation, and in turn, technological innovation into economic, social, and cultural transformation."[1] This metamorphosis would transform practically all aspects of human life.

In addition to great innovation, it was also an age of discovery and imagination, as our understanding, curiosity and speculation about our universe grew significantly. By 1900, humanity had already identified eight planets orbiting our Sun, as well as multiple moons, including two small and perplexing celestial bodies orbiting Mars. Indeed, Mars was the subject of constant public and scientific speculation. It had become a common belief that an alien civilization existed on Mars. As early as 1838, amateur Scottish astronomer Thomas Dick speculated that there could be as many as 12 billion Martians on the Red Planet.[2] Whether or not Dick's Martian census was based on verifiable facts or logic, the notion of a vast civilization on Mars thrived during the nineteenth century. Schemes were hatched to communicate with our Martian neighbors though such imaginative methods as massive flaming drawings (big enough to see from Mars) of the Pythagorean Theorem on the surface of Earth, or even using enormous mirrors to reflect sunlight that could burn messages on the surface of Mars.[3] As outlandish as these (and other) concepts were, they would certainly be considered the precursors of today's Search for Extraterrestrial Intelligence (SETI), a group that searches for signals from space. Marc Hartzman, author of *The Big Book of Mars*, stated,

> More than a hundred years ago, Martians weren't a thing of science fiction. They were thought to be science fact—beings who evolved earlier and thus were superior in intelligence. So how could we show them that we humans are pretty smart too? Their ingenuity may have been misguided, but the infectious and inherent desire to find life outside of Earth has only grown in intensity. Once future scientists knew there were no Martians, it just meant they had to look further. And with the discovery of radio astronomy, the search for extra-terrestrial intelligence finally began to extend well beyond the planet next door.[4]

Speculation regarding an advanced civilization on the Red Planet were bolstered by Giovanni Schiaparelli and Camille Flammarion, who surmised not only that there were canals (or canali) on the Red Planet, but also the likelihood of abundant vegetation on the Martian surface. While Schiaparelli was not convinced that the "canali" were anything other than naturally occurring waterways, an American amateur astronomer, Percival Lowell, was inspired by the concept of canals on Mars, and decided to advance the work that Schiaparelli had started. In 1895, he released the first of a series of books speculating about the ancient civilization on Mars who had constructed the networks of canals.

With all of these competing mainstream theories, an ancient Martian civilization seemed highly probable rather than farfetched, and popular fiction was drawn to the prospect of alien life and human exploration of space. As early as 1865, Jules Verne had written *From the Earth to the Moon*, a tale of humans traveling to the Moon, and several decades later, H.G. Wells wrote *First Men in the Moon*, in which Earth explorers encounter lunar extra-terrestrials. Fiction also hypothesized about the prospect that intelligent beings from other worlds could threaten Earth. Based on this type of speculation, H.G. Wells penned one of his more famous works, *The War of the Worlds* (1898). This novel was the first *well-known* alien invasion story (there had been less successful yarns pre–Wells), depicting a Martian invasion of the British countryside. Variations on Wells' alien invasion theme were told by authors throughout the upcoming century.

The First Movies

Within this backdrop, a new and innovative form of entertainment materialized in the late nineteenth century: motion pictures. This was an invention in which a progression of images on a film strip created the illusion of continuous movement. Arguably, the first "real" motion picture on record was released at the Society for the Development of the National Industry in Paris, France, on March 22, 1895. Produced by brothers Auguste and Louis Lumière, it was called *La Sortie de l'usine Lumière à Lyon* (Exit from the Lumière Factory in Lyon). This 46-second film, showing laborers leaving a factory, marked the start of a major new industry that would influence society substantially. Early filmmakers quickly began to learn the art of film production, and their topics rapidly became more ambitious.

These founding filmmakers soon understood the value of music within this new artform. According to film music expert Jon Burlingame, "As far back as 1895 when the Lumière Brothers were experimenting with film in Paris they came up with the notion of a piano not only to help cover up the noise of the projector, but it also was quickly discovered that music could provide a kind of emotional underpinning for viewers."[5]

It remains a popular belief that music and sound effects played a negligible formal role in the production and presentation of silent films, but the early film viewing experience was often anything but "silent." Music would often play a crucial formal and informal role in the exhibition of films. Music almost always accompanied early films not only to conceal projector noise, but also to musically reflect the action onscreen. Film music expert Paul Cuff from the University of Warwick in the U.K. states that throughout the silent era, "the public experience of filmgoing was invariably aural as well as visual. Audiences encountered soundscapes as varied as the spaces in which films were projected: fairgrounds, variety theatres, music halls, movie palaces."[6] Musical selections were often chosen from classical music and popular repertoire of the day. As the complexity of motion pictures progressed, original scores were occasionally commissioned.

The precursors of film scoring formally began shortly after the invention of motion pictures. An early science fiction film helped to lay the groundwork for what would soon become the new musical composition genre of film music. In 1902, French illusionist and film director Georges Méliès directed *Le Voyage dans la Lune* (*A Trip to the Moon*), based on Jules Verne's 1865 novel, *From the Earth to the Moon*. Drawing on his illusionist background, Méliès produced innovative special effects that enthralled audiences. According to Alissa Wilkinson of *Vox*, Méliès employed "things like time-lapse photography, multiple exposures, dissolves, pyrotechnics, theatrical machinery, and more...."[7] She also noted that Méliès worked at "a time of burgeoning scientific exploration and big dreams about the future of mankind. The filmmaker tapped into those through his experimentation with effects, and through stories he told tales of discovery."[8]

Méliès did not commission an original score for the production, but an English composer and pianist, Ezra Read, composed a special score to accompany this film in 1903. He called his music "A Trip to the Moon: Comic Descriptive Fantasia." The manuscript for this composition, lost and forgotten, was discovered by researcher Martin Marks quite by chance in the British Library in 2006. According to Marks, he found it "within a bound volume of miscellaneous piano pieces from 1903. On the front cover is printed a 'Synopsis' containing a list of the score's 24 different segment headings. These precisely describe the scene content of the imaginative and hugely successful film *Le Voyage dans la lune*...."[9] Because Read's music is only tangentially associated with *Le Voyage dans la Lune,* it is not considered the first original film score.

Many scholars believe that the art of film music had its true genesis with the release of *The Assassination of the Duke of Guise* (1908), directed by Charles le Bargy and André Calmettes. This 18-minute film is "the earliest documented film for which an original score was written," said Ben Erickson of MovieMusicUk.com.[10] Le Bargy and Calmettes approached one of the most prominent living composers of the day to score their film, Camille Saint-Saëns. He accepted their offer and began to develop music for each scene as he watched the film. This included using sections from his unpublished Symphony in F major "Urbs Roma" (1856), as well as new music. Structurally, according to Erickson, the score "is divided into five distinct tableaux which Saint-Saëns used to determine the overarching musical form of the score."[11] In so doing, he applied his operatic expertise to help define how films should and would be scored for decades to come. Erickson wrote that Saint-Saëns "had behind him decades of experience in the tradition of grand opera, a progressive familiarity with early recording technology, and the finest team of artists hitherto witnessed in film."[12]

However, since the score was not embedded and synchronized in the film as they would be with the advent of talkies, the Saint-Saëns score was rarely performed in conjunction with the movie. This was frequently the case when the film arrived in the United States. American audiences of the time were unlikely to enjoy this production with Saint-Saëns' groundbreaking score.[13]

In 1910, Thomas Edison released what was almost certainly the first American-made science fiction film, *A Trip to Mars.*[14] The film tells the story of a chemist who discovers a powder that can reverse gravity. He uses it to travel to Mars, where he discovers alien creatures. The film, produced for the Kinetoscope market, was directed by American writer-director Ashley Miller, who directed 133 films between 1909 and 1933.[15] Manufactured by Edison, Kinetoscopes were devices with which individuals could view films through small peepholes positioned at the top of the machine. This type of movie viewing did not lend itself to musical accompaniment, but Edison was adamant that his film needed to be supported by music. To help ensure that proper music was used, Edison provided specific suggestions for the style and placement of music. According to Trinity music professor Simon Trezise, they were "frequently issued in conjunction with the release of films from around 1910."[16] These pieces usually drew from well-known classics that Edison or his directors thought suited the stories and scenes. While *A Trip to Mars* is unlikely to have had original music, Edison's early cue sheets were another important advancement toward more formal film scores.

Over the next few years, several space-related science fiction films were produced, many with Mars-centric plots. This included a loose adaptation of Charles Dickens' *A Christmas Carol, A Message from Mars* (1913), considered the first full-length science fiction film made in the United Kingdom. In 1918, the Danish film company Nordisk Film produced *A Trip to Mars* in which humans travel to Mars and find a civilization of peace-loving vegetarian Martians—a far cry from the Martian invaders described by H.G. Wells.

From the newly formed Soviet Union came several early science fiction space films. One of the best known of these films was 1924's *Aelita* (aka *Aelita: Queen of Mars*), in which a worldwide Communist revolution is followed by a Communism attempt to conquer the universe. Based on Alexei Tolstoy's 1923 novel of the same name, the film tells the story of a Soviet engineer who travels to Mars and leads a worker uprising against the oppressive Martian capitalist elite.

As was the case with silent films produced by their western filmmaking counterparts, *Aelita*'s producers believed that the film needed the bravado of an original score. They hired composer Valentin Kruchinin, who had composed popular pieces in the Soviet Union such as "Little Bricks" (*Kirpichiki*) and *Mine No. 3* (*Shakhta No. 3*).[17] As was the fate of many silent film scores of the time, however, little of it survives. According to Philip Hayward, "The original score for the film, performed in an orchestral version during its premiere run in Moscow, only exists in fragments and it cannot be ascertained to what degree the Martian sequences were accompanied by music that attempted to communicate alien culture through stylistic markers."[18] It has been reported that Kruchinin utilized a theremin in his score; this may have been the first time the electronic instrument was used in a motion picture score. (The theremin was used widely in 1950s science fiction films, but it is unlikely that Kruchinin's use of the instrument influenced American science fiction composers in that decade. It is highly doubtful that they had heard Kruchinin's score.)

What may have been the first full-length original score for a space-related film accompanied a German documentary called *Wunder der Schöpfung* (the English version was called *Our Heavenly Bodies*), released in 1925 during the Weimar period. It was co-written by Hanns Walter Kornblum and Ernst Krieger and directed by Kornblum, who had made a shorter film about Einstein's Theory of Relativity in 1923. *Wunder der Schöpfung* provides an overview of the solar system and the universe as it was known at the time. The ambitious documentary took over two years to film, highlighting such topics as planetary physics, the origins of the solar system, gravitation, stars and galaxies.[19] According to Michael Cowan, Reader in Film Studies at the University of St. Andrews, "It's a quite self-consciously 'imaginative' film, which uses animation and trick cinematography to visualise theoretical knowledge."[20]

The filmmakers enlisted the help of a prominent composer-conductor, Ignatz Waghalter, to write a dedicated score for the film. Waghalter had just returned to Berlin from the U.S. after serving as the general music director and first conductor of the New York State Symphony Orchestra, the predecessor to the New York Philharmonic. According to Waghalter's great grandson David Waghalter Green, Waghalter "was appointed to lead the musical operations for UFA (Universum Film-Aktien Gesellschaft) film studios. He received a very lucrative contract. Part of that involved him writing the score for *Wunder der Schöpfung*."[21] Waghalter was one of the most accomplished conductors and composers of his day, highly regarded as an opera composer. This made him well-suited to enter the burgeoning field of motion picture composition. "He was a man who knew how to craft visual images into music," Green commented. "One of the reasons why he would have written a film score was that he had a remarkable melodic gift. He had an extraordinary melodic imagination, and had a tremendous facility for translating scenes, personalities, and moods into music. He was a late Romantic composer."[22]

Waghalter was well practiced at musically interpreting personalities. At dinner parties and other similar gatherings, the composer would create impromptu musical interpretations of his guests. It is unknown if the guests were always happy with their musical avatars, but this would have been useful training for developing thematic materials for motion pictures.

Like many of the original silent film scores of the 1920s (particularly in pre-war Germany), the *Wunder der Schöpfung* score was lost. Nonetheless, based on Waghalter's other compositions in that period (particularly within the genre of opera), the *Wunder der Schöpfung* score would most likely have been based heavily on late romantic orchestral and operatic composition. "[H]e would *not* have composed a modernistic score. He would not have written exclusively atonally," said Green. "Waghalter saw music as a means of communicating."[23] Waghalter had "an emotional connection" with his audience, according to Green. "[S]ince it was a visual film, I am sure Waghalter was able to convey a sense of wonder, a sense of mystery ... he was a man who knew how to craft visual images into music."[24]

If true, Waghalter's approach to film scoring would have been comparable to many of the great early Hollywood composers. David Green believes that if his grandfather had landed in Hollywood rather than New York in the 1920s, he may have become one of the great film composers, since he approached his scores like such composers as Max Steiner and Franz Waxman.[25]

Wunder der Schöpfung premiered in Berlin with one critic describing Waghalter's score as a "sensation."[26] But like most silent film scores, it was forgotten within a few years, and was not among the manuscripts discovered by his grandson decades later.

Note: Ignatz Waghalter developed a close friendship with renowned physicist Albert Einstein, a passionate music lover and violinist. Einstein once said, "Life without playing music is inconceivable to me.... I live my daydreams in music. I see my life in terms of music...."[27] Waghalter and Einstein would periodically meet to play chamber music together. Green does not know if his grandfather's friendship with the greatest scientific mind of the age inspired or influenced his *Wunder der Schöpfung* score, but he does say that his grandfather was very much interested in the sciences.

Metropolis

Perhaps the most notable original score for a silent science fiction film accompanied director Fritz Lang's epic *Metropolis,* released in 1927. While this film was not a space-based story, it has a futuristic grandeur and ambition that would impact not only space-related science fiction for the next century, but the entire motion picture industry. (*Metropolis* was released the same year as *The Jazz Singer,* the first film to synchronize picture and sound; it led to the birth of the talkies.)

Metropolis is based on a dystopian novel by Thea von Harbou (Lang's wife) about a repressive society in the distant future where the capitalist ruling class live in spectacular skyscrapers on the surface, while the working class endure a torturous life underground. According to Craig Lysy of MovieMusicUk.com, the lower class toils "endlessly to operate and maintain the great machines that power the city. They share not in the profits, nor any of the benefits, which go solely to the ruling elite."[28] Against this backdrop, the protagonist Freder encounters a young woman named Maria who possesses a prophetic gift and predicts the arrival of a "Mediator" who will create a new Utopia. Meanwhile, a malevolent inventor named Rotwang builds a robot that bears a striking resemblance to Maria. The robot is designed to be an agent of chaos, to enable Rotwang's ascent to power.

Metropolis was a massive project that took 17 months to film, utilizing approximately 36,000 extras. It was estimated to have cost over five million Reichsmarks.[29] This extraordinary budget also included an ambitious musical score by German composer Gottfried Huppertz. Lang worked with Huppertz on three prior films, including *Die Nibelungen* (1924), for which Huppertz composed his first film score.

Lang and von Harbou did not want the score to merely adorn their

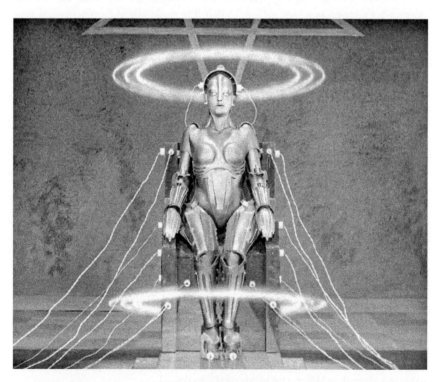

The robot (the Maschinenmensch) in the 1927 silent film *Metropolis*.

film as musical window dressing or just to fill the silence. They had very specific ideas about how the music should support the film and they provided Huppertz with input on placement of music as well as the musical styles to be used in various scenes—reminiscent of how modern directors and composers "spot the music" (determine where music will be placed in a film). To assure the best teaming of film and music, Huppertz was enlisted early in development so that he could immerse himself in the plot and understand the characters, enabling him to develop character themes as soon as the actors were cast. Huppertz played the themes to the actors prior to filming scenes, "to bring them into the proper mood."[30]

Huppertz's score "drew on established scoring traditions to emphasize dramatic and narrative aspects of the film (rather than the futuristic strangeness of its scenarios),"[31] according to Phillip Haywood, editor of *Off the Planet: Music, Sound, and Science Fiction Cinema*. In so doing, Huppertz may have helped establish a school of scoring science fiction films focusing on character and dramatic action rather than attempting to musically depict strange, futuristic or alien scenes. This is the school of composing John Williams effectively used 50 years later with his score to *Star Wars*.

Sixteen themes were composed for *Metropolis*. The first was "The Metropolis Theme": bright, optimistic music reflecting the seemingly idyllic city and its elite citizens. Craig Lysy describes it as a "gorgeous refulgent major modal statement, which resounds with proud horns regale [*sic*] that offer a testament to its architectural magnificence and grandeur."[32] However, beneath this idyllic setting are the working class (or proletariat) who literally live underground. This starkly contrasting world is musically portrayed by heavy, unrelenting music in minor keys, "carried by kinetic pounding drums, cycling trilling woodwinds, dire horns, and dark bass, all joined in a syncopated mechanistic rhythm that speak [*sic*] to the massive machines they maintain."[33] Huppertz also deftly integrates familiar themes to draw on the audiences' musical memory (and emotions).

To represent the revolutionary theme of the workers, Huppertz interweaves "La Marseillaise" (the French national anthem) into the score. It is heard when "the False Maria" leads a mob to destroy the machines. Film music expert Emilio Audissino stated, "The music here provides a negative comment of bottom-up revolutions in general by presenting the famous French anthem in a rhythmically distorted minor mode."[34]

Another familiar theme is the thirteenth-century Gregorian chant "Dies Irae" (the Day of Wrath) to portray the villain Rotwang. This may be the first time that "Dies Irae" was utilized in a motion picture. It would become a staple of motion picture music decades later in such films as *It's a Wonderful Life*, *The Shining*, *Home Alone* and *Close Encounters of the Third*

Kind. In fact, John Williams (who wrote the music for the latter two films) frequently used variations of the chant to suggest impending doom.

Huppertz's score often seemed fitting to accompany a ballet. The film's dramatic narrative, teamed with the fact that it was silent (despite the compelling score), magnifies even more the ballet-like feel of the production.

Metropolis premiered in Berlin on January 10, 1927, supported by a 66-piece orchestra. At the conclusion, "[u]nending applause brought the creators and the production staff to the apron stage over and over again, including Gottfried Huppertz, who put up the background music and conducted himself."[35]

Despite the score's initial success, there is much debate regarding the impact of Huppertz's music on the developing film scoring business. Bob McQuiston of the Classical Lost and Found website states, "The richness of the score undoubtedly served as an example to such European expatriate Hollywood composers as Max Steiner, Erich Wolfgang Korngold and Franz Waxman"[36]; but Audissino expressed doubt whether Huppertz's music had any influence on Hollywood film scoring. Audissino speculated that Steiner, Waxman, Korngold and even later composers such as Williams were unlikely to have heard the Huppertz score. When *Metropolis* arrived in the United States, on the rare occasions that Huppertz's music was played at all, the screenings would only feature a small number of the score's themes.[37] Soon after that, the score disappeared for decades.

Metropolis was also a box office failure, bringing in only 75,000 Reichsmarks (the film cost 5.3 million Reichsmarks to produce). In addition to receiving numerous poor reviews at the time, another contributing factor toward its poor reception was the fact that it was praised by Adolf Hitler and Joseph Goebbels. This was just a few years after Hitler attempted to overthrow the Munich government, and several years before he assumed power in Germany.

The *Metropolis* score fell into oblivion for a multitude of reasons. In addition to the film's box office failure, the rise of the Nazi Party and the outbreak of World War II, which eventually devastated Germany, assured that innumerable films and musical scores were completely lost. It was only years later that the score was rediscovered, but in the meantime, "[a]ll sorts of musical accompaniments had been used to be coupled with the film—the most famous in recent times was Giorgio Moroder's 1980s pop-music compilation," stated Audissino. "Huppertz's score was restored and reinstated only in the first decade of the 2000s, and despite that there are still some screenings of the film that employ different music."[38]

***

Fritz Lang and Thea von Harbou collaborated on another science fiction film before the end of the decade—and this one was a space film: *Frau im Mond* (*Woman in the Moon*), which premiered on October 15, 1929, in Berlin. Based on von Harbou's 1928 novel *The Rocket to the Moon*, the film depicted a privately funded mission to the Moon that included descriptions of multistage rockets. It would be decades before humans landed on the Moon, and even longer before the private sector began funding major space efforts.The plot also reflected the current events of that time. Only three years earlier, Robert Goddard launched the first liquid fuel rocket in the United States, and during the same year that the film was released, renowned Russian rocket pioneer Konstantin Tsiolkovsky published a paper hypothesizing about multiple stage rockets. For the first time, speculation of human exploration of space was beginning to look less like science fiction and more like a real possibility.

Like *Metropolis*, *Frau im Mond* featured an original score. Composer Willy Schmidt-Gentner was one of the most successful and prolific film composers in the German film industry. However, despite *Frau im Mond*'s visionary subject matter, Lang and von Harbou had not kept pace with the latest technologies in filmmaking. Talkies were now becoming the standard in the film industry, particularly in the U.S. Filmmakers who had not transitioned to this new technology were left behind; and any film score that was written for one of the final silent films was likely to be forgotten forever.

Science Fiction Talkies of the 1930s

By the early 1930s, the film industry had almost entirely transitioned to sound films, and music was playing a substantially different role in the new era. With the ascent of talkies, scoring techniques began to mature rapidly. "At first, these scores were mostly concerned with setting a general mood and highlighting the drama," stated conductor Ransom Wilson. "But gradually film composers began to experiment with writing specific music for different characters and plot elements in the film (as their colleagues in the world of opera had been doing for some time already)."[39]

Legendary composers including Steiner, Korngold, Waxman and Alfred Newman began to establish many of the norms of film scoring that are still used today. They were heavily influenced by classical and opera composers Richard Wagner, Johannes Brahms, Gustav Mahler, Richard Strauss and others. As Chloé Huvet of the Institute of History of Representations and Ideas in Modernities wrote of these founding composers of film music, "Educated by major figures in the production of European

Art music from the second half of the 19th century, and experienced in the writing of operas, operettas, and musicals, the pioneers of Classic Hollywood scoring quickly adapted to the necessities of film accompaniment."[40]

The Sound of Science Fiction

Not all early space-related sound films used traditional orchestral music. The first film of this genre in the sound era did not feature music inspired by the late Romantic period of classical music. Produced by Fox in 1930, *Just Imagine* was an unlikely science fiction musical comedy that was filled with popular—but somewhat campy—songs of the day. According to the website She Blogged by Night, "It's a romantic musical science fiction comedy set in the then-futuristic year of 1980. It was designed to be a vehicle for comedian El Brendel, as well as an entertaining, uplifting version of the future for audiences in the middle of the Depression and Prohibition."[41]

Visually, this film was clearly influenced by the dystopian classic *Metropolis*. Mathew J. Bartkowiak noted, "[W]hile *Metropolis* influenced the visual style of Fox's production, the former presents in unequivocal terms a negative and oppressive portrait of technological progress and aims to persuade its audience that the future bears more distress than the present; by contrast, the 1930 film promotes technology as a positive force."[42]

Everything is not as idyllic as it appears in the fictional 1980 depicted in this film. While airplanes have replaced cars, and there are innumerable remarkable futuristic advances, personal liberty and identity have been greatly curtailed. People now have numbers, not names, to identify them. Marriages are determined by tribunals, pills have replaced food and alcohol, and babies come from vending machines. Within this backdrop, a man named J-21 is disappointed when a marriage tribunal denies him the right to marry LN-18, the woman he loves, because he has not distinguished himself enough in society. As a result, he volunteers to pilot a rocket to Mars with a scientist named Z-4 and a man who has just been revived after being in a coma since 1930 (he was struck by lightning while playing golf). The odd trio successfully reaches Mars, where they encounter Martians; hijinks ensue. Upon their return to Earth, J-21 is granted permission to marry LN-18.

Just Imagine was directed by David Butler, who went on to a long film and TV directing career. The score was written by Hugo Friedhofer, who wrote music for dozens of films in the 1930s and 1940s; almost all of these compositions were uncredited within the films—including on *Just Imagine*.

The final film was a failure in virtually all respects. As "She Blogged by Night" wrote, "The problem with *Just Imagine* is that it pretty much fails as romance, musical, and comedy."[43] It would be many years before anyone attempted a science fiction musical comedy motion picture again.

Long Live the King of Science Fiction

As the film industry adjusted to the merging of recorded sound in film in the 1930s and early 1940s, science fiction movies also began to evolve. The most successful and well-known "non-space" science fiction film to appear in this period was the 1933 film *King Kong*. The plot itself was literally a dream (or nightmare) come true for screenwriter Merian C. Cooper who had a dream one evening of a giant gorilla rampaging through New York City.[44] Upon wakening, he realized that this was a great premise for a movie and successfully pitched the story idea to RKO's David Selznick as an epic re-imagining of the "Beauty and the Beast" story. The film was co-directed and produced by Cooper and Ernest B. Schoedsack.

In their adaptation of Cooper's dream, a filmmaker-showman named Carl Denham sets sail aboard a ship called the *Venture* to the mysterious Skull Island to film a movie. There they find a giant ape named Kong. Kong falls in love with a young actress named Ann Darrow, leading to the famous climax at the top of New York City's Empire State Building.

RKO insisted that music from their archives be used to score the film rather than hiring a composer and an orchestra. At the time, RKO was suffering from financial problems and needed to save money. Cooper was adamant that his vision for the film needed to be supported by a large original orchestral score. He was so passionate about this that he used $50,000 of his own funds to hire the head of the RKO music department, Max Steiner. Steiner had already established himself as one of the top film composers of the time (and he went on to compose for such films as *Gone with the Wind* and *Casablanca*).

While Steiner was not a fan of horror and fantasy films, *King Kong* was an exception. He later recalled, "I thought it was just great. It was made for music. It was the kind of film that allowed you to do anything and everything, from weird chords and dissonances to pretty melodies."[45] Steiner wrote an expansive score that added significantly to the overall quality of the film, but in doing so, also helped establish many of the norms and practices that are still used in film music composition today. According to Steven C. Smith, author of *Music by Max Steiner: The Epic Life of Hollywood's Most Influential Composer,*

King Kong is the most influential music score of all time. Because it completely established the grammar of film music ... and Steiner is the guy who figured out not just how to write music around dialogue, but how to write themes for characters and shape them subtly throughout a film—exactly what John Williams does in a *Star Wars* film, or the composers for a Marvel film do today.[46]

To support Steiner's grand score, he was only allowed an orchestra of upwards of 46 players. According to Steven Smith, "To create a fuller sound, Steiner and [Bernard] Kaun used stratagems Max learned in his theater days": Numerous musicians played more than one instrument at any given moment during the recording.[47]

As Gottfried Huppertz had done for *Metropolis* six years earlier, Steiner musically references the Wagnerian opera and sets a film scoring precedent that would be used for decades. According to a *Gramophone* review, " [Steiner's] use of Wagnerian leitmotifs—for the sailors, for Ann, for Kong himself—was 'rediscovered' in *Star Wars* and remains in continual use today."[48]

Steiner wrote four primary themes to musically tell this cinematic story. The first was a three-note theme that was used to portray different aspects of Kong as the mega-hominid "leading man" that evolves over the progression of the film. Initially, the theme is used for primal effect, but as the plot develops, and Kong falls in love with Ann (Fay Wray), Steiner effectively twists the theme as it is revealed that Kong is not merely a savage beast. Craig Lysy observes that the theme "varies from the monstrous and primal, to tender when he is bewitched by Ann's presence."[49] Steiner also interweaves primary themes for Ann and the island's native inhabitants, as well as for the ship's crew.

With these themes or leitmotifs, Steiner draws directly from methods that Richard Wagner and other composers had employed to great effect in nineteenth-century operas. But Audissino points out:

A distinction should be made between the Wagnerian use of leitmotif and the one used in Hollywood. Royal S. Brown, the musicologist, called what you find in Hollywood music a 'condensed' leitmotif. In motion pictures you don't have the space/room to produce the lengthier and more intricate leitmotific variations that you have in Wagner's musical dramas. The idea was basically imported from Wagner in a condensed form; a leitmotif is the association of music with a specific character or dramatic situation in the film.[50]

King Kong was an enormous box office success and saved RKO from financial collapse. The film had cost RKO $672,000 to produce, and even though it was released during the darkest days of the Great Depression, it generated $5.3 million in sales. Its success was far more profound than just box office profits. While relatively primitive by modern standards, special effects and storyline played a significant role in future films—including space-based pictures. Noted film critic Roger Ebert described *King Kong* as "the father of *Jurassic Park*, the *Alien* movies and countless other stories in which heroes are terrified by skillful special effects. A movie like *Silence of the Lambs*, which finds its evil in a man's personality, seems humanistic by contrast."[51]

Perhaps the best-known space-related productions of the 1930s and early 1940s were the serials *Flash Gordon* (1936) and *Buck Rogers* (1939). Serials typically did not use original scores, but largely incorporated uncredited music borrowed from other films. For example, *Flash Gordon's Trip to Mars* (1938) and *Flash Gordon Conquers the Universe* (1940)—as well as *Buck Rogers*—used stock music that composer Franz Waxman had composed for *Bride of Frankenstein* in 1935. Nonetheless, the music compensated for weak plots and clunky visual effects. Even though the Waxman stock music had not been specifically written for the serials, the music still helped define their melodramatic, adventurous sound. In fact, these serials and their heroic soundtracks would help to inspire George Lucas as he was contemplating *Star Wars* in the 1970s.[52]

Things to Come: The Changing Role of Film Music

One of the most ambitious science fiction–space movies of the 1930s was a British film called *Things to Come* (1936). Based on H.G. Wells' 1933 novel *The Shape of Things to Come,* the film foresaw a post-apocalyptic future where society collapses as a result of war and disease. The story then reveals that after a century of chaos, technology eventually triumphs and there is a mission to the Moon. Wells' plot reflected many of the social and political forces at play in the mid–1930s, as Nazi Germany was growing in power and the Communist Party was a constant source of anxiety.

Things to Come boasted an impressive creative team. Director William Cameron Menzies had already directed several films, and he later served as art director and/or production designer on such films as *Gone with the Wind* and *It's a Wonderful Life*. Producing the futuristic drama was Alexander Korda, who had previously produced *The Private Life of Henry VIII* and *The Scarlet Pimpernel*. In addition, Wells himself played a significant role in the film, collaborating with Menzies and Korda in its development.

Wells was also instrumental in determining the musical direction of the film. He believed that the score should play an integral role in advancing the story, not just serving as background music or window dressing. To make sure that the film had the type of music that he envisioned,

Wells approached the prominent British composer Arthur Bliss to write the score. Bliss, the composer of such works as *A Colour Symphony, String Quartet in A Major* and *Hymn to Apollo*, had never scored a motion picture. Nonetheless, he had been intrigued by the new film music genre for over a decade and had even written an essay discussing film music in 1922, "Those Damned Films." At the time, he had viewed many silent films and wrote that the people responsible for matching the music to the films "know not their job."[53] He added that if that trend continued, the overall films would suffer, but if they "get some composer to collaborate with the producer and write those special cinema noises.... What a proud day it will be for some of us to be featured as the sound-producing experts on a real live million-dollar movie!"[54] Bliss' appraisal should also be considered with the understanding that it was written in the silent film era when music selections varied wildly from film to film and from theater to theater.

Bliss' chance to elevate film music came 12 years later in 1934 when he was delivering a series of lectures on contemporary music. One attendee was H.G. Wells, who was impressed by Bliss' lecture and invited the composer to lunch. During the lunch, Wells offered him the opportunity to compose music for the upcoming *Things to Come*. Wells had been contemplating the marriage between film and music well before his meeting with Bliss. In his 1929 book *The King Who Was a King*, he articulated his thoughts on the development of motion pictures as well as film music. Regarding the latter, Wells stated, "Behind the first cheap triumphs of the film to-day rises the possibility of a spectacle-music-drama, greater, more beautiful and intellectually deeper and richer than any artistic form humanity has hitherto achieved."[55]

To achieve this "spectacle-music-drama," Wells wanted Bliss to approach the composition as he might approach a concert piece. He instructed Bliss to compose the music first, before the script was complete, and they would adapt the film to match the music.[56] Bliss began the score in 1934 and in March 1935, before production started, he recorded portions of the music with the London Symphony Orchestra. Wells later stated, "The music is a part of the constructive scheme of the film, and the composer, Mr. Arthur Bliss, was practically a collaborator in its production.... Sound sequences and picture sequences were made to be closely interwoven. The Bliss music is not intended to be tacked on; it is part of the design."[57]

As idyllic as this arrangement seemed to Bliss and Wells, Alexander Korda had other plans on how to integrate the musical score. Korda overruled Wells' promise to Bliss and demanded that the music be modified to match the film rather than the other way around. When Bliss refused to modify his music, Lionel Salter, a composer and music editor, made the necessary edits to the music. Salter later wrote, "I was charged with 'tidyings-up and surgery,' a job I felt privileged (and somewhat overawed) to do, as he (Bliss) had been one of my musical heroes."[58] Musical hero or not, substantial "surgery" was needed to bend Bliss' music to the final film. According to Stephen Lloyd, "None of the movements that Bliss recorded (nor for that matter in the Suite) corresponds precisely to what is heard in the soundtrack."[59]

Later in 1935, the revised soundtrack was recorded by the London Symphony Orchestra; the conductor was London Films' young music director Muir Mathieson. The London Symphony Orchestra's role in this film would change the perception of film music forever. This was the first of many film scores that the London Symphony Orchestra would perform over the following decades, setting the standard for future motion picture music recordings. According to the London Symphony Orchestra website,

> Until that time, recorded film music had consisted essentially of work by small bands and groups performing theme songs and pieces of short background music. But with the commissioning of Sir Arthur Bliss to compose a score performed by a full symphony orchestra for [*Things to Come*], the face of film music was changed forever—not only in Britain but also around the world.[60]

As for the soundtrack itself, "Bliss captured the mechanical crescendo and diminuendo not just through dynamics and orchestration … but through eclectic stylistic references," according to western music expert Matthew Riley.[61] Riley observed that the opening fanfare echoes Tchaikovsky's Fourth Symphony, while in the "Evacuation," Bliss used a "gradual replacement of orchestral instruments by the clinking of anvils in this allusion to Wagner's *Das Rheingold*."[62]

While there may have been stylistic similarities to Wagner, film music reviewer Craig Lysy stated after assessing the score, "we realize that Bliss' conception was not leitmotif, but rather set pieces woven together to support the film's narrative arc." However, Bliss' full original concept was effective: "Taken in totality, Bliss' music offers a remarkable musical journey, which speaks to the fall and rebirth of civilization, where from out of darkness and despair is born a refulgent Utopian joy. So pleased was Bliss that he created a concert suite for his score, which survives to this day."[63]

Things to Come, then the most expensive film yet produced in England, premiered on February 21, 1936. Though not a tremendous box office success, the film did receive generally favorable reviews. *The Daily Telegraph* called it "unforgettable," but also pointed out that it had flaws by paying tribute to the fascist dictators of the time. "Ralph Richardson, as the Boss, shouts too much on the same key—after all, Herr Hitler and Signor Mussolini, whatever their other qualities, are wonderful mob speakers."[64]

Bliss' music also fared reasonably well with reviewers. Even *The Times*, which was critical of the quality of the music in the film, did not blame Bliss: "As we know from the concert performance, Mr. Arthur Bliss has not failed to make good use of his opportunity, but another power has intervened to nullify his work. For the sound in this film is so grossly over-amplified that the music becomes mere noise."[65]

In addition to the role of the soundtrack, the music also promoted the film through a suite that Bliss arranged based on the film score. Conducted by Bliss, this piece was first performed in September 1935 at the Henry Wood Promenade Concert in Queen's Hall in London; it has served as the most effective ambassador for the music of the film—and is still occasionally performed to this day. Regarding a 2014 performance at Carnegie Hall in New York City, musicologist Bryon Adams stated that Bliss' *Things to Come* score is "considered to be one of the finest achievements by a British film composer, music on a level with scores by Vaughan Williams, Malcolm Arnold, and William Walton. In a prophetic anticipation of John Williams, Bliss concludes the suite drawn from his music for *Things to Come* with a broad Elgarian tune that hails Wells' cloudless, technologically perfect future."[66]

Note: Queen's Hall was destroyed during World War II. After the war, the Henry Wood Promenade Concerts—now known as BBC Proms—moved to Royal Albert Hall.

***

The End of the Beginning

With a small number of exceptions, the 1930s and 1940s did not offer a significant number of films related to space travel, and most of the science fiction films were often monster films and serials. Popular movies tended to be focused on adventure, intrigue, war and screwball comedy. Real-life events also played a significant role in popular entertainment as the world endured years of depression followed by worldwide war. It was not until the 1950s, when a new threat to "peace on Earth" emerged, that space-related films became popular.

2

The Evolving Sound of Space
The Sound of the 1950s

It was not until the 1950s that film composers wrote music that audiences would associate with space when they heard that music separately from the film. In contrast to the optimistic orchestral pieces that would reign years later, the space-related music of this period was often foreboding, reflecting the public mood and anxiety of the time. World War II had ended only a few years earlier, but that conflict was replaced by the Cold War with the Soviet Union.

During World War II, tremendous advancements were made in rocketry and other essential precursor technologies of the space race. These developments were still almost exclusively associated with mass destruction—particularly combined with the terrifying power of atomic weapons. Unlike every previous conflict in human history, the next war had the potential to destroy civilization and possibly every living creature on Earth. As a result, the fear of nuclear war became a consistent theme in films of the 1950s. According to academic librarian Rebecca Saunders,

> The threat of a nuclear holocaust bombarded the cultural imagination. 1950s horror films' preoccupations with science, space, and invasions clearly represent collective anxiety about a nuclear attack, foreboding scientific advancement, and subversive agents of ideological opposition. In general, science experiments combined with military intervention are portrayed in '50s cinema as both the cause of terrifying problems and also the source of a solution.[1]

This national (and international) anxiety, teamed with constant advancements in technology, had a significant influence on the music that would accompany science fiction and space films. In contrast to the traditional approach that Gottfried Huppertz had taken with *Metropolis*, science fiction films in the 1950s would often try to musically simulate the strange and alien nature of the subject matter. As such, the 1950s was likely the first decade in which a style of motion picture music was associated with space, often based on electronic sounds rather than traditional orchestral music. According to film historian–musicologist William H. Rosar, '50s SF films "are unique musically in one respect because they are virtually the only films of any film genre in that period to have a distinct instrumental sonority associated with them—that of the theremin."[2]

> ### Sidebar: The Invention of the Theremin
>
> The theremin was invented by accident in 1920 by a Russian radio engineer named León Theremin. The inventor was attempting to use sound waves to create proximity sensors to detect approaching objects. He noticed that when he moved his hands between two antennas, he could manipulate the high-pitched sound that his contraption was emitting. A competent cellist, he realized that his device could be used as a musical instrument. According to *Smithsonian Magazine*, Vladimir Lenin was so enthralled by the invention that he sent Theremin on tour to Europe and the United States to demonstrate the new Soviet invention and sound.

The Day the Earth Stood Still

Electronic instrumentation had been used in such movies as the Hitchcock thriller *Spellbound* (score by Miklós Rózsa), as well as the science fiction film *Rocketship X-M* (music by Ferde Grofé). The esteemed film composer Bernard Herrmann helped define what space would sound like during the 1950s. Herrmann was selected to write the music for director Robert Wise's classic 1951 alien visitation film *The Day the Earth Stood Still*.

Film producer Julian Blaustein had been looking for a science fiction story to metaphorically reflect the tensions and paranoia of the atomic age, when he came across a short story called "Farewell to the Master." Written by Harry Bates in 1940, the story serves as the basis for *The Day the Earth Stood Still*. Bates was paid $500 for the rights to his story.[3]

While the film portrayed the story of an alien visitor and the threat of destruction, this threat was really a metaphor for the fear, paranoia and irrational behavior that permeated human interaction in response to the prospect of nuclear annihilation. As film musicologist Anthony Bushard wrote, the movie "is a wonderful medium through which to examine a society's collective consciousness and is a primary example of culture."[4] Bushard also observed that the film "elevated the emerging genre of cinematic science-fiction above 'junk or kiddy fare' and addressed more mature themes than one would normally encounter at a Saturday matinee."[5]

Herrmann was hired by legendary composer Alfred Newman, 20th Century–Fox's music director. (Newman's 20th Century–Fox fanfare is heard at the beginning of the film—and hundreds of others.) An extended version of this fanfare was used 26 years later at the opening of *Star Wars* (see "Return of the Fox Fanfare" below). Herrmann had scored Orson Welles' masterpiece *Citizen Kane* as well as such films as *The Magnificent Ambersons* (also by Welles), *All That Money Can Buy* (an Oscar winner for Herrmann), *Anna and the King of Siam* and *The Ghost and Mrs. Muir*. He was no stranger to the alien invasion genre, having conducted the orchestra for Welles' 1938 *War of the Worlds* radio broadcast.

Herrmann composed an innovative and eerie score utilizing orchestra as well as some non-traditional instruments—most notably, two theremins. Professor Rebecca Leydon explains that Herrmann's use of the theremin is only "the most conspicuous of several unusual instruments in the score." These instruments included "a pair of Hammond organs plus a large studio organ, electric violin, electric cello, electric bass (one of each),

A flying saucer lands on the National Mall in Washington, D.C., at the beginning of the 1951 film *The Day the Earth Stood Still*.

a trio of vibraphones and an electric guitar." Herrmann so effectively conveyed the mood of the film as well as the fear regarding a nuclear apocalypse, that the theremin became the staple instrument for B space movies as well as post-apocalyptic monster films.[6]

The instruments that Herrmann did *not* use are also of interest. Craig Lysy called Herrmann

> a consummate innovator who always sought to bring new and dynamic methods to scoring films. His decision to remove the acoustic instruments of the string and woodwind sections of the orchestra and to augment his ensemble with the alien, otherworldly sounds of the Theremin, vibraphone, and celesta was a masterstroke. His six motifs were all carefully conceived and expertly applied, fully supporting in scene after scene the film's narrative.[7]

As noted earlier, Herrmann's score is far more complex and varied than just the ominous sounds of theremins and other foreboding cues. During scenes where Klaatu and Bobby visit Arlington National Cemetery and the Lincoln Memorial, Herrmann writes extremely reverential music, using trumpets and horns to match the solemn atmosphere at these national sites. The music helps temporarily relieve the audience from the tension regarding Klaatu's mission on Earth, but also is a reminder of the horrors and sorrow of war.

An unfortunate legacy of Herrmann's score may have been the unbridled use of theremins to depict alien creatures and monsters in B-movies, but his *Day the Earth Stood Still* composition was a truly innovative piece. As Mathew Bartkowiak observed, the score was the

> first of its kind to present a total orchestral complement of acoustic, electric, electronic instruments (and multiple theremins) that were subjected to intricate mixing and tape-cutting techniques. It may turn out that future audiences are drawn to this film more because of its unique musical colors and structures than its film techniques, which have now become dated.[8]

Film reviewer Jon Burlingame echoes this sentiment: "There are so many bad science fiction films in the 1950s that take their musical cue from the brilliance of Herrmann's accomplishment and sort of ruin it by the end of the 1950s. I think by the end of the 1950s nobody wanted to go near a theremin because it had been so misused in so many bad science fiction pictures."[9] As a result, Herrmann's score has suffered from association to second-rate imitators of his original score.

Herrmann rose to the level of one of the greatest film composers of all time in the 1950s and 1960s, most famously writing the scores to such Alfred Hitchcock classics as *Vertigo*, *North by Northwest* and *Psycho*. While he did not write a significant number of space-related pieces for the rest of his career, he returned to the space genre in the late 1950s. The first of these pieces, "The Outer Space Suite," was written in 1957 for the CBS television music library, to be used in science fiction television programming. In fact, the music was used in several episodes of the series *The Twilight Zone*. Herrmann also wrote several scores specifically for *The Twilight Zone*, including a Season 1 space-based episode called "The Lonely" (1959). Set in the future, this episode tells of a convict sentenced to 50 years in solitary confinement on an asteroid, millions of miles from Earth. When he arrives, he finds a human-like robot (or gynoid) named Alicia with whom he eventually falls in love. Herrmann writes an effective score that Jon Burlingame described as "absolutely gorgeous, because he's again using an unusual combination that sort of harkens back to *The Day the Earth Stood Still*, but is more specifically space-oriented; harps, vibes, muted brass, organ, percussion—deployed in a way that makes outer space absolutely beautiful."[10]

Forbidden Planet

Hermann was not alone to innovate with electronic sounds in the 1950s. In 1956, *Forbidden Planet*, the science fiction adaptation of Shakespeare's *The Tempest* (with a healthy dose of Freudian psychological theory), incorporated an electronic score like no previous film—and perhaps no film since. Based on a story by Irving Block and Allen Adler, the film was directed by Fred M. Wilcox, best known for directing Lassie movies. In the twenty-third century, the starship C-57D is sent to the planet Altair IV to investigate the fate of a group of settlers who arrived there years earlier.

The film features a soundtrack that may be unique in motion picture history, an all-electronic score by Bebe and Louis Barron. Neither of them had ever scored a full-length film, and were not professional musicians. While they had both studied music, it was not until Louis took an interest in soldering electronic equipment that they began manipulating electronic sounds in the late 1940s. By 1950, they had produced their first musical pieces (called "Heavenly Menagerie") that had been assembled by recording electronic sounds on magnetic tape, then cutting and reassembling the tape. This time-consuming process was still not refined enough to contribute to a Hollywood film, but was an important proof of concept for the couple.

After further refinements of their craft, their big break came in 1955 when they crashed a party honoring artist Miriam Svet, the wife of MGM president Dore Schary. At the party, they managed to corner Schary and described their expertise in recording electronic sounds and how these recordings could be used in motion pictures. Louis Barron later recalled that during their conversation, Schary insisted that they come to Hollywood and score *Forbidden Planet*. Schary had a different recollection of their initial meeting. His first impression of the Barrons was that they had the disheveled appearance of an "unmade bed."[11] When the Barrons asked him if he would be willing to listen to their electronic recordings, Schary recalled, "I told them that we were returning to California the next morning and that I had no time to oblige them. To assuage their obvious disappointment, though, I promised that if they were ever in California I'd be pleased to listen with an open ear and mind."[12]

Not long after this encounter, to Schary's surprise, the Barrons moved to California and took him up on the offer to visit him. Despite his initial skepticism, Schary was impressed with their technology and invited the Barrons to contribute their skills to the film. According to musicologist James Wierzbicki, this was not an offer to write the film score, "but simply to create electronic sounds that might possibly be used." The producer still intended to commission a traditional score,[13] and had hired composer David Rose. Rose, music director of MGM Records and a composer for TV's *The Red Skelton Show*, had already scored over a dozen films. However, after Rose had composed several cues using traditional orchestral methods, the producers were not pleased with his efforts and released him from the production.

Rose was so unhappy with his release from the film that according to Donald John Long of *Film Music Monthly*, "[he] burned all the sheet music of his discarded score for *Forbidden Planet*, except for his beautiful main title theme."[14] He later recorded the theme and released it, stating that it was "inspired" by the film.

Now in the unlikely position of scoring the entire film with their electronic techniques, the Barrons had to overcome the limitations of their equipment. To create a full melodic score was nearly impossible. They would also need to remind Schary of this fact. Schary provided consistent input regarding each scene, such as the moods and overall feel that he wanted the Barrons to achieve with their score. Bebe Barron recalled Schary asking, "Can you do fear?" Bebe replied, "Well, that's all we could do, really, is fear."[15] The harsh electronic sounds did not lend themselves to joyous or loving feelings. Nonetheless, this limited palette of emotional sound was effectively used during one of the critical moments of the plot. Bebe recalled, "In the scene where the scientist, Morbius, was dying himself, we used the circuit as it was dying. and you could tell he was going through hell." These sounds were not always predicable, and the Barrons felt as though their electronic circuits almost had lives of their own—and a certain level of free will.[16] They emphasized this in a 1964 interview:

We design and construct circuits, which function electronically in a manner remarkably similar to the way lower life forms function psychologically.... Most remarkable is that the sounds, which emanate from these electronic nervous systems, seem to convey strong emotional meaning to listeners. There were no synthesizers or traditions of using electronic music when we scored the film, and therefore we were free to explore "terra incognito" with all the surprises and adventures.[17]

As unorthodox and seemingly random as their methods were, the Barrons' music did not completely break with all established film compositions norms. As Rebecca Leydon explains, "*Forbidden Planet* fabricates a non-tempered pitch universe and a set of bizarre timbres, replacing the classic Hollywood score's associative use of key-centers and themes with an idiosyncratic leitmotif technique based on the behavior and 'life cycle' of sound generating circuits."[18]

Other music scholars have observed more traditional musical practices used in the Barrons' score. According to musicologist David Cooper, the Barrons' score, "at least partly functions through principles of pitch construction that, although attenuated, are comparable to those found in more conventional 'symphonic' scores of the period."[19] While the Barrons' electronic effects tended to be too abstract to create themes or traditional motifs, their score did "employ specific motives associated with the character Robby, the Krell civilization, the 'monster from the Id,' and more abstractly, the emotion of love, but it also embodies tonal relationships which prioritise the pitches D♭, F and B."[20]

In recent years, *Forbidden Planet* has often been hailed as one of the most innovative space films of the 1950s, but it was a box office disappointment. Neither the literary references in the plot nor the score's innovative use of sound resonated with reviewers or theatergoers at the time, and the film was often categorized as a B-picture with a large production cost.[21]

Forbidden Planet was the only major Hollywood film score that Bebe and Louis Barron worked on. This was partly a result of the tepid response to the film, but also the fact that the Barrons were not acknowledged as composers in the credits. The MGM legal department was concerned over a potential backlash from the musicians' union if they defined the Barrons' work as a "score" when no musicians actually played on it.[22] The two Barrons were finally credited with creating "electronic tonalities."

The Barrons' work is now considered a milestone in the use of electronic music in film and other musical genres. As Craig Lysy stated,

This score was audacious in its conception, bold, innovative and constitutes a seminal event in the history of film score art.... The electronically generated oscillatory patterns created by the Barrons served as the progenitor of the modern synthesizer, which would arise eight years later and be embraced by cutting edge composers seeking a new sound and method of scoring films.[23]

As for the full impact of the production, according to Ian Olney of York College of Pennsylvania, "*Forbidden Planet* elevated science fiction as a Hollywood genre, effectively reintroducing it to audiences as a brand of cinema capable of stimulating the intellect as well as the imagination. Its influence did not end there."[24]

Leith Stevens and George Pal

Despite the proliferation of electronic music in science fiction, not all space scores and science fiction scores of the 1950s were electronic and/or avant-garde. One of the most prolific composers of space films that decade relied on traditional orchestral compositions. Composer Leith Stevens wrote the music to such films as *Destination Moon, When Worlds Collide* and *The War of the Worlds.* For all three films, he worked with producer George Pal, the predominant creator of high-end science fiction films of this era. While he never reached the heights that George Lucas or Steven Spielberg achieved decades later, Pal was arguably the most respected producer in the genre at the time. "I do think the George Pal movies were great populist entertainment," notes film music historian Jeff Bond. "[His films had] a higher profile than a lot of the other science fiction movies being made at the time because they were in color and they were lavish compared to all the giant bug movies and monster movies...."[25]

A Juilliard-trained composer, Stevens had worked as an arranger and conductor for CBS radio during the 1930s. He also had experience in both the classical and jazz music worlds. His Piano Concerto in C Minor was heard in the 1947 film *Night Song* (the first of his music used in a movie) and he wrote an all-jazz score for the 1954 film *The Wild One.*

In 1950, Stevens scored his first space-related film. He teamed with Pal and director Irving Pichel on *Destination Moon,* based on a novel by Robert Heinlein entitled *Rocketship Galileo.* Heinlein's story was ahead of his time, prognosticating a privately funded space program after government funding collapses. Scientist Dr. Charles Cargraves, industrialist Jim Barnes and a retired general named Thayer privately develop an atomic rocket called *Luna* to mount the first human landing on the surface of the Moon. In contrast to many other films of the time, the story realistically depicts government bureaucracy and regulations as well as public protests regarding an "atomic" rocket, in addition to outlining the physics and challenges of sending humans to the Moon.

Stevens took his role as composer very seriously and reportedly spoke to several scientists, including Wernher von Braun, to "get an idea what space was like in order to create it musically."[26] Stevens researched the science, imagery and engineering of space for three months before starting on his score. According to Cy Schneider, who wrote the liner notes for the 1960 soundtrack, "The result was a startling, particularly dramatic score which became immediately popular. The music evoked new feelings, new mental pictures ... it investigated a musical world never before probed or propounded so sharply."[27]

Stevens initially considered a "wildly atonal score," what he called "a musician's score,"[28] but reconsidered this approach. While his fellow musicians may have appreciated these types of musical works, Stevens also understood that "if he was going to get any audience reaction through the music, or any emotional result, he would have to abandon that idea and try to create the unreal effects with strange orchestral color."[29]

With this in mind, he constructed a score that effectively reflected the grandeur of space, but also displayed a sense of mystery, danger and foreboding. Unlike many of the scores that followed, *Destination Moon* did not try to create alien sounds, but used the orchestra to convey danger, tension and wonder, not unlike a suspense movie of that age. This is reflected in his opening theme music, which elicited an ominous sense of anxiety and wonder as the credits scroll up the screen, quite reminiscent of the *Star Wars* crawl. It is unclear whether George Lucas was influenced by the opening scene from *Destination Moon.*

Stevens' score was not limited to ominous orchestrations. Once the crew members are on their way the Moon, they have a meal of coffee, sandwiches and bananas, as pastural, slightly whimsical music plays; the melody would have been just as well suited to a Western film as a family rides their wagon across the prairie. This is followed by a short scene where Joe, the ambivalent radar and radio operator, plays his harmonica. (Fifteen years later in 1965, American astronaut Walter Schirra played "Jingle Bells" on his harmonica aboard the Gemini VI-A mission.)

Soon after the harmonica concert, complications arise when an antenna fails to deploy, and the crew members are forced to conduct a spacewalk. Stevens' "In Outer Space" is a "shimmering violin-based section, an otherworldly sense of musical dislocation during the woodwinds' part, adjoining passages for harp, a hauntingly beautiful part for harps and flutes accompanying the travelers' sense of awe at their voyage, and an action theme that is one of the more memorable ever written to accompany a realistic space flight."[30] While primitive by modern standards, the scene may have been the most realistic depiction of the space environment yet portrayed on film. Stevens' musical underpinning of the scene was also important. According to Jon Burlingame, "Leith Stevens, of all the Hollywood composers, was really the first composer who was given an opportunity to think about how to portray space in music,"[31]

Stevens was not the only composer to provide music to *Destination Moon*. Clarence Wheeler, who specialized in music for short films (including the Woody Woodpecker cartoons), was given the opportunity to write for the zany animated bird in *Destination Moon*. In a rare comical moment in an otherwise serious film, an animated short is projected to convince investors to pay for the Moon mission. The animated film, starring Woody Woodpecker, provides a lighthearted overview of the mission as well as the physics of gravity and inertia. Wheeler wrote the music for the entire animated sequence in the exact style he would have on any other Woody Woodpecker film he composed. This segment was not unlike the animated instruction video in *Jurassic Park* starring an animated DNA strand.

The year after *Destination Moon* appeared, George Pal produced another space-related drama, *When Worlds Collide* (1951). Based on a 1932 novel of the same name by Philip Wylie and Edwin Balmer, the film is a spacefaring version of the Noah's Ark story, opening with heavenly-sounding music and a quote from Genesis. The action begins when an astronomer in South Africa discovers that a star called Bellus is less than eight months from a catastrophic collision with Earth. Orbiting Bellus is a planet named Zyra, which is a comparable size to Earth and will survive the cosmic collision. Zyra could be home for a new human civilization. Skepticism abounds, however. The apocalyptic news is initially mocked by the international community, motivating a cadre of scientists and industrialists to independently build a spaceship (or Ark) to transport a small group of humans, plants and animals, as well as a collection of human knowledge and achievements, to Zyra.

Stevens was called upon again to score this film. As with *Destination Moon*, he took a more traditional orchestral approach. According to musicologist William Rosar, "The musical language for Stevens' score for *When Worlds Collide* is similar to *Destination Moon*, but much more highly charged and forceful, undoubtably in response to a story that depicts … the end of the world."[32]

Stevens also employed non-western musical sounds to add depth to the score. "Much of Stevens' score is based on a faintly Middle Eastern–sounding theme he calls simply 'Bellus and Zyra,' a melodic idea that employs two tonics," said Rosar. "Stevens uses different versions of the theme as a unifying element throughout the score."[33]

Two years later, Pal and Stevens teamed up for a third space-related film: *The War of the Worlds*. The film was based on the 1897 novel by H.G Wells, the novel that had also inspired Orson Welles' infamous radio broadcast in 1938. Paramount had been considering a film adaptation of *War of the Worlds* as early as 1925, when they purchased the rights to the story directly from Wells. At that time, they had planned for Cecil B. DeMille to direct the film, but that production never materialized. When Pal took control of the project a quarter century later, he enlisted Byron Haskin to direct. Haskin had directed over a dozen movies at that point, including Disney's *Treasure Island*.

Another key player in the film was Paramount's head of production, Don Hartman. Initially, he had been skeptical regarding the quality of the film, telling Pal that "this script is a piece of crap and this is where it belongs," tossing into a waste basket.[34] But over time, Hartman apparently warmed to the film's concept, and even became a passionate advocate regarding the quality of the score. In fact, he approached Pal during production and stated that he had screened *Gone with the Wind* to assess what qualities made that film great. Hartman continued, "Not the least of its great qualities is the magnificent, dramatic score. It enhanced the drama beyond comprehension. You need to take great care in dubbing and scoring *War of the Worlds* as it will add immeasurably to your picture."[35]

As with his two previous space-related films, Stevens wrote a traditional orchestral score. William H. Rosar noted that it "has a contemporary, late 40s-1950s feel to it (that is 'contemporary' by Hollywood standards), is primarily melodic (or motific) but at the same time relies heavily on musical color, featuring a variety of unusual or novel orchestral effects."[36] Stevens did selectively use a small number of electronic instruments, such as the Novachord (considered the world's first commercial polyphonic synthesizer), but most exotic musical sounds in the score were produced by standard orchestral instruments.

None of the exotic sounds were used to define the Martian invaders; they do not have a musical theme at all. Pal wanted their motivations to remain a mystery, later stating, "We would never show the point-of-view of the Martians despite the pleas of the front office."[37] Rather than creating a musical "Martian theme," the approach of the Martian vehicles is represented by a high-pitched electronic humming noise—or the shrill sound of their heat rays. These sounds were almost entirely created through electronic instruments and equipment. As described by Steve Rubin in a 1977 *Cinefantastique* article, "The alien sounds produced by the Martian war machines, the sinister power surge and resulting enfilade, was an effect achieved entirely by electric guitars."[38] Other sounds were created by oscillators to generate "alien sound-feed-back. Using these sound circuits, the engineers perfected the spine tingling 'ping, ping, ping' of the heat ray generator" as well as the searching sound of the alien eye and other sounds.[39]

Stevens' musical accompaniment is used sparingly and subtly, but at times it is thrust into the foreground to extraordinary effect. One notable example is a scene where the local pastor walks into the battlefield as the levitating Martian vehicles approach. Stevens' music seems to contrast with the inherent danger of the scene. As the pastor walks slowly toward the approaching Martian war machines, he holds a Bible up in front of him and recites parts of Psalm 23: "Thou anointest my head with oil; my cup runneth over...." But the music is not tense or predictive of the fact that the pastor will soon be vaporized. The music is slow, somber and reserved, reflecting a spiritual feel rather than that of impending doom. As film and television music expert Jeff Bond observes, "[Stevens] doesn't score the suspense and the fear of that scene, but he scores the serenity of this priest and his [faith] and I think that makes it much, much scarier."[40]

This was one of the first space film scores to draw from Gustav Holst's "The Planets." According to Bond, Stevens does not get nearly as much credit for his innovative references to Holst as he should. "He did that in a more original way than John Williams did later, when Williams was referencing Holst in *Star Wars*. Leith Stevens used these major chords out of the Mars movement from Holst's 'The Planets' without really aping the structure and coming up with his own approach."[41]

The War of the Worlds was both a box office and critical success. According to *Variety*'s 1953 review, the alien invasion film is "a socko science-fiction feature, as fearsome as a film as was the Orson Welles 1938 radio interpretation[42] ... [W]hat starring honors there are go strictly to the special effects, which create an atmosphere of soul-chilling apprehension so effectively [that] audiences will actually take alarm at the danger in the film."[43] Clearly, much of the "soul-chilling apprehension" is a result of Stevens' music.

Stevens had written effective music for some of the most successful space-related films of the early 1950s, but his musical approach did not remain in the public psyche. "One explanation might be that Stevens took an in-between approach," stated Emilio Audissino. "Having only introduced some electronic elements in an otherwise more traditionally styled score, Stevens might have been sidelined by the more experimental works of Herrmann or the Barrons."[44] Since the new sound was moving toward electronic music, the traditional sound, while still quite effective, did not stand out in the public consciousness. It did not seem new. Audissino compares this with the arrival of *Star Wars* in the 1970s. "Had Williams used more electronics in *Star Wars*, his score would have probably not been that groundbreaking,"[45] because (with several notable exceptions) composers had been using strange electronic sounds to musically portray space for more than two decades. "It depends on the contexts: futuristic music against the clichés of Romantic music and Romantic music against the clichés of futuristic music, respectively," said Audissino. "Either way, there is a choice that is decidedly on one side and that goes against the conventions of the genre. By not choosing one side and keeping in the middle, probably Stevens played safer but failed to be remembered as an innovator."[46]

Bond explains that there were also other biases that worked against Stevens at the time. "Science fiction was not a greatly respected genre. Bernard Herrmann was probably the only true 'A-list' composer to score a science fiction film since *The Day the Earth Stood Still* was taken more seriously.... *The Day the Earth Stood Still* has this great pedigree and Herrmann is a greatly respected composer...."[47] Stevens was certainly a successful film composer, but never approached the level of success that Herrmann did in the 1950s and 1960s.

Jon Burlingame commented, "It's kind of a shame that he is not as well remembered for these early science fiction scores. I think it's because Leith Stevens was operating from a more conventional orchestral approach. What Stevens was doing was still very effective dramatically ... it deserves more attention than I think it's gotten."[48]

3

Entering the Final Frontier

The 1960s and Early 1970s

The prospect of nuclear annihilation remained a potent fear as the world entered the 1960s. It was also a time of rapid social and technological shifts. The election of John F. Kennedy as president of the United States seemed to inject the country with a sense of youthful energy.

A powerful symbol of this energy was space exploration. Yuri Gagarin became the first human in space on April 12, 1961, and just a few weeks later, on May 5, Alan Shepard became the first American in space. Twenty days after that, on May 25, 1961, in front of a joint session of Congress Kennedy announced the goal of landing humans on the surface of the Moon by the end of the decade. He reiterated this goal the following year at Rice University, when he spoke his famous words, "We choose to go to the Moon in this decade and do the other things, not because they are easy, but because they are hard, because that goal will serve to organize and measure the best of our energies and skills, because that challenge is one that we are willing to accept, one we are unwilling to postpone, and one which we intend to win, and the others, too."[1] True to the goal set down by the president, eight years later, *Apollo XI* landed on the lunar surface, and Neil Armstrong and Buzz Aldrin became the first humans to step on the Moon.

During the 1960s, both the United States and the Soviet Union made extraordinary progress toward opening the door to space exploration. It seemed as though this momentum would continue perpetually. The prospect of human missions to Mars and exploration of the rest of the solar system not only seemed possible, but inevitable.

This was reflected in some notable television shows and films of the 1960s, as well as in the music that was written to support these productions. The ominous electronic sound of space music was already fading as the 1960s began. Heroic and romantic orchestral compositions began to re-emerge, reflecting an optimistic and adventurous mood that arose as the space race began to accelerate. The television shows *Lost in Space* and *Star Trek* appeared in the mid–1960s, both with distinct orchestral music and generally optimistic visions of the future of human space exploration (despite the fact that the Robinson family was "lost" in space). These shows, particularly *Star Trek,* would inspire generations of space scientists and engineers. The music that accompanied them also played a role in inspiring the public. In her PhD dissertation for the University of Michigan, Jessica Leah Getman wrote,

> In *Star Trek*'s title cue, in which the space theme accompanies visuals of imaginary planets, vast fields of stars, and the *Enterprise* flying through them, this musical language contributes to the sense of heroic exploration and collaborative accomplishment attributed to the *Enterprise* crew as they travel across the galaxy. In turn, this coding reflects back to remark on the United States, painting it as both a land of opportunity and a unified nation in its prime, continually reaching beyond its technological and social boundaries, conquering not only the problems of this world, but those beyond it as well.[2]

✳✳✳

Not all the television shows of the 1960s had the impact of *Star Trek*. Many science fiction shows of the early 1960s were far less than awe-inspiring. This included the British series *Fireball XL5*, which was a space-based puppet show, and the American animated space adventure *Space Angels*. Both premiered in 1962.

British composer Barry Gray (who went on to score *Space: 1999* and *Thunderbirds*) composed music for the *Fireball XL5* series. According to Lee Thacker of Setthetape.com, Gray's *Space Angels* scores were "bold and brassy orchestral pieces" and also had elements of jazz. The main theme, "Fireball," was "a very bouncy piece of pre–Beatles pop, which is just ridiculously catchy." It made the British pop charts.[3]

Paul Horn was the composer of record on *Space Angel*. Despite his jazz lineage, he wrote a short, highly melodramatic theme, vaguely reminiscent of Leith Stevens' opening music of *Destination Moon*. However, most episodes featured very little music. Much of the music that was featured would better be described as sound design than musical scoring. The show would have little musical or cultural impact. (Horn studied transcendental meditation in India with teacher Maharshi Mahesh Yogi at the same time as the Beatles.[4])

In 1962, Hanna-Barbera's futuristic cartoon *The Jetsons* premiered. *The Jetsons* followed the success and the model of *The Flintstones*, but rather than a "modern Stone Age family," *The Jetsons* depicted a family living in the year 2060. By this date, apartment buildings among the clouds and flying cars were the norm. Strictly speaking, *The Jetsons* was not a space-based show (since it still mostly took place within Earth's atmosphere), but it was inspired by the burgeoning space age.

To score this futuristic family story, Hanna-Barbera called upon Hoyt Curtin, a veteran composer for many of the animated series of the time. Jon Burlingame calls Curtin the "the king of television cartoon music."[5] Curtin was responsible for Hanna-Barbera's primetime shows *The Flintstones, Top Cat, Jonny Quest et al*. His music for *The Jetsons* would often be reminiscent of his work on *The Flintstones*, with both employing jazzy music. According to Burlingame, "The jazz approach to the scoring of many Hanna-Barbera shows was directly attributable to Curtin's love of big-band music,"[6] Curtin once said, "These cartoons are not World War Three. They are happy...'Happy' to me is jazz."[7]

The Jetsons' most memorable musical element was unquestionably its jazzy theme song that would serve to introduce the main characters with a small ensemble of vocalists singing "Meet George Jetson, his boy Elroy, daughter Judy, Jane his wife." Curtin initially recorded the theme song with a small band, since Hanna-Barbera did not have substantial faith in the series. But after receiving positive feedback from the network, Curtin was asked to write a new score for a large band. According to Curtin, "Instead of writing a whole new score ... I just had musicians listen to, on headsets, the first tryout with a small band. I wrote an arrangement to include the large group, all the strings and everything."[8]

Running for just one season, *The Jetsons* probably did not make a significant impact on the public perception of space, but Curtin's music did reflect the new, optimistic sound of space and the future. In fact, his jazzy theme would live on long after the original show was cancelled. During the 1980s, *The Jetsons* grew in popularity and two additional seasons were produced. The theme song even began to be played on popular radio stations. According to David Wharton of the *Los Angeles Times*, "On a given day, the tune might play between Twisted Sister and Genesis on any one of several rock'n'roll radio stations in Los Angeles. George and the family have an animated video on MTV, and *The Jetsons* theme, re-recorded in stereo, recently reached No. 9 on Billboard magazine's retail sales charts."[9]

Doctor Who

Doctor Who, arguably the most iconic television show in British history, premiered on November 23, 1963. It went on to become the longest running science fiction television show in history with over 850 episodes between 1963 and today (with a gap in production between 1989 and 2005).

The show had a rocky start, airing one day after the assassination of American President John F. Kennedy. As a result, its ratings were extremely low, motivating the BBC to re-air the pilot episode a week later, November 30.

Produced by the BBC, *Doctor Who* follows the journeys of an alien simply known as the Doctor. He travels through time and space aboard his TARDIS (Time and Relative Dimension in Space), a vehicle that looks identical to a British police box on the outside, but is far bigger on the inside.

During the early years of the show, music was not a high priority. The early music in the series served the role of sound design rather than a soundtrack, used to set the mood or advance the plot with electronic and other unusual sounds. Nonetheless, from the first episode, *Doctor Who* made a musical statement with its driving and seemingly unrelenting theme song.

As with most shows of the time, the composition of appropriate opening theme music was one of the top priorities, and show producer Verity Lambert had a clear concept of what she wanted. She had listened to an unusual performance by a French avant-garde band, Les Structures Sonores. Their music sounded like the product of electronic instruments, but their compositions were played on glass and metallic sculptures called Sound-Structures that had been custom-built for them.[10] Les Structures Sonores played a form of music called "musique concrete"; the style, advanced by French composer Pierre Schaeffer, was defined by *Encyclopædia Britannica* as an "experimental technique of musical composition using recorded sounds as raw material…. The fundamental principle of musique concrète lies in the assemblage of various natural sounds recorded on tape (or, originally, on disks) to produce a montage of sound."[11]

Lambert wanted to emulate that sound for the new *Doctor Who* series, but the production could not afford to hire Les Structures Sonores. As a result, she approached BBC Radiophonic Workshop: Founded in 1958, they specialized in innovative and unusual electronic music that "created the soundscapes of alien worlds and imagined futures, conveyed the wonders of nature and introduced generations of audiences to the possibilities of electronic sound and music."[12]

Australian composer Ron Grainer was hired to write the theme music. Grainer had moved to London in 1952 and became a successful television composer. His music for *Giants of Steam*, a 1963 documentary about Great Britain's railway system, caught the attention of Verity Lambert. While she had a clear idea of the musical sound she wanted for *Doctor Who*, she gave Grainer the somewhat vague instruction that she wanted something "with a beat, radiophonic, 'familiar yet different.'"[13] Grainer took this task seriously, retreating to his private beach in Portugal to write the *Doctor Who* theme. The end result was contained on a single page of manuscript paper with "just the famous bass line and a swooping melody."[14] According to Mark Ayers of the Effectrode Thermionic website, Grainer's manuscript outlined a "few harmonic changes, and these are marked out almost entirely by the movement of the bass line, with only sparing use of inner harmony parts to reinforce where necessary."[15]

This manuscript was handed off to Delia Derbyshire, a composer, musician and master of electronic music and sound at the BBC Radiophonic Workshop. Derbyshire turned Grainer's initial concept into the theme song that is now famous around the world.

Derbyshire had joined the Radiophonic Workshop in 1960 and proved to be a genius at manipulating and recording sounds. Born in 1937, she had become fascinated with abstract electronic sounds as a child when World War II air raid sirens left an indelible mark on her psyche.

Upon receiving the short manuscript, she began to interpret Grainer's unusual guidance. "On the score he'd written 'sweeps,' 'swoops,' 'beautiful words,' 'wind cloud,' 'wind bubble,'" with very little clarity regarding what he meant by these instructions. Nonetheless, she must have interpreted his suggestions well enough: She said that Grainer was "tickled pink" when he heard the final product.[16] She remained humble and self-effacing, recalling, "It was a magic experience. I couldn't see how it was going to sound. It was Ron's brilliant oral imagination."[17]

The groundbreaking collaborative theme was both an eerie yet driving piece of electronic music, largely produced by manipulating analog tapes. According to Amy Mulligan of the Museum of Electrical Invention, Derbyshire and the Radiophonic Workshop also "used white noise, plucked strings, played with oscillators and 'wobulators' to create the notes and sounds you hear. Then the tapes were spliced together, sped up, slowed down to create something that resembled music."[18]

Like *Forbidden Planet*, this song was entirely electronic. "The most remarkable thing is that nobody actually plays it," said Derbyshire. "The music was constructed note by note without the use of any live instrumentalists at all."[19] Unlike *Forbidden Planet*, the *Doctor Who* theme has a tonal melody, and Derbyshire did not harness electronic circuits as the Barrons had on their groundbreaking score.

While Derbyshire believed that Grainer was "tickled pink" over her arrangement, it may not have been for the reason she assumed. According to Adam Blackshaw of the National Film and Sound Archive of Australia, "When Grainer heard the final recording, he was dumbfounded and quizzically asked Derbyshire if she had written the piece.... Grainer wanted to give Derbyshire credit as a co-composer but it was against BBC policy at the time."[20]

To this day, there are varying opinions on who deserves more credit for the iconic theme, Grainer or Derbyshire. Composer David Arnold is of the opinion that they are both equally important: "Without the composition, the realization wouldn't have happened, and without the realization, the composition wouldn't perhaps have gotten to the level that it did."[21]

Regardless of who played a more significant role in writing the song, only Ron Grainer and the Radiophonic Workshop would be properly acknowledged for their role in the composition. As a result, Derbyshire's work on *Doctor Who* and other projects with the Radiophonic Workshop went unacknowledged for years. It was only in later years that her extraordinary contribution to electronic music—and her role in one of the most iconic themes in television history—became fully known.

The iconic theme is only the best-known music associated with *Doctor Who*. Every episode needed to be scored, requiring several composers to contribute to the first few years of production. Two of the more influential composers during *Doctor Who*'s early days were Dudley Simpson and Tristram Cary. Cary was an accomplished composer, having scored numerous films, concert pieces and a six-part BBC production of *Jane Eyre*. He was also a pioneer of "musique concrète." Between 1964 and 1966, he composed music for over two dozen episodes of *Doctor Who*, firmly leaving his musical imprint on the show. Cary was arguably best known for providing music for the first six episodes that introduced the Daleks, the cybernetic aliens that became the most prominent villains of the entire *Doctor Who* franchise. Cary created a completely "alien" sound to musically depict these villains. According to musicologist Alexander Walls, "Cary uses musique concrète techniques to create abstract soundscapes; the public's unfamiliarity with this adds to the otherworldliness of Skaro and its inhabitants, making up for deficiencies in sets and special effects. 'The Daleks' showcases how well early *Doctor Who* represented alien soundscapes."[22] Cary noted that the episodes "definitely called for electronic music," and that "the largely atmospheric tracks are mostly made by manipulating real sounds mechanically."[23] As mentioned earlier, these early scores often blurred the line between music and sound design. According to Ethan Iverson of *The Atlantic*, "At first, the show's background music was minimal. Exotic atmosphere was frequently supplied by a generic electronic hum, as lo-fi as the rubber-suit monsters and cardboard spaceship consoles."[24]

The individual who almost certainly had the largest musical impact in the first run of shows (1963–1989) was Dudley Simpson, who served as the primary composer of the science fiction show from 1964 until 1979.

Simpson had written the music for such BBC shows as *Moonstrike* and *Kidnapped*. On the set of *Moonstrike*, he was approached by Mervyn Pinfield, *Doctor Who*'s associate producer, to write music for a three-part story for Season 2 (1964), "Planet of Giants." Simpson, who had never written music for science fiction, was invited to view the highly unusual *Doctor Who* set. It featured, among other strange objects, a giant telephone and other large props to make the human actors look diminutive. Confronted with these massive set pieces, Simpson recalled thinking, "How am I going to write this music? ... Hello, I've only got a dozen instruments."[25]

Twelve instruments were an overstatement. As it turned out, during his entire tenure with the show, he was not allowed to exceed eight musicians to record the scores. For "Planet of Giants," his small ensemble included a piccolo for the small characters and a tuba for the giants. He also used percussion, clarinet, horn, trumpet, trombone and piano, but was only given five musicians for the second and third episodes. As a result, he had to be both efficient and creative in how he handled his ensemble. Simpson recalled, "The music came as the last item of the budget. They made it clear to me that if we were going to have music at all it had to be done on the cheap."[26]

Nevertheless, Simpson was enthralled by his work on the show, taking great pride in his compositions. He recalled,

> I used to sit up all night doing *Doctor Who*. It used to be such a rush. I would have to deliver music to my copyist at all hours. I got pulled up once by a policeman, who said I'd been past him three or four times each way. I said, "It's all right, I'm delivering music." "What for?" he asked. When I told him, he said, "What? *Doctor Who*? Well, you'd better be going on your way, then."[27]

By the time the fourth Doctor, Tom Baker, had arrived, the musical scoring had become far more integral to the show—in no small part because of Simpson's continuing role. Simpson had essentially become the series' "house composer," writing a wide variety of pieces for chamber ensembles to support the show. He had also moved away from the heavy use of electronic music so prevalent in the series' early days. According to Ethan Iversen of *The New Yorker*, Simpson hit his peak in an episode called "The Pyramid of Mars": "[It] includes the definitive 'mad scientist at the pipe organ' cue."[28]

During the first run of the show, *Doctor Who* contained several distinct phases of musical style. The music would largely follow the Radiophonic style of composition until 1969. After that, the music shifted to the chamber ensemble style that Simpson specialized in. After Simpson left in 1979, the score reverted to primarily electronic music until the end of the first run of the show in 1989.[29] There was a hiatus until 2005, when the show was rebooted and Murray Gold became the primary composer for the next 12 years. Segun Akinola assumed that role in 2018.

Lost in Space

Doctor Who may not have been a full-fledged space-related show (it was more focused on travelling through time), but a new American show premiered in 1965 that embraced a future where humans would travel to other planets. This show was unquestionably responding to the accelerating space race with the Soviet Union. *Lost in Space* was created by Irwin Allen, who had produced several SF motion pictures in the early 1960s, including *The Lost World* and *Voyage to the Bottom of the Sea*.

Lost in Space was a space-based adaptation of Johann David Wyss' 1812 novel *The Swiss Family Robinson*. Over 30 years in the future, in 1997, the Robinson family, along with Major Don West and a robot, set out on a flight to an Earth-like planet around the star Alpha Centauri. Their spacecraft is the *Jupiter-2*, a saucer-shaped vehicle reminiscent of the spacecraft in *The Day the Earth Stood Still*. Dr. Zachary Smith, a saboteur who bungled and found himself trapped aboard during lift-off, causes the ship to become hopelessly lost in space. Each week, the crew of the *Jupiter-2* had new adventures in space and on alien planets.

Lost in Space used several composers during its three-year run, but the person who most significantly set the tone was John Williams. Williams had already composed scores for dozens of television shows and films and had just completed his contract with Universal. Professionally known as "Johnny" Williams at the time (a well-known British actor named John Williams was active then), he was hired to compose the theme music as well as to score several episodes.

Williams used a traditional, bright orchestral scoring style "that is easily apprehended by television audiences," rather than relying on electronic sound.[30] Williams described this musical style years later when explaining his similar approach to *Star Wars*: "It is not music that might describe *terra incognita*, but the opposite of that, music that would put us in touch with very familiar and remembered emotions."[31]

Williams' first task was to write the theme song, the first of two opening themes he wrote for the show. According to Dye Family Professor of Music Ron Rodman of Carlton University, this theme is "humorous quasi-style pop tune that had several musical-narrative topics embedded."[32] Accompanying the animated opening credits, Williams wrote a pulsing musical section using flutes and piccolos to musically portray

the animated computer lights flashing on the screen as part of the opening title sequence. The main melody then begins "with trumpets playing
a quasi-heroic gesture completed by a more comical pop-style chromatic
gesture, followed by calamitous descending chromatic runs in the trumpets, flutes, and piccolos again."[33] In a rare use of electronic instrumentation, Williams also employed an instrument with no formal name. It
was developed by Paul Tanner, who had previously been trombonist with
the Glenn Miller Band. According to Jon Burlingame, the instrument was
"part theremin and part ondes martenot"[34] and could more accurately
control an electronic pitch than a standard theremin. (Note: An ondes
martenot is an electronic instrument invented by Maurice Martenot that
created electric pulses at two supersonic sound-wave frequencies using
radio tubes.)

By the time *Lost in Space* Season 3 rolled around, Williams was
tasked with writing a new, more dramatic theme song—one that would
become far more identified with the show. After a countdown prelude that
was accompanied by "heavy stinger cords,"[35] the theme breaks into a more
majestic descending horn section, followed by a "campy 1960s rock style
section."[36] This theme, far more "hummable" than the original theme, was
recycled (and rearranged) in both the 1998 *Lost in Space* motion picture as
well as the television reboot that premiered in 2018.

With the exception of the original theme music, Williams did not use
electronic instruments for the remainder of his duration on the show, and
he made very little use of strings. "We had a pretty healthy brass section,
eight or ten," he recalled. This was supplemented with woodwinds and
percussion, which was "a little more generous than the Universal ensemble typically would be."[37]

Lost in Space was Williams' first space–science fiction composition
job. According to Ron Rodman, "Williams' proclivity to compose in the
neo–Romantic and light classical 'pop' styles originates in *Lost in Space*.
Throughout the run of the series, Williams' music was recycled (along
with occasional contributions from other composers), and reiterated tonal,
melodramatic, and conventional orchestral tropes."[38]

"I guess the intention was probably to be pretty straight with it,"
stated Williams. "But some of it, even at the time, was kind of campy.... I
did get a little broad fairly quickly. I sometimes think in my mind that it
was kind of a precursor of *Star Wars* in a way, because [the series] had the
robots, the various characters, and a broad musical treatment."[39]

While he only wrote music for four episodes, his contributions set the
musical tone for the series and his cues were frequently recycled throughout the run of the show. These cues would often be intermixed with the
music of other composers, including Alexander Courage (who had

already begun writing music for *Star Trek*,[40]), Leith Stevens), Herman Stein and Joseph Mullendore. Stock music was also be woven into the show. Perhaps the most famous piece of borrowed music was Bernard Herrmann's score for *The Day the Earth Stood Still*. During the Season 1 episode "War of the Robots," Will Robinson, Dr. Smith and the Robot encounter a malevolent robot while Herrmann's "Gort" theme sounds to indicate its sinister nature. This music was also heard in the series' unaired pilot.

As "campy" as *Lost in Space* was, the show lived on for decades in repeats, introducing new generations to the Robinson family and the musical style.

Star Trek: A New Frontier for Television

"Space. The final frontier. These are the voyages of the starship *Enterprise*." These now-famous words were heard on televisions around the United States on September 8, 1966. The new NBC space drama *Star Trek* marked the beginning of a shift in science fiction space television programming, and the beginning of a new major franchise.

The show began at a time when the space race was accelerating to its climax. In 1966, the year that *Star Trek* premiered, the Soviet Union had successfully sent the Luna-9 robotic lander to the surface of the Moon. That same year, the U.S. launched the *Saturn 1B* rocket (a precursor to the *Saturn V* rocket that brought men to the Moon three years later) and conducted the first successful docking of two spacecraft when the *Gemini VIII* spacecraft docked with the *Agena* in Low Earth Orbit. Neil Armstrong was the command pilot on that mission, three years before he became the first human to step on the Moon.

Taking place in the twenty-third century, *Star Trek* follows the crew of the USS *Enterprise* on a five-year mission "to explore strange new worlds; to seek out new life and new civilizations; to boldly go where no man has gone before." The ship is commanded by the bold and swashbuckling James T. Kirk. Other crew members include Mr. Spock, first officer and science officer (who was half-human and half-Vulcan); Leonard McCoy, the ship physician; Lieutenant Uhura, the communications officer; Lieutenant Commander Montgomery Scott, the chief engineer; Lieutenant Hikaru Sulu, helmsman; and Ensign Pavel Chekov, navigator. Together, the creators and cast not only changed expectations of what a science fiction television show could aspire to, but also broke through the social barriers of the time, featuring an African American woman and a Japanese man as bridge officers at a time when most authority figures on TV were played by white men.

Star Trek creator Gene Roddenberry knew that music was an essential ingredient for his new series, and he had very strong feelings on the topic, specifically regarding electronic music. He was so opposed to the electronic-theremin sound of the 1950s that he told composer Alexander Courage, "I don't want any of this goddammed funny-sounding space science fiction music, I want adventure music."[41] Roddenberry was more specific with his preferences in another interview when he said, "Give us Captain Blood!" Courage would channel another swashbuckling composer named Robert Farnon, who composed the score for the 1951 film *Captain Horatio Hornblower*.[42] The opening notes of that film are remarkably similar to the opening notes of the *Star Trek* theme. This similarity was not purely coincidental. While it was commonly believed that Roddenberry's vision for *Star Trek* was to be a space-based version of *Wagon Train* (a popular television show that premiered in 1957), his vision for *Star Trek* was that it should be "Horatio Hornblower in outer space."[43] The Hornblower film was based on a series of books written by C.S. Forester and first published in the 1930s about a fictional Royal Navy Officer during the Napoleonic Wars. Roddenberry saw Captain Kirk as a futuristic version of Hornblower.

Roddenberry considered numerous composers to write the first episode and the theme music, including the renowned Franz Waxman and Elmer Bernstein, as well as rising talents Jerry Goldsmith and John "Johnny" Williams. However, Desilu musical director Wilbur Hatch approached Alexander "Sandy" Courage to ask, "How would you like to write the theme for this thing, and we'll see if Roddenberry likes it?"[44]

Courage had written for numerous television scores, including *Wagon Train*. He had also orchestrated some major films (*My Fair Lady*, *The Agony and the Ecstasy*) as well as uncredited orchestration of *North by Northwest* and *Ben-Hur*. He was not a fan of science fiction, however, calling the entire genre "marvelous malarkey."[45] Nonetheless, he took on the task and apparently Roddenberry liked what Courage wrote, and Courage signed on for the original pilot called "The Cage." For it, he wrote an iconic theme that would become his best-known composition by far. He later commented, "Little did I know when I wrote that first A♭ for the flute that it was going to go down in history."[46]

The theme took Courage about a week to compose, drawing inspiration from two contrasting songs. Courage later recalled the first of these songs was "an old Hebridean tune from the outer islands of Scotland, because I wanted something that had a long, long feel to it."[47] He wanted to place the Hebridean-like tune over faster-moving, adventurous music. The inspiration for the faster-moving section was a 1930 song called "Beyond the Blue Horizon."[48] He recalled, "I wanted to make all of the scales go way out, and I wanted the intervals to be long, and I wanted to have a kind of exotic feel to it."[49]

Roddenberry advocated a female voice to play a central role to the theme. According to Courage, Roddenberry particularly liked the seductive sound of soprano Loulie Jean Norman. "That really got to Roddenberry," Courage stated. "Because he was quite a sexpot and anything that had to do with a woman's voice was just right for him. So, he mixed in more soprano and less of the instruments than I would have wanted."[50] Norman's voice was featured only during the first season of *Star Trek*. The song was remixed for the second and third seasons without Norman's vocals, to avoid paying the singer royalties.

Roddenberry was certainly not opposed paying royalties to himself. Anyone familiar with the opening credits of *Star Trek* may have also noted that Alexander Courage is not the only person credited for the theme song; Roddenberry is also credited. Roddenberry did not co-write the song, but he did write lyrics to go along with the music. The lyrics were never used in the show—and probably were never intended to be used—but Roddenberry insisted on receiving 50 percent of the royalties for Courage's theme music. Roddenberry merely needed to justify being listed as a co-composer so that he could share in the royalties. He was quoted as saying, "I have to get some money somewhere. I'm sure not gonna get it out of the profits of *Star Trek*."[51] Roddenberry's special lyrics were not as inspirational as the television show he created.[52]

This was, predictably, a source of tension between Courage and Roddenberry. To help smooth things over, Roddenberry sent Courage a letter in October 1967, trying to convince the composer that he had agreed to share credit. Roddenberry wrote,

> Perhaps this will help refresh your memory—in my old office, the small bungalow across the lot, you and I sat down one afternoon and discussed sharing the credits on the music. I recall very distinctly that you shook your head and stated that you would naturally prefer not to split the money on the theme but, on the other hand, since this was the way it was and since we were working so closely together on the concept you would go along with it.[53]

This letter does not appear to have alleviated Courage's irritation, and he only scored two episodes in the first season. According to producer Robert Justman, the fact that Courage only scored two episodes was at least partially because Courage had already committed to arrange music for the film *Doctor Dolittle* (1967). Justman added, "Nevertheless, owing to the 'royalty' issue, it's no wonder Sandy Courage lost all enthusiasm for the series and liking for Gene Roddenberry. Despite my efforts to convince him to score second-season episodes, Sandy never returned to *Star Trek*."[54]

Most of the *Star Trek* music was written by other composers. Courage was joined in the first season by Fred Steiner, Joseph Mullendore, Gerald Fried and Sol Kaplan, who would play a much larger role in establishing the musical tone and emotional depth for the franchise within each episode. This was not necessarily an easy task. According to Jeff Bond, author of *The Music of Star Trek*, "These guys were all confronted with something that had never been done before."[55] This included musically portraying the ship itself (very much a character in the show), as well as inventing the sounds of exotic planets, traveling at warp speed, and engaging in battles with hostile alien species in space. *Star Trek* was not the first television series to prognosticate about humanity's spacefaring adventures and battles in the future, but the show was far more thoughtful and cerebral than the space-based shows that had come before.

The composers also needed to overcome the limitations of the show. Nobody knew that *Star Trek* would eventually be considered one of *the* groundbreaking series of the 1960s. Thus, at times they had to contend with constrained budgets and sometimes limited special effects technology. The music would often compensate for these limitations. "They all had to think about how to address those ideas through music and augment the visual effects that were cutting edge for the time, but they were not as immersive as they are now," stated Bond. "Even though they couldn't put tremendous money into costumes, like you would see now with *Game of Thrones*, the music kind of fleshed out the costumes and the makeup and made you feel like all this stuff was more real."[56]

The composer who arguably made the largest impact on the musical sound of *Star Trek* was Steiner. According to Bond, "Although Courage laid down some of the most basic thematic material of the series and established the overall orchestral tone of the show's scoring, it was Steiner who really fleshed out its composition style in his early *Star Trek* scores: richly orchestral, with dark, heavy textures in brass and low strings."[57]

Best known for his musical contributions to the courtroom drama series *Perry Mason*, Steiner had worked extensively on other TV shows such as *Rawhide*, *Gunsmoke* and *Hogan's Heroes*, as well as *Lost in Space*. Wilbur Hatch invited Steiner to join the *Star Trek* team based on the composer's work on *The Twilight Zone*, where he was required to demonstrate similar stylistic flexibility as he would in the new space show.

Steiner quickly become one of *Star Trek* producer Bob Justman's preferred composers. "As soon as I heard his music, I was hot for it," recalled Justman. "[His] music was broader in a way; he was kind of like the John Williams of that time; broad, sweeping themes, very melodramatic style of music."[58] This relationship was particularly important for Steiner. While Hatch had hired Steiner, Justman almost certainly had more day-to-day influence on the scoring of the show.

Television composers in the 1960s had to work under a different set of union rules than they do today. Current-day TV composers (of record) write scores for specific episodes and are acknowledged for their contribution. This was not necessarily the case in the mid–60s because of union rules. Composers would often write music that was reused in numerous episodes and intermixed with the music of other composers. Steiner recalled, "On my first assignment, I was writing music for three different episodes in one session. That was quite a way to break in."[59] Rather than having an original score for every episode, shows made heavy use of library music. "It was music composed not to any specific episode or scene," according to Bond. "A composer would come in and say 'Here's a piece of fight music'—'Here's a piece of sad music'—and they would produce maybe a half-hour of music like this." Composers frequently had no idea which episode would feature their music, or how it would be utilized. Steiner recorded a substantial amount of library music. "They were almost all variations of cues that he had written for the show, and he would just record different versions with different tempos and different emphasis."[60]

As a result of this non-individual system, it was very difficult to determine who scored music for each episode in the original series. As Bond researched his *Music of Star Trek*, he was able to identify which composers contributed to each episode. He scoured cue sheets and other valuable materials, and interviewed composers and producers to shed light on the contributions of each composer. Bond recalled, "Tracing individual music cues from the original *Star Trek* to their composers can be an act of archaeology worthy of Indiana Jones."[61]

The Influence of *Star Trek*

The *Star Trek* franchise influenced the world well beyond the confines of science fiction, perhaps more than any other science fiction franchise. The show (and subsequent productions) inspired generations of space scientists and engineers, and the music within each episode also helped to inspire the public. As with any effective film or television music, one only needs to hear the music (separate from the show) to relive the original emotions or have flashbacks to specific scenes. While the various scores for the original *Star Trek* series were not always among the greatest music in TV history, they were highly effective at supporting a groundbreaking series—and enabling people to conjure the emotional impact of their favorite episodes through music.

2001: A Space Odyssey

Television was not the only source of innovative space content in the 1960s. There was a major cinematic milestone in 1968: the release of Stanley Kubrick's *2001: A Space Odyssey*. Kubrick's directorial mastery was magnified by the fact that the film was released just a few months prior to the *Apollo VIII* mission in which humans orbited the Moon for the first time, and a little more than a year before Neil Armstrong and Buzz Aldrin put the first footprints on the Moon. Audiences justifiably had faith that the future of space exploration was limitless. According to Mekado Murphy of the *New York Times,* "One year before Apollo 11 touched down on the surface of the Moon, Stanley Kubrick's astonishing film helped prepare audiences for what it might look like to get there…. While the movie has much more than the Moon on its mind, it primed a generation of people for sights their eyes might not have otherwise believed."[62]

The film was a collaboration between Kubrick, who had directed such films as *Dr. Strangelove* and *Spartacus,* and science fiction author and futurist Arthur C. Clarke, the author of *Childhood's End, The City and the Stars* and *The Hammer of God.*

Kubrick had expressed interest in working with Clarke as far back as in 1953,[63] but their formal partnership began in March 1964, when Kubrick wrote Clarke a letter proposing "the possibility of doing the proverbial 'really good' science fiction movie."[64] Kubrick added that his interest was focused on three main premises, "(1) The reason for believing in the existence of intelligent extra-terrestrial life. (2) The impact (and perhaps lack of impact in some quarters) such a discovery would have on Earth in the near future. (3) A space probe with a landing and exploration of the Moon and Mars."[65]

As it turned out, many of the key plot elements had already been mapped in a 1948 Clarke story, "The Sentinel." That story even included the discovery of an alien artifact. This would be the basis of the monolith discovered on the Moon in *2001* that was emitting a signal to Jupiter. Clarke's initial premise was then broadened to become a spacefaring version of Homer's *Odyssey* intermixed with references to Friedrich Nietzsche's novel *Also sprach Zarathustra.* As Michael Benson wrote, Nietzsche's philosophy is reflected through the message that "mankind is merely a transitional species—sentient enough to understand its animal origins but not yet truly civilized."[66]

The pedigree of the creators matched with the philosophical, scientific, spiritual references made *2001* unlike any previous space-based film, but Kubrick knew there was another critical ingredient to achieve his full vision: music. This musical ingredient could not be satisfied by the electronic sounds of the 1950s, nor the music that had come into vogue in motion pictures in the mid–1960s.

The director had always envisioned tracking his film with the music of nineteenth- and twentieth-century classical composers, but the studio initially insisted that an original score be composed. Composer Alex North was hired, but after receiving a significant portion of this score, Kubrick reverted back to his original plan to track the film with classical pieces (see *2001: The Score That Almost Was* below).

The most impactful of these musical selections was an 1896 tone poem by the romantic–early modern German composer Richard Strauss (1864–1949), based on Nietzsche's *Also sprach Zarathustra*. This piece famously accompanied the opening sequence as well the transitional (or evolutionary) moment when a proto-human (or hominid) called Moon Watcher discovers how to use a bone as a weapon, enabling his tribe to rise above other proto-human "tribes," thus gaining a dominant position in the food chain. From a musical perspective, this scenario was quite appropriate. In a letter to Otto Florsheim of *The Musical Courier*, Strauss himself described his inspiration for the piece, writing that he was trying "to convey in music an idea of the evolution of the human race from its origin, through the various phases of development, religious as well as scientific, up to Nietzsche's idea of the Übermensch (superman)."[67]

Whatever Strauss' original hopes were for "Also sprach Zarathustra," the piece had remained relatively obscure prior to *2001*'s release. Its use in the film catapulted the initial bars of the composition to new levels of fame, and it became the musical theme most associated with space (with the possible exception of the *Star Trek* theme) until the release of *Star Wars* in 1977. It also became ubiquitous in popular culture, invoking images of the conquest of space. One immediate example occurred during coverage of the *Apollo XI* landing in 1969: The BBC used "Also sprach Zarathustra" to accompany portions of their coverage of the historic Moon launch.[68] According to Emil de Cou, musical director of the Pacific Northwest Ballet, Strauss' piece had been so effectively co-opted for space that "[s]omehow when you think about 'Also sprach Zarathustra,' you don't think of Nietzsche, you think of Kubrick."[69]

The rest of the film is also tracked with selections from the classical repertoire. After the film's opening "Dawn of Man" section, the timeline fast forwards several million years to the twenty-first century. A Pan American (Pan Am) space plane is engaged in a space ballet as it approaches and docks with a rotating space station, accompanied by "The Blue Danube," an 1866 composition by Austrian Johann Strauss II (1825–1899), also known as "The Waltz King." "Johann Strauss II's Blue Danube waltz and the spaceship floating together is a marvelous juxtaposition of movement in the endless void of space," said Jeff Rush, chair of the Film and Media Arts Department at Temple University's School of Theater, Film, and Media Arts. He added that the music is not intended to perfectly reflect the action but Kubrick respects "the abstraction that's built into the music ... [T]he music opens the film up to all kinds of possibilities."[70] (Despite Richard Strauss and Johann Strauss II sharing the same last name, they were not related.)

The music by Richard Strauss and Johann Strauss II was used to convey wonder, but also to express a sense of familiarity and the progression of the human race. However, Kubrick also effectively used contemporary, avant-garde compositions to musically represent the unfamiliar— or alien. Central to this musical approach is the music of György Ligeti (1923–2006).

Born in Romania in 1923, Ligeti became one of the most prominent avant-garde composers, generating musical pieces that the *Encyclopædia Britannica* described thusly: "Specific musical intervals, rhythms, and harmonies are often not distinguishable but act together in a multiplicity of sound events to create music that communicates both serenity and dynamic anguished motion."[71] In short, Ligeti's music presented a sound that would seem unnerving and even alien to audiences of the time.

Kubrick employed music from three of Ligeti's compositions, including the 1961 orchestral piece *Atmosphères* and his 1966 choir piece *Lux Aeterna*, and *Requiem* for choir and orchestra written between 1963 and 1965. These musical selections, as well as the long intervals without music,

A Pan American space plane approaches Space Station V in *2001: A Space Odyssey*.

worked extraordinarily well at portraying both the majesty of space, but also the often-unnerving elements of the film. According to film scholar and musicologist Emilio Audissino, by selecting both tonal and non-tonal music, Kubrick is also helping to bridge our perception of space music. The 1950s had seen the use of non-tonal music (often electronic) to depict a more ominous, sinister perception of space. "In *2001*, we have the same futuristic music by Ligeti—as well as Richard and Johann Strauss—very tonal—very old fashioned music. Kubrick created a contrast between the modernistic and classical sound."[72]

The Ligeti music is extremely non-tonal and often non-rhythmic. It would be an unfamiliar sound to most moviegoers of the late 1960s. With that in mind, Kubrick used the Ligeti music to evoke something alien, far from our realm of understanding—as well as arousing a sense of anxiety from the audience.[73] As the subject matter became more alien and unnerving as the film progressed, Ligeti's work was used extensively. Almost the entire recordings of *Atmosphères* and "Kyrie" from *Requiem* were used in the film. "It was bold of Kubrick to trust that his audience would stay put for what amounted to a seventeen-minute avant-garde concert with visual elements added," noted Alex Ross. "But he seemed to grasp the formal logic in Ligeti's futuristic sound—the Requiem is influenced by the polyphonic masses of the fifteenth-century composer Johannes Ockeghem—and saw how it could unify his jumble of images."[74]

As was the case with "Also sprach Zarathustra," *2001* also boosted Ligeti's fame. According to Christine Lee Gengaro, "Although Ligeti was enjoying some notoriety in the 1960s, it was Kubrick's use of his pieces in *2001* that introduced the composer to a massive audience."[75]

Despite this significant expansion of his name recognition, Ligeti, who was still producing music (unlike both Strausses), was not happy with the situation. Shortly after viewing *2001* in September 1968, he wrote a letter to a friend expressing displeasure that the publisher had allowed his music to be used in the film. He wrote that *2001* was a "piece of Hollywood shit."[76] He was so upset that he took legal action, but in the end received only a $3000 settlement.

Ligeti's displeasure with Kubrick faded in the following years. When Kubrick directed *The Shining* (1980) and *Eyes Wide Shut* (1999), Ligeti granted permission for his music to be used in those films in exchange for a healthy royalty. In his book *György Ligeti: Music of the Imagination*, Richard Steinitz notes that Kubrick and Ligeti developed a mutual respect, "In Kubrick, Ligeti recognized a willingness to explore and take risks, a tireless concern for detail and obsessive pursuit of perfection similar to his own."[77]

✳✳✳

There were some additional factors to distinguish Kubrick's musical philosophy from other films. In addition to shrewd selections of musical tracks, Kubrick did not believe in fading out the music at the end of scenes. "He often edited the music as little as possible, opting to cut or add images rather than compromise the composer's musical idea."[78]

Kubrick was also a master of silence. In a 1968 interview with *Playboy* magazine, Kubrick noted that the film was two hours and 19 minutes, but there was only 40 minutes of dialogue. "I tried to create a visual experience, one that bypasses verbalizing pigeonholing and directly penetrates the subconscious with an emotional and philosophical content."[79] In many ways, these silences added to the tension of the film just as much as the music did—and may have reminded the audience of the isolation and silent vacuum of space.

Reaction

While the film would be praised as a masterpiece in time, initial reaction during some early screenings was less than stellar. Dan Chiasson of *The New Yorker* compared the early premieres around the country with the legendary opening of Stravinsky's "Rite of Spring" in 1913,

> when Parisians in osprey and tails reportedly brandished their canes and pelted the dancers with objects. A sixth of the New York première's audience walked right out, including several executives from MGM. Many who stayed jeered throughout. Kubrick nervously shuttled between his seat in the front row and the projection booth, where he tweaked the sound and the focus. Arthur C. Clarke, Kubrick's collaborator, was in tears at intermission.[80]

After these disheartening screenings, Kubrick went back to the editing room, reducing the length of the film by 17 minutes.[81] When *2001* was released again, the film received significantly better (yet mixed) reviews. Among the prominent critics of Kubrick's musical choices was Jerry Goldsmith. Goldsmith, who had composed the score for *Planet of the Apes,* released the same year, argued that music should not be forced into a film. He complained, "*2001* was ruined by Kubrick's choice of music. His selections had no relationship, and the pieces could not comment on the film because they were not part of it."[82] Despite Goldsmith's criticisms, *2001*'s classical score was an overwhelming success, not only within the framework of the film but also as a soundtrack album. It sold so well that a follow-up album was issued.

2001: The Score That Almost Was

The extraordinary symbiosis between classical music and film that occurred in *2001: A Space Odyssey* almost did not happen at all. While Kubrick had been considering using a classical repertoire to score the film from the early stages of its development, MGM had insisted that an original score be composed.

Kubrick and Clarke contemplated several composers to write the film score. At first they considered Carl Orff, whose most famous work was the intense choral and orchestral piece *Carmina Burana*. According to Christine Lee Gengaro, author of *Listening to Stanley Kubrick*, "Before the cameras rolled, Carl Orff's *Carmina Burana* inspired Kubrick and Clarke, who were apparently so taken with the dramatic music that they briefly discussed commissioning the score for the film from Orff."[83] Kubrick even approached Orff, but he declined because he was 71 years old and "too old to take on such an undertaking."[84] Bernard Herrmann was also considered. Herrmann had written the score for *The Day the Earth Stood Still* as well as numerous Alfred Hitchcock's films, but he was eliminated from contention because his fee was too high, and Kubrick was already significantly over budget on the production.

Eventually, Alex North was hired to score the film. North was best known for his innovative music for 1951's *A Streetcar Named Desire*, writing the first jazz-based score in a major motion picture. North had also worked with Kubrick several years earlier on *Spartacus*. He appeared to be a perfect composer to score the groundbreaking space film.

North began the process of scoring *2001* with palpable zeal and emotional ownership. It would prove to be an extraordinarily challenging job. He was under significant stress during this process, particularly since he knew that Kubrick had become quite enamored with the temp track that had been assembled for *2001*—much of which would be heard in the final version of the film. According to Michael Benson, author of *Space Odyssey: Stanley Kubrick, Arthur C. Clarke, and the Making of a Masterpiece*, North was "plagued throughout by the unsettling sense that nothing he could compose would truly compare to two Strausses and Ligeti."[85] Thus North suffered from stress-induced muscle spasms and back pain. As a result, he was unable to conduct the 91-piece orchestra during the recording session.[86]

North's stress level intensified during the months prior to the film's release. Communication between Kubrick and North almost completely broke down. North only received sparce and cryptic updates from Kubrick regarding the musical spotting. Nevertheless, North had composed and recorded over 40 minutes of music, with the obvious expectation that it would be used (in part or in full) in the final cut.

It was at the New York screening of *2001* in April 1968 that North first (allegedly) discovered that none of his music been used. According to Alex North, he was completely surprised and embarrassed.

Kubrick later claimed that North *had* been informed prior to the premiere that his score would not be used, stating that North had not adequately followed his instructions to use the "temp tracks" as a basis for his compositions. Kubrick also said that North "wrote and recorded a score which could not have been more alien to the music we had listened to, and, much more serious than that, a score which, in my opinion, was completely inadequate for the film."[87]

Whether or not North had pre-knowledge of his score being scrapped, Jon Burlingame believes this result was preordained:

> In a way, it is not unlike *Star Wars* in that it's a unique moment in film music history. Stanley Kubrick—even in the years before he made *2001*, was never a big fan of original scores. He had always intended to use classical excerpts in *2001*. It was only the pressure of MGM at the last minutes that he tried to use a composer since they were horrified by the thought that someone would think that MGM was too cheap to hire a composer.[88]

Kubrick did not have much respect for modern film composers, at least when compared the great classical composers. He stated, "They are not a Beethoven, a Mozart, or a Brahms. Why use music which is less good when there is a multitude of great orchestral music available from the past and from our own time."[89]

Whichever version of these events was true, North and Kubrick never spoke again. But the composer's score lived on. North did not want it to fall into obscurity, and even released recorded excerpts. The composer considered adapting portions of it into a symphony and even contemplated using it in a piece to honor the *Apollo 13* mission.[90] None of these grand aspirations would come to fruition in North's lifetime (he died in 1991), but the music was brought back to life in 1993. North's friend Jerry Goldsmith recorded North's *2001* score with the National Philharmonic Orchestra at Abbey Road Studio in London.[91] Over a decade later, in 2007, North's original recording was released, allowing film music aficionados to compare and contrast how well North's score would have enhanced (or diminished) Kubrick's film.

***

It is impossible to know how well North's score would have been received compared to the classical selections that were ultimately used, but Kubrick's blending of imagery, plot and music resulted in some of the most iconic moments in film history—and elevated the level at which space films would be judged for the next several years. For a time, Kubrick's masterpiece reigned supreme in the world of space movies. These were years in which original orchestral scores had fallen out of favor in large Hollywood productions. Jon Burlingame called this "a period of time when movie directors and producers are really rejecting the traditional orchestral score in favor of pop and rock and R&B, and soul sounds."[92] This trend dramatically changed in May 1977 when *Star Wars* was released.

Planet of the Apes

On March 27, 1968, less than a week before *2001: A Space Odyssey* arrived in theaters, *Planet of the Apes* was released. Unlike *2001*, which was unequivocally a space film, *Planet of the Apes* was far more ambiguous regarding whether it was a space film or not. Based on the 1963 novel by Pierre Boulle, *La Planète des singes*, and adapted for the screen by Rod Serling of *Twilight Zone* fame, the film was directed by Franklin J. Schaffner. Schaffner had made his name in television on such shows as *The Ford Theater Hour, Person to Person* (hosted by Edward R. Murrow) and *A Tour of the White House with Mrs. John F. Kennedy*. He later won an Academy Award for his direction of the 1970 film *Patton*.

Planet of the Apes opens with a crew of astronauts landing on a mysterious planet on November 25, 3978, just over 2000 years after they had departed Earth in the year 1972. They are amazed to discover that the indigenous humans on the planet have not developed language skills and are dominated by English-speaking apes. The protagonist, Taylor (Charlton Heston), is captured and dumbfounds his captors with his ability to speak, but then is treated like a sideshow "attraction" in a circus. As the plot develops, Taylor tries to understand the evolutionary process which apes were descended from humans, as opposed to on Earth where human are distant descendants to apes. He asks Dr. Zaius, "How in Hell did this upside-down civilization get started?" It should be noted that both *2001* and *Planet of the Apes* were examining the topic of evolution, but in dramatically contrasting ways.

To score this post-apocalyptic drama, veteran composer Jerry Goldsmith was hired. Goldsmith had been composing for film and TV for over a decade, including the films *The Sand Pebbles, Stagecoach* and Schaffner's *The Stripper*, plus several episodes of the *Twilight Zone* TV series.

According to Goldsmith, Schaffner ceded the music decisions to him: "I did the suggesting. He did the understanding, knew what I was talking about. I said it should not be an electronic score, not gimmicky, and wanted to do it with a normal orchestra. I did not want to do the obvious on this."[93]

Goldsmith may have been adamant about the use of a "normal" orchestra, but his *Planet of the Apes* score was not traditional tonal music. He favored an avant-garde approach, utilizing a 12-tone score (or Chromatic scale). In so doing, he constructed one of the most unusual and chaotic scores ever written for film. "Goldsmith resolved early for his music to speak to the primal and inverted nature of the ape world and so abandoned the use of traditional melodic constructs, instead drawing inspiration from modernist composers such as Bartok and Stravinsky," according to film reviewer Craig Lysy.[94]

To project a chaotic and alien feel with the score, Goldsmith was highly inventive. "For this avant-garde effort Goldsmith assembled a remarkable array of percussive, acoustic, ethnic and non-traditional instruments," said Lysy. This even included stainless steel bowls from the composer's own kitchen.[95]

The end result was music that sounded alien; something that was not indigenous to Earth. This was an important musical device. As Jon Burlingame explained, director Schaffner "basically gave a direction to Jerry which is 'Make sure people know that we're *not* on Earth,' which is a classic instance of audience misdirection. We come to believe that we're on this far-off planet, ruled by apes ... yet by the end of the movie, that highly unusual soundscape is the grandest instance of misdirection, since we've been on Earth the whole time."[96]

The musical misdirect—advancing the upside-down world narrative—begins at the first moments of the film. In fact, Goldsmith also dispenses with traditional tonal opening theme music completely. Instead, according to JerryGoldsmith.com, he "opens his avant-garde score ... introducing his bizarre Main Title for the apes themselves through some dissonant percussion and a mischievous flute melody that darts round the screen, supported by piano and the 'whooshing' sound of those horns. 'Crash Landing' is a lengthy action cue as the survivors escape their sinking ship."[97] Traditional instruments were used in non-traditional ways to achieve these unusual effects. According to Goldsmith, "For the swoosh of air effect in the desert scenes, I used French horns with their mouthpiece turned around backwards."[98] However, as Taylor sees the Statue of Liberty, rather than utilizing a dramatic musical cue—or a return to tonal music—Schaffner and Goldsmith opt for a scene that is free of music. The only other sound that can be heard are the waves washing in and out.

It is worth noting that the Boulle novel *La Planète des singes* did *not* include the plot twist that Taylor was on Earth the entire time. That major story element was added by screenwriter Rod Serling.[99]

1968–1976: The Pre–*Star Wars* Years

Several other space-related motion pictures and television shows materialized in the decade prior to the release of *Star Wars*. None would have nearly the impact of *2001: A Space Odyssey*, *Star Trek* or even *Planet of the Apes*, but some would make a cultural impact and/or offer new spins on "space music."

One of the more unusual ones was *Barbarella*, released in the same year as *2001* and *Planet of the Apes* (1968). *2001* and *Apes* had serious plots, but *Barbarella* was anything but serious. It embraced the sound, culture and sexual revolution of the late 1960s. According to Josh Robertson of Groovy History, *Barbarella* "is not a good movie, but that is almost beside the point. Jane Fonda in revealing and outrageous futuristic fashion, reveling in a future that was all about sexual freedom—that was the point."[100]

Based on a French comic book series, *Barbarella* was produced by Dino De Laurentiis and directed by Frenchman Roger Vadim, who was married to Fonda at the time. Barbarella (Fonda) is asked by the president of the United Earth Government to voyage into space to locate a scientist who created a weapon capable of destroying humanity. As Robertson stated, *Barbarella* is "[a] pleasure-seeking, galaxy-hopping adventurer … [T]he titular heroine came to define an aesthetic, sort of a groovy and mod vision of science fiction that envisions the galaxy as a humorless nightclub where everyone gets lucky but nobody seems to enjoy it."[101]

Music would provide the proper mood and rhythm of this very "groovy" film. At first, Vadim hired French film composer Michel Magne, who had scored dozens of films, including the 1962 Jackie Gleason movie *Gigot*. For reasons never disclosed publicly, Vadim discarded that entire composition.[102] He then hired songwriters Bob Crewe (who had written songs for the Four Seasons and many other performers) and Charles Fox (later known for writing or co-writing theme songs for TV's *Laverne and Shirley*, *Happy Days* and *The Love Boat*) to compose and record the *Barbarella* soundtrack. This music was supplemented by the Oscar-winning composer of *Lawrence of Arabia*, Maurice Jarre (who went uncredited on *Barbarella*).

The final product was an outrageous science fiction reflection of the counterculture of the late 1960s. Dan Goldwasser of Soundtrack.net opined that for the most part, the score

> is like a band having a jam session. Punchy brass, electric guitars, and even orchestral interludes ("The Sex Machine") give the whole album a really eclectic (if not slightly schizophrenic) personality. I have to admit—it might be as cheesy as it comes, but it's just a lot of fun to listen to. Included at the end of the album are instrumental lounge covers of the songs performed by

Young Lovers. It's smooth and should fit in right at home in any bachelor pad.[103]

Charles Fox recalled that the score "was meant to be futuristic; it was a spoof, you know. But I did get a chance to do electronic things mixed in with some classical things, too, actually. …Some of it—like when Barbarella's flying around with Pygar and the winged angel—is very Baroque sounding."[104]

The *Barbarella* music attracted a retro-cult following that has lasted until this day, but since *Barbarella*—and its music—were more reflection of culture of the late 1960s rather than excitement about space exploration, the music would have little influence on the public's perception of the sound of space.

Movies set in space were not limited to western film producers in this time period. Based on a 1961 novel by Stanisław Lem, *Solaris* (1972)—the Soviet Union's answer to *2001*—was directed and co-written by one of the country's most respected filmmakers, Andrei Tarkovsky. He had directed such films as *Ivan's Childhood* (1962) and *Andrei Rublev* (1966).

The film tells the tale of the crew of a space station orbiting a planet called Solaris. When the crew members experience physical and psychological stress, psychologist Kris Kelvin is sent to the station to help them deal with their emotional crises. By the time he arrives, almost all the crew members have disappeared, and one has killed himself. The two remaining crew members have had mental breakdowns. To add to the strange situation, Kelvin encounters his wife Khari, who had committed suicide ten years earlier on Earth. He finally learns that the other crew members had encountered similar "visitors" instigated by an unknown sentient intelligence on the planet.

Tarkovsky initially planned to release the film without any musical score; he asked composer Eduard Artemiev (or Artemyev) *not* to write music, but "to build an ambient, mechanical soundscape."[105] Artemiev was an up-and-coming film composer who specialized in electronic music. Although Tarkovsky had wanted only an electronic soundscape, Artemiev convinced him that a musical score would be appropriate. He did this by appealing to Tarkovsky's love of Bach. Artemiev interweaved Bach's Chorale Prelude in F-Minor into the film but also made heavy use of electronic sounds—and the score would be anything but traditional. Artemiev wanted his music to sound like it was "composed of sounds of terrestrial life as if processed by the ocean."[106]

To achieve these sounds, he used an orchestra in completely unorthodox ways, as though it was "one giant synthesizer." His score at times was so subtle that it became almost completely inaudible. He commented,

"It occurred to me that we could introduce orchestral sounds, voices, tapping of the strings light as the rustle of grass, very subtly."[107] Apparently Tarkovsky approved of the concept and they were able to create "a special musical language. The surrounding world, with the help of the orchestra— the clusters of soft sounds emerge, almost inaudible, sometimes overlapping. The viewer may not even notice them."[108]

Solaris premiered at the 1972 Cannes Film Festival, winning the Grand Prix Spécial du Jury. It played in only five Soviet Union theaters, but still sold over ten million tickets over time. Eventually, in 1976, film critic Roger Ebert wrote, "*Solaris* isn't a fast-moving action picture; it's a thoughtful, deep, sensitive movie that uses the freedom of science-fiction to examine human nature. It starts slow, but once you get involved, it grows on you."[109]

British moviemakers still had science fiction aspirations, envisioning a future in which humans master space exploration. An ambitious television show appeared in 1975, *Space: 1999.* While it was a British production, it was focused on the American television market and enlisted a number of American writers and actors, including the lead actor, Martin Landau, who played Commander John Koenig. The British response to *Star Trek, Space: 1999* was the creation of the husband-and-wife team Gerry and Sylvia Anderson, whose TV credits included the Supermarionation series *Thunderbirds* and the live-action *UFO.*

Twenty-four years in the future, after humanity has taken the next logical steps in space exploration, humanity constructed Moon Base Alpha on the lunar surface. A massive explosion at a nuclear waste dump on the far side of the Moon rips the Moon from the Earth's orbit and thrusts it—and the inhabitants of Moon Base Alpha—into the depths of space. There they encounter aliens and have other adventures. The special effects–heavy show was the most expensive TV series ever made at that time, costing roughly $6.5 million to produce and an additional $275,000 per episode.[110]

Veteran television composer Barry Gray was recruited to compose the music for the show's first season. Gray scored numerous television shows and also collaborated on several projects with the Andersons, including *Thunderbirds* and *UFO.* It was during these earlier jobs that he had shown the ability "to create a huge sound from a relatively small orchestra."[111] Gray had a significantly larger orchestra for this series, and the Andersons knew that he would provide a high-caliber orchestral score that could elevate their series.

However, musician union rules in Britain were similar to those in the U.S. at the time. There were limitations on how much music any one composer could contribute to a series in Britain. Gray was only allowed to score five out of every 13 episodes. To fill in the rest of the season, library tracks, cues composed for other shows, cues written by other composers and classical pieces such as Tomaso Albinoni's "Adagio for Strings and Organ in G Minor" and Gustav Holst's "Mars, The Bringer of War" were used.[112]

Nonetheless, Gray established the musical feel for the show, starting with the dynamic theme music that he co-wrote with Vic Elmes. The theme, both orchestral and at times funky, was recorded in December 1973 using a 52-piece orchestra; after that, Gray would regularly use orchestras of between 32 and 38 pieces throughout Season 1.[113] In addition to the traditional orchestral instrumentation, he also used electric guitars, alternating between a big, brassy, orchestral sound and a funky rock'n'roll piece—creating a unique sound. According to Ian Fryer, author of *The Worlds of Gerry and Sylvia Anderson*, the theme brought "a real sense of awe and majesty to each episode, the opening fanfare announcing to the world, 'Watch this, it's important.'"[114]

Gray used an orchestra for each episode, consistently creating a big sound, while experimenting with musical styles to suit shifting alien circumstances. As observed by reviewer Gary Dalkin, "The more imaginative nature of the programme allowed Gray to introduce elements of both avant-garde electronics and dynamic rock, and fuse these with his grandiose, often tenderly romantic orchestral writing to unique effect."[115]

Gray was not invited back for the second season. The series' success depended overwhelmingly on the market in the United States, resulting in constant pressure to conform to American television norms of the time. The first season was not picked up by any of the major American networks. As a result, a major restructuring of the show was ordered. This included a change in composers.

An attempt to appeal more to the American audience included the hiring of British jazz musician and composer Derek Wadsworth.[116] Wadsworth had previously scored a modest number of TV shows and had worked as a session musician for Dionne Warwick, George Harrison and Tony Bennett.

For the new theme music, Wadsworth received very specific instructions from the producers. Gerry Anderson was looking for a driving piece with a feel reminiscent of the *Hawaii Five-O* theme (composed by Morton Stevens). Wadsworth noted that Anderson wanted him "to inject a similar kind of energy to give the show an exciting kick start."[117] In a three-hour session, Wadsworth recorded three versions of the new theme song—all entirely orchestral. Once Anderson chose the version he favored, Wadsworth began to "doctor" the piece, inserting electronic sounds as well.[118]

The final product indeed had drive. J.K. Donnelly wrote,

"Wadsworth's title music is fast and kinetic with a rock backbeat, and led by a synthesizer melody with brass and electronic blasts and 'spangles.'"[119] Nonetheless, Wadsworth's theme did not have nearly the flair that Gray's original music had. In fact, Gray's original theme had many more of the qualities that made the *Hawaii Five-O* theme so effective.

According to film studies expert K.J. Donnelly, "Some of Wadsworth's music sounds patently close to 'easy listening music.' It is less orchestral than Gray's, with a small string section which was used only occasionally. Instead, Wadsworth's music is much more rhythmic, with jazz-rock beats and some disco grooves."[120] Much of the music produced by both composers may now be dated, but Gray's music has stood up far better to decades of evolving musical tastes.[121]

Despite the substantial budget and sophisticated special effects, *Space: 1999* was canceled after two seasons, largely out of a belief that it ran counter to American television preferences of the time. Had the show been released two years later, after *Star Wars* appeared in theaters, the show's destiny may have been substantially different.

4

John Williams
and *Star Wars*, 1977

A Turning Point in Space Music

The classic 20th Century–Fox fanfare echoed in movie theaters throughout the United States in May 1977. A moment of silence followed, and then blue typeface words appeared on a solid black background: "A long time ago in a galaxy far, far away..." Audiences were then jolted to attention as the fortissimo brassy downbeat of an orchestra thundered and the large, bold letters STAR WARS receded into the dark, starry backdrop.

What followed was one of the most iconic films in movie history, with a dazzling and uplifting score by John Williams.

The release of *Star Wars: A New Hope* on May 25, 1977, revolutionized moviemaking and transformed expectations of film scores as well as orchestral music in general. It was an unparalleled milestone that also changed how "space music" could and should sound.

This watershed moment was largely enabled by the success of a seemingly unrelated movie, *American Graffiti* (1973). Set in 1962 and based on George Lucas' life experiences, *American Graffiti* told the story of some young friends during their last night together one summer. The film was produced for a relatively small budget (under $800,000) and became a sleeper hit, pulling in a profit of more than 50 times what Lucas had spent on the film. Its financial success, combined with favorable critical response, enabled Lucas to pursue something bigger, bolder and far more outlandish: *Star Wars*.

With *Star Wars*, Lucas blended several genres. According to John Williams expert Emilio Audissino, "Lucas' concept was a saga which blended Sci-Fi with ancient myth, technology and fairy-tale magic, comics with epics, future with past."[1] Lucas noted,

When I did *Star Wars* I consciously set about to recreate myths ... the classic mythological motifs. And I wanted to use those motifs to deal with issues that existed today.... What these films deal with is the fact that we all have good and evil inside of us and that we can choose which way we want the balance to go. *Star Wars* was made up of many themes.[2]

Lucas did not limit himself to classic western mythology; he borrowed from Japanese filmmaker Akira Kurosawa's 1958 samurai film *The Hidden Fortress*, as well as from the writings of mythologist Joseph Campbell, with whom Lucas became close friends. Lucas explained, "I've tried to take the ideas that seem to cut across the most cultures, because I'm fascinated by that and I think that's one of the things that I really got from Joe Campbell, was that—what he was trying to do is find the common threads through the various mythology, through the ... religions."[3]

Lucas' vision was unlike anything being produced by Hollywood at the time—and that was problematic. Since the film was not a traditional science fiction film or a traditional fantasy film—and reflected such a diverse number of genres—Lucas initially had trouble selling it to a studio. According to Emilio Audissino,

Star Wars—which was a strange beast because it wasn't clear whether it was sci-fi or fairy tale—it also had some story dynamics that looked like a Western. *Star Wars* was rejected by a couple of studios before landing at Fox. The producers were not really convinced by the marketability of the film because the genre was not clear. If you have a clear genre, it is much easier to market. And even if considered sci-fi, sci-fi as a genre was not considered profitable at the time.[4]

While 20th Century–Fox eventually bought *Star Wars*, the studio had little faith in it. In fact, *Star Wars* was only initially released in 42 theaters nationwide. Distribution expanded to 1750 as the popularity of the film exploded.

The role of the score cannot be understated in contributing to *Star Wars'* ultimate success. Selecting the proper music had always been an element of George Lucas' overall vision of the film. He had even written the *Star Wars* script while listening to both symphonic music and classic Hollywood scores. As a result, Lucas almost decided to take an entirely different musical direction for *Star Wars*. Stanley Kubrick had demonstrated a model that could potentially be used in Lucas' new film. Lucas had spotted *Star Wars: A New Hope* with temporary music that included classical selections as well as film music of the 1930s and '40s, specifically the works of Erich Wolfgang Korngold. Growing fond of these musical selections, Lucas was considering *not* commissioning an original score at all but using his temp track selections as the final musical backdrop.

Fortuitously, his close friend Steven Spielberg intervened, convincing

Lucas to hire composer John Williams. Two years earlier, Williams had composed the orchestral music for Spielberg's blockbuster *Jaws*. In a 1975 conversation, Lucas told Spielberg, "I want a classical score. I want the Korngold kind of feel about this thing. It's an old-fashioned kind of movie, and I want that grand soundtrack that they used to have on movies."[5]

As Lucas recalled, Spielberg replied, "The guy you've got to talk to is John Williams. He did *Jaws*, I love him, he's the greatest composer that ever lived. You've got to talk to him!"[6]

Lucas heeded Spielberg's advice and met with Williams, and the composer explained why he believed that *Star Wars* needed an original score.[7] Williams said that well-established classical pieces can be very challenging to integrate as film scores, particularly on a film like *Star Wars*. Using classical pieces often does not allow a film composer to "develop [the music] and relate it to a character all the way through the film. For instance, if you took a theme from one of the selections of Holst's 'The Planets' and played it at the beginning of the film, it wouldn't necessarily fit in the middle or at the end.... I felt that the film wanted thematic unity."[8] The combined arguments of Spielberg and the composer convinced Lucas to hire Williams to write an original score.

In the tradition of Max Steiner decades earlier, Williams preferred not to read scripts before writing the music, because he knew that a film's final cut is often significantly different than what he would have envisioned by reading the script. Williams said, "I remember seeing [*Star Wars*] and reacting to its atmospheres and energies and rhythms. That for me is always the best way to pick up a film—from the visual image itself and without any preconceptions that might have been put there by the script. Having said that, I don't even remember if George Lucas offered me a script."[9]

As Williams prepared to write his score, Lucas provided specific input regarding the music that would support his space opera. In an interview, Lucas mentioned that the temp track that Williams would have heard used many of the same pieces he had listened to while writing the script: "And with Johnny, you can say, 'I want something that feels exactly like this, you understand the emotion here and the emotion there?' ...He knows exactly what I'm talking about, and he'd really be conscientious about getting the director's vision on the screen."[10]

Williams delivered a massive (approximately 800 pages) orchestral score. To fully realize his creation, the London Symphony Orchestra (LSO) was hired. The 86-piece orchestra began recording the *Star Wars* score on March 5, 1977, at England's Anvil Studios. This was the same studio where Williams had recorded *Fiddler on the Roof* and *Jane Eyre*. While Williams was familiar with the venue, this was the first time he had ever used an established symphony orchestra to record a film score. The original plan was to hire an orchestra of freelance musicians, but Lionel Newman, music director of 20th Century–Fox, suggested they hire the London Symphony Orchestra. But this did not mean that the prestigious orchestra had any interest in recording a film score.

Fortunately, composer-conductor André Previn was the orchestra's music director at the time. Both Williams and Newman knew Previn well, because Previn had scored and conducted the music for numerous films. Thus, Williams had no hesitation in calling Previn to ask, "How would it be if we borrowed your orchestra for this recording?"[11] Previn agreed, beginning one of the great partnerships between Hollywood and an established symphony orchestra.

Based on Lucas' original musical inspirations, Williams created a score that harkened back to adventure series such as *Flash Gordon*, harnessing a musical style that echoed the golden age of Hollywood in the 1930s. According to Chris Malone, "Williams saw the temporary music track as an inspiration to develop his own swashbuckling music that embraced the brassy and heroic sound of film composer Erich Wolfgang Korngold's 1930s and 1940s films for Warner Brothers, in particular *Kings Row*."[12] Other clear influences on Williams' score were Igor Stravinsky's "Rite of Spring" and "Mars" from Holst's "The Planets."

An example of the Korngold influence is heard in the opening fanfare. Korngold's 1942 film *Kings Row* and that of *Star Wars* have many similarities. In addition to the fact that both compositions are written in the B♭ Major key, Alex Ross of *The New Yorker* observed that the opening themes of these two films "share a fundamental pattern: a triplet figure, a rising fifth, a stepwise three-note descent."[13]

Stravinsky's influence is also obvious in the original *Star Wars* film, most notably when R2D2 and C-3PO are perambulating in the Tatooine desert prior to their capture by the Jawas. Williams' music bears a similarity to "Part II: The Sacrifice: Introduction" in Stravinsky's "Rite of Spring" as R2D2 and C3PO separate and walk into the unknown.

Gustav Holst's famed 1916 composition "Mars: Bringer of War" from "The Planets" (Op. 32) weighs heavily in Williams' score as well. This influence is clear as the *Millennium Falcon* is caught in a tractor beam and pulled toward the Death Star. Williams' pulsating music closely echoes the opening section of "Mars," using a very similar ostinato pattern. The Holst paraphrasing is even more pronounced after Luke and Han race from the Death Star, just before it explodes. Williams uses a repeating D♭ Lydian triad (A♭, D♭, G) over C, the chord Holst used in the final measures of "Mars." Although, while Holst completes "Mars" with a harsh chord, Williams' use of the D♭ Lydian chord is followed by the explosion of the Death Star to complete the cue.

The composer reaches even further back into the library of musical knowledge to the fourteenth century. As Gottfried Huppertz had done in his 1927 score for the silent film *Metropolis*, Williams integrates variations of the Gregorian chant "Dies Irae" into his musical canvas. This piece of music (and interpretations of it) have been used in operas, films and other musical pieces for centuries to convey a sense of doom. The first clear reference of this piece in the original *Star Wars* trilogy occurs when Luke discovers that his Aunt Beru and Uncle Owen have been killed by the Imperial Storm Troopers. Luke views their charred remains as the Force theme plays, followed by a clear echo of "Dies Irae" representing his pain and loss. References and allusions to "Dies Irae" appear throughout the original *Star Wars* trilogy, as well as many other scores Williams composed over subsequent decades.

Based on his extensive use of musical references, some pundits have claimed that Williams lacks originality or is even guilty of plagiarism. However, Williams has followed a long tradition in film, opera and classical music composition; musical ideas and phrases have been borrowed and adapted for centuries. Johannes Brahms was accused of stealing materials on more than one occasion. When asked about the similarities between his Symphony No. 1 in C minor and Beethoven's Ninth Symphony, he replied, "Any ass can see that."[14] In the case of Williams, University of Memphis music professor Jeremy Orosz describes the *Star Wars* composer's treatments of these musical phrases as "paraphrases." Orosz notes that Williams "uses pre-existing material as a creative template to compose new music at a remarkable pace."[15]

Williams has become a master of using these musical references to elicit a sense of familiarity from the audience. He then evolves the initial musical idea to comply with the needs of the plot, character or emotion, thus expanding the initial musical phrase into something new.

Themes, Leitmotif and Wagner

Another significant influence on Williams' *Star Wars* scores was Richard Wagner—not necessarily through musical paraphrasing, but thematic techniques. According to Nicholas Meyer, director of *Star Trek: The Wrath of Khan*, "You can draw a straight line from Wagner to Strauss to Korngold to John Williams."[16]

Since Lucas wanted *Star Wars* to have an operatic quality, Williams incorporated Wagnerian drama and leitmotif in the score. "The composer fancied the film as a grand space opera with strong themes of good versus evil so it was agreed that an operatic approach, using the leitmotif technique, should be adopted," Chris Malone wrote in his paper "Recording the *Star Wars* Saga." Malone observed that Williams utilized "a melody or chord progression to signify a character, emotion or locale. Wagner's four-opera *Ring Cycle* is perhaps the best-known classical use of leitmotif and Williams has certainly acknowledged that fact."[17]

According to music scholar Frank Lehman, Williams uses 23 individual leitmotifs in the original *Star Wars* Trilogy and 61 in all nine primary *Star Wars* films. In most cases, these themes are not isolated from the other thematic material. Williams frequently built new themes based on the basic tonal structures of earlier themes. As the story evolved over the three motion pictures, so too did the music. In his usual self-deprecating manner, Williams downplayed how deliberately he musically unified all three films, brushing off any comparison to what Wagner accomplished in *Ring Cycle*:

> I think if the score has an architectural unity, it's the result of a happy accident. I approached each film as a separate entity. The first one was completely out of the blue, but the second one was of course connected to the first one; we referred back to characters and extended them and referred back to themes and extended and developed those. I suppose it was a natural but unconscious metamorphosis of musical themes.[18]

Whether or not this was a happy accident, the music of the original trilogy is remarkably well unified and progresses effectively to support the characters and plot. Lucas explains:

> John's music tells the story. Each character has a theme that develops and interacts with the themes of the other characters; the musical themes connect the themes of the stories and make them resonate. He also creates an emotional context for each scene. In fact, you can have it both ways, because you can play a scene against the emotions that are in it because the music is there to tell you the truth.[19]

The major themes and leitmotifs in the original film include:

The Main Theme ("Luke's Theme")

In a film franchise packed with iconic themes, "Luke's Theme" is almost certainly the most recognizable, serving multiple roles within the franchise. "With its opening orchestral blast, [the] cue tells us that we are in for a tale that is larger than life, something extraordinary, something from the realm of myths," observes Mark Richards of *Film Music Notes*. "The cue, which functions both as main title music and as a theme for Luke Skywalker, retains this mythic feel throughout its entirety and yet is surprisingly diverse in its musical material."[20]

Williams recalled that the opening of the film "was so visually stunning ... that it was clear that that music had to kind of smack you right in the eye and do something very strong."[21] He also noted, "when I thought of a theme for Luke and his adventures, I composed a melody that reflected the brassy, bold, masculine and noble qualities I saw in the character.... When the theme is played softly, I tended towards a softer brass sound. but I used fanfare-ish horns for the more heraldic passages."[22]

To contrast the A section of the theme, Williams explained that the B section "was lyrical and romantic and adventurous also."[23] Together, Williams composed one of the most memorable themes in motion picture history and was able to enthrall generations of *Star Wars* fans from the first note of the original film.

The Force

One of the most significant and enduring themes or leitmotifs of the entire *Star Wars* trilogy is the music that Williams wrote to signify the Force—the mystical energy force that "binds the galaxy together." As Williams explained, the Force represents "the spiritual-philosophical belief of the Jedi Knights, and the Old Republic. Like the Princess' theme, it has a fairy tale aspect rather than a futuristic aspect."[24]

In contrast to character-centric themes or music associated with an object (the Death Star, for example), this music "is a prime example of Williams giving shape to something completely absent onscreen to the point that it becomes an element as tangible as characters and location," according to Maurizio Caschetto.[25] This description is consistent with most of the accepted definitions of "leitmotif."

The Force theme appears early in *Star Wars: A New Hope* as Luke contemplates his place in the universe. Alex Ross of *The New Yorker* wrote of the celebrated scene in which

> young Luke Skywalker looks longingly toward a horizon lit by twin setting suns, dreaming of a life beyond the desert planet Tatooine. Williams writes a melancholy, expansive G-minor theme for solo horn, which is soon taken up by full strings. Akin to the noble C-minor melody that Wagner writes for Siegfried, this leitmotif represents not only Luke but also the mystical medium known as the Force.[26]

This theme is not limited to quiet moments of reflection or spirituality. It is used quite flexibly throughout the film and the entire franchise. Mark Richards of *Film Music Notes* wrote,

> The gentle statements set the theme's melody softly in lyrical instruments like the horn, strings, or winds.... In its more aggressive, militaristic settings, the

melody assumes a loud and strident tone in the trumpets and/or trombones, and there is usually a heavy accompaniment in the rest of the orchestra that suggests the emotional weight of the situation at hand.[27]

Perhaps the most mystical use of the music occurs when Luke speeds down the Death Star's equatorial trench in his X-Wing fighter, attempting to destroy that facility. As he gets ready to fire, the mystical force theme is heard with shimmering strings while Obi-Wan Kenobi's voice echoes in Luke's head, urging him to "use the Force" rather than rely on the accuracy of the computer guidance system.

The Force theme is played again moments later, but this time in a military march style as Luke, Han and Chewbacca walk down the aisle of the grand hall to receive their medals from Princess Leia.

The Cantina

One of the few stand-alone pieces in *Star Wars* was "The Cantina," used to create the musical ambiance of the scene set in the raucous and seedy Cantina bar at Mos Eisley spaceport. To musically capture the sound he was hoping for, Lucas posed a question to Williams: "Can you imagine, several creatures in a future century finding some 1930s Benny Goodman swing band music in a time capsule or under a rock somewhere—and how they might try to interpret it."[28] In response, Williams composed two cues for the Cantina bar for a jazz ensemble rather than orchestra. This ensemble included steel drums, two saxophones, drums, trumpet, clarinet, a Fender Rhodes piano and an Arp Synthesizer.[29] Both songs had very "terrestrial"-sounding names. The first was called "Mad About Me" and the second piece "If I Only Could Let Go and Cry."[30]

This musical contrast was very important. There were as many different stories to be told within that bar as there are in real-life bars on Earth. Thus, while the songs were not primary themes within the film, they reflected the shared energy of all the individuals and stories intermingling at the Cantina.

Leia's Theme

Another critical theme in this trilogy is Williams' music for Leia. Williams stated, "The princess theme is very romantic. The first time Luke sees her, he says how beautiful she is. It really is a fairy-tale princess melody."[31] However, this theme does far more than evoke love. It defines her complexity as a human being, reflecting not only her femininity, but also her strength; she is not the stereotypical "damsel in distress" prevalent in old Hollywood cliffhangers. Justin Chandler of CBC observed:

> The melody of Princess Leia's theme is built of two distinct cells that reflect her character's inherent contradiction. The first is an upward leap of a major sixth, from the dominant to the mediant. While large melodic leaps tradition-ally imply heroism and confidence … the melody's second component, and the one Williams develops more fully, outlines a falling third using an 8th and two 16th notes, and keeps the tune hovering around the unstable second, third and fourth scale degrees. This is Leia's vulnerability and yearning, the private side of the woman who, in public, is the leader of the Rebellion.[32]

As with most Williams themes, he twists, turns and evolves them through variations and creative instrumentation to evoke emotion, ten-sion, longing, wonder or whatever else needs to be conveyed.

Leia's theme is not exclusively used to depict Princess Leia; Williams uses a variation for one of the film's most dramatic scenes: The death of Obi-Wan Kenobi. Luke makes eye contact with Obi-Wan and the Force theme sounds just before Obi-Wan is struck down by Darth Vader. The music then quickly transitions into the Leia theme. "I used part of the prin-cess theme in the beginning of it…. I took the dramatic license because it was the most sweeping melody," commented Williams.[33] Obi-Wan Kenobi has just been killed by Darth Vader, and now Luke, Leia, Han, and the droids are escaping to the *Millennium Falcon*.

Impact

In contrast to Alex North's experience with *2001: A Space Odyssey*, Williams exceeded the musical expectations of the director. George Lucas acknowledged this at the 44th Life Achievement Award Gala Tribute to John Williams: "*Star Wars* was meant to be a simple hero's journey. A fan-tasy for young people. And then John wrote the music, and he raised it to a level of art that would stand the test of time."[34]

Star Wars was a worldwide sensation, and the soundtrack album quickly became the bestselling film score album in history. The film and its music resonated with the public like few previous others, filling a cul-tural void. "In less than six months it broke the box-office records set by *Jaws*," wrote film historian Michael Matessino. "Once again, the music played a strong role in the global phenomenon. By late summer, a disco version became America's number one song, and in November, Zubin Mehta conducted an entire concert of *Star Wars* music at the Hollywood Bowl." Williams also won numerous awards, including three Grammys and an Oscar.[35]

"I think that John Williams changed the way we think about film music," commented composer Jeff Russo (*Star Trek Discovery* and *Star Trek: Picard*). "Certainly, he changed the way we think about fantasy space music. From a narrative standpoint, he has changed the way we think about music for movies."[36] Indeed, the genre of film music had been following another trend until this moment. According to Jon Burlingame, *Star Wars* "comes on the heels of a period of time in Hollywood; in film scoring; 1967–1974 or so; where the sounds of pop and soul and R&B are dominating movies. If you look at *The Graduate* and *Easy Rider* and *Midnight Cowboy* ... this is a period of time where movie directors and producers are really rejecting the traditional orchestral score."[37]

Once again downplaying his role, Williams praised Lucas, stating, "I have to credit the film for a lot of this. If I had written the music without the film, probably nobody would have heard of the music, it was a combination of things and the elusive, weird, unpredictable aspect of timing that none of us can quite get our hands around."[38]

The Empire Strikes Back

Three years after the release of *Star Wars* came the much-anticipated sequel *The Empire Strikes Back*. Predictably, there was skepticism whether the magic of *Star Wars* could be repeated, but these doubts were quickly dispelled. In fact, *The Empire Strikes Back* is often considered the strongest film in the original trilogy for both plot and music.

After the colossal success of *Star Wars,* it would stand to reason that Lucas would not have any problems financing his follow-up film, but this was not the case. "Lucasfilm nearly went broke independently financing *Empire*; a last-minute bank loan was necessary to ensure completion," stated Paul Scanlan of *Rolling Stone.* "And the eventual profits from *Empire* led to another problem: Lucas' company, based chiefly in Los Angeles, began to mushroom."[39]

In spite of these challenges, the film proceeded on schedule for a 1980 release. Williams was again called upon to put this new space adventure to music. According to Williams, "I wanted to try to develop material that would wed with the original and sound like part of an organic whole: something different, something new, but an extension of what already existed."[40] He composed a massive score, mixing the old themes with highly effective new ones. The full score contained roughly 117 minutes of music, and was once again recorded by the London Symphony Orchestra, utilizing anywhere from 60 to 100 musicians.[41] Chris Malone said that the completed score "is justifiably one of the great achievements in film scoring...."[42] Gary Arnold of *The Washington Post* called *Empire* "[a] more impressive and harrowing magic carpet ride than its fundamentally endearing predecessor...."[43]

Williams expanded his original themes and introduced new and powerful new cues that advanced the story and manipulated the emotions of the audience. Some of these new themes include:

"The Imperial March"

What may well be the most popular theme of the entire franchise is "The Imperial March," or Darth Vader's theme. Heavily influenced by Frédéric Chopin's 1839 Sonata No. 2 in B-flat Minor (more commonly known as "The Funeral March") and with echoes of "Dies Irae," Williams channels the chilling composition into a bold and militaristic theme to project Darth Vader's strength and a sense of doom. According to composer Juanjo Molina, "['The Imperial March'] is used as a counter-theme. As we see the struggle of good and evil in the history, musically we can also appreciate how we have the main music, protagonist, and its corresponding antagonist in the figure of Vader and his leitmotif."[44]

The musical picture that Williams paints is not of one-dimensional evil. He builds in complexities and seemingly conflicting elements. According to musicologist Doug Adams, "In an ingenious move, the entire first half of the melody is entirely major, even to the point of arpeggiating major chords. However, its harmonization is built upon third-related minor chords, which gives the theme a Sousaesque popular sensibility, but with a heart of stone."[45]

As with most of Williams' themes, he evolves the "Imperial March" melody and harmonies throughout the film and the trilogy. By the end of *Return of the Jedi*, the theme is a hollow echo of its previous glory.

"The Imperial March" was first heard by the public three weeks prior to the opening of *The Empire Strikes Back*, when Williams conducted it during a Boston Pops Concert on April 29, 1980.[46]

Han and Leia's Theme

As the burgeoning romance between Han Solo and Princess Leia develops in earnest, Williams responds with music to accompany and evolve this relationship. In so doing, the composer exhibits his skill of morphing earlier pieces into new themes. According to Doug Adams of *Film Score Monthly*, "This theme represents Williams' most literal minded connection of thematic material within the *Star Wars* scores. Introduced in *Empire*, Han Solo and the Princess' theme takes up where Leia's theme left off. Both begin with Williams' signature romantic rising major sixth interval before settling downwards."[47]

The theme is used to the greatest emotional effect as Han is about to be frozen in carbonite, as Leia says, "I love you," and Han replies, "I know!" As steam rises from the floor, Han is lowered into the chamber. Tortured variations of the love theme build until a violent eruption of steam shoots up from the chamber as Han Solo is frozen. Charlie Brigden of FSR wrote,

> The Love Theme is reprised tinged with brass that gives it a tragic feel, with the orchestra rising to a truly operatic tone as Han is lowered into the depths of the machine. As the smoke clears, "The Imperial March" appears, played by the very top of the brass, and as the slab of carbonite is lowered and slammed onto the metal floor, a subdued and doom-laden Love Theme is played.[48]

At the end of the story, another sweeping rendition of the theme leverages the emotions of the audience. Lando Calrissian and Chewbacca depart on the *Millennium Falcon*; Luke and Leia look out the window as Luke puts his arm around her. Just then, the Han and Leia theme plays to signify that Leia is in love with Han Solo. It also serves as an emotional reminder to the audience in 1980 that they would need to wait another three years to see the resolution to the story.

Yoda

Not all the new thematic music was composed for the original *New Hope* characters. A new character was introduced in *The Empire Strikes Back*: Yoda, the 900-year-old Jedi Master who had been in hiding on the planet Dagobah since Darth Vader decimated the Jedi Order. As with many of his other themes, Williams constructs the Yoda theme from elements of his previous *Star Wars* themes:

> I mean we would have the Princess Leia theme as the romantic theme in the first film, but then we'd have Yoda's music, which was unexpectedly romantic, if you like, in the second film, but not such a distant relative, musically speaking, intervallically/melodically speaking to Princess Leia's music. So you can marry one theme right after the other ... you can interplay them in a contrapuntal way, and it will be part of a texture that is familial.[49]

Williams went on to compose extraordinary music for the final film of the trilogy, as well as six additional films, but the evolution and creation of music for *The Empire Strikes Back* was arguably the high point of his compositional expertise for the franchise, one on par with the composer's greatest film scores.

Return of the Jedi

Movie audiences around the world were left with a major cliffhanger at the conclusion of *The Empire Strikes Back*. Han Solo was frozen in carbonite and shipped off to Jabba the Hut, and Luke learned that Darth Vader was his father. As such, *Return of the Jedi* was almost certainly the most anticipated film of the original trilogy when it opened on May 25, 1983. The reviews were not as strong as for the previous two films, but that would have little impact on the film's success. The cultural phenomenon that was the *Star Wars* trilogy transcended reviews. As Paul Scanlan of *Rolling Stone* observed,

> *Jedi* is something more than a sequel. When people start lining up more than 24 hours before the first show, as they did across the country on May 24th, it's not just to learn how Luke Skywalker works out his father problem. The arrival of a new *Star Wars* picture has become a social and cultural event, not to mention a box-office bonanza.[50]

This third episode of the *Star Wars* trilogy was directed by Richard Marquand, who had directed the World War II spy film *Eye of the Needle* as well as the horror film *The Legacy*. Lucas had played a less direct role in the production of *The Empire Strikes Back*; he took a much more hands-on role in the third *Star Wars* film.

Return of the Jedi proved to be extremely challenging for Marquand and Lucas. According to Lucas, "*Jedi* almost killed everybody, every department, from costumes to building monsters to the sophistication of the mechanics to the special effects. Everything was very, very hard on everybody. This one was grim for me, just as bad as *Star Wars*, just as bad as directing."[51] But Lucas knew that regardless of how challenging the film was, Williams would provide a score that would elevate it and advance the story.

Themes and Leitmotifs

Williams employed and evolved themes that had been introduced in the first two films. The "Luke" theme is again interwoven throughout. The Han and Leia theme is also prominent as the two characters are reunited after Han is rescued (and unfrozen).

The theme that evolves most significantly is "The Imperial March."

At the start of the film, the theme represents Darth Vader's strength. It is as confident and militaristic as it had been during *The Empire Strikes Back*. As the story progresses, Williams twists the theme as Darth Vader turns back to the light side of the Force, but he is mortally wounded as he hurls the emperor into the massive chasm on the new Death Star. Vader lies wheezing on the ground as Luke embraces his father, who has found redemption, and the once menacing and grand "Imperial March" is now played by a single harp as though it is a faint echo of its previous grandeur. Musicologist Frank Lehman stated,

> Williams strips away the march's militaristic trappings, leaving behind a sputtering shadow of the theme, orchestrated with such extraordinary delicacy that part of it seems to evaporate with each new phrase. With a final, hollowed-out rendition on a solo harp, the old dark lord expires, and the once-unstoppable "Imperial March" achieves a small measure of peace.[52]

The Emperor's Theme

The most important new theme introduced in *Return of the Jedi* was "The Emperor's theme." The emperor did not appear at all (he was only referred to) in *Star Wars: A New Hope* and made only a brief appearance as a holographic projection in *The Empire Strikes Back*. In *Return of the Jedi*, he finally appears in person as a fully developed character and the center of evil in the galaxy.

The emperor was brilliantly played by Ian McDiarmid, his makeup and costuming effectively bringing the character to life. But the character would not have been perceived by audiences as being nearly as evil, formidable or even seductive without Williams' music. According to *Film Score Monthly*, "The Emperor's theme exudes wicked malice with a series of minor triads.... There is a tenuous harmonic relationship between this and Vader's theme where each is set for distantly related, pure minor chords."[53]

Frank Lehman noted that these minor triads "progress chromatically, in a kind of violation of natural musical law." Lehman quoted music theorist James Buhler, who stated, "The music gives the impression that only a very powerful sorcerer, perhaps only a god, could animate these chords thus."[54]

For the first time in the trilogy, Williams introduces a chorus to add color and weight to this sinister theme. Lehman added,

> The brooding, wordless male chorus that intones Palpatine's theme reinforces the sense of eldritch unease that the character exudes. Unlike "The Imperial March," the Sith lord's music is not overtly threatening, but mysterious and beguiling, like a dark siren's call. The leitmotif draws from an old association

in film and classical music that wordless choruses stand in as the voice of the divine—a technique especially favored by Williams' old Hollywood mentor, Alfred Newman.[55]

Luke and Leia Theme

A "Luke and Leia" theme is also introduced. Even though Han and Leia's romantic relationship progressed to a new level in *The Empire Strikes Back*, there is still the looming prospect that Luke and Leia may have romantic feelings for one another. Williams had even written a "torrid" love theme for Luke and Leia that was never used for *Star Wars*. It was eventually revealed that the two characters were siblings.

Thus, Williams wrote a new theme, not representing torrid love, but the strong bond of siblings. The new theme projected "emotional maturity and melancholic color in the melody," according to Charlie Brigden of Filmschoolrejects.com. "Williams works up to the revelation slowly, with some beautifully sad and tender phrasing from the strings amongst which he weaves the 'Force Theme.'" Brigden added, "When he finally tells Leia the truth, the 'Luke and Leia' theme is played on the higher strings with celeste twinkling under it, emphasizing the familial bond as well as the power of the Force. Leia says, 'I know. Somehow, I've always known,' and this awareness of the spiritual connection between them cements that they are indeed brother and sister."[56]

As with most of his other themes, the "Luke and Leia" music interacts naturally with the other thematic material in the trilogy. Just as Leia tells Han that that Luke is her brother, the score transitions seamlessly from the "Luke and Leia" theme to the "Han and Leia" theme.

According to David Collins of the *Star Wars Oxygen* podcast, the "Luke and Leia" theme is essentially constructed from the DNA of the "Luke" theme when Williams uses a heroic 5th, rather than "the romantic love interval" (major 6th) that Williams uses for his other love themes. "Even though we don't hear it in the movie a lot, it actually signified something very symbolic in a musical sort of way."[57]

With the completion of his third *Star Wars* score, Williams had accomplished something rare in film scoring history. As Lucas said in a 1983 *Rolling Stone* interview, the *Star Wars* trilogy totaled

[s]ix hours and 15 minutes' worth of films, and you're talking about maybe five and a half hours' worth of music. It's the underpinning, a grease that each movie slides along on and a glue that holds it together so that you can follow it. There's always been a scene or a moment in which the music connects so strongly with the visual that it sends shivers up my spine every time I see

it. It's happened in all three pictures. Johnny's always gotten that moment for me.[58]

Star Wars Trilogy Impact

The impact of *Star Wars* reached well beyond the film industry. According to *Star Trek* actor-director Jonathan Frakes, "It has popularized symphonic music.... And made it economically viable in many ways."[59] While the scores to the *Star Wars* trilogy were not the first film music to become repertoire for major symphony orchestras, they legitimized the performance of film music by major orchestras. This impact was magnified when John Williams was named the nineteenth conductor of the Boston Pops Orchestra in 1980 after the passing of the legendary Arthur Fiedler. When Williams arrived in Boston, film music was undervalued by major symphony orchestras; in fact, Williams was often treated with disrespect by orchestra members. This changed during his tenure.

"I think we owe John Williams a tremendous debt in terms of the growing respect for film music in the concert hall," stated Jon Burlingame. "By the time that he leaves the Boston Pops in 1993, it's much more widely accepted that film music is not only worthy of performance by legitimate symphony orchestras, but it's also what the public wants."[60]

Motion Picture Music

This impact was perhaps most greatly felt within the film scoring industry. For over a decade prior to Lucas' film, orchestral scores had largely fallen out of favor. With the release of *Star Wars: A New Hope* (and to a lesser extent, *Jaws*), large orchestral scores, primarily inspired by romantic classical composers, not only came back into fashion, but were practically compulsory for major adventure motion pictures—particularly space films. Jason Zumwalt of Udiscovermusic.com observed that Williams' *New Hope* score "was the beginning of the modern American film score. Not only would he go on to shape how we 'heard' our favorite movies by providing the music for films such as the *Indiana Jones* series ... but his influence on every other film composer cannot be denied."[61]

The arrival of *Star Wars* also inspired an entire generation of young composers. "The original *Star Wars* floored me," recalls *Star Trek: The Next Generation* composer Ron Jones.

I was just graduating from college. The only place near us where it was playing was the Cinemara Dome in Seattle. We go there and there's this huge line and

by the time we got in, they got to Tatooine and they're basically playing Johnny's version of the "Rite of Spring." I just said, "Oh yeah! This is great!" I'd
already decided that I was going to Hollywood anyway after college.... I think
seeing that film really set a lot of us on a trajectory of what grand film scoring
can be and what that landscape is. I always gravitated to full orchestra.[62]

Return of the Fox Fanfare

Williams' powerful and memorable orchestral score raised the bar
for what audiences would expect for film music for decades to come. However, it was not just Williams' score that became ingrained in the public
consciousness. For people of a certain age, the 20th Century–Fox fanfare
music became synonymous with the opening notes of Williams' iconic
Star Wars score. Even when the Fox theme heralds the beginning of other
films, many viewers will hum the opening notes of *Star Wars* or mime the
downbeat of a conductor leading the orchestral Williams theme. As Tim
Greiving of the *Los Angeles Times* wrote, "The logo became inseparable
from *Star Wars*, and its catchy call-to-arms triggered a Pavlovian drool
in filmgoers waiting in the pregnant pause before the giant golden title
slammed onto the screen."[63]

This symbiosis between the Fox fanfare and Williams' score was not
accidental. The two pieces of music were joined deliberately, creating a
highly unusual musical and emotional bond between a film score and a
studio logo sequence.

Over the previous several years, the Fox fanfare logo sequence was
being phased out, but George Lucas was personally enamored of it and
specifically requested it in his film. In the liner notes for the 1997 release
of the *Star Wars* soundtrack, Mike Matessino wrote, "It was George Lucas'
inspired creative stroke to reintroduce it when Fox released *Star Wars* in
1977."[64] Using the fanfare helped link the film to the golden age of Hollywood; as noted by film composer David Newman, "[The logo-fanfare]
harks back to a storied past." The fanfare sets up the *Star Wars* theme perfectly, helping to set the tone of the movie. Newman adds that it was as
though, "We're going to sit down and listen to a story, like we're kids."[65]

The logo theme was written in 1933 by Newman's father, legendary
film composer Alfred Newman, who had been hired by movie mogul Dar-
ryl F. Zanuck, creator of 20th Century Pictures. Two years later, the studio
merged with Fox Film Corporation and "20th Century–Fox" was born, the
new company retaining the logo sequence and music produced for 20th
Century Pictures. However, the early version of the fanfare consisted of
only the initial brass opening sections. It was not until 1954 that the full

version of the fanfare, featuring a dramatic string section, was written by Newman in response to Fox's request for an extended sequence for the CinemaScope version of the logo. This extended version is associated with the *Star Wars* franchise.

Williams was uniquely suited to incorporate the classic fanfare into his opening theme. He had worked as a pianist for Alfred Newman on several film scores at Fox. According to Greiving, Williams "counted [Newman] as a mentor and friend."[66] Honoring his past mentor, Williams set out to integrate the two pieces, writing the *Star Wars* theme in B-flat major, the same key as Newman's Fox fanfare, treating the fanfare as though it were part of his own composition.

Nonetheless, bringing back the Fox fanfare was more easily said than done. The *Star Wars* team could not locate the master recording for the Fox music, so they resorted to making a copy directly from the soundtrack of 1954's *River of No Return*. As a result, there was a significant difference in sound quality between the Fox fanfare recording and the new *Star Wars* recording, but this may have worked to their advantage. According to Chris Malone, in his paper "Recording the *Star Wars* Saga," "It proved to be an inspired choice as, not only were both the *Star Wars* 'main theme' and 'Fox fanfare' composed in B flat minor, the difference in sound quality from the 1954 recording of the 'Fox Fanfare' to the dynamic and powerful recording of the *Star Wars* music ensured audiences would be in for an aural treat."[67]

In addition to sharing the same key signature, Williams' score complemented the studio fanfare brilliantly. Williams recalled,

> I tried to construct something that again would have this idealistic, uplifting but military flair to it. And set it in brass instruments, which I love anyway, which I used to play as a student, as a youngster. And try to get it so it's set in the most brilliant register of the trumpets, horns, and trombones so that we'd have a blazingly brilliant fanfare at the opening of the piece.[68]

With the unprecedented success of *Star Wars* and the equally passionate response to Williams' music, the 20th Century–Fox fanfare was thus reborn. When the first of the *Star Wars* prequels, *The Phantom Menace*, hit the big screen in 1999, it was accompanied by the famous studio sequence. Many theatergoers literally cheered as the Fox fanfare announced the beginning of a new *Star Wars* epoch. Fox's role in *Star Wars* continued through the next two films.

But all good things must come to an end (at least for a little while). In 2012, Disney purchased Lucas Films. Since Fox was no longer the distributor of the franchise, Disney decided to remove the Fox fanfare from the beginning of the *Star Wars* films. Predictably, this decision generated a minor uproar with purist *Star Wars* fans.

David Newman was also not pleased. Since his father's music had been deliberately fused to the *Star Wars* franchise, he believed it was a mistake to remove it. "You can make a case that it is integral to the movie," said Newman. "It's not just a logo, so taking it out diminishes the effect of the movie."[69]

Newman as well as *Star Wars* fans did not have to wait long for the Fox logo fanfare to be returned from exile. A new hope arose in 2019 when Disney completed the purchase of 20th Century–Fox. Later that year, the Fox fanfare logo was reunited with the Lucas-produced *Star Wars* films. However, the Fox fanfare would not be used in any of the productions that followed: *The Force Awakens*, *Rogue One*, *The Last Jedi*.

For new films produced by the Fox division, the storied studio logo sequence (including Alfred Newman's fanfare) would also be preserved, but with modification to the company title. Disney rolled out a new version that resembles the pre–1935 logo so that the large block letters now read "20th Century Studios."

David Newman believes this was a good decision by Disney. "These media companies are very important to the world, not just to their shareholders. I don't think Disney's brand could ever suffer from anything like that." However, Newman is also of the opinion that since the two pieces of music were intentionally linked, the fanfare should remain on all *Star Wars* films featuring Williams' opening theme.[70]

In an interview with film music journalist and Williams biographer Tim Greiving, he agreed with Newman that the fanfare should not have been removed in the first place: "It felt like a brutal piece of surgery when the fanfare was removed." Greiving was less critical of how Disney resolved the controversy. "It's smart business for a company that traffics in nostalgia, but it was also the right decision from an artistic and emotional standpoint. Good on Disney."[71]

Close Encounters of the Third Kind

> "John Williams is my oldest collaboration and I depend
> on Johnny more than I've depended on anybody to
> rewrite my movies musically—and put them a rung
> higher than I ever could reach."—Steven Spielberg[72]

Not all the space-related film composers in the late 1970s were attempting to replicate *Star Wars*. In fact, Williams himself produced a radically different musical sound later in 1977 for *Close Encounters of the Third Kind*.

Close Encounters was released just as NASA's *Voyager* spacecraft was being launched into deep space, carrying greetings from the people of Earth to potential extra-terrestrial life. This included a pictographic representation of Earth's location in the solar system as well as a "Golden Record" that contained music and sounds of Earth (see "Music in 'Real' Space").

In the same period, a SETI scientist at Ohio State University detected a strong signal from space of unknown origin—and NASA had just landed the *Viking* spacecraft of the surface of Mars looking for signs of life (unsuccessfully). The search for extra-terrestrial life was very much in the public consciousness during this period. (Dr. Gilbert V. Levin believed that his Labeled Release experiment on *Viking* did find evidence of organic life, but NASA dismissed the results, stating that it was a sign of an inorganic chemical reaction.)

Close Encounters was written and directed by Steven Spielberg and released on November 16, 1977. The title of the film was based on a real classification system that had been developed by astronomer and UFO expert Josef Allen Hynek. His classification system defined different levels of human interaction with alien beings. This classification system is described in the original trailer for the film:

- Close encounters of the first kind: Sighting of an unidentified flying object.
- Close encounters of the second kind: Physical evidence of a UFO.
- Close encounters of the third kind: Actual contact....

Spielberg's story would depict all three categories of "encounters" as a small group of people are mysteriously drawn to Devils Tower, Wyoming, where the first formal contact between aliens and humanity occurs in the film.

The genesis of the film was linked with a film that Spielberg had directed when he was 17 years old, *Firelight* (1964). *Firelight* told the story of the first contact between humanity and extra-terrestrials. "In a way, he had lived with *Close Encounters* since he was a child," related *Close Encounters* actor Bob Balaban. "And he had a vision in a real palpable sense of what this movie should feel like when you experience the movie."[73]

The Musical Language of Extraterrestrials

After the massively successful score for *Jaws*, Spielberg knew that John Williams needed to score his ambitious alien contact film. Although *Close Encounters* was released six months after *Star Wars*' theatrical bow,

Williams had been actively working on Spielberg's alien film well before he was recruited by George Lucas. According to Ray Morton, author of Close Encounters of the Third Kind: The Making of Steven Spielberg's Classic Film, "By the time Williams collected his golden statue [Williams' Oscar for his *Jaws* score], he was already hard at work on *Close Encounters*."[74]

This time, Williams took a radically different approach. In his *Star Wars* score, the composer harkens back to the sound of late-romantic classical music, as well as the Hollywood composers of the 1930s and '40s. In his *Close Encounters* score, Williams embraced an avant-garde sound like that of György Ligeti, reminiscent of Kubrick's use of Ligeti's music in *2001* to depict the alien elements of that film.

One would think the musical scores of *Close Encounters* and *Star Wars* were written by two different composers. Unlike *Star Wars*, *Close Encounters* does not open with a rousing fanfare—or any theme music at all. The title *Close Encounters of the Third Kind* appears in white letters with solid black background in complete silence as the names of the cast members are projected on the screen. But then, wrote Craig Lysy of MovieMusicUk.com, "slowly, and almost imperceptibly from out of the blackened formless void we bear witness to violins mysterioso ascending with kindred strings, which is soon joined by orchestra and chorus in a chromatic crescendo that crests powerfully as the screen explodes with the light of desert dunes beset by fierce wind sounds."[75]

As for the rest of the score, the music was integrated with the story like no other film before it. The music was a core element of the plot. Spielberg did not want to fall into old Hollywood alien contact clichés, in which the aliens spoke in "stilted English the way aliens did in so many bad science fiction films."[76] He also did not want his extra-terrestrial visitors to be telepathic or communicate in any of the other worn-out methods that became popular during the 1950s. After conversations with Williams and others, Spielberg "decided that it would be original, unique, and beautiful to have the terrestrials and extra-terrestrials talk to one another using music."[77] According to Spielberg, "I had first thought mathematics would be the common language between intergalactic species, but I thought it would be much more emotional if music was how we spoke to one another."[78]

Creating this musical alien language was perhaps the most challenging element of Williams' score. Spielberg approached him during the early stages of pre-production and asked him to come up with an appropriate combination of five musical notes that the humans and aliens could use to communicate with one another.[79] This would essentially serve as a "doorbell" to alert humanity that alien beings wanted to begin a conversation. The theme could not be overly complicated. "John spent a lot of time coming up with those five notes," recalled Spielberg. "John said that it can't sound like a song—and it can't sound like a fragment.... He decided mathematically that it would be five notes."[80] Williams played over 300 five-note combinations to Spielberg. Out of these options, they both eventually agreed on the now-famous notes.

The five-note motif—D, E, C, C (octave lower), G—would represent a musical greeting from visiting aliens. Spielberg and Williams also combined the musical greeting with a sign language system to accompany each note. They used a real system created by Hungarian composer Zoltán Kodály (1882-1967) to help teach the young children the fundamentals of music. Together, an alien tonal and sign language were created.

Spielberg and Williams chose this musical language for artistic reasons, but the concept resonates with SETI's Artist in Residence, composer Felipe Pérez Santiago:

> I believe music is a universal language for all humans and even for a lot of living beings on our planet. Music transcends physical, ideological, generational, language frontiers, and it's certainly a universal way of communication. So, I think it's natural to use music or sound (traveling frequencies) as a way of communication to outer space.[81]

Whether this contention by Santiago is correct or not, humanity has no way of knowing how alien civilizations may communicate with each other or with other species. For all we know, the great galactic language may well be music.

As noted earlier, Williams channeled contemporary and even avant-garde sounds influenced by such composers as György Ligeti and Krzysztof Penderecki. As Joshua Barone of the *New York Times* wrote, the *Close Encounters* score is "atonal and elusive, full of amorphous sound that rarely coalesces into melody."[82] This atonality serves to effectively contrast and underscore the melodic motifs scattered throughout the film and then climax in the final minutes of the extra-terrestrial tale. "He used that in a progressive—I would say dramaturgical way—throughout the film," commented Emilio Audissino. "The interesting thing in the score is that there is a progression from atonality to tonality. We start with this music that is very much like the other side of *2001*—the Ligeti atonal music that we hear in *2001*."[83]

Spielberg and Williams draw upon expectations that have been stoked for decades. Hollywood had often depicted aliens as mortal threats to humanity, using atonal music to define the nefarious invaders. With these preconceived perceptions firmly in place, Spielberg presented 1977 audiences with brightly illuminated alien spaceships as they terrorize occupants of pickup trucks and kidnap young children. Adding to the tension, we do not see the aliens "in the flesh" until the last third of the film. "The director is telling us 'They are coming,'" stated Emilio Audissino. "'They might be threatening' and the music plays around with that idea. Then there is a progressive discovery that they are fascinating creatures, not coming to Earth to conquer and destroy."[84] In this case, the use of music is similar to what Williams had done in *Jaws*. The music serves as a surrogate for the unseen shark; except in the case of *Jaws*, the shark does not turn out to be a benign aquatic creature.

Atonality is not the only musical tool Williams wields to escalate anxiety. He also employs two well-known pieces of music to evoke an almost Pavlovian musical response; one originated in the thirteenth century and the other was written in the twentieth century. As Tom Schneller, Ithaca College music professor, explained, "*Close Encounters* is dominated by two motives that reinforce Spielberg's 'two-handed Wonder/Terror approach,' to use Todd Alcott's phrase. Each is derived from a melody associated with opposite ends of the conceptual and emotional spectrum: "Dies Irae" and 'When You Wish Upon a Star.'"[85]

As he had in *Star Wars: A New Hope*, Williams uses the Gregorian chant to project a sense of peril. "Dies Irae" first appears just after the Roy Neary character (played by Richard Dreyfuss) encounters an alien spacecraft for the first time. As he sits in his pickup truck reading a map by a railroad crossing, bright lights shine down on his vehicle and the electrical systems in his truck go haywire. Nearby mailboxes rock to and fro, and the railway signals are activated when there is no train in sight. As quickly as the episode started, it stops, and everything is quiet. He then speeds off as the "Dies Irae" variation thunders in the background. Williams uses this theme to advance the prospect that these aliens may be a threat not only to humanity, but immediately to Roy.

The "Dies Irae" variation also represents Roy's evolving mental state as he is tormented by uncontrollable visions of Devils Tower in Wyoming. "I used a four-note motif for Neary, which in my mind had to do with his obsession with the mountain," Williams recalled. "I was trying to get inside Neary, really, to play musically his obsession with this unseen thing."[86]

Allusions to the thirteenth-century chant are heard several additional times, perhaps most dramatically when Roy and Jillian are on their quest to reach Devils Tower. Schneller wrote:

> Williams uses the "Dies Irae" motif most conspicuously during the sequences in Wyoming as Roy and Jillian drive across the country in a reckless, frantic search for Devils Tower. Plowing through fields and crashing through roadblocks, they are in the throes of an ecstatic madness. The music here is at once exuberant and foreboding, and its apocalyptic undertones resonate with

particular intensity as we see the lonely car hurtling through an abandoned, desolate landscape littered with the bodies of (apparently) dead cattle.[87]

We eventually discover that the aliens are benevolent and that "Dies Irae" and the atonal musical elements were used as a "red herring" to divert and manipulate the audience.

"Dies Irae" was also chosen to accompany this film because of another film that influenced *Close Encounters*: the Disney animated masterpiece *Fantasia* (1940). Spielberg wanted to mirror *Fantasia*'s "Night on Bald Mountain" scene, both in imagery and sound. The music that accompanies this scene in *Fantasia* was Modest Mussorgsky's same-name composition "Night on Bald Mountain," which utilizes variations on "Dies Irae." In fact, the image of Bald Mountain played a role in Spielberg's selection of Devils Tower; the scene where alien clouds encircle Devils Tower looks quite similar to the Bald Mountain in the Disney film.

Williams also uses another familiar theme: "When You Wish Upon a Star," written by Leigh Harline and Ned Washington and famously sung by Jiminy Cricket in the Disney animated film *Pinocchio* (1940), is subtly integrated into the last moments of *Close Encounters*. Unlike "Dies Irae," this theme only appears at the climax as it becomes clear that these alien visitors are friendly.

The climax of both story and music begins when the alien "mothership" arrives at Devils Tower. In this epic scene, when humanity and the visiting aliens finally begin direct communication, Williams composes a kinetic musical exchange between the intimidating mothership (larger than Devils Tower) and the almost insignificant humans. The humans begin the musical conversation with an electronic keyboard playing the five-note greeting, but their conversation eventually is taken on

Humans and aliens communicate with music at Devils Tower in *Close Encounters of the Third Kind*.

by an oboe. Then Williams uses the big, deep sound of a tuba to represent the aliens in this unusual exchange of information. The piece eventually develops into a fast-paced duel between tuba and oboe. Williams had considered generating the entire conversation on electronic instruments but, according to Craig Lysy of MovieMusicUk.us, "[h]e felt that the Moog synthesizer was too automated as to sound, inhuman. As such he reasoned that the difficulty of playing these two acoustic instruments served to make the aliens more relatable. Additionally, the low register resonating power of the tuba fully embodied the stunning enormity of the Mothership."[88]

It has now become abundantly clear that these aliens are not likely to be potential conquerors or destroyers of humanity, but the musical sequence still generates a significant amount of tension as the musical dual speeds up and a highly mechanical and non–human-sounding manner. But finally, in the final 30 minutes of the film, "[t]here's a sense of deliverance to it," recalls Williams. "An absence of tension. [That] everything is going to be all right. Our world and their world are going to come together. There is nothing to fear. That's the part of the music that I find most successful even today."[89]

As Roy Neary is escorted by his alien hosts into the mothership, the music resolves into full tonality and a feeling of wonder. To help solidify the transition between anxiety and wonder, the familiar and unexpected melody subtly echoes in Williams' score: the first seven notes of "When You Wish Upon a Star." The song is heard in Williams' score as Roy achieves his dream and is escorted into the alien mothership with his new extra-terrestrial friends. This selection was not a musical whim by Williams. Spielberg had planned to use the song as far back as when he was writing the first draft of the script; "I pretty much hung my story on the mood that song created, the way it affected me emotionally."[90] Williams added that "When You Wish Upon a Star" was in *Close Encounters*, disguised, for the sense of mystique. "It is a beautiful song and it meant a lot to Steven, and there are strong associations, fantastic associations with it. Most people don't even notice it, and that's all right, too. It may be just a kind of artistic conceit, I suppose, but it has some meaning to us. That should be enough of a reason"[91] Spielberg explained that this was the moment that Roy essentially "becomes a real person. He loses his strings, his wooden joints, and he goes on that ship knowing what he's doing."[92]

Released six months after *Star Wars*, *Close Encounters* showed musical naysayers that Williams could not be placed into a compositional box. Between his scores for *Close Encounters* and *Star Wars*, he demonstrated extraordinary musical diversity and imagination. Williams remains proud of his work on *Close Encounters*, noting, "Over the years, *Close*

Encounters of the Third Kind has remained one of my favorite Steven Spielberg films. With its depiction of the long-awaited visit of the radiant and loving extra-terrestrials, the fascinating premonitions of the little boy, and the five-note musical motif used to communicate with our other-worldly guests, the film offered a rich and unusual canvas on which to present the music."[93]

5

The Post–*Star Wars* 1970s

In the wake of George Lucas' juggernaut space opera, a flurry of space-related films and television shows materialized in the late 1970s. There were now new expectations for production value as well as the caliber of music that would accompany science fiction films and TV shows.

Battlestar Galactica

The show that seemingly mirrored *Star Wars* the most was ABC's *Battlestar Galactica*, premiering on September 17, 1978. This space adventure was created and produced by Glen A. Larson, the successful writer-producer of popular TV shows such as *Quincy M.E.*, *McCloud* and *Switch*.

Battlestar Galactica was set in a star system far far away—within our own galaxy. Loosely based on the Book of Mormon, a civilization comprised of 12 human colonies are in constant warfare with a race of robotic villains called the Cylons. After a sneak attack, the colonies are destroyed and only one Battlestar (their most powerful class of war ship), *Galactica*, as well as a fleet of private ships, survive. Led by the Battlestar *Galactica*, the rag-tag convoy heads out into deep space, searching for the lost colony, Earth.

To support and elevate this ambitious, special effects–heavy show, an impressive orchestral score was needed for each episode, something that was practically unheard of in TV at the time. To take on this challenge, Larson hired composer Stu Phillips, who he had worked with on *McCloud* and *Quincy*. While Phillips was not a "space enthusiast," he had some experience writing space-related music, including an album called "Music for Outer Space" in 1956, and then music for a short film on John Glenn in the 1960s.[1]

The studio objected to the hiring of Phillips and pressured Larson to hire a "bigger" name in film or television scoring. "He had to fight for me," recalls Phillips. "The studio had spent $14 million, which was a lot of money in those days for a television show, and they had other named composers in mind, but [Larson] stuck with me. I was loyal to him and he was loyal to me."[2]

After the studio relented, Larson showed Phillips the first cut of the *Battlestar* pilot film in advance of a screening by studio executives. This first cut ran approximately two hours and 40 minutes, an unusually long duration for a television movie. The film also had no musical cues or final sound effects yet. To compensate for these missing elements, temporary music (a temp track) was essential before the studio executives viewed the film. Larson's first assignment to Phillips was to select a temp track. According to Phillips, he said, "We need music. We need a lot of music."[3]

Phillips and Don Woods, a sound editor and part-time composer, tracked the entire show with classical selections and film cues, as well as some of Phillips' previous music. Phillips recalled that studio executives, after viewing the pilot, said, "Oh, we love the music."[4] This created other challenges, however. Phillips would need to write a score that matched or exceeded these expectations. With this in mind, Larson asked him to write music that sounded as similar as possible to the temp music (without plagiarizing)—largely to accommodate the network executives who had loved the temporary music.[5]

Phillips succeeded, writing opening theme music and a score that had a brassy and heroic sound reminiscent of *Star Wars*. The problem was, it was bigger and brassier than most television shows could afford. Television shows of the 1970s rarely used symphonic music. According to composer Bear McCreary, who scored the reboot of *Battlestar Galactica* in the early 2000s, "It was mind-blowing that he could do a score that symphonic and big on TV" in that era.[6]

To bring Phillips' score to life, the Los Angeles Philharmonic was hired. It was highly unusual for an established orchestra to record music for a television show, but the Philharmonic management hoped that they might attract a younger audience if they established such a partnership. The fact that the *Star Wars* score had made such an impact—and had greatly magnified the name recognition of the London Symphony Orchestra—almost certainly influenced their decision.

With the orchestra committed to the project, there was still an important remaining question: Who would conduct the orchestra? When the head of the Philharmonic inquired during a meeting, Phillips raised his hand and declared, "I am."[7]

A deafening silence and several skeptical looks followed, but then Larson spoke up: "If Stu says he can do it, he can do it." According to Phillips, "Glen stuck his neck out. He didn't know if I could do it, and I didn't know if I could do it. I'd never conducted a 100-piece orchestra before."[8] Nonetheless, Phillips did successfully conduct the L.A. Philharmonic, providing an essential ingredient for the new space adventure.

Even though the show had a significant budget, Phillips' music helped compensate for weaker elements of the production. A Filmtracks. com review notes, "Phillips' music achieved that which the show's budget could not in other production elements: the awe of space. By compensating for some of the shortcomings of the cheesier sets, costumes, and special effects, the heroic and occasionally melodramatic score provided the necessary element of fantastic, space-journeying marvel."[9]

Battlestar also faced another challenge—one that was not production related: a lawsuit. Coming 16 months after *Star Wars,* the series and music were unquestionably inspired by the Lucas film, but 20th Century-Fox believed that the show went well beyond being merely inspired by the film, accusing NBC–Universal of stealing the idea for the show from *Star Wars,* citing 34 similarities.[10] The Ninth District Court stated, "[A]t a minimum, it is a close enough question that it should be resolved by way of a trial. We intimate no opinion whether the films are substantially similar as to either idea or expression, but state only that reasonable minds could differ on those key factual issues."[11]

The plot and technological creation of *Battlestar* were the lawsuit's primary focus, but the Fox legal department was also concerned that Phillips' *Battlestar* music may also have plagiarized John Williams' *Star Wars* score. As a result, Williams was dispatched to visit a *Battlestar Galactica* recording session to provide his opinion in this matter. "Of course, they asked the wrong person," stated Phillips. "Because John is the last person in the world who would ever accuse anyone of ripping off anything—that's not his style." Williams attended the session for over an hour and reported back to Fox that he had found no evidence of plagiarism by Phillips.[12] Phillips did not even remotely blame Williams for this accusation. "Please do not hold John Williams at fault for visiting the *Battlestar* session," Phillips said. "It was not his idea to do so. He was asked by the legal department of Fox to do this. John is too nice a person to have done this on his own."[13] A settlement was eventually reached and *Battlestar* was cancelled after one season. It is unclear whether the show's cancellation was part of the settlement (the terms of the settlement have not been released). Its cancellation was likely a result of a combination of production costs, ratings and the lawsuit.

Nonetheless, Phillips had produced scores that not only elevated the show but were highly unusual for television at the time. According to Jon Burlingame, "This was really a high point in Stu Phillips' career.... Phillips really rose to the occasion with a grand scale, swashbuckling score."[14]

After its cancellation, *Battlestar* quickly faded from the public consciousness, but over time, Phillips' music began to inspire interest in the show again. "It went into the dumpster for a while," said Phillips, but the *Battlestar Galactica* fan club became very active in the 1990s trying to generate enthusiasm in bringing the show back. Not until the reissuing of the album on CD did the broader support for a reboot begin to build. "That sparked some interest and people started posting it online. Suddenly there was new interest and I started getting calls from orchestras to send them scores to perform—all over the world. It started to get a new life."[15]

One year after *Battlestar Galactica* was released, Glen A. Larson released another space-related television show called *Buck Rogers in the 25th Century*, and again Phillips was hired to score the show. In contrast to *Battlestar*, this show was intended to be tongue-in-cheek and intentionally over-the-top.

As Phillips was preparing to score the initial episodes, Larson's only instruction was "Give me a ballsy sound!" According to Phillips, "That was Glen's thing. He always wanted a ballsy sound. He liked trombones, and tubas, and timpani and all the growly low stuff—he loved that." However, the theme music would not be "ballsy." Larson decided to write the theme song himself, a song that was more pop-oriented than symphonic. "His theme was kind of like a country waltz … and it was kind of unusable in most cases within the scores…" recalled Phillips. "What I did is write a new theme of my own and used that a basis and kept using that theme throughout the show."[16]

Buck Rogers lasted two seasons but did not enjoy the long-term popularity (for both the show and music) that *Battlestar Galactica* did.

The Black Hole

Disney charged into the space genre, hoping to not only produce a film equal to Lucas', but one that would also surpass the *Star Wars* magic. Their cinematic vehicle was the $20 million *The Black Hole*, released on December 21, 1979. Instead of riveling *Star Wars*, the film was described by David Weiner of *The Hollywood Reporter* as

> more akin to *20,000 Leagues Under the Sea* in outer space with throwback trappings: an uneven mix of Gothic drama, kiddie adventure, clunky dialogue and characters, cool-but-derivative robot designs and retro-styled rockets amid a very colorful palette, a wonderfully moody John Barry score, and spectacular visuals thanks to signature animation techniques and ingenious, matte-based special effects.[17]

In 2130, the spacecraft USS *Palomino* is returning to Earth after a long deep-space mission. They discover the USS *Cygnus*, a ship that had mysteriously vanished years earlier, in orbit around a black hole. At first, they believe the vehicle is abandoned, but then discover that the great scientist Hans Reinhardt is the sole survivor and has created a race of cowled drones to run the ship, as well as storm-trooper–like security robots and a Darth Vader–like robotic bodyguard named Maximillian. Eventually it is discovered that the drones are actually the *Cygnus* crew members, stripped of their humanity and individuality.

The *Black Hole* plot was darker than typical Disney films and it would have become the company's first PG-rated production, but the decision was made to release it under the Buena Vista division of Disney, rather than under the main Disney brand.[18] The decision was logical from another perspective. The film's director, Gary Nelson, was concerned that adult audiences would automatically assume that any Disney movie would be a children's film, thus would not attract adult audiences—which would be necessary if they were to rival *Star Wars*.[19]

Nelson understood the significant role that John Williams' score had played in *Star Wars*' overall success. The music supporting *The Black Hole* needed to rival that level of music. Veteran composer John Barry was called upon for this daunting task. Barry was best known for his scores for the James Bond franchise (including *Moonraker,* a Bond film that came out the same year and also contained space battles). The composer had also written music for films such as *Born Free, The Lion in Winter* and the low-budget space drama *Starcrash.*

Barry began to compose a score that, according to Craig Lysy, reflected "the concept of this bottomless three-quarters swirling thing, the black hole, [that] was the film's central image to me and the thought behind the movement of the main theme."[20] With this concept in mind, Barry produced a spellbinding waltz that reflected the unrelenting nature of a black hole. As music reviewer Joe Marchese opined, "This dizzying, swirling waltz-meets-march Main Title throbs with urgency, and the use of the waltz form is a most unexpected stylistic choice that pays off."[21] Originally conceived as "*The Poseidon Adventure* in space," Barry's score also at times features foreboding music that is reminiscent of Williams' music for that cruise ship disaster film.

The Black Hole was one of the last movies to use what had already become a musical anachronism, the overture. Motion picture overtures were usually reserved for major epic films like *Ben-Hur* or hit musical adaptations such as *My Fair Lady*. By adding an overture prior to the primary thematic music, Disney was clearly making a statement regarding the quality of the film they had produced. Contrasting with the swirling, foreboding theme music, the overture is a more upbeat and traditional, clearly influenced by Williams' *Star Wars* fanfare. Craig Lysy described the theme as "a retrograde inversion of John Williams' *Star Wars* main title theme."[22] As with Williams' score, Barry's score appears to have been influenced by Erich Wolfgang Korngold's *Kings Row* theme. Lysy stated, "I must say that Barry's approach is a clever twist and perfectly conceived. The music is a classic march that opens with a heroic fanfare started first in the upper register and then repeated mid-range over militaristic timpani."[23]

The Black Hole failed to match Lucas' film on any level and received generally poor reviews. While it was profitable, it quickly faded from the public memory. A major factor in the limited impact of the film is that it was released just two weeks after *Star Trek: The Motion Picture* appeared in theaters.

The Black Hole was the first film score recorded digitally.

6

Alien and the Return of *Star Trek*

Jerry Goldsmith in 1979

Jerry Goldsmith had an extraordinary year in 1979. He had already established himself as one of the premier film composers of his time, having written music for *Patton*, *The Omen* and *Chinatown*, as well as the science fiction films *Planet of the Apes* and *Logan's Run* plus numerous episodes of the 1960s TV series *The Twilight Zone*. In 1979, he composed two of his best remembered scores: *Star Trek: The Motion Picture* and *Alien*.

Both were space-based, but the plots and music of these productions contrasted dramatically. Goldsmith's *Star Trek* music was written in the traditional romantic classical style, but his *Alien* score was written using more modern and avant-garde compositional techniques. Goldsmith demonstrated not only his extraordinary range and ability, but also how the music in space-based films did not need to follow a single school of composition. In this sense, Goldsmith's success in 1979 was very similar to the success that John Williams had enjoyed in 1977.

Alien

The first of these films to debut was *Alien*. The space horror flick was presented on May 25, 1979, at the Seattle International Film Festival and then went into general release on June 22. A horror movie set in space, the film featured the famous tagline, "In space, no one can hear you scream." The story takes place on a space tug called *Nostromo,* traveling back to Earth with its crew members in stasis for the duration of the long flight. However, the crew is awakened when a distress signal comes from a nearby moon. That moon contains an aggressive alien species that will kill the entire crew except for Warrant Officer Ripley.

For Goldsmith, fear would serve as a productive motivator to inspire

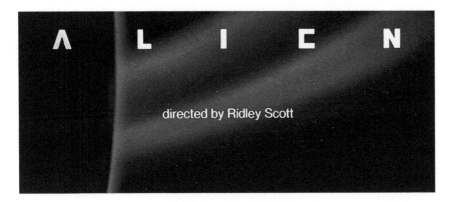

Opening credits of *Alien*.

music for this film. The composer recalled his first screening: "I remember to this day this one scene when he [Brett] was looking for his cat in this dark chamber on the ship.... I was absolutely terrified. I kept reminding myself, 'It's just a movie, it's just a movie.' It really scared the shit out of me."[1] The composer had originally intended to introduce *Alien* with a more traditional romantic sound, stating that the opening music of the movie should represent "the great unknown."[2] He envisioned an optimistic sound to musically misdirect the audience. He recalled, "I thought 'Well, let me play the whole opening very romantically and very lyrically and then let the shock come as the story evolves.' Don't give it away in the main title.... It didn't go over too well."[3] Director Ridley Scott and film editor Terry Rawlings were not enthusiastic about this approach. They instructed Goldsmith to compose a new opening cue that would represent the true mood and progression of the film. According to Goldsmith, "I wrote a new main title, which was the obvious thing, weird and strange, which everybody loved." However, Goldsmith did not love it; "The original one took me a day to write and the alternate one took me about five minutes."[4]

Goldsmith's revised opening theme effectively projects a mysterious and threatening feel. Charlie Brigden of RogerEbert.com described the film version of the theme music as "obtuse and esoteric... [It] uses wind and string effect influenced by Polish composer Krzysztof Penderecki originally intended to be used later in the picture."[5]

Goldsmith employed a mix of orchestral and exotic sounds, but according to Mauricio Dupuis, author of *Jerry Goldsmith: Music Scoring for American Movies*, "the most remarkable part of this score is how it mixes a symphonic orchestra with unusual tribal and folkloric instruments."[6] These included a didgeridoo, an aboriginal instrument; a conch shell or shell trumpet; a serpent wind instrument that is considered an ancestor of the tuba; and a shawm, an oboe-like instrument from the Middle East.[7] Goldsmith also made use of the Echoplex, a custom-built device created to produce an unusual echo effect when music was recorded through it. He had used this equipment extensively in his Oscar-nominated score for *Patton*.

As effective as Goldsmith was at musically projecting a creepy atmosphere, silence is also a potent device to elevate the sense of terror in the film. An example of this occurs after the face-hugging alien is detached from Kane's face. As the crew carefully searches the room, there is no music, just the sound of Kane's breathing—which elevates anxiety as much as a tense piece of music. These extended periods without music are effective throughout the film.

The relationship between Jerry Goldsmith and Ridley Scott was not harmonious after the new theme music was composed. The two men had significant creative differences. Goldsmith was asked to rewrite numerous cues, but many of these revised cues were excluded from the final film. Scott and sound editor Terry Rawlings eventually replaced portions of the score with entirely different pieces of music. In one case, during a scene where acid is burning through the deck of the ship, they replaced Goldsmith's cue with music that Goldsmith had written for the John Huston film *Freud* in 1962. Goldsmith was particularly unhappy about this: "Everyone would say 'Look how wonderful that music works'—I said, 'It stinks! It's all wrong.'"[8]

The decision that appears to have angered Goldsmith the most was the replacement of his revised end credit music. This time they would not swap the cue with another Goldsmith composition; instead, they inserted Howard Hanson's Symphony No. 2 (The Romantic). Rawlings later stated, "I don't think he ever forgave me for using Howard Hanson for the end of the film."[9]

Rawlings appears to have been correct. During a 1986 interview, Goldsmith said that working on *Alien* was "one of the most miserable experiences"[10] of his career (RogerEbert.com). But Scott was happy with the end results and stated, "Jerry Goldsmith's score is one of my favorite scores. Seriously threatening but has beauty. It had beauty, darkness and seems to [play] the DNA of some distant society."[11]

Later in life, after had had more time to reflect, Goldsmith attributed his conflicts with Scott to the director's inexperience at the time. "Ridley is a brilliant filmmaker—he's a brilliant visualist. I think that was just his second film and he wasn't as articulate then about what the music should do." As a result, Goldsmith noted, Scott wanted him to replicate the visuals through music, "and music can't replicate the visuals. It's not what it's supposed to do.... Let me do the emotional."[12]

A recording of Goldsmith's full original score was released by Intrada in 2007, enabling film music lovers to compare and contrast each version of the score.

Star Trek: The Motion Picture: The Emergence of a Franchise

Alien made a significant cultural impact and led to a franchise of films over the next several decades. But Goldsmith's "other" space film of 1979 had an even more substantial cultural impact. *Star Trek: The Motion Picture* launched the only science fiction film franchise that would truly compete with *Star Wars*.

Since the cancellation of the *Star Trek* TV series in 1969, the popularity of the reruns had been growing steadily and spawned a subculture of fans called "Trekkies." Series creator Gene Roddenberry had been contemplating a *Star Trek* film or a return to TV since the early 1970s. In a 1974 letter to a couple of *Star Trek* fans, Roddenberry was quite confident that a *Star Trek* film was imminent. "The status of the *Star Trek* theatrical film has gone from fair to good. Perhaps very good!"[13] In the mid–1970s, NBC expressed interest in launching a new live-action *Star Trek* series. However, Paramount had estimated that the cost of creating just the sets, props and costumes would cost roughly $750,000. Because of these high costs, they informed NBC that production could only move forward if NBC committed to four episodes up front. NBC declined, derailing any attempt of returning *Star Trek* to TV in the 1970s.[14] Paramount also had other reasons for hesitation. The popularity (and profit) from the original series had never been higher and Paramount feared that if a new series was introduced, it would undermine the value of the original series. Essentially, they did not want the old *Star Trek* to have to compete with a new *Star Trek*.

Thus, the circumstances were not favorable to produce a new series or film until another space film was released in 1977. With an expanding *Star Trek* fanbase and the release of *Star Wars*, Roddenberry and Paramount finally determined that the time was right to unite the *Star Trek* cast in what would become *Star Trek: The Motion Picture*. The film set the cast against a mysterious energy cloud named V'Ger that was approaching Earth and causing general mayhem in the galaxy. The *Enterprise*, sent to intercept the cloud, discovers that V'Ger is an old U.S. space probe called *Voyager 6*, believed to have fallen into a black hole years earlier. Damaged by its trans–black hole voyage, the probe encountered a machine race that dramatically enhanced the spacecraft and enabled it to complete its mission and find its creators on Earth.

Roddenberry assumed the role of producer and invited Robert Wise to direct. Wise was perhaps best known for directing the film adaptations of *West Side Story* and *The Sound of Music* (winning Academy Awards for both) but had also made a major contribution to the science fiction genre with his direction of *The Day the Earth Stood Still* twenty-eight years earlier. So confident was Paramount in the film's prospects that they staged the largest press conference held at the studio since the 1950s to announce that Wise would direct.[15]

Music played as critical a role in the success of the film as the plot and special effects. Wise had worked with Jerry Goldsmith on the 1966 film *The Sand Pebbles*. Goldsmith had in fact been approached to work on the original *Star Trek* series, but had to decline because of a scheduling conflict. He was quite pleased to be given a second chance, "It's serendipitous that years later, I came back to this project," he stated.[16]

Goldsmith had a daunting task. Expectations were extremely high for the film and his score. "Goldsmith had two main tasks to overcome," according to the JerryGoldsmithOnline.com website. "Firstly, to write an equally dramatic score as John Williams had achieved with *Star Wars*, but make sure it wasn't duplicated, and secondly to write a brand-new theme for one of the most popular franchises ever produced."[17]

Goldsmith was adamant about not reusing any of the TV series' original music, later stating, "When I was asked, I said I'd love to do the movie, but on the condition I wasn't saddled with the television theme."[18] They agreed his request, but his first attempt at a theme song was not successful. Upon hearing Goldsmith's initial theme, Wise was not satisfied. Wise later recalled, "The main theme was underdeveloped. I called a few people to hear the music. Everybody agreed it didn't work, so I had to tell Jerry."[19]

A dejected Goldsmith spent the next month reworking the opening music. When Wise heard the new version, he asked Goldsmith, "Why didn't you come up with that in the first place?"[20] Goldsmith had written a brassy and uplifting theme that Craig Lysy described thusly: "Filled with the spirit of adventure, abounding with the indomitable human quest to explore, Goldsmith's music resounds with the noble and forthright optimism of Gene Rodenberry's vision. Propelled by trumpets eroica, this piece launches the Star Trek rebirth with a glorious and inspiring optimism not often felt."[21]

The new opening fanfare would eventually rival or possibly exceed the fame of the opening music for the original series. Goldsmith reused the theme in *Star Trek V: The Final Frontier*, and it reached the height of its notoriety when it later became the opening theme music for *Star Trek: The Next Generation*.[22]

The new theme was integrated and manipulated throughout the film.

Goldsmith constructed a more nuanced and emotional version of the theme, called "The Enterprise," as Kirk and Scotty inspect the newly renovated USS *Enterprise* from a shuttle craft, a clearly emotional experience for "Admiral" Kirk, who had left the *Enterprise* years earlier. James Southall described the musical variation: "[A] majestic, rhapsodic piece, it is essentially a fantasy on Goldsmith's main theme, underscoring a sequence in which absolutely nothing happens (we just get repeated shots of the ship from a variety of angles); this is film score as ballet. It can never fail to send a shiver down the listener's spine."[23]

Significant technical issues plagued the film, and some scenes and sound effects had not been completed as the premiere date approached. Goldsmith's score helped to save the film. It filled many of the gaps where sound effects had not yet been added. "Thank goodness we had Jerry's score," said Wise. "I told him that music would take the place of sound effects. He really saved us."[24]

The V'Ger theme was a prime example of the musical substitution for sound effects. According to Jeff Bond, author of *The Music of* Star Trek, "The core of the [*Star Trek: The Motion Picture*] score is Goldsmith's evocative material for the V'Ger probe itself, which is daringly symbolic and elaborate."[25] In some cases, Goldsmith used musical sound effects to compensate for the lack of traditional sound effects or other shortcomings of the film. As an example, he used the Blaster Beam, Craig Huxley's innovative instrument (a mix of both a stringed and percussion instrument). According to Jeff Bond, "The effect is immediately imposing, powerful, and unearthly, instantly establishing the V'Ger entity as incomprehensible, alien and threatening."[26] Craig Lysy described the V'Ger theme as featuring "recurring ostinatos first by harp and later by piano. Ethereal horns, religioso pipe organ and mesmerizing arpeggios that resound as the mechanistic power of the blaster beam and rumbling bass underscore V'Ger's staggering enormity and power."[27]

Goldsmith introduced most of the major themes early in the film, one of them before the main fanfare sounds: "Ilia's Theme," which James Southall from MovieWaves.net describes as Goldsmith's "beautiful, longing theme of love and regret, culminating in the briefest of hints of his *Star Trek* march."[28] It not only musically identifies the navigator of the *Enterprise*, but also the romantic feelings between her and *Enterprise* first officer (under Kirk) Commander Will Decker.

This music also served as an overture prior to the main theme. As with the opening of *The Black Hole*, the filmmakers were harkening back to the age of big, epic movies that often boasted extensive overtures—or movie musicals (Robert Wise had directed two of the most successful movie adaptations of musicals). Few people remember the overture for *Star Trek:*

The Motion Picture, however. It served little purpose in the film and, like the *Black Hole* overture, was a musical anachronism.

Another cue introduced early in the film was the Klingon theme. This music does not play a significant role in the overall film, but it became one of the most durable themes in the *Star Trek* franchise. Appearing just after the opening fanfare as three Klingon Birds of Prey approach V'Ger, the driving, visceral music is reminiscent of the third movement of Ralph Vaughan Williams' Symphony #4 in F minor. Mauricio Dupuis noted that Goldsmith's theme "envisages a rhythmic pattern of tubas and trombones as well as a grave string pizzicato, with a fundamental timbric help provided by Javanese rattles (angklungs) played as castanets. Against this background, the horn section draws a simple phrasing starting with two repeated notes, divided by a fifth."[29] The result is a primal, warlike sound that effectively portrays the warrior race.

"The Klingon thing was instinctual," Goldsmith recalled. "I knew that there was a barbaric quality about them, a primitive quality, and they were the aggressors.... I did want to get that into the music, and that was the sum of the intellectual rationalization. I guessed they were the bad guys and they were attacking, so I figured we needed a battle cry for them."[30] Goldsmith's Klingon theme achieved canonic status within the *Star Trek* franchise, not only used by Goldsmith himself in *Star Trek V: The Final Frontier* but also in *Star Trek: The Next Generation* and other spinoff series.

Some of the most expansive music that Goldsmith composed for the first *Star Trek* film played as the *Enterprise* enters the swirling clouds surrounding the mysterious V'Ger. Once again, the music helps compliment or even compensate for special effects (both visual and sound) that were not always at the level that Roddenberry and Wise were hoping for. To elevate the sheer awe of this scene, Goldsmith wrote swirling music, suggestive at times of Bernard Herrmann's dizzying *Vertigo* theme. From the JerryGoldsmith.com website: "Goldsmith initially captures the mysterious craft by traditional orchestral means with a lush string passage and a Herrmannesque piano motif that carries the *Enterprise* deep inside."[31]

As the *Enterprise* continues to penetrate the cloud, Spock takes an unscheduled spacewalk to mind-meld with the mysterious V'Ger. Like *2001*'s stargate sequence, this extended scene featured mesmerizing lighting effects created by designer Douglas Trumbull. As Spock enters V'Ger's inner sanctum, he approaches a glowing manifestation of Ilia "and we hear her theme rise upon horns, ultimately culminating is a thunderous crescendo as they mind meld," wrote Craig Lysy. "The cue ends with a diminuendo as Spock drifts back to a waiting Kirk's arms."[32]

Goldsmith's inventive musical imagination is at the core of the success of the movie. There are few people who believe that *Star Trek: The Motion Picture* was a great film, but it was successful enough to relaunch the *Star Trek* franchise.

The Wrath of Khan

Star Trek: The Motion Picture, a very expensive film to produce, suffered from numerous problems in production. Nevertheless, it still generated a healthy profit and solidified the decision to produce additional *Trek* films. But studio executives wanted to produce the next film on a much smaller budget. Paramount president Michael Eisner believed that if they could make a better film, and on a more reasonable budget, they might develop a franchise to rival *Star* Wars.[33]

To guide this leaner production, Nicholas Meyer was hired to direct. Meyer had written and directed the 1979 time-traveling thriller *Time After Time* and scripted the 1976 Sherlock Holmes film *The Seven-Per-Cent Solution* based on his novel. He had never written or directed anything like *Star Trek* and often commented that he had never really watched the original television show.[34]

The new director's first task was to review potential scripts. This proved to be a helpful process for Meyer to understand the franchise and the characters. Having reviewed five scripts, he came to fully realize that the James T. Kirk character was truly based on Horatio Hornblower—a character model that Roddenberry had intended when he first conceived the original show. With that revelation in mind, Meyer wrote an original script—one that would prove to be quite controversial. Since Leonard Nimoy was hoping to leave the franchise, Meyer's story would feature the death of Spock.

In Meyer's story, Kirk and the *Enterprise* crew battle Khan, a genetically engineered villain. (Khan's sidekicks are also genetically engineered.) At the end of the story, Spock sacrifices himself to save the *Enterprise*. But first he mind-melds with Dr. McCoy, transferring his memories to the doctor. During Spock's later funeral, his body is shot into the new Genesis Planet, providing a glimmer of hope that he might return.

Meyer knew he needed a big orchestral sound to support the story. In fact, orchestral music is part of Meyer's family DNA. His grandfather was a Boston Symphony Orchestra violinist and his mother a concert pianist; his father, a psychiatrist by profession, was also an accomplished pianist. "I grew up with music. I am a music fool. I am an orchestra-holic," commented Meyer. "I believe that the orchestra is the greatest human invention." He added that the individual players are just like us (vices and all), "but when you put them together—and they play Beethoven—they transcend themselves. I have a kind of fanatic loyalty and need that revolves around orchestras."[35]

Meyer (and Paramount) considered bringing back Jerry Goldsmith, or even Miklós Rózsa (the composer for Meyer's *Time After Time*) to score the film, but the production could not afford either composer. Meyer began the process of listening to demo tapes, hoping to find a new composer. According to the director, "There were two people who really interested me: One was a composer named John Morgan and the other was James Horner."[36] One composer truly stood out. "I met and hired master Horner, a young man who spoke with a vaguely English accent," recalled Meyer.[37] Horner had been born in Los Angeles but had spent his early years in England before returning to the U.S. As a result, he always spoke with a slight British accent.

Upon hiring the 28-year-old Horner, Meyer was very clear from the start what he was looking for musically. He told Horner, "This film doesn't take place in outer space. This movie takes place on the ocean. This movie is Captain Horatio Hornblower. It's got to sound like the ocean—and what sounds like the ocean? [Claude] Debussy's *La Mer* [The Sea]—That's what I want."[38]

Like Meyer, Horner had little previous exposure to *Star Trek*, with one notable exception: He had been invited by Jerry Goldsmith to view the recording sessions for *Star Trek: The Motion Picture* in 1979. Unbeknownst to Horner at the time, this would be an extraordinary training session for what would become his biggest film scoring job yet.

Meyer also wanted to move *Star Trek* in a new direction. Horner recalled, "They didn't want to repeat the theme of [the first *Star Trek* movie]—they wanted a new theme. Nick wanted it to be seafaring. They didn't want to reuse or reference anything of *Star Trek* #1—that was history now."[39]

This musical exclusion did not include the original show. Horner begins the new film with the opening notes of the 1960s *Star Trek* series, "to establish a strong, nostalgic link to the time of the original series," observed Jeff Bond. Horner then launched his new theme music that Bond describes as "an exciting six-note repeating horn motif over a meandering string line that ascends sweepingly to a climax in the film's brassy eight-note title melody."[40] In deference to Meyer, the theme has a strong feel of nautical voyages of Hollywood past. The main title sequence also features a secondary, slightly melancholy theme, played on strings. While it can be considered an extension of the Kirk theme, it is also closely linked to the *Enterprise* as well as the close friendship between Kirk and Spock.

Horner believed that the score should only have a small number of themes. "I believed that you had to have two—maybe maximum three—that an audience could keep track of," he recalled. "Three themes would be the principal themes and then have a motif or two that were very short, but narrated other things.... [T]he motif would be short blasts of things."[41]

An example of this approach occurs when Horner mingles the Kirk theme with the friendship (B-theme) theme as the *Enterprise* leaves the drydock moorings. Jeff Bond wrote, "As the ship actually begins to move, Horner adds a heraldic three-note fanfare to the repeating figure from the main title, alternating between the two motifs to give an effect of gathering energy until the repeating motif bursts free along with the starship into a soaring rendition of the main melody."[42] This musical sequence also harkens to the music of great sea battles by Korngold in such films as *Captain Blood*.

Horner's musical depiction of Khan was also effective. For Khan, Horner wrote a short war-like motif using French horns and rapid percussion. "It helps you know right away that it's Khan's music.... It was something I could play that was a short burst of power."[43]

These short blasts of the Khan motif countered other themes. For example, in a sequence called "The Battle of the Mutara Nebula," Horner intertwines the Khan motif with both the Kirk theme and *Enterprise* motif as the course of the battle sways back and forth. These musical cues inform the audience of the progress of the battle scene—musically hinting at who currently has the upper hand. Horner stated,

> The chases could be very easily theme-driven because there was a lot of battle music. I had to musically say who was what—and what was who—and who was damaged ... and that helped a great deal knowing how the battle was going. I think that is really important when you're having long battle sequences. Otherwise, it's just action music.[44]

The relationship between Kirk and Spock crescendos on screen and musically as the Genesis device explodes and the *Enterprise* achieves warp drive just in time. The melancholy Kirk-*Enterprise* (B) theme plays as Kirk views the creation of a new life-filled planet materializing before his eyes— and then realizes that Spock is not at his post. The music continues as Kirk frantically runs to Engineering—to confirm his fear. McCoy and Scotty hold him back and as McCoy says, "It's too late." The Spock theme gently sounds. After a period of no music, Spock slowly dies from radiation exposure as variations of the Spock theme return. Kirk kneels on the other side of the transparent protective barrier and Spock says, "I have been, and always shall be, your friend." Horner recalled, "I wanted to make much more of Spock than had ever been done before, and that unique undercurrent of the film between Spock and the captain." This central relationship had not been thoroughly explored musically before. "I wanted to tell the story of two men and their friendship, and that's what I gleaned out of the series and out of the first movie. The closer I could play that bond during the movie, the more I could make of that bond's separation when Spock dies, the more I could break the audience's heart at the end of the movie."[45] This emotional moment is solidified as a bagpipe plays "Amazing Grace" during Spock's funeral.

With a full production cost of only $10 million, *Star Trek: The Wrath of Khan* premiered on June 4, 1982, and soon became a fan favorite—often cited as the best *Star Trek* film ever made. It demonstrated that sometimes less is more. Meyer believes that the significantly smaller budget may have worked to his advantage. He quoted legendary American musical theater composer and lyricist Steven Sondheim saying, "Content dictates form. Less is more. God is in the details." Meyer expanded on that thought, stating, "Art thrives on restrictions.... The employment of imagination, sometimes in place of money, can be very rewarding."[46] He was correct in this case. *The Wrath of Khan* brought in $80 million in box office receipts.[47]

Two years after the shocking death of Spock, the next installment in the franchise, *Star Trek: The Search for Spock*, was released on June 1, 1984. Meyer refused to direct this edition after they had changed the ending of *The Wrath of Khan*. According to Meyer, however, "I still felt passionately that Spock ought not to be brought back to life and in any case, bringing dead people back to life was something I didn't know how to do, because, I suppose, I have trouble believing such a thing is possible."[48] As a result, Leonard Nimoy, who was now apparently happy to have his character resurrected, directed the film.

Nimoy had originally intended to hire his friend, composer Leonard Rosenman, to score *The Search for Spock*, but the studio insisted on bringing back James Horner "given the success of the prior film, and the continuity of storyline, and the continuity of Horner's soundscape would strengthen the narrative."[49]

As the third *Trek* installment began where *The Wrath of Khan* left off, it should come as no surprise that Horner's *The Search for Spock* music was quite reminiscent of his earlier score. This similarity begins with the opening theme music, in which he musically flips his previous theme. He uses *Wrath of Khan*'s B-theme, the friendship theme, as the primary (A) theme in the new film. This is logical since the film focuses on Kirk's grieving process and then the prospect that he might be reunited with Spock.

The Search for Spock served as a transition film. It was not one of the better *Star Trek* films, but it was essential to set the stage for future films, most notably by resurrecting Spock. Other key plot elements that were established in the third *Star Trek* installment were the death of Kirk's son (stoking his hatred of the Klingons) and the destruction of the *Enterprise.* As a result, the now-renegade crew takes command of a Klingon Bird of Prey.

The Voyage Home

Star Trek: The Voyage Home begins not long after *Search for Spock* left off. Nimoy also directed this film in which the crew faces the challenge of traveling back in time aboard a Klingon Bird of Prey to twentieth-century Earth. Once there, with the help of marine biologist Gillian Taylor, they transport a pair of humpback whales to the future to help save humanity from destruction caused by powerful whale-speaking aliens. Returning to the *Trek* franchise as a screenwriter, Nicholas Meyer developed a plot with many comedic moments.

However, based on his growing reputation in the film industry, James Horner was now an "in-demand" composer whose fee was beyond what the new *Trek* film could afford. As a result, Leonard Nimoy was finally able to recruit his friend Leonard Rosenman, who had scored numerous television shows and well as such films as *Fantastic Voyage, Beneath the Planet of the Apes* and *The Jazz Singer.*

Rosenman joined the production before the script was completed. Making good use of this time, he and Nimoy brainstormed the role that music should play in this film. They agreed that a more selective approach would be adopted to determine which scenes were given musical cues. According to Rosenman, there is "less music in this film than in any other science fiction film. Most science fiction films are wall-to-wall music." There is only 31 minutes of music in *Star Trek: The Voyage Home.*[50]

As Jeff Bond wrote, "The final result was one of the most unusual *Star Trek* movie themes, a heroic six-note theme and variations played against a rapid-fire four-note brass figure."[51] Inspired by the unusual plot location, twentieth-century San Francisco, and the unlikely premise, Rosenman composed more styles of music than could be found in any other *Star Trek* film at that time. His efforts were supported by the 98-piece piece L.A. Philharmonic Orchestra.[52]

A new theme was Rosenman's first priority. His first attempt was a variation on the original Alexander Courage theme, but Nimoy was not enthused about it. According to Rosenman, "Leonard said, you know, it's not fun, it's not cheerful."[53] Undeterred, Rosenman went back to the musical drawing board to come up with something more fun and cheerful. The result was an uplifting, brassy piece that would fit right in at a holiday pops orchestra concert. According to James Southall, it was a "delightfully upbeat main theme, which has the requisite amount of heroism but also a delightfully deft, light feel to it, reflecting the nature of what is to come."[54]

While previous *Star Trek* productions would have comedic moments, *The Voyage Home* was the first true comedy of the original motion pictures. To support the plot's comedic element, specifically in two scenes with Pavel Chekov, Rosenman composed a couple of zany pieces. The first is heard when Chekov attempts to escape from a U.S. aircraft carrier as we hear an energetic Russian-inspired scherzo, loosely based on Tchaikovsky's "Manfred" No. 5. Chekov's escape does not go as planned and he is sent to a hospital after nearly falling from the deck of the aircraft carrier. Kirk, McCoy and Gillian attempt to rescue him with a gurney, beginning another comedic chase. For the madcap race through the hospital halls that ensues, Rosenman wrote oompah-like music that he compared to circus music or a Charlie Chaplin–like chase.[55]

The Voyage Home also featured jazz for the first time in a *Star Trek* film. At first Nimoy suggested that Rosenman write music that was reminiscent of Gershwin, but Rosenman replied, "No, no, no, no; let's do something entirely different than any other *Star Trek*, and it's set in San Francisco, so let's use jazz. I mean, that was really alien!"[56] They decided to also hire a jazz-fusion band, the Yellowjackets, to create two pieces that would help create the proper musical ambiance for a time-traveling, late-twentieth-century whale rescue tale.

Star Trek: The Voyage Home was a tremendous commercial success and Rosenman's score was nominated for an Academy Award—the first *Star Trek* score to be nominated since Jerry Goldsmith's nomination for *Star Trek: The Motion Picture.*

Star Trek: The Final Frontier

Goldsmith was brought back for the next *Star Trek* film, 1989's *Star Trek: The Final Frontier*. For this fifth *Trek*, William Shatner took the helm as director, his first directorial experience for a major motion picture. (His only previous directorial experience was several episodes of his TV series *T.J. Hooker.*) In this edition, the *Enterprise* crew follows a Jesus-like rogue Vulcan named Sybok (Spock's half-brother) in search of "the garden of Eden" (or Sha Ka Ree) on a planet at the center of the galaxy where a god-like entity allegedly resides.

To musically elevate this spacefaring saga, Goldsmith began with the opening notes of Alexander Courage's original TV theme. He then recycled his brassy *Motion Picture* fanfare; this created controversy among some *Trek* fans who had not seen the original motion picture. Unaware that Goldsmith had written the fanfare for the original film, *Star Trek: The Next Generation* fans accused the composer of stealing the *TNG* theme.[57]

Goldsmith also brought back his original Klingon theme. This time the Klingons, who only appear briefly in the original motion picture, play a much more substantial role. As noted by Mauricio Dupuis, Goldsmith is able to provide more depth, "applying a more incisive use of brass, additional percussion, pizzicato strings, and a ram's horn."[58]

Some of the film's most interesting music cues are Goldsmith's new compositions. For example, as the *Enterprise*, with Sybok on board, enters a vortex that will lead them to Sha Ka Ree, their Garden of Eden–like destination, Goldsmith taps his knowledge of heavenly, ethereal music, introducing "a quasi-religious theme, powerfully performed by brass, while strings convey a sense of wonder as the doubters start to believe that perhaps this is the Final Frontier" (according to a review on JerryGoldsmith. com). "The ideas are further developed for a shuttle trip to the planet surface as rhythm adds pace and anticipation to the 'God' theme."[59]

While Goldsmith was able to write some compelling music to support *The Final Frontier*, it was not enough. The film received poor reviews and is often ranked as one of the weakest *Trek* films—if not *the* weakest).

The Undiscovered Country

With the hopes of repeating the success that he had enjoyed with *Wrath of Khan*, Nicholas Meyer returned to direct *Star Trek: The Undiscovered Country* (1991). The first step in achieving this goal was selecting a title. *The Undiscovered Country* was based on a line from Shakespeare's *Hamlet*. Meyer had originally intended to use this title for his first *Star Trek* film, *The Wrath of Khan*. But the title was far more suitable for this later film.

More than any preceding film edition of *Star Trek, The Undiscovered Country* reflected world affairs at the time. The film was in production as the Cold War between the Soviet Union and United States was ending and shortly after a State Department official, Francis Fukuyama, wrote his controversial paper "The End of History?" and declared that the "triumph of the west, of the Western *idea*, is evident first of all in the total exhaustion of viable systematic alternatives to Western liberalism."[60] Nevertheless, there were hardliners on both sides who were skeptical or even fearful of the "new world order."

The Undiscovered Country mirrors these events, as the Klingon Empire is facing collapse and reaches out to the Federation to negotiate a long-term peace. Hardliners on both sides, resistant to change, try to scuttle the peace process.

Meyer had originally hoped to again recruit James Horner to score the film, but the composer was no longer an affordable option. Meyer considered using excerpts from Gustav Holst's "The Planets," but copyright issues for that composition (and all other Holst compositions) were complicated.[61] Thus, he began the search for a new composer.

Both Meyer and film editor Ronald Roose reviewed (separately) demo tapes for prospective composers. They both became enamored with composer Cliff Eidelman. According to Eidelman, "Nick told me that they both came together with my tape in their hands."[62] Meyer hired Eidelman and told the 26-year-old composer, "This is a movie about the Klingons—a brooding, war-like people. Listen to the opening of Stravinsky's *Firebird*. That's the sort of thing I'm after."[63] Eidelman was inspired by this meeting (not having seen the script yet) and came back to Meyer within 24 hours and said, "I think I have the main title."[64] Meyer agreed.

Meyer and Eidelman found themselves well aligned regarding the musical philosophy of the film. This may in part have been based on Meyer's considerable knowledge of film scores and classical music. "We were able to relate on another level," recalled Eidelman. "He could talk about music in a musical language way."[65]

As Meyer had suggested, the opening theme had overtones of Stravinsky's *Firebird*, but was also influenced by Holst's "The Planets" and at times had the feel of Bernard Herrmann. The piece alternated between brooding, foreboding music, countered by Holst-like rhythmic brass and strings. This foreboding musical feel was woven throughout the film, depicting the progressing conspiracy and deceit being perpetrated within the storyline.

This is countered by Eidelman's *Enterprise* theme, which Craig Lysy describes as "a bright and noble major modal statement carried by horns eroica. The theme is emblematic of both Captain Kirk and the *Enterprise*."[66]

Eidelman was given an orchestra of 90-plus players to record the score (according to MovieMusicUk.com, the orchestra had 86 players), including an unusually large percussion section. To bolster the large percussion section, Eidelman visited a warehouse that was filled with percussion instruments from around the world, owned by famed percussionist Emil Richards.[67] Richards also played as a percussionist on the recording.

Eidelman was also the first *Trek* film composer to use a chorus in a score: "Halfway through writing the score, I decided that it was a good idea to punctuate the Klingon ice planet with an aggressive percussive choral sound." He originally was not sure what words should be sung during this choral piece, but came up with a perfect solution. "As Kirk and Bones are heading down into the prisons of the ice planet, I have the choir sing 'To be or not to be' in Klingon."[68] References to *Hamlet* were an ongoing theme in the film. During an earlier scene, the *Enterprise* command crew have dinner with Klingon Chancellor Gorkon and General Chang (played by Christopher Plummer) and discuss the "original" Klingon text of *Hamlet*. General Chang then says, "taH pagh taHbe"—"To be or not to be" in Klingon, adding, "You have never heard Shakespeare until you've heard it in the original Klingon."

There had been some skepticism about hiring such a young composer, but according to Nicholas Meyer, when they began recording on the 20th Century–Fox scoring stage, "it quickly became apparent that something remarkable was taking place. Visitors to the session as well as those connected to the film came into the booth and listened with mounting excitement to what everyone recognized as a great score and one that would define and elevate the film."[69] Eidelman recalled, "The room was on fire."[70] According to *Music of* Star Trek author Jeff Bond, the *Undiscovered Country* score "was a departure from earlier *Star Trek* movie scores in almost every respect."[71]

Star Trek: The Undiscovered Country received positive reviews and brought in over $96 million, more than three times the production budget. By the time that this sixth *Star Trek* film arrived, the franchise had begun to move in a new direction with the successful TV series *Star Trek: The Next Generation*.

7

The 1980s

As a new decade began, the shadow of *Star Wars* still prevailed. In fact, in 1980 its long-awaited sequel *The Empire Strikes Back* was released—a film that arguably surpassed the quality, story and music of *A New Hope*. In this period, several space-related films of varying quality appeared. One of the first entries of the 1980s was based on a 1930s comic strip.

Flash Gordon

Perhaps the most unusual of the space films of the early '80s was *Flash Gordon*, released in the U.S. on December 5, 1980. Produced by Dino De Laurentiis and directed by Mike Hodges, this campy production was a live-action adaptation of the King Features comic book of the same name. De Laurentiis had been interested in adapting *Flash Gordon* into a major motion picture as far back as the 1960s. To assure that he maintained control of the story, he even turned down an offer in the 1970s from up-and-coming film director George Lucas to purchase the *Flash Gordon* rights. His rejection of Lucas' offer would eventually lead to De Laurentiis' opportunity to finally develop his film.

After being turned down by De Laurentiis, Lucas developed an original science fiction concept, *Star Wars*. *Star Wars*' extraordinary success provided De Laurentiis the catalyst that he needed to produce a major motion picture adaptation of *Flash Gordon*, one that he hoped would match the success of Lucas' film.

De Laurentiis was not looking to clone *Star Wars*. His film would pursue a substantially different style of filmmaking. Rather than striving to produce designs and effects as realistic as possible, *Flash Gordon* would be filmed with a retro–comic book look and feel, and with a tongue-in-cheek storyline (although there are varying opinions on whether De Laurentiis intended the film to be tongue-in-cheek).

This retro approach did not diminish the role of the musical score. While stylistically different than the other big space films of the time, *Flash Gordon*'s full orchestral score was consistent with the original serial productions of the 1930s. The serials used orchestral library music, largely written by Franz Waxman from his *Bride of Frankenstein* score.

However, an alternate approach was also used to provide the musical backdrop of the film. It had been their intent to employ a traditional orchestral score, but director Hodges suggested the addition of original songs from the British rock band Queen. This suggestion was not instantly embraced by all involved. According to Queen guitarist Brian May, "The biggest challenge was getting Dino De Laurentiis on board, because he was the man in charge—the creator of the whole thing." In fact, De Laurentiis may have been oblivious to who Queen was, having reportedly asked, "But who are the queens?"[1]

Despite Dino's initial hesitation, Queen was hired to contribute songs to *Flash Gordon*, even though they were already extremely busy with other projects. At the time, they had just finished their album "The Game" and were gearing up for a major concert tour. Adding a major motion picture—which they had never done before—added to an already packed schedule.

At this point, De Laurentiis and Hodges still intended to commission an original orchestral score, but with Queen songs strategically placed throughout the movie. Brian May had a different idea. He was of the belief that Queen was capable of scoring the entire film. When asked years later whether science fiction films need orchestral scores, he replied,

No, perhaps they don't. You know, if we could actually do this in a kind of rock style, it could really break some barriers.... And I was determined that not only would we do kind of highlights, but we would do atmosphere and we would be an organic part of the film, and I think it's the first time it was ever done, and I'm immensely happy that it's become sort of part of folklore.[2]

May did not get his wish to produce the entire score, but Queen did produce energetic music that was placed throughout the film—and became the most memorable musical elements of the movie. As Queen began the process, the band members wrote some songs based on early rushes of the film. According to May, when it was presented to Hodges and De Laurentiis, "There was a horrible moment when Mike jumped up and down saying, 'It's brilliant, it's brilliant,' and Dino sat there with a face ashen and white as a sheet and obviously didn't enjoy it, and when it came to the theme I had written—you know, 'Flash'—well, Dino said, 'It's very good, but it is not for my movie.'"[3] De Laurentiis did not prevail with this contrary perspective, allowing Queen to write an assortment of songs that

Max Bell of udiscovermusic.com describes as, "the fusion of trademark Queen rock guitars and lavish synth accompaniment."[4]

Queen's best-known contribution to *Flash Gordon* was unquestionably the main theme, "Flash," which starts off with pulsating bass (with piano and drum) and the famous "Flash, Ahh!" lyrics, followed by a more melodic B section. The song is a duet between Freddie Mercury and May, with Roger Taylor providing additional vocals and harmony. May plays almost all the instruments on the recording. In addition to his distinctive guitar playing, he also played a Bösendorfer Model 290 Imperial grand piano—a piano with 97 keys, rather than the standard 88 keys, and an Oberheim OBX synthesizer.[5]

"Flash" was one of two Queen songs in the film that featured lyrics. The other was the high-octane final song "Hero," with classic Brian May guitar riffs. The remaining Queen songs were instrumentals, with heavy use of guitar and synthesizer. This includes "Battle Theme," which uses the same basic guitar riffs as would be used in "Hero," as Flash and the Hawkmen attack Mingo City to save Dale Arden from her forced marriage to Ming. "It is the film and the soundtrack's most triumphant moment," opined Daniel Ross of *The Quientus*, receiving this accolade "both compositionally and for the way it evokes the recklessness of a load of semi-clad flying beardies attacking a spaceship."[6]

"The Attack" then shifts to May's guitar rendition of Richard Wagner's "Wedding March" (or "Bridal Chorus") for Ming's over-the-top wedding to Dale. The rendition is reminiscent of his guitar performance of "God Save the Queen" on the 1975 Queen album *A Night at the Opera*. As Daniel Ross wrote,

> Brian May's performance of "The Wedding Theme" as a multi-voiced guitar solo must be the high watermark. Tasteless and shamelessly decadent, it captures the brazenness of Flash as a whole, but works along the same lines of May's performance of the National Anthem on the roof of Buckingham Palace in 2002. It was utterly ridiculous, but enough people found it cool to make it an iconic moment.[7]

As noted earlier, May did not get his wish to score the entire film. A hybrid approach was eventually used, with an orchestral score and Queen songs inserted in appropriate scenes. To compose the orchestral portion of the music, veteran composer Howard Blake was brought on board. Blake had written the score for Ridley Scott's 1977 film *The Duellists* and composed music for several TV series.

Blake entered during a stressful period in the production. Queen had recruited cellist and composer Paul Buckmaster to write the orchestral scores, but according to Blake, "'I was brought in [during] a crisis situation when it was found that the composer nominated by *Queen* had for some reason been unable to complete 'more than one minute' of a score for the film."[8] This was a major problem since they were swiftly approaching their release date. They were so anxious to have a score produced that Blake recalled arriving on a Thursday and being asked, "Do you think you could write a new score by Monday?" They also told him that they wanted most of the two-hour film to be scored. Completely flabbergasted, Howard answered with complete candor: "Nobody on Earth could write it by Monday," and emphasized that it would probably take until Monday to complete the contractual paperwork.[9]

Blake did work at an accelerated pace: In ten days, he wrote an orchestral score that would utilize an 80-piece orchestra. As he recalled, "I nearly killed myself from extreme exhaustion.... And I wouldn't like to do it again,"[10]

Blake maintained a cordial relationship with the Queen band members, brainstorming and collaborating with them. "I remember Freddie Mercury singing the idea of 'Ride to Arboria' in his high falsetto and I showed him how I could expand it into the orchestral section now on the film, with which he seemed very pleased."[11]

After a grueling schedule to complete the music on time, Blake later learned that large portions of his score were replaced with synthesized music, including at the climax of the film. "I wrote an absolute stunning piece of music, and they took it out of the film."[12]

The final product was indeed a hybrid of both approaches, featuring Queen songs as well as Blake's orchestral scoring and the synthesized music. The opening credits list both Queen and Blake, first displaying "Music Composed, Performed and Produced by Queen" followed by "Orchestral Score Composed and Arranged by Howard Blake." Despite tension and hard feelings, the collaboration between Queen and Howard Blake did seem to work musically. Max Bell notes some specific examples of this. "The fusion of a lovely Mercury melody and Howard Blake's score on 'Kiss (Aura Resurrects Flash)' ... is the logical closer on side one just as the May and Blake collaboration on 'The Hero' is the ideal coda."[13]

Nevertheless, Blake's contributions have been largely forgotten. The members of Queen are generally considered the musical artists of record on the film. This perception was bolstered by the fact that the *Flash Gordon* original soundtrack album was composed entirely of Queen music. The soundtrack made the charts, including a Gold Record in Britain. It reached number 23 on the American charts.

***

E.T. the Extra-Terrestrial

Arguably the most successful space film in the early 1980s (with the exception of the *Star Wars* sequels) was Steven Spielberg's *E.T. the Extra-Terrestrial*, released on June 11, 1982. It was Spielberg's follow-up to *Close Encounters*, but audiences now had the expectation that the director's alien visitors were friendly based on *Close Encounters'* final scenes.

E.T. tells the story of an alien stranded on Earth and the young boy who helps him get home. In contrast to *Close Encounters*, which was focused on a global scale, *E.T.* was an intimate tale. As film music expert Emilio Audissino explained, "*E.T.* is a story about a very private moment—a very private encounter between an Earthling boy and the extra-terrestrial. It is a continuation because at that point we know that for Spielberg extra-terrestrials are not frightening."[14] This would have a significant impact on the styles of music used to set the emotional tone of the film.

John Williams was enlisted to score this new alien encounter film. "*E.T.* seemed wonderful to me when I saw it," he recalled. "I think Steven was a little worried about it because E.T., he's not really beautiful. He's an odd-looking little creature. I remember Steven saying, 'Do you think the public will embrace this creature?'"[15] Spielberg's worries were partly dispelled when Williams first played his score for the director on the piano. Spielberg exclaimed, "I loved it. It was great. And I could not wait for the scoring session."[16] Williams recorded the score with an 80-piece orchestra on the old MGM scoring stage.

As he had for *Star Wars*, Williams defined the characters through themes or leitmotifs for the aliens, E.T., the mysterious government official and the friendship between E.T. and Elliott, as well as the bicycle flight scenes. Unlike what he had composed for *Star Wars*, he did not write a grand opening fanfare, but a far more subtle musical beginning. As the opening credits appear on a black background, dark and almost sinister music is heard, not dissimilar to Goldsmith's opening of *Alien*, Williams' opening music for *Jurassic Park*—or even *Close Encounters* itself. However, this initial threatening music is merely a misdirect. The initial atonal, threatening music, as Audissino observed,

> soon moves to the presentation of the *E.T.* theme, played by the piccolo flute over images of a bright starry night—and it's a very sweet theme. Williams states musically, this time from the beginning, that this extra-terrestrial is not a threat at all. And indeed, atonal music is used in the film to depict the adult humans: *they* are the menace now.[17]

Only hints of the full main theme are heard in these opening moments. The theme will be slowly revealed as the story develops. "We may have had the first few notes of this emotional theme suggested early on," said Williams. "Then three or four more notes, then finally the whole theme. So finally, when you hear it all, there's something vaguely familiar about it. You've been prepared for four reels to actually hear this melody."[18]

These early musical moments are essential and firmly establish the critical role of the music in this film. No dialogue is spoken in the opening moments. The narrative is driven entirely by the action on screen and by the music providing the emotional and intellectual context. At this stage of the film, Williams' music is equal to, and sometimes more important than, the characters on screen or the cinematography.

Williams noted that he teased the audience with hints of this music as the story develops, but only presents the full treatment of the theme when Elliott and E.T. ride through the woods on Elliott's bicycle and take flight as they go over a cliff. According to music theorist Frank Lehman,

> As E.T. and Elliott approach the inevitable flying bicycle scene, the music grows and grows, increasing in anticipation and tension until the turning point when the bike lifts up and takes flight. The wondrous and famous Flying Theme majestically sweeps through the orchestra, climbing over the moon and landing safely.[19]

Williams: "I remember working very hard on that flying theme. I was concerned about getting just the right, soaring melody, which for me as a musician was a serious challenge.... What would the orchestra say? What would the leaps of melody be? What could possibly be good enough to accompany a film like this?"[20]

This would become the film's most iconic scene. And while it is visually memorable (the bicycle in front of the Moon becomes the Amblin logo), the fully revealed "Flight" theme is unquestionably the crucial ingredient that makes the entire segment work.

As with many of Williams' most recognizable theme compositions (*Raiders of the Lost Ark, Star Wars*, etc.), there is a musical "B section." Composer Hans Zimmer noted (referencing the *Raiders* theme, but speaking of Williams' broader body of work), "There's always the bravura part of the John Williams composition ... and then comes the B part. It's less well known, but it's so beautifully crafted. I always think that's the part he writes for himself."[21] In the case of *E.T.*, the sweeping "A section" gives way and a "B section" is introduced that feels both musically giddy, but also seems to build energy, almost like an airplane accelerating down a runway until it reaches a climax and returns to the A theme. Craig Lysy described this second theme as being more "fluid and lyrical," but it is "where the theme soars and evokes a sense of wonderment, propelled by sumptuous strings and horn declarations."[22]

The full score has a substantial musical range. As exhibited in the earlier wistful renditions of the *E.T.* theme on piccolo, Williams creates other, more intimate themes. When Elliott and E.T. are in the bedroom for the first time, their friendship develops with another quiet and tender theme played at first by a single harp. This music is built from the same DNA as the E.T. theme, using many of the same notes, but rearranged like a musical anagram, once again creating a sense of familiarity.

Williams also employs more sinister-sounding music. The mysterious government officials, led by a man with keys dangling from his belt, is musically foreboding, played with bassoons and bass clarinets. The piece is quite reminiscent of *Star Wars'* "Imperial March." It does not convey the same sense of doom that the "Imperial March" projects, and is far more subtle, but it nonetheless leaves the audience wary regarding the intent of the officials. Even this material is revealed to be a musical misdirect. At first "Keys" and his government minions are shown as just silhouettes, then just their legs and torsos are shown, and then finally we see the true face of "Keys" and it is not evil. In fact, he could almost be interpreted as an adult version of Elliott.

Perhaps the most impressive and complex segment of Williams' score begins after E.T. returns to life. Helped by his bicycle-riding friends, Elliott escapes with E.T. to attempt to reunite the alien being with his people. A chase ensues, accompanied by almost 15 minutes of uninterrupted orchestral music. During this extended orchestral cue, Williams weaves in many of the primary themes as the chase literally takes twists and turns. Jon Burlingame said, "The composer, of course, rose to the challenge. And what's more, Spielberg went the extra mile to ensure that Williams could make just the right musical statement, especially during the climactic bike chase leading up to the finale and E.T.'s departure."[23]

In this case, the music literally drove the scene. According to Williams, he was having problems keeping the orchestra properly synchronized with the action on screen. Spielberg offered a solution: "I will take the film off the screen so that you can play the music with the orchestra, with its natural phrasing, in the way that it ebbs and flows in its own way. Then I will conform the film to what is the best musical performance."[24] This allowed Williams to perform the piece without having to worry about synchronizing perfectly with the action on screen; Spielberg would match the footage to the music. This was very unusual. Williams said,

> We usually have to slavishly phrase the music to the cuts of the film.... I think part of the reason that the end of the film has such an operatic sense of completion—a real emotional satisfaction as well; as satisfaction from what we see—may be in part a result of this wedding of the musical accents with Steven's film editing.[25]

The result was a rare matching of film and music working as equal partners to advance the plot and stoke emotions. By the time E.T. boards his ship, the main flying theme plays at full volume, then it switches back to the original E.T. theme played with a piccolo as the spacecraft door closes. But it is not a sad moment. "We could look at what is happening in the story as being very sad," said psychologist Dr. Siu-Lan Tan. "These are farewells. And at the very end, we hear this coda. This fanfare that's very triumphant. That is saying that we're looking at this from Elliott's viewpoint. That it's not a loss, but it's almost like saying 'Mission Accomplished. We got E.T. home.'"[26]

E.T. is less a story of aliens and more a story portraying the wonder of youth and friendship. As such, Williams' score displays Peter Pan–like nostalgia more than composing music that screams "space score."[27] The music helps define and drive the relationship between E.T. and Elliott. "Through their friendship they are both healed and the music needed to speak to this for the film to succeed."[28]

Spielberg's initial worries that audiences would not warm to the strange-looking alien proved to be unfounded. *E.T. the Extra-Terrestrial* became an enormous hit, delivering a significant return on the studio investment. The film cost only $10.5 million and pulled in earnings of $793 million. Williams later observed, "I don't think the expectations would ever compare to what the results were."[29] He added, "Once we saw it with an audience, you could see that this emotional connection was made between the children, E.T., and the audience."[30]

The Right Stuff

Extra-terrestrial life and alien civilizations were not the only subject matter for space films of the early 1980s. Humanity's desire to venture into space was the topic of the 1983 movie *The Right Stuff*, based on the Tom Wolfe book. It told the story of the early days of the American space program, from the breaking of the sound barrier by Chuck Yeager up until the end of NASA's Mercury program. The film was directed by Philip Kaufman, who had directed such films as *Invasion of the Body Snatchers*, *The White Dawn* and *The Wanderers*.

Robert Chartoff and Irwin Winkler, both known for producing Sylvester Stallone's *Rocky* films, produced the American space program drama.

Best known for his work on the James Bond films, John Barry was originally hired to provide the film's musical score. However, Kaufman and Barry had differences of opinion regarding the musical direction of the project. According to Barry, "It was going very well, and then there were certain problems on the movie down the line, and [Kaufman] needed an excuse for delaying the production. The details are a little foggy now, but I've always remembered my association with Kaufman was also one of the most dishonest pieces of behavior I've ever encountered in the movie industry."[31]

With the departure of Barry, Chartoff and Winkler approached Bill Conti, who had worked with the two producers on the *Rocky* films. Conti was asked to mimic as closely as possible the temp track that had been assembled. The temp track was comprised of such pieces as Holst's "The Planets," Tchaikovsky's Violin Concerto in D Major and Henry Mancini's music from Kaufman's *The White Dawn*. All three clearly influenced Conti's final score. It is not unusual for composers to capture the spirit of temp pieces without plagiarizing. However, Conti emulated these compositions so closely at times that he acknowledged the pieces in the end credits of the film.

Tchaikovsky's Violin Concerto in D Major was clearly an influence on the Mach 1 cue and serves as a general triumphant theme. Conti's cue for John Glenn bears a striking resemblance to "Mars" from Holst's "The Planets." Despite these strong similarities, Conti composed an effective score—and won the Academy Award for Best Score in 1984. But *The Right Stuff* was a box-office failure.

Note: John Glenn made a run for president of the United States in 1984, hoping that the film would help propel him to the White House. His presidential campaign did as well as *The Right Stuff* did at the box office.

The Last Starfighter

Arthurian legend and interplanetary space battles unite in the 1984 film *The Last Starfighter*. Written by Jonathan R. Betuel, the movie was a 1980s version of the King Arthur "sword in the stone" story, except in this case, the main character was American teenager Alex Rogan, who lives in a trailer park. Rather than pulling a sword from a stone, Alex gets the high score on a video game named Starfighter, but this was no ordinary video game. Furnished by a "con man"–like alien named Centauri (played by Robert Preston, best known as the titular con man in *The Music Man*), the game serves as an audition to find humans who may have "the right stuff" to become a Starfighter. Centauri transports Alex to the planet Rylan where he trains to become a Starfighter to help defend "the Frontier against Xur and the Ko-Dan Armada." After all the other Starfighters are wiped out by Xur, Alex is left to save the universe as the last Starfighter.

Director Nick Castle had only directed one previous full-length film, 1982's *Tag: The Assassination Game,* but he already had an impressive and eclectic career. Just out of film school he was co-recipient of an Oscar for the 1970 short film *The Resurrection of Bronco Billy.* (After winning that award, Castle joked, "It was all downhill from there."[32]) He wrote several successful screenplays, including *Escape from New York,* and played Michael Myers (aka The Shape) in John Carpenter's *Halloween.*

The Last Starfighter was far more challenging than *Tag: The Assassination Game.* This space adventure relied heavily on a new technology called CGI (Computer-Generated Imagery) to produce most of the space-based visual effects. No other film to date had utilized this technology as extensively as *The Last Starfighter.* With a production budget of only $15 million, the success of the film depended on this new technology.

If matched with the right music, the score could help compensate for potential shortcoming of the visual effects resulting from the new technology. As was the case with many other directors in the post–*Star Wars* era, Castle wanted to commission a big, epic space film score on the level of *Star Wars.* Composer Craig Safan was hired to accomplish this task. Safan had worked on over a dozen films and TV shows over the previous decade, including *Tag: The Assassination Game.*

Safan faced a significant challenge: When he screened the film for the first time, it was almost devoid of special visual effects. Since CGI was a time-consuming process, these effects had not yet been added. There were extensive sections where the screen would go black. According to Safan, "There would just be a little white dot going across a black screen and they'd say something like 'That's the Kodan warrior ship'.... I don't even know if I saw [the CGI ships] until after I scored the picture. I had to imagine it."[33] As a result, a significant portion of the score was written as Castle stood over Safan's shoulder describing what was happening in the film.

Another challenge was that Safan's compositional background was primarily writing electronic scores. He knew well that in the post–*Star Wars* era, that approach would not be viable. "With *Starfighter,* if I try to do this all electronically, I'm going to get fired," recalled Safan. "The studio is definitely thinking *Star Wars,* and they're going to want to hear a big, giant orchestra. They're not going want to hear weird music or electronics, or *Forbidden Planet....* They're going to want to hear big melodies played by brass instruments."[34] Nonetheless, he was still able inject electronic sounds into the score. He stated, "There's quite a bit of electronics mixed in with the orchestra, but it's still basically a big, melodic, romantic score." He also did not want to simply imitate some of the Holst-heavy scores of the previous decade, writing his score with the influence of Jean Sibelius, particularly his style of orchestrating and use of horns.[35]

The recording took place at the MGM recording stage using a 90-piece orchestra. To achieve a big sound, he fortified some of the instrumental sections. "I just used a giant orchestra using 6 horns, 6 trumpets, quadruple woodwinds—and on top of that, a bunch of electronics."[36]

For better or worse, Safan knew that his score would be compared to John Williams' music for the *Star Wars* original trilogy, but he did not want to mimic Williams. He recalled,

> Rather than having so many little leitmotifs like John Williams uses in *Star Wars*—even though I do have a few different leitmotifs—most of it is done with one melody. That melody is played slow, it's played fast, it's played in 3/4, it's played in 4/4; I thought of it as the heart theme, because what I thought this film has going for it is that it has a lot of heart and a lot of emotion. That's what this melody can be used as…. It's pretty much a one-theme movie.[37]

Rather than developing a theme for every character and situation, Safan was able to use variations of the same basic theme to advance the story.

The Last Starfighter never approached the heights that *Star Wars* had achieved. The film cost approximately $15 million and pulled in roughly $29 million, receiving mixed reviews. However, Safan's energetic score was generally well regarded at the time, with the *New York Times* calling it Safan's "adrenal music."[38]

Composer Craig Safan conducts his score of *The Last Starfighter* (courtesy of Craig Safan).

Despite a disappointing initial reception, the film grew in popularity over time, generating discussions of the prospect of potential remakes and sequels. Safan is not at all surprised that the film has remained popular. "[Nick Castle] was very meticulous with the script.... Nick is very story-oriented. I think that's one of the reasons that this film has lasted as long as it has. It has a really good story. It's not just about going out in space and fighting aliens."[39]

Castle's script was not the only major factor in *Last Starfighter*'s long-term popularity. Safan's score played a substantial role in this success. The score has lived on as a popular concert piece. According to Safan, "*Starfighter* is thrown into lots and lots of those film music programs. After all, how much John Williams music can you play?"[40] If conductors want to diversify the content of these concerts, concerts that are heavy on Williams and Goldsmith, "they throw in *Starfighter* because it's not as well known—and sounds fresh...." This popularity began soon after the film was released. "I got a call from Erich Kunzel from the Cincinnati Pops," recalls Safan. "He was doing a space program and he asked if I could do something—and I said 'What?'" It had never crossed his mind that the score would become popular concert music. The performance by the Cincinnati Pops was recorded and according to Safan, "That was the beginning. He [the conductor] was doing *Star Wars*, he was doing some Jerry Goldsmith stuff, a Broughton piece—so I was in good company.... When I wrote it, nobody was performing film music."[41]

The Last Starfighter also has rare distinction of being adapted into an off off–Broadway musical in 2004, one of the few science fiction films to be musically staged in the theater.

Star Trek Returns to Television

Arguably the most significant milestone in space-based television of the 1980s, as well as the *Star Trek* franchise as a whole, was the arrival of *Star Trek: The Next Generation* (*TNG*). The show premiered on September 28, 1987, with the two-part pilot "Encounter at Farpoint." While the series received mixed reviews, it ran for seven seasons, eventually becoming the highest-rated syndicated television show of the time, and it spawned four motion pictures and three additional TV series. It also expanded how music could be utilized to elevate a science fiction TV series.

The concept of a new *Star Trek* series had been proposed on many occasions since the end of the original series. It was not until the mid–1980s, with the success of the *Star Trek* feature films, that the idea of a new series achieved a critical mass of support, prompting Paramount to ask

Gene Roddenberry to develop one. This was a long time coming for Roddenberry, who had attempted to create a live-action TV series back in the 1970s once *Star Trek* reruns had become increasingly popular. According to Robert Justman, a producer of both the original *Star Trek* series as well as the first season of *Next Generation*,

> In the mid–1980s, Paramount realized that they were making zillions of dollars on this old television show and if they had a new one, they could milk the cow again. Gene had a peculiar way of getting people onto whatever show he was doing. I knew enough to know that when he called me to go to lunch and screen some films to look at the special effects, a new show was in the offing.[42]

Expectations and pressure were extremely high for the *Star Trek* reboot. The new show would feature an entirely new cast aboard the USS *Enterprise* 1701-D, and the action would take place approximately 100 years after the events of the original show. The new cast would be led by British Shakespearean actor Patrick Stewart, but Roddenberry was initially skeptical whether Stewart was a suitable choice to take the helm of the *Enterprise*. His style and look were nothing like that of William Shatner's Captain Kirk. Roddenberry's hesitation was quite apparent to Stewart. "It was very odd with Gene because I was dragged into an audition for him in his living room the morning after I'd been seen doing something at UCLA. My meeting lasted about six minutes, and then it was perfectly clear I was not wanted in that room any time longer. It was Gene who said, 'What the hell? I don't want a bald, middle-aged Englishman.'"[43] As fate would have it, that bald, middle-aged Englishman's Captain Jean-Luc Picard would become one of the most popular characters in the franchise, arguably more popular than Captain Kirk.

With the overall series premise established, Roddenberry and Justman were adamant about using large orchestral scores to help define the new series. At that time, according to executive producer Rick Berman, "A lot of people were using synthesizers and very simple music. We did a more expensive and more complex process because Gene wanted a rich, full orchestra that we would record in the big studio at Paramount for each episode." However, Berman also did not want the scores to sound "science fiction-y," as though they were written in the 1950s-1960s.[44]

Justman supervised the scoring of *The Next Generation* during the first season. As notes by Jeff Bond in *The Music of* Star Trek,

> Justman had overseen the scoring on the original series and favored the kind of up-front dramatic music that had been a hallmark of the show.... The evolution of *Star Trek: The Next Generation* scoring style derived from the different philosophies of co-producers Robert Justman, veteran of the original show,

and Rick Berman, the man who was to eventually take over full production of the show after Justman's departure at the end of the first season.[45]

Justman's authority was not absolute. According to Bond, composer Ron Jones was Justman's first choice to compose the music for the new *Star Trek* series, but Paramount preferred another composer. Veteran TV composer Dennis McCarthy was hired to compose music for the two-part pilot episode. Not only had McCarthy scored such science fiction shows as *V* and the new *Twilight Zone* in the 1980s, he had also worked on numerous popular TV shows such as *MacGyver* and *Dynasty*. McCarthy had also spent nine years on the road with country music star Glen Campbell in the late 1960s and 1970s, playing and arranging songs. His time on the road helped him to develop other skills that proved invaluable for his new *Star Trek* gig. He was quite skilled at quick and often significant changes to musical arrangements, and was accustomed to tailoring his music to the tastes and strengths of his employers. These skills were essential in scoring the new *Trek* series.

Writing the music for the pilot was not an easy assignment. McCarthy and the producers knew that they needed to win over the original fans to ensure the show's success. The opening theme song would play a crucial role in achieving this goal. Berman and Justman wanted this theme to emotionally connect the audience with the earlier *Star Trek* productions. They asked McCarthy to "meld" the Alexander Courage piece with the Jerry Goldsmith march from the original *Star Trek* movie.

The two pieces fit together quite well. As the opening sequence begins, McCarthy repeats the opening notes of the Courage fanfare several times and then dramatically transitions into the Goldsmith theme, fusing the two pieces and linking the new series with the earlier show. The finished product quickly became the "quintessential *Star Trek*" theme to many fans and arguably popularized the Goldsmith music more effectively than the original film had. As expressed by Jonathan Frakes, who played Commander Riker on the show, "Like John Williams and *Star Wars*, Goldsmith's themes for *Star Trek* reminds everyone viscerally, emotionally, and subconsciously of *Star Trek*. The feeling that the show creates is mysteriously created by a composer of that level—and he imbues us with that. Even if you just hear the first few notes of the theme...."[46]

Based on his successful hybrid arrangement of the opening theme music, McCarthy was asked to score "Encounter at Farpoint," setting the initial musical tone for the series. McCarthy soon realized that the producers had contrasting scoring philosophies. Berman came from the school of "don't let the music get in the way" while Justman preferred bigger, "in your face" music. This would remain an area of mild tension during the first *TNG* season, and Berman's influence was already impacting the music. McCarthy recalled that during the second episode he scored, "Haven," he mistakenly assumed he would still have a free hand shaping the sound of the show. He wrote a whimsical Irish-like violin piece; after dubbing the cue, he asked the producers how they liked it. He was told in no uncertain terms *not* to do that again, because it was whimsical and melodic.

When Justman left the show after the first season, Berman rose to the position of executive producer. He had worked on television and film production for years, previously serving as Director of Drama Development at Warner Brothers. At Paramount, he oversaw such shows as *Cheers, Family Ties* and *MacGyver*. During his period as Paramount's Vice-President for Television Movies and Miniseries, the decision was made to create the new *Trek* series. Berman was selected to work directly with Gene Roddenberry. Berman recalled, "The general opinion was that Roddenberry was a cranky old bastard and nobody wanted to have anything to do with him, but since I was the lowest ranking vice-president, it was like 'Let *him* do it.'"[47]

Berman had well-defined opinions regarding the role of music in the series. In addition to his requirement that the music not be too "science fiction-y," he believed that the music should play a more subtle role in the storytelling than had been the case in *Star Wars*. Berman said, "One of the things that meant a lot to me was that the music should not be overbearing—and that it should not call a lot of attention to itself. It has always been a problem to me when the music is too big."[48] He did not like films where the audience could easily surmise that a character was evil because of a musical cue. This style of thematic music, or leitmotif, was heavily used by John Williams in the *Star Wars* franchise. Composer Jay Chattaway, who joined the composition team in later seasons, explained,

> The real philosophy was—*Star Trek* vs. *Star Wars* musically. The *Star Trek* producers seemed to want to believe that the *Star Trek* audience was much more intelligent—and could make up their own minds whether a character or species was really good or evil. That's the big difference in the psychology between *Star Trek* and *Star Wars*. *Star Trek* wants the listener-viewer to make up their mind as to the purpose of the people.[49]

Berman had set the musical parameters for the show, but producer Peter Lauritson oversaw the day-to-day musical life in post-production. In contrast to Berman, who claims never to have watched *Star Trek* prior to his work on *Next Generation*, Lauritson had been attentively following the efforts to launch a new *Trek* series. "I had been a big fan of the films and the original series," he recalled. "As things progressed, I felt more and more like I was the right person to jump in and help this thing get off the ground."[50]

The role of music was significant in Lauritson's vision of a new *Star Trek*, and he saw this as an opportunity to take a productive role in the scoring process. "I've been a major music person all my life. I was interested in learning more and being more involved in orchestral stuff. I was impressed by how much it could add to a film or television program." He also understood how impactful a musical score was to a space-related series:

Space is vast, and it has that epic quality—when you think of the ocean or the west—it has that same type of vastness to it. It is adventure. It's life and death. The stakes are high in space and so the music has the opportunity to be big and make big statements and bring great import to what's going on. It was just exhilarating the way that music could play in a space film or series.[51]

While this grand musical vision had the potential to be at odds with Berman's directive, Lauritson and Berman found a balance during the hectic production schedule. According to Berman,

When we would do our sound mix every week or ten days, and we had X number of music cues and the big question was, did they work? Were they too loud? Too soft? Should they be moved a little bit? Were they too hokey? Too big? Very often we would drop a cue or move a cue. I never did that without Peter and I think there were numerous occasions where Peter did it without me.[52]

Had they been using a small ensemble, these musical demands might not have been too challenging for the composers. But every *Next Generation* episode required as much as 30 minutes of orchestral music. Fortunately, McCarthy was as adaptable as any television composer of the time. His years on the road with Glen Campbell had honed his skills. Campbell often asked him to make substantial adjustments and quick changes to arrangements. Being given even a week to produce a score was more than sufficient for McCarthy.

As prolific and adaptable as McCarthy was, a single composer could not handle the high volume of music needed on this weekly series. To remedy this problem, they also hired Robert Justman's first choice, Ron Jones, as a full-time *Next Generation* composer.

Jones was working on three TV series and scoring a low-budget movie when he received the call to join the *Star Trek* composing team. He recalled that he was at Glen Glenn Sound when someone asked, "Hey, Ron, did you hear about the new *Star Trek*?" and Jones replied, "Ah, that'll never work." But a couple weeks later, a friend told him that they needed another composer on the series "because if only one person did it, they'd die."[53]

Concealing his skepticism regarding the prospects of the *Star Trek* reboot, Jones arranged for a meeting at Paramount and was offered the job as the second full-time *TNG* composer.

His relationship with the *Trek* producers was not always harmonious. While Berman had complete faith in McCarthy to maintain his musical "prime directive"—dictating that music should not be too "big"—he was a little more hesitant with his praise of Jones. Berman said, "We butted heads a little bit because there were times when I thought his cues were wonderful and there were times when I thought his cues called a little too much attention to themselves."[54] Years later, he recalled reading claims by Jones that he did not think music was essential or it needed to be boring. According to Berman, this was "Nonsense! I just thought that in the case of Ron's music, there were a number of occasions where the music was too big and too flourishy. But Ron was a very talented composer."[55]

Jones did understand the parameters that had been set. As long as the composers adhered to Berman's musical directive, they were given flexibility to decide how to effectively convey the feel, rhythm or emotion for each episode. Jones colorfully explained, "It wasn't like working for dictators. It was actually like working for the mob. They say, 'Go kill Vinny!' They don't tell you how to kill Vinny. They just expect Vinny to be killed."[56]

As the series progressed, various guest composers were featured. One was Jay Chattaway. According to Chattaway, "Ron Jones was not available for one of the shows and the producers wanted to have a different sound for an episode and put out a call." Not long after his demo tape was sent to the *Star Trek* producers, Chattaway's agent called him and said that the *Trek* people wanted to meet with him." Chattaway replied, "I don't want to do television."[57]

Chattaway was initially hesitant about becoming a full-time composer on a weekly series since he had established himself as a motion picture composer. "I was cranking my way through the big movie world. I'd done like 30 motion pictures, like Chuck Norris and Stephen King films."[58] Nonetheless, he met with the *Trek* producers and was surprised that rather than a traditional interview or audition, they had him spot (determine the placement and style of music cues in an episode) the music for an actual show. "We all sat around and watched the show. They gave me their input as to what they thought the music should be and where it should go. The head of music said, 'Don't listen to what other composers have done. Just do what your version of a big space epic should look like and sound like and go for it.'"[59]

Chattaway had done some TV composition, but this experience had primarily been for documentaries, most notably for oceanographer and filmmaker Jacques Cousteau. His work with Cousteau contributed significantly to solidifying his future with the *Trek* franchise. Chattaway's first *Next Generation* episode, "The Tin Man," was about an alien lifeform living in the vacuum of space. The Tin Man character reminded Chattaway of a big whale in space, and since Chattaway had previously recorded the sounds of whales off the coast of California for Cousteau, he incorporated the whale recordings into the score. Chattaway recalled, "I think that's the item that the *Star Trek* producers gravitated toward. 'Hey, this guy's writing music for whales, so he must be the right guy for us.'" Chattaway said that after "The Tin Man," "I didn't hear much for the rest of the season, but then did another episode—then got a call from Peter Lauritson saying that they wanted me to be a regular on the show."[60]

With McCarthy, Jones and Chattaway on the payroll, the *Next Generation* producers had an extraordinary depth of musical talent at their disposal. According to Lauritson, "We worked pretty well with all of them. They all had different things going on. Dennis was strong with the French horn sound. Jay leaned a little heavier on strings. Ron Jones had a little more variety in his scores, but it always was pretty interesting stuff."[61]

The fourth *Next Generation* season ended up being Jones' final period on the show. In his book *The Music of* Star Trek, Jeff Bond noted, "Jones' refusal to live by the stylistic dictates of the series was ultimately his undoing. While Dennis McCarthy strove to meet the challenge of Berman's musical vision, Jones continued to write in a style he felt best suited the episodes...."[62]

The Sound of *Star Trek*

By the third season, *Star Trek: The Next Generation* had developed a distinct musical sound—and even had some recurring themes. According to Ron Jones, this was a natural evolution in the music. When the series began, the producers were concerned about the prospect of alienating the original *Star Trek* audience, "so we sort of scored it as though it was a continuation of the original series and then gradually changed not only the sound but the overall progression of the show." Jones added that it "ceased being the stepchild of the original series."[63]

As the show moved further beyond the shadow of the original show, new sounds were introduced by the composers and sound effects technicians. Jones took this very seriously and tried to account for the physics of music. How would music (sound waves) change in varying atmospheric pressure or gravity levels? He recalled that, here on Earth,

[w]e have 60 miles of atmosphere pressing down on us ... and sound waves operate a certain way here, but if you were on Mars, there's not enough oxygen

so you could play the loudest music possible, and it wouldn't carry. I would take into account those sort of physical demands—and imagine 300 years in the future—by then, Jimi Hendrix is classical music.[64]

Jones was hypothesizing about a topic that was not centuries in the future or the product of alien civilizations. As will be discussed in a later chapter, how these physical factors impact the sound of music are already being observed in space and in other extreme environments. According to astronaut Chris Hadfield, the lack of gravity on the human diaphragm in space has a definite impact on singing in that environment. Lower atmospheric pressures can also impact the sound of some instruments and prevent humans from whistling or using some woodwind instruments.[65]

How can these exotic sounds be recreated on the surface of Earth? At the time *The Next Generation* was being produced, standard sound effects studios typically had a limited array of equipment, often only Fairlight and Synclavier synthesizers. According to Jones, "If you were on a different planet or a Klingon spaceship, you needed a whole new set of environmental sounds." To simulate potential "alien" sounds, the *Next Generation* composers would sample a wide range of exotic instruments, including Japanese Kotos, Arabic whistles and other instruments and sounds. "We had to use everything possible," notes Jones. "Plus electronics and echoes and delays and reverbs. We had six percussions. Most TV shows don't even have six players."[66]

Chattaway also recalled creating new sounds to accommodate the show's wide-ranging demands. This included using an Electronic Wind Instrument that was played by one of their woodwind players. That instrument could utilize sounds that are digitally sampled from unusual sources. "We had a Data episode when we were debating whether or not he could show emotions. We digitally sampled a garden hose and some other electronic sounds," said Chattaway. "The woodwind player could trigger those sounds with his mouth and add emotional control over instruments that were inanimate."[67]

Next Generation even made use of instruments that were carved from gourds that were on display at the Orange County Art Museum in Los Angeles. Jones contacted the artist responsible and asked, "Can I use those on a *Star Trek* episode?" Jones continued:

[The artist] said "Wow! I never thought anyone would ever use these." I said, "We're looking for a weird sound. These are just weird enough that they might work." So he lent us the use of these gourds that were in the museum....[68]

These experimentations helped boost the show's overall quality, not only by expanding their library of exotic sounds, but also enlarging the emotional palette that they could draw from to advance the plot. This was particularly helpful in defining the unrelenting cybernetic villains: the Borg. These half-machine, half-organic bad guys were introduced during the second season in the episode "Q Who." During this episode, the *Enterprise* is visited by the omnipotent, Loki-like nemesis Q. When Q tells Picard, "You're not prepared for what awaits you," Picard confidently replies, "How can we be prepared for that which we do not know? ... But I do know that we are ready to encounter it." To put Picard to the test, Q propels the *Enterprise* 7000 light years from their original location. The *Enterprise* then encounters a Borg spaceship, which Jones described as "a cube of plumbing flying around in space with carbon-based beings."[69] Jones wrote a score that projects a constant state of anxiety as well as defining the Borg in unrelenting and almost industrial musical sounds.

Having successfully created the sound of the Borg, Jones was the obvious choice to score a special two-part Borg cliffhanger straddling Seasons 3 and 4, "The Best of Both Worlds." He produced an unsettling score that perfectly suited the relentless Borg. According to Fandom.com,

> The composer's chilling theme for the Borg, often voiced by eerie synthesized chorus, dominates "The Best of Both Worlds." It forms the basis for some of the score's exciting action-oriented material. In the episode's quieter moments, Jones' scoring is subtle yet melodic, with colors and harmonies chosen to evoke emotion without overpowering the onscreen drama.[70]

✳✳✳

The music aboard the *Enterprise* did not always represent the alien or serve to subtly support the emotions of each scene. Music played a significant role in the fictitious life on the *Enterprise*. The ship boasted quite a musical crew. Commander Data (Brent Spiner) played the violin and sang in multiple episodes and films. There are several scenes during which Commander Will Riker (Jonathan Frakes) plays his trombone. Frakes said,

> I had lunch with Maurice Hurley, an executive producer on the show, in the first season. He picked my brain about my interests. That's where I revealed my interest in jazz and the fact that I played the trombone. Before Season 1 was over, I was in the Holodeck with Minuet (a holographic character) in an episode called "11001001," playing my trombone. I thought it was a really cool thing to embrace. I didn't play well, but I did play loud.[71]

Frakes was pleased to find that these musical scenes created a bond between him and other trombone players throughout the world, thus expanding the reach of *Star Trek*. In fact, this musicianship in space was closer to reality than it was to science fiction. As will be highlighted in an upcoming chapter, music has already played an important role for astronauts in space and has enabled astronaut-musicians to connect with musicians on Earth, not only expanding interest in "real" space, but displaying the value of music in space.

In 1991, Spiner sang lead vocals on an album called *Ol' Yellow Eyes Is Back*, featuring guest instrumental performances by *Star Trek* cast members (including Stewart and Frakes). Dennis McCarthy produced the album.

Perhaps the most memorable example of crew musicianship occurred in the Season 5 episode "The Inner Light" (1992). It was the first of two episodes directed by Peter Lauritson and the teleplay was by Morgan Gendel. In it, the *Enterprise* encounters an alien probe that connects directly with Captain Picard's brain. Picard collapses on the bridge and awakens in the village of Ressik on a planet called Kataan. He goes on to live the life of an iron weaver named Kamin who is married with two children. Kamin teaches himself to play a Ressikan flute, and plays it frequently and passionately for the rest of his life on Kataan. At the end of Kamin's life, Picard awakens on the *Enterprise* deck where only a few minutes have passed, but in his mind, 40 years had elapsed. When the *Enterprise* brings the alien probe into the cargo bay, they find a box containing Picard's flute, which becomes a powerful reminder of the other life that he lived on Kataan.

According to Jay Chattaway, who scored the episode, they did not want to use a traditional flute because it would need to be held sideways, blocking a large portion of Stewart's face. Instead, they selected an instrument similar to a pennywhistle that would be held straight out, allowing an unobstructed camera view of Stewart's face. There was even a very specific reason for the flute being metallic rather than wood. Since metalworking was the main industry on that part of Kataan, it was culturally appropriate to create a flute made of metal.[72]

One of the episode's core emotional elements was a recurring song that Picard played during his alternate life—a theme that became one of the most beloved musical works in the *Trek* franchise. Chattaway recalled,

That tune came to me in about 20 minutes. I had a script and an instruction for a lullaby-type piece. The way *Star Trek* works, you also need to have an alternate piece. It was supposed to sound sort of like Gaelic or something that might sound folksy. I thought, "This is the one. This is perfect," but then I wrote the alternate tune, so I tried really hard to write one that wouldn't be as good. I was thinking, "Boy, I really hope they don't pick that one." Fortunately, they picked the right one and that's the one that we pre-recorded.[73]

The alternate theme was used as the basis for Jeff Russo's theme music for *Picard* 28 years later.

Since Stewart did not play the flute—and since the instrument was not functional anyway—professional flutist Brice Martin was hired. Even though the TV flute did not actually play music, Stewart learned the song on a pennywhistle, enabling him to accurately give the impression that he was playing the song on the Ressikan flute.

Stewart learned the song well enough on the pennywhistle that he played it on stage years later. Chattaway recalled, "We did one concert with [Stewart] at a convention and he actually came out and played with the band, which was fun."[74] Picard's flute song has had a substantial life beyond "The Inner Light." Chattaway composed multiple versions of the Picard's flute song, including a long orchestral version for a world *Star Trek* orchestral tour ("Star Trek: The Ultimate Voyage") that he occasionally conducted, starting in 2016. This concert series visited over 100 cities worldwide. As noted by conductor Justin Freer in a *Los Angeles Times* interview, "I admired so many of these composers and so much of what the producers and directors created over the years. What better way to celebrate it than to marry some of the great music of the franchise to many of its great visuals?"[75]

Orchestral concerts of this kind have grown in popularity, particularly for space-related music. Concert halls that once would have shunned film or TV music now put these scores to good use to attract new audiences. Chattaway said,

> So many symphonies are not able to make their budgets based on playing Beethoven and Brahms in the concert halls. So, they started playing a lot more film scores using the actual symphony orchestras accompanying films. Now more people are coming in to see this event. Young kids are coming in to see *Harry Potter*, but now played with the Philadelphia Orchestra. It has brought in a whole new generation of people to listen to symphonic music.[76]

In 2006, Picard's flute was included in a Christie's auction of *Star Trek* props. The estimated auction price was posted as $800–$1200, but in the end, the flute was sold for $48,000.[77]

Despite thematic and philosophical differences between *Star Trek* and *Star Wars*, both franchises boldly advanced the orchestral tradition of scoring. As Chattaway said, these orchestral scores create

> a long-lasting impression. It's not like the beat of the week. It's always been music that will last through the ages, and I think that has been a big part of why even the original series is still popular and it doesn't sound all that dated because it is still a symphonic approach to scoring music. Classical music has lasted since it was invented and will probably extend through the ages and I think that's what gives *Star Trek*, and space music in general, longevity.[78]

Star Trek: Deep Space Nine

The success of *Star Trek: The Next Generation* reenergized the *Trek* TV franchise and substantially expanded the fanbase for Roddenberry's vision. According to Graeme McMillan of *Time*,

> [W]hen the show finished in 1994, it had become the highest-rated drama in syndicated television, boasting 15 to 20 million viewers a week. This was far beyond anything managed by the original *Star Trek*.... This kind of success took the show far beyond any expectation of "cult" and transcended what was expected of genre television in general. *Star Trek: The Next Generation*, somehow, made nerd culture mainstream for the first time.[79]

As a result of this success, three additional TV shows and four motion pictures were produced. The first was *Star Trek: Deep Space Nine* (*DS9*), which premiered in 1993. In contrast to the first two *Trek* live-action series, *DS9* took place aboard a space station of the Cardassians (an antagonistic alien race). The station was positioned near a wormhole that provided access to the Gamma Quadrant on the other side of the galaxy.

The series' central character was Starfleet Commander Benjamin Sisko, who had lost his wife during the conflict with the Borg. Since *DS9* took place on an alien space station, it had the feel of a mining town in the old American West, with a wide array of characters and villains passing through "town."

Produced by Rick Berman and Peter Lauritson, *DS9* leaned heavily on composers Dennis McCarthy and Jay Chattaway. Creating an individual musical sound for *DS9* was especially important. The music had to reflect a unique and alien environment (aboard an alien space station), but at the same time, it also could not deviate too far from the *Star Trek* sound that had been established in *The Next Generation*.

The theme music again played a significant role in establishing a musical identity for the show. Berman and Lauritson had originally hoped to hire Jerry Goldsmith to pen this new theme music, but Goldsmith had scheduling conflicts that prevented him from taking this job. The show had several talented composers at its disposal—and Dennis McCarthy was asked to tackle the *DS9* theme music. The composer indicated that he was so committed to the franchise that he would do it free if asked, although this was almost certainly an exaggeration.

Berman again had specific ideas regarding the title music. It needed to have a much different sound than Goldsmith's *TNG* theme. *DS9* would be a lonely place built by a militaristic species. McCarthy composed a majestic piece that both reflected the loneliness of deep space, but also echoed Goldsmith's original theme. According to Jeff Bond, "McCarthy's *DS9* title theme was an atmospheric, haunted yet somehow noble horn melody that beautifully captured the isolation of the station and the quixotic nature of its inhabitants."[80]

While many of the musical parameters that Berman and Lauritson had established in *TNG* remained, McCarthy, Chattaway and other composers were able to expand the musical canvas beyond that of *TNG*. Peter Lauritson noted, "It was about what was going on interpersonally between all people who came and went on *DS9*, so there was a different verve on that series...."[81] Bond wrote that in the pilot episode, McCarthy "broke every rule of current *Star Trek* music, sporting funky source music for Quark's bar, militaristic percussion for its confrontations with the Cardassians, even a striking atonal string cue to characterize the bizarre interior of the series' space wormhole."[82]

As the show progressed, other story-driven avenues materialized, enabling the composers to express themselves in new ways. An example of this was the introduction of a holographic lounge singer, Vic Fontaine, during Season 6. According to Jay Chattaway, who scored the Fontaine episodes,

> He'd sing the "Rat Pack" Frank Sinatra type of thing. But he wasn't just a lounge singer, he was also clairvoyant. He could tell if people were in love or if they weren't or tell them their future. He was played by Jimmy Darren, who was a singer and actor as well. That sort of broke up the normal routine of scoring *DS9*. Now we could do jazz, and that was my background. I got chosen to do most of the jazz episodes.[83]

The holodeck provided a unique vehicle for character development as well as stories and sets that would not be possible within the confines of the space station (or starship). During a Season 7 episode, "Badda-Bing, Badda-Bang," Avery Brooks (playing Captain Benjamin Sisco) was able to demonstrate his musical gifts. An accomplished jazz singer and pianist, he and the Vic Fontaine character duetted "The Best Is Yet to Come." Chattaway recalled, "Nobody knew how good Avery Brooks' voice really was. They did this duet called 'The Best Is Yet to Come.' We recorded it live. Jimmy Darren, who's a professional singer, did okay, but then Avery came in and [hit] it out of the park. He was so outstanding. What a strong voice and it was perfect."[84]

Voyager

The next *Star Trek* series of the *Next Generation* franchise began airing on January 16, 1995. *Star Trek: Voyager* returned to life aboard a starship. Rather than depicting life on the *Enterprise*, the new show took place on the USS *Voyager*, which finds itself on the far end of the galaxy. It was the first *Trek* series under the UPN (United Paramount Network) structure. "*Voyager* was the first 'corporate' *Star Trek*," stated Chattaway. He continued:

> While Paramount had been involved, it had still been at an arm's length. But *Voyager* was now a "UPN" production, so there were more people giving opinions regarding what the music and show should be. They wanted a lot more action in *Voyager*. And there is now the female captain and there is a gentler approach.... The amount and the type of music in *Voyager* was much more adventurous and much more action-oriented. As the Borg began to play a larger role in the show, per episode, there was much more music.[85]

Jerry Goldsmith returned to the *Star Trek* franchise to write the *Voyager* theme music. He once again composed a grand orchestral piece, one that contrasted significantly with what he had written for *Star Trek: The Motion Picture* (and later used as the *Next Generation* theme). According to the JerryGoldsmithOnline.com website, Goldsmith

> chose not to do the obvious and provide another epic theme as per *Star Trek: The Motion Picture*, instead writing a beautiful, sweeping theme perfectly accompanying the images of space and *Voyager* flying past planets and nebulas. It is a fantastic accompaniment to the opening credits but also a wonderful listen without the visuals.[86]

Chattaway was tasked with composing for the pilot, which needed to feature more action. The studio also wanted significantly more music than had typically been used in *Deep Space Nine*. For a two-hour pilot, Chattaway wrote approximately 90 minutes of music.

In what was now a tradition in the *Star Trek* universe, there were musical performances by cast members in this new series. Starting in the Season 3 episode "The Swarm," music was used as a device to explore the holographic doctor's desire to expand beyond his original programming, similar to how Data's musicianship and painting helped him to explore humanity. Robert Picardo, who played the Doctor, had suggested the Doctor's musical proclivities. According to Picardo, "My simple suggestion that he become a fan of opera became a plot point—a way into that story." In this episode, Picardo was called on to sing pieces from Puccini's *La Bohème*. However, the Doctor starts having lapses in memory, and he begins to wonder whether these episodes were a result of dedicating a large portion of his program to interests (singing opera, etc.) outside his primary programming.[87]

According to Picardo, the Doctor's love of opera was a perfect way to explore his limits. "Art makes you appreciate the natural world. It enhances the human experience. So why wouldn't it enhance the holographic experience as well? I think opera became symbolic of the Doctor's desire to make himself a fully realized individual—not just a narrow application medical hologram."[88]

For the rest of the series, the Doctor's love of both listening to and performing opera became a central trait of his character, as well as a vehicle to explore new storylines. It became particularly useful when a new crew member came on board, a former Borg, Seven of Nine (played by Jeri Ryan).

As Seven began to acclimate to life on *Voyager*, the Doctor became an unlikely teacher. Picardo recalled, "That was a culmination of an arc of stories I had with Jeri where the Doctor took it upon himself to help her reclaim her humanity; by having role-playing to learn appropriate behavior in different situations." Brannon Braga asked for suggestions on how the Doctor could play a role in this—and possibly replace the relationship that the Doctor and Kes had developed over the previous seasons. "Finally, in teaching Seven how to behave on a date, he falls in love with her," said Picardo. "When I read the script and saw that we sing 'You Are My Sunshine' I thought 'Oh my God! They got this public domain and that's the only reason why we're singing this song."[89]

Enterprise

The final post–*TNG* series was *Star Trek: Enterprise*, which premiered on September 26, 2001. Taking place two centuries earlier than *TNG*, *DS9* and *Voyager*, *Enterprise* told the story of the original starship *Enterprise*. For this first new *Star Trek* of the twenty-first century, Rick Berman wanted to try a new approach for the theme music. All previous shows had utilized grand orchestral themes, but to inject new energy into the series—and possibly attract new audiences—they employed a pop song called "Faith of the Heart" (or "Where My Heart Will Take Me" in *Enterprise*).

This was the first *Star Trek* theme song that was not composed specifically for use in *Star Trek*. It had been written by songwriter Diane Warren and originally performed by Rod Stewart in the 1998 film *Patch Adams*. With the selection of the song, Warren became the first female composer to write a *Star Trek* theme. According to Berman,

> I met Diane Warren who was a major songwriter—one of the top
> Grammy-winning songwriters—and I think she was a *Star Trek* fan to some
> degree. She was going to write something, but then, she played me this song
> "Faith of the Heart" which just seemed to resonate with me a great deal about
> what *Star Trek* was about.[90]

English tenor Russell Watson sang the new version as a montage of images of historical space events (both real and from the *Star Trek* canon) appeared with the opening credits. "I thought that the song and the visuals were lovely," Berman opined.[91] However, the new musical approach was not favorably received by many *Star Trek* fans. "We got a tremendous amount of criticism for it," said Berman. "We essentially got a zillion 'How dare you.' A good 80 percent thought it was disastrous. ...The person to blame for that would undoubtably be me. I just thought that it would be good to have some sort of vocal theme because we wanted the show to be different."[92]

Despite the use of this voice-based pop song, they had not abandoned the long tradition of using orchestral scores in each episode. Dennis McCarthy had even written orchestral opening theme music for the series on his own time—just in case there was an issue with the vocal song. That theme was not wasted. It was used as the closing music for the series.

The orchestral scores remained the show's musical underpinning, but the music also evolved from season to season as the show tried to build a stronger audience. By the third and fourth season, there was pressure to integrate more synthesizers within the orchestral sound. Since McCarthy's (and Chattaway's) experience was primarily orchestral scoring, they hired a new composer, Kevin Kiner. According to Kiner, "The producers were struggling to modernize the *Star Trek* sound.... I think for me they were trying to inject some youth and some modern film score sound into the final two seasons."[93]

Kiner used "more percussion and more on the ostinato strings," admitting that it was challenging to keep the score "current": "It's hard to define what makes a film score sound more current—what the zeitgeist is.... I've been doing this for 36 years and I definitely don't use the same licks and the same motifs that I did 36 years ago."[94]

As a result of these changes, the orchestra was reduced to 38 pieces (from 50), supplemented by electronic instruments. The end result was more of a hybrid sound than had been used on any previous *Trek* production.

Star Trek: Enterprise did not resonate with audiences as much as the previous shows, and the producers were constantly adjusting the storyline to build more interest. As a result of disappointing ratings, the show ran for only four seasons, the final episode airing in May 2005.

Star Trek: The Next Generation of Motion Pictures

"We all know that the power and the emotion that can be created by music is just unmeasurable."—Jonathan Frakes[95]

Star Trek: First Contact

"Jerry Goldsmith was the sweetest man and his music
from *Star Trek* was legendary."—Rick Berman[98]

Arguably the strongest of the *Next Generation* films was *First Contact,* directed by *Star Trek* cast member Jonathan Frakes. Over the previous several years, Frakes had established himself as a director within the *Star Trek* franchise. "One of the great pleasures on the Paramount lot was going to 'Paramount University,'" recalled Frakes. "When I was learning to direct, I would go the scoring stage and see [McCarthy] at work with 80, 90 musicians—some of the finest musicians in Los Angeles. All kinds of studio musicians. It was a great part of my experience on the show."[99]

Star Trek: First Contact reintroduced the most popular *TNG* villains, the Borg. The action starts just as the Borg begin an assault on Earth. Just in time, Picard and the *Enterprise* destroy the Borg cube, but not before a spherical escape pod flees. The sphere passes through a temporal portal with instantaneous results: To their horror, the *Enterprise* crew sees that Earth has now been completely assimilated by the Borg. The Borg had gone back in time to assimilate humanity centuries earlier. Hoping to restore the original timeline, the *Enterprise* follows the Borg through the temporal portal to the mid–twenty-first century.

Jerry Goldsmith returned to the *Star Trek* franchise to score the time-traveling tale. "Jerry Goldsmith was just a prince," recalled Rick Berman. "We screened the film for Jerry and we were very much in sync. In most cases, we relied on Jerry's incredible experience with *Star Trek* and his knowledge and talent."[100]

This sentiment was shared by Frakes. "One of my fondest memories is going with Rick to Jerry Goldsmith's house in the flats of Beverly Hills," he recalled. In the studio above his garage, Goldsmith said, "Well, here's what I'm thinking," and then played the opening theme to *First Contact*. "Rick and I looked at each other and I smiled and thought, 'I have really arrived,'" said Frakes.[101]

Rather than the driving upbeat music that he had written for *Star Trek: The Motion Picture,* Goldsmith wrote a sweeping and slightly melancholy theme that Berman called "noble and strong—a main theme that has a sense of dignity and strength that the picture calls for."[102]

As the opening credit sequence draws to a close, the music shifts to a starker sound, the "ominous, metallic signature of the Borg," according to film reviewer Adam Dean.[103] In fact, this section of music was not written by Goldsmith but by his son Joel. Jerry had accepted the job while he was still working on another project, *The Ghost and the Darkness.* Joel, an accomplished composer in his own right, was recruited to help his father score the film. This included writing some major cues, such as the Borg theme used throughout.

As a result of the scheduling pressure, the Goldsmiths composed only 72 minutes of original music for the film (of which 22 minutes were composed by Joel). Nonetheless, it was an effective score that wove together new themes along with some familiar motifs from previous films, such as the Klingon theme that Jerry Goldsmith had composed for the original motion picture. The Klingon theme was now used as a heroic theme for Worf.

One of the film's most captivating musical moments comes in the final scene, after the Borg's plan to rewrite history has been undone. An alien spacecraft descends at the settlement in Bozeman, Montana, and a hooded alien and two crewmates step out as the music swells. The alien removes his hood to reveal that he is a Vulcan. Adam Dean wrote,

> Goldsmith creates a finale piece bristling with awe, emphasizing thoughtful woodwinds and strings for this historic *Star Trek* moment. The second portion of the cue deals with Picard saying goodbye to Lily. Goldsmith closes the cue with a touching moment and an heroic flourish as the *Enterprise* warps back to their own time.[104]

Frakes later spoke of "the privilege" of working with Jerry Goldsmith and called him "one of the people at the top of the craft in the history of the genre. He couldn't have been nicer and couldn't have been more collaborative and couldn't have been more of a genius."[105]

First Contact held a special place in Goldsmith's heart. He was quite proud of the work that he did on the film: "To me, it's the best *Star Trek* film I've done. I loved the script so much…. It's a wonderful chance to let it all loose—a broad canvas—romantic canvas—that's hidden inside of me. It's one of the things I love about these pictures. It's kind of cathartic…."[106]

First Contact received positive reviews and generated an impressive worldwide box office

Sidebar:* The Goldsmiths Did Not Write All the Music in *First Contact

The character of Dr. Zefram Cochrane was musically defined by twentieth-century rock 'n' roll music played at top volume. When Cochrane is first introduced in a makeshift bar, Roy Orbison's "Ooby Dooby" thunders from the jukebox. Later in the film, when Cochrane, Will Riker and Geordi La Forge lift off toward space aboard the *Phoenix* (atop a converted ICBM), Steppenwolf's "Magic Carpet Ride" screams from the speakers. Big orchestral scores may be the essential musical underpinning of the *Trek* franchise, but other types of period music have been successfully integrated into both film and television productions of *Star Trek*.

of $146 million, with a production budget of approximately $45 million. As such, the film guaranteed the viability of additional *Star Trek* films.

Star Trek: Insurrection and *Star Trek: Nemesis*

The final two films featuring the *Next Generation* cast did not have the success and quality of *First Contact*. Jonathan Frakes and Jerry Goldsmith teamed once again in 1998 for *Star Trek: Insurrection*, about a race called the Ba'Ku who live on a planet with cellular regenerative properties—essentially a planetary Fountain of Youth. However, a race called the Son'a, in partnership with a rogue Starfleet admiral, attempts to relocate the Ba'Ku and steal their planet. The Son'a are in fact a group of Ba'Ku children who had broken away years earlier and undergone the ravages of time and bioengineering. The plot tests whether the Federation is willing to stand by its high ideals during a time when they are being challenged on many fronts. Craig Lysy wrote, "The story explores Machiavellianism, which espouses that 'Might Makes Right' and that evil means may be used to achieve a 'Greater Good.'"[107]

Goldsmith once again comes through with an emotional score. The main theme represents the Ba'ku. It's a sweeping, pastoral sound reminiscent of Aaron Copland (or even Randy Newman's score for *The Natural*). The piece starts with harp, moving to woodwinds, piano and then strings. According to Lysy, the Ba'ku theme "speaks to the idyllic beauty of the planet Ba'ku. Imbued with a wondrous gentle elegance and animated by woodwinds, we find ourselves transported to an ideal existence where infirmity and death have long been vanquished. There is also the ethereal and transcendent Mystical Theme, a woodwind lover's dream come true, which speaks of the utopia that is Ba'ku."[108] The peaceful serenity of the Ba'Ku theme is interrupted by the revelation that the villagers are being spied upon as Data disengages a forcefield that had been concealing the observation post. The music changes dramatically as "Goldsmith enters with electronics then explodes with an aggressive orchestral action piece."[109]

Goldsmith also added some subtle symbolism in his musical depiction of Data. According to Peter Lauritson, "Jerry was one of those composers who could sneak up and just grab you.... In [*Insurrection*], because Data was an android, Jerry utilized clockworks in his score. It was subtle, but I'm sure people subconsciously picked up on it."[110]

After the pastoral start to the film, Goldsmith's *Insurrection* score is primarily action-based, reminiscent of some of his other action scores. According to James Southall, Goldsmith "seemed to use the 1998 *U.S.*

Marshals (which is, I think, a hugely underrated score) as his template for virtually all the action music he wrote thereafter—there's a certain sparseness to the sound that hearkens back to his 1970s scores."[111]

The final *Next Generation* motion picture installment was *Star Trek: Nemesis* (2002). It was Stuart Baird's third (and final) directorial job on a major motion picture after directing *Executive Decision* and *U.S. Marshals*, both scored by Goldsmith. In *Nemesis*, a Captain Picard clone takes over the Romulan Empire. Picard and the *Enterprise* must thwart his nefarious plot.

For *Nemesis*, Goldsmith did not compose a substantial opening theme. The film starts with the opening notes of the Alexander Courage theme, then transitions into a short, driving theme, heavy with percussion as the viewpoint descends to the Romulan Imperial Senate on Romulus. According to Jeff Bond, Goldsmith revisits a motif that he used in the original motion picture:

> It may have been just because of the temp track, but he had this cello motif—of this busy, pumping piece of music that went all through the first *Star Trek: The Motion Picture* score, but he never really used that motif again in his later scores. He revisits music in a couple of cues in *Star Trek: Nemesis*. I have no idea if he knew this was going to be his last *Star Trek* score, but it brings [Goldsmith's music] full circle.[112]

Overall, the *Nemesis* score lacks the complexity and emotional charge of many of Goldsmith's previous *Trek* scores. *Nemesis'* most memorable musical moment was a rendition of "Blue Skies" sung by Data at Riker and Troy's wedding. ("Blue Skies" was reused in the first episode of *Star Trek: Picard* in 2020.)

Nemesis was one of the final major motion pictures that Goldsmith scored (only followed by *Looney Tunes: Back in Action*). He passed away on July 21, 2004. Goldsmith was one of the most successful composers in motion picture history, working on some of the greatest films of the past half-century, but he was always particularly proud of his decades creating the music of *Star Trek*.

8

Space: The 1990s

"Sci-fi is a genre that allows you to do anything, because
your responsibility to truth and reality is different."[1]
— David Arnold

The beginning of the 1990s was a time of worldwide transition. The Berlin Wall fell in 1989, and two years later the Soviet Union collapsed. This led to what was called the New World Order in which the United States was the only remaining superpower. These events had a direct impact on the future of space exploration. In the aftermath of the Soviet Union breakup, there were concerns that former Soviet nuclear and space scientists would sell their talents to rogue states or terrorist groups. To help diminish this prospect, the United States built a partnership with Russia: the Shuttle-Mir program, in which astronauts and cosmonauts would visit the Russian Mir space station aboard both the U.S. Space Shuttle fleet as well as the Russian Soyuz capsules. This partnership was beneficial to both countries and eventually led to the International Space Station partnership.

Indeed, humanity seemed to be taking steps that would move us closer to the vision of a unified planet as portrayed in *Star Trek*, and *Star Trek* was approaching the height of its TV popularity at this time. The success of *The Next Generation* (and subsequent *Trek* shows) helped stimulate new space-based TV series in the 1990s: *Babylon 5*, *Space Above and Beyond* and *Stargate SG-1*, all of which leaned heavily on orchestral scoring. Many featured newer faces in the science fiction music genre. The 1990s also saw a plethora of space-related motion pictures.

Babylon 5

The *Babylon 5* pilot appeared in February 1993 and the full-fledged series began in January 1994. The series was conceived by J. Michael Straczynski, a well-established TV writer (*Murder, She Wrote*; *The Real Ghostbusters*; *He-Man and the Masters of the Universe*). *Babylon 5* was a groundbreaking series, one of the first TV shows to utilize CGI effects. The series also followed a continuous story arc, told over multiple seasons. While this practice has been common in recent years, it was not standard for mainstream television shows (except for soap operas) to feature multi-season story narratives. Most series (including *Star Trek*) produced episodes with self-contained plots.

Taking place 250 years in the future, the five-mile-long *Babylon 5* space station, operated by Earth Force, is positioned in "neutral territory." The massive facility is home to a quarter million humans, aliens, diplomats, business owners and others, living and working together. As the series progresses, two major plotlines emerge. An ancient spider-like race called the Shadows schemes to begin a galactic war, and in parallel, a totalitarian conspiracy takes place on Earth. The *Babylon 5* crew plays a central role in thwarting both threats. The show had a much "edgier" tone that *Star Trek*, delving into politics, religion, drug addiction and many other mature topics. Straczynski wanted to create an "adult approach to sci-fi. What *Hill Street Blues* did for cop shows."[2] *Babylon 5* was certainly not the near-utopian society that *Star Trek* envisioned.

Establishing the proper musical sound was essential. Nevertheless, budget constraints limited *Babylon 5* to a single composer (whereas *Star Trek* employed several). As the *Babylon 5* pilot, "The Gathering," was being produced, Straczynski hired rock musician turned film composer Stewart Copeland (the drummer for The Police) to write its music. However, by the time the series was greenlighted, Copeland was recording a new album, preventing him from becoming the series' full-time composer.[3]

Straczynski turned to Christopher Franke, best known as a member of the German electronic band Tangerine Dream. Like Copeland, Franke was not a typical choice to produce an orchestral film score. His experience had been primarily focused on electronic (popular) and experimental music. Franke had received some classical training, but undoubtedly it was his background in musical experimentation that solidified his position as *Babylon 5* composer. According to Franke, "They looked into a certain group of people who are known for their openness and certain experiments. I was the lucky chosen."[4] Straczynski, pleased with his new composer, stated, "I wanted for *Babylon 5* to have a sense of scope and scale. And his music is emblematic of that. It is unabashedly dramatic. Unabashedly operatic. And it elevates the scenes that it appears in."[5] In another interview, he added, "[Franke] far exceeded what Stewart did for us, good as that was. There's some killer stuff coming, very aggressive, very moving and powerful. His piece for 'And the Sky Full of Stars'—'Requiem for the Line'—is brilliant, sad, emotional, brave … just nifty."[6]

Babylon 5 provided a unique opportunity for Franke. "For me, science fiction shows are much more interesting because typically, I like to innovate when I write music. So that's usually my home. To do a cross between sound effects, unusual instruments and the classic orchestra."[7] Franke was also fortunate to be philosophically well-aligned with Straczynski and producer John Copeland regarding the role and style of music that should support the series. The level of trust established between them was so strong that at one point, Straczynski simply requested that the composer "break my heart. Just break my heart. And he was always able to do that,"[8] knowing that Franke needed no more instruction to compose the proper music.

While Franke was granted an unusual degree of musical freedom, the show could not afford a large orchestra for every episode. But Franke compensated:

> I like to combine simply the best of the two worlds. I need this acoustic dirt produced by live instruments and the ability to play so well between two semitones. All this micro-tonality and acoustic dirt is just something which is very refreshing. I like these noises; a synthesizer sounds too clean. On the other hand, the natural instruments have weaknesses like frequency, range, dynamics, and control ability. Therefore I like to combine the best of the two worlds.[9]

For the orchestral elements of the scores, the music was recorded by Berlin Film Symphony Orchestra at Franke's sound stage in Berlin. These recordings were never recorded with a "full" orchestra. Even when the score required a full orchestra, Franke never assembled more than 24 musicians at a time. Once these recordings were complete, he mixed all the orchestral and electronic elements into the final score. The process had some advantages.[10] If any section needed to be re-recorded, he did not need to call back the entire orchestra. (This practice also made him a pioneer in remote soundtrack recording, a method that became far more common and practical during the 2020 COVID-19 pandemic.)

The end result: scores that averaged 25 minutes of music each week. This accounted for roughly 50 percent of the length of each episode. It was quite common for large portions of the visual effects to be absent when the musical scoring began. "There could be a hole as long as a minute where there is a black picture describing what happens," recalled Franke. "Then I get color copies of certain drawings or sketches and we talk verbally about the content and movement of those special effects."[11] Franke then composed music based largely on what he imagined the scene would look like.

Despite the heavy reliance on special effects, what made *Babylon 5* stand out was its characters and complex plots. These played a substantial role in Franke's musical decision-making. "In the end, it's about people.

It's about the choices. It's about the consequences of their choices."[12] He also musically anticipated future events to create a series-wide continuity. "So instead of just scoring what we see, I tried to implement what this will lead to or the consequences. The music in *Babylon 5* is interpreting the past or the future. *Babylon 5* all the time goes into the past or the future because it doesn't have a constant time axis."[13]

As early as the third season, Franke was able to bring many of these elements together. In the episode "Severed Dreams," when Captain Sheridan declares *Babylon 5's* independence from Earth, Franke utilized a chorus:

> These voices are very special to me because they can be very haunting or human, but if used wisely and not too often, human voices are like pearls in an arrangement and can really make your emotions stir. I need to transcend sometimes something which is not materialistic, which is like the energy of thoughts, the pureness of people's behavior, then I really like to use the human voice and try to process it so they don't sound like the Italian operatic sound.[14]

Franke's volume of music was critical to the show's success. According to film music expert Jeff Bond,

> Franke's pulsating, textural scores for the series have always functioned perfectly with its slick CGI visuals, focusing on atmosphere and pacing in conjunction and conspiring to keep the viewer's attention off the show's simple fly-by-night sets and props and on the intricate interweavings of fate, interpersonal relationships and galactic politics that keep viewers (all 20 of them) tuning in week after week.[15]

But according to Bond, Franke's individual production of the *Babylon 5* music may have limited the melodic and harmonic variation from episode to episode. "The individual episode scores, however, are almost indistinguishable, and too often the cues just wander along from synthetic crescendo to crescendo as they underscore each episode's dramatic brinksmanship and plot points."[16]

While *Babylon 5* never reached the popularity of the *Star Trek* franchise, it established and retained a strong fanbase and spun off several TV movies and series. None achieved the audience or quality of the original series.

Stargate

Star Trek was not the only franchise to influence space-related science fiction in the 1990s. The 1994 motion picture *Stargate* inspired a highly successful TV franchise several years later (see *Stargate SG1* below).

Conceived and written by Roland Emmerich and Dean Devlin, the film tells the story of a Stargate (found during an archaeological dig in Egypt) that can instantaneously transport people to distant galaxies (based on the Einstein-Rosen bridge concept). The first crew to use the Stargate finds themselves trapped on a distant planet, and they attempt to decipher how to use the Stargate to get home. Meanwhile, a malevolent alien is trying to kill them and hopes to destroy human civilization on Earth.

Young composer David Arnold was an unlikely choice for this film. *Stargate* was to be a big-budget film and Arnold had only worked on one full-length, low-budget film, *The Young Americans.* At the time he was selected for the *Stargate* job, he had just begun work at a video store in London. As fate would have it, his *Young Americans* music impressed *Stargate* executive producer Mario Kassar. According to Arnold, Kassar particularly liked "Christian Requiem," a big piece that Arnold had written for chorus and orchestra. "They liked the idea and sound of it. And I was cheap and enthusiastic," recalls Arnold.[17] The composer was flown to California to meet with Emmerich and Devlin. Arnold recollected, "I'd never had a meeting with anyone. The movies I'd worked on were stupid films with friends, so everything came about in a slightly accidental, slipshod, random way. I never had to audition or do anything that meant that I was up against anyone."[18]

On the plane to California, he read the script. "I didn't really know what I was doing. I'd read some articles in movie magazines about screenwriters pitching a script."[19] With this in mind, he decided that the *Stargate* music should be "somewhere between *Lawrence of Arabia* meets *Star Wars.*"[20] This idea seemed to resonate with Emmerich and Devlin and they asked Arnold to send them some thematic ideas. To his surprise, after delivering his initial ideas, Emmerich and Devlin offered him the job less than a week later.[21] "I was amazed that Roland and Dean were giving their big-budget film to a complete unknown, a composer who'd only done one three-million dollar British movie that didn't even get released in America. So either Roland and Dean were either stupid or incredibly trusting."[22] Since composers with his level of experience are rarely given major composition jobs, Arnold conceded, "I was expecting to wait 15 to 20 years for something like this…."[23]

He did not waste the opportunity. He set to work with the desire of being musically authentic to the film. "It's a big, slightly 'camp,' over-the top, special effects space adventure with people in it who you like," said Arnold. "It felt like the score needed to meet the demands of the film."[24] Keeping true to his original "*Lawrence of Arabia* meets *Star Wars*" concept, Arnold began to listen to Egyptian music, particularly Egyptian percussion, to help construct the proper mood for the film. He partnered with noted Egyptian percussionist Hossam Ramzy, known as Egypt's Ambassador of Rhythm, who had worked with Led Zeppelin and other performers to inject Egyptian sounds and rhythms into their music.

While percussion plays a prominent role, the score is highly melodic. According to Arnold, "I'm a huge fan of melody. I love something idiosyncratic for the piece rather than something that sits underneath and apologizes for itself. I definitely wanted it to be a voice in the film. Part of that was naivete."[25] Nonetheless, he did not overwhelm the film with melodies. "In *Stargate,* the only person that the music really evoked was Ra. I was composing for the overall film as opposed to characters. It was a broader kind of musical painting in terms of discovery, wonder and sorrow."[26]

When Ra makes his appearance, Arnold wanted to convey the wrath of an ancient god. "He's coming and you have better be on your best behavior—[it would] be best to get out of the way. So you have that which is the grand aspect of it…. It's so theatrical that you can't ignore the scale and the size of it."[27] Arnold contrasted this grand sound with the more subtle and hair-raising music to portray Ra, which he described as "[t]his slinky, evil, winding, slimy kind of presence. A slithering unknowable danger. The sort of thing that you'd like to avoid. Kind of like putting a wet hand on your shoulder or finding something crawling down the back of your neck."[28]

But Ra is also the religious figure and that side of Ra had to be portrayed musically. "You've got the two themes. You've got the [charm] where everyone in a kind of religious way is celebrating him—or announcing him with chanting. Then you have the slimy violins who paint the ultimate side of him."[29]

The score was recorded by the 85-piece Sinfonia of London and conducted by Nicholas Dodd. Arnold recalled, "I was absolutely petrified. It was the biggest thing I'd ever done obviously…. But bloody hell, it sounded amazing in that room!"[30] He said his completed score had the lyrical quality of *Lawrence of Arabia,* but also "that kind of Hollywood, grandiose energy that John Williams had so completely captured for *Star Wars*— which kind of said 'space' for a long time. That sound said 'space movie.' I think we got the kind of DNA of both of those things right, but we also made something a little idiosyncratic. A lyrical action score."[31]

Jeff Bond commented that Arnold's score also gave musical nods to Williams' *Close Encounters* music, James Horner's *Brainstorm* and *Aliens,* and Elmer Bernstein's music for *The Ten Commandments.*[32]

Stargate received mixed reviews, but it significantly exceeded expectations at the box office. With a production budget of roughly $55 million, the film brought in just under $200 million.

Independence Day

After the success of *Stargate*, David Arnold was hired by Roland Emmerich and Dean Devlin to score their next big-budget film, *Independence Day* (1996). It was an alien invasion film loosely based on H.G. Wells' *War of the Worlds*, but also referenced innumerable other films and other popular culture tropes.

In this second Emmerich-Devlin film, Arnold did not want to simply mimic what he had done on *Stargate*. Both films had space-related plots, but Arnold believed the films were in fact from two different genres: "*Stargate* seemed more like fantasy and *Independence Day* seemed more like science fiction. So there was more of an anchored, rooted sense of Earthliness in *Independence Day*, because it related mainly to people."[33]

Scoring *Independence Day* was no small task. This film was bigger than *Stargate* in every respect. "There was a set of expectations for [*Stargate*]," recalled Arnold. "I don't think people had really expected *Stargate* to be anything that much, but it became something quite big. With *Independence Day*, there was the expectation that it would be good—and it had to be good."[34]

This realization was highly stressful to the composer. "There were times when I would kneel down on the floor of my hotel room with my head in my hands—unable to conceive of anything that would work for a scene." He eventually determined that a melodic approach would be needed just as it had been with *Stargate*. This time, the story did not require a *Lawrence of Arabia* feel, but something akin to an American patriotic anthem. "It seemed to me that what it needed was a kind of national anthem, but for the world. I noticed that many of the national anthems around the world have a descending base line, whatever the top melody is doing."[35]

This anthem was closely associated with the character of President Whitmore (portrayed by Bill Pullman). The music needed to represent the "every man" and project nobility. "That's the key word for *Independence Day*," stated Arnold, "because the film is about how people retain nobility while facing what might be the end of the world."[36] Devlin was so happy with the final result that he commented, "You can leave it up to a Brit to write some of the most rousing and patriotic music in the history of American cinema."[37]

Contrasting the "every man" nobility of President Whitmore, Arnold approached the aliens from a completely different emotion place. The *Independence Day* aliens had no individuality, and the music had to reflect a feeling of unrelenting impending doom. "There's a line where someone compares the aliens to locusts," recalled Arnold. "So, you don't want to find a theme for a creature, because that would lead you to believe that it's the one controlling everything."[38] In fact, Arnold's concept for the alien theme did not come to him through his usual creative process. It came to him in dream.

Arnold occasionally had fever dreams associated with the terror of being unable to finish a score on time, but this dream was far more productive. In this case, he dreamt that he was at the Los Angeles Guitar Center and several keyboards were on display. Naturally, he "played around" on the keyboards and noticed that one of them had a preprogramed setting that said, "Alien Invasion." "I pressed the button and listened to it and thought, 'Well, that sounds pretty good.'" The composer was able to wake himself and hummed the melody into a Walkman so that he would not forget it. When he listened to it in the morning, the dreamed melody was just as good as he remembered. His "dream theme" was used in the movie.[39]

Arnold said that there was no way to write music big enough to symbolize the destruction of human civilization. "So, I've composed a death march for the world, which spells out 'die' in Morse code.... It's dash, dot-dot-dot-dash, and I play it on two African jum-jum drums and a Japanese daiko drum."[40] In a reversal of fortunes, as the Earth forces plan for their counter-offensive, the Morse code theme was turned against the aliens, becoming the only form of communication between the nations of the world. All other communications were either disrupted or could be monitored by the invaders.

In total, the composer wrote roughly two hours of orchestral music for a motion picture that was two hours and 21 minutes long, significantly more than had been written for *Stargate*. To perform his massive score, a 90-piece orchestra and a 46-person choir was utilized under conductor Nicholas Dodd, who had also conducted the *Stargate* score. A FilmTracks.com reviewer observed, "No plug remained un-pulled for *Independence Day*, with all the snare-ripping, wild piccolos, blaring trumpets, and cooing choral elements necessary for such a story."[41]

Despite mixed reviews, *Independence Day* was the top-grossing film of 1996, generating rumors of a potential sequel. While Arnold's music unquestionably played a role in the film's success, he was not invited back to compose for the sequel, *Independence Day: Resurgence*, produced in 2016.

Even though David Arnold is a fan of the space genre as well as real space exploration, *Independence Day* was his last space-related film. He regrets this immensely, stating, "I think basically all films should be set in space. I can't think of a film that if you put it in space, it wouldn't be better."[42] While he was (probably) only partly serious with this observation, he believes that the science fiction genre can provide more freedom to a composer:

> When you're in the realms of fantasy and fiction, your responsibility to the humanity of it is slightly different. When it's about real things and real people, then I think your responsibility to it is grounded in a way that fantasy isn't. What that does musically is, it releases you from the shackles of formality. Because the world that you're engaging with is not real, it unties you from the ideas of expectation and allows you to do unusual things.[43]

Stargate SG-1

Stargate lived on—but on the small screen. The film inspired a series of TV productions, starting with *Stargate SG-1*. That series featured many of the movie's characters, as well as some new ones, engaged in weekly adventures traveling through the intergalactic portal known as the Stargate. Created by Brad Wright and Jonathan Glassner, the series premiered in July 1997 and generated several spinoff shows and direct-to-video films.

The original film boasted David Arnold's impressive orchestral score; Wright and Glassner knew that big sound was essential for their new series. They hired Joel Goldsmith, who had co-written the *Star Trek: First Contact* score with his father, Jerry Goldsmith, and had scored such TV shows as *The Outer Limits* and *Diagnosis Murder*.

Goldsmith's initial task was to provide the show with its own signature sound, while musically connecting the series with the original film. To achieve the latter task, he crafted a modified version of Arnold's original theme music to establish both the mood of the new show and to accommodate the length of a television opening credit sequence. Other themes composed by Arnold were used. According to Goldsmith,

> [A] lot of those themes were really quite appropriate to use. Then as we started to add more of our own characters, Thor, etc., then I started to develop more themes of my own. Also, I didn't want to pound David's themes into the ground. They're very recognizable themes, and they're terrific, but I also didn't just want to completely bash the audience over the head with them every week.[44]

The studio rejected Goldsmith's original score for the pilot episode "Children of the Gods." Recalling his experience with the pilot, Glassner stated,

> I was unhappy with the score. The guy who scored the whole rest of the show, Joel Goldsmith, he'd set up a beautiful, beautiful score for "Children of the Gods" and the studio felt that it was not exciting enough—and actiony

enough—and they made us re-score it by tracking music from the movie. They cut up pieces of the track from the movie and put it in there.[45]

This was not an isolated occurrence. The producers had very strong opinions about their shows' music, which occasionally generated friction with their composer. According to Goldsmith,

> On a few occasions I was exceptionally proud and excited about a specific piece that I had written for a show and was absolutely flabbergasted when both Brad and Robert couldn't stand the piece, they just hated it. And ironically there have been times when I seriously doubted the effectiveness of a cue and they just loved it. Sometimes it can be difficult to judge the quality of your own work.[46]

While Wright and Glassner craved the sound of a full orchestra for *Stargate SG-1*, limited budgets made this impossible. Goldsmith simulated an 80-piece orchestra with synthesizers, but occasionally hired two or three musicians to supplement the synthesized score, in order to produce a more convincing orchestral sound.

The show was seen in dozens of countries and ran for ten seasons. Over that time, additional composers were hired, such as Kevin Kiner, who would write for *Star Wars: Rebels* and *Clone Wars*; and Neal Acree who was best known for writing music for video games and some TV movies.

Stargate SG-1 and the subsequent productions almost certainly introduced far more people to the Stargate universe—and David Arnold's themes—than the original film had in 1994.

Space: Above and Beyond: Shirley Walker

A little more than a year after the final episode of *Star Trek: The Next Generation*, the ambitious series *Space: Above and Beyond* was launched by Glen Morgan and James Wong. Morgan and Wong had become friends in high school and then both attended Loyola Marymount University's School of Film and Television. They served as producers on the TV series *The Commish* and executive-produced *The X-Files*.

The concept for *Space: Above and Beyond* emerged from a college class taken by Morgan and Wong, examining the fiction of war. According to Morgan, when they were considering space show concepts, he said, "I love the World War II genre," so we said, "Let's do World War II in space."[47] *Space: Above and Beyond* takes place in the year 2063, as an Earth colony is attacked by an alien species known as the Chigs. The series follows "the Wild Cards," a group of elite Marine pilots on the front lines against their alien enemies.

It was always intended for music to play a prominent role in the space war drama. Morgan recalled that they wanted it to reflect the score of their favorite World War II film. As he recalled, "I'd been searching for that kind of Jerry Goldsmith, *Patton* kind of sound" to bring the show musically to life. One of the series' visual effects artists, Glenn Campbell, steered them in the right musical direction: On location in Australia, Campbell presented Morgan with a Sony Walkman containing a tape with music composed by Shirley Walker and asked, "What about this?"[48] The recording was Walker's score to *Batman: The Animated Series*. According to Morgan, he said yes within ten seconds of hearing the music.

In a heavily male-dominated profession, Walker had already become one of the industry's most successful female composers. Starting off as a synthesizer player on *Apocalypse Now*, she began orchestrating and conducting for dozens of films and TV shows, then scored *The Flash, Falcon Crest* and *Batman: The Animated Series*. She had also worked as an orchestrator and conductor for rising film composers Hans Zimmer and Danny Elfman.

When Walker arrived to begin scoring *Space: Above and Beyond*, she received some very simple instructions from Morgan and Wong. They asked her to try to capture the sound of *Patton* or *Tora! Tora! Tora!*, both scored by Jerry Goldsmith. (Morgan conceded, "Jim and I are like musical dopes. I'm sure she'd be laughing her head off at us."[49]) Morgan and Wong occasionally provided temp track music, but Walker pushed back on this; she did not want to be influenced by temporary musical selections. She wanted to view the scenes and come up with her own ideas.[50]

Walker particularly enjoyed writing the show's opening theme music:

> I really wanted to embody the military presence, and it has a lot of drums in there. The nature of the melody is such that it's coming down and going back up. It puts them out in space and brings them back to their home planet. This continual return to home for replenishing and then going out to fight the bad guys.[51]

To achieve the sound that the producers and Walker were looking for, Fox approved the budget to hire an orchestra, which was not common at the time for a TV series. But this budget was not limitless: They could only afford a (roughly) 30-piece orchestra, largely comprised of horns and percussion, and augmented by synthesizers.[52]

In addition to the big militaristic sound, Walker was also able to musically portray the characters, their intentions and their emotions. Morgan said,

> The great thing about Shirley Walker—she told me things about the characters that I didn't really know or may not have understood, through her music.

For example, the Shane Vansen character was in search of revenge. Her parents and some of her family had been assassinated by the Silocates—and the theme for Shane was a kind of a round because that's all revenge was—you were kind of a dog chasing its own tail. There was no (musical) outcome.[53]

The musical portrayal of the commanding officer, Lt. Col. McQueen, reflects more of an inner conflict. According to Morgan, the McQueen theme is like a call to arms, but "it kind of like dies out—it flattens. It's not a call he wants to answer. It's just heartbreaking."[54]

Walker was accomplished at interweaving these themes, particularly as the characters interacted or came into conflict. According to Morgan, "The Vancen round could then intertwine with the McQueen call to arms—and the theme could be played backwards or just instruments would play through this scene—another instrument would play through that scene—and then they would all come together either triumphantly or tragically."[55]

KQED reviewer Marc Hasan observed that Walker had

a gift for knowing exactly how much pity, heroism, and tragedy to score before stepping back, and it also allowed her to replay her militaristic theme in more intriguing arrangements, shifting the colour of brass in the "Ray Butts" suite, or giving it scorching desperation using high register strings and trumpets at the beginning of "Stay with the Dead."[56]

Despite Walker's success, she struggled her entire career overcoming the "boys club" mentality within the film and TV scoring profession. She said that she never technically "lost" a job because she was a woman, but according to Morgan, she often was not "offered" premier composition jobs because of the conception that the best composers were men—or that women only wrote "feminine music." Walker observed that the industry often believed that all female composers should share the same musical style of British composer Rachel Portman:

The fact that Rachel is succeeding in the way that she is, I think, makes those of us who aren't writing "feminine'" music—I mean, quirky, feminine, sweet stuff—again, we just have to keep pushing a little harder. It is unfortunate that there are people who see women as being so frail that they couldn't carry the stress of a score, and particularly, of a major score.[57]

Despite these obstacles, Walker would almost certainly have continued to break new ground for female composers. However, as a result of complications from a stroke, she passed away on November 30, 2006, at the age of 61. At the time of her death, Walker had composed scores for more major motion pictures than any other American woman, elevating the role of female composers within the Hollywood power structure. "She really was a trailblazer,"[58] stated Morgan. He recalled that Walker fought to advance talented female composers, and also furthered the careers of some of the top male composers. According to Morgan, "She taught Danny Elfman to orchestrate—this is never mentioned"; she also mentored Hans Zimmer, who is currently at the pinnacle of the film scoring world. While her status within the entertainment industry was not as high as it should have been, Walker had received the respect and admiration of many people in the industry. This admiration enabled Morgan to leverage his friendship and professional relationship with Walker to hire other talented musicians. When he was searching for a composer for *Intruders*, his relationship with Walker helped him recruit his preferred candidate: "I talked Bear McCreary into scoring *Intruders* because I worked with Shirley Walker. He said, 'I'll do this score if every week you tell me a Shirley Walker story.'"[59]

McCreary recalled that he only met Walker once and was "absolutely starstruck,"[60] but he was heavily influenced by her:

> My personal story with Shirley Walker picks up after she died. I had already
> started scoring *Battlestar Galactica*. There was one episode in particu-
> lar called "Dirty Hands" in the third season where I was drawing upon this
> sound of a Dobro guitar, which is a very common instrument in Southern
> blues. I had first heard this instrument on *Batman: The Animated Series* in an
> episode called "The Forgotten." It was so bluesy, cool and I just remembered
> it.[61]

McCreary was frustrated that even though Walker was "the first woman to score a studio, major budget film in the history of film,"[62] the Academy Awards did not include her in the "In Memoriam" segment after her death. McCreary was so upset over this exclusion (or oversight) that he wrote a scathing commentary about the Academy on his blog. The next day he received an email from one of Walker's family members inviting him to her public memorial.

According to Glen Morgan, *Space: Above and Beyond* had provided a perfect vehicle for Walker. She was particularly inspired by the depiction of heroes. Morgan recalled that just a few weeks before Walker's passing, she told him, "I like when you guys write about heroes. You wrote about heroes well. Let's do that again."[63] It was in these types of scores—for these types of characters—that her true personality was shown. Morgan stated, "What you hear in *Batman* and *Space* and the stuff she did for *Black Stallion* ... that music really is Shirley Walker. She was so passionate. Quick to laugh. Quick to roll her eyes." Morgan recalled the "matronly"-looking Walker attending a screening of *Final Destination,* and as a plane blows up and kids are blown out of the plane, she laughed hysterically and said, "This movie fucking rocks!"[64]

Note: The musical makeup of *Space: Above and Beyond* was not exclusively orchestrally based. Walker and the producers injected some popular music to add personality and depth. An example of this occurred in the fifth episode, "Ray Butts." Legendary Marine pilot Ray Butts, a man obsessed with pancakes and the music of Johnny Cash, leads the Wild Cards on a secret mission. Near the end of the episode, his ship is caught in the gravitational pull of a black hole. Reconciled that he will not survive, he says goodbye to the squadron and turns on Johnny Cash's iconic song "I Walk the Line." As the ship is pulled deeper into the black hole, the Cash song is distorted by the impact of intense gravity.

Galaxy Quest

In 1987, Mel Brooks directed *Spaceballs*, his outrageous parody of *Star Wars*. After the success of that movie, it seemed almost inevitable that a film parody of *Star Trek* would eventually follow. It took 12 years, but in 1999, *Galaxy Quest* was released. Inspired by *Star Trek*, this film was based on the premise that an alien civilization called the Thermians had received broadcasts of a *Star Trek*–like TV series called *Galaxy Quest*. They do not understand that the series is a work of fiction; in fact, they believe that the episodes are recordings of actual events—or "historical documents." So impressed are they with these "historical documents" that they remodel their entire society based on the lessons and technology of *Galaxy Quest*. When their civilization is threatened by an evil reptilian warlord, they come to Earth to seek help from the crew of the NSEA *Protector*—who in actuality are simply unemployed actors.

The film was originally going to be directed by Harold Ramis of *Ghostbusters* fame; after he dropped out, Dean Parisot was hired. Parisot's directorial experience had been almost exclusively in television, on such eclectic shows as *Northern Exposure*, *Reading Rainbow* and *E.R.* Nonetheless, there was a certain logic in his ascent to this gig. In addition to the fact that he was a huge *Star Trek* fan, his TV background provided valuable experience that could be applied to a film about a fictional TV series.

As with any *Star Trek* production (or *Star Trek*-like production), the music was a critical ingredient for success. They turned to composer David Newman, a member of the most prominent family dynasty of Hollywood composers and musicians. This dynasty included his father, composer Alfred Newman; his uncle, conductor Lionel Newman; his brother Thomas Newman and his cousin, Randy Newman. David had established himself as one of the top Hollywood musicians and composers in his own right, scoring such films as *The War of the Roses*, *Matilda* and *Anastasia*. He was also quite proud of the fact that he was a *Star Trek* fan who had played violin for the orchestra (under Jerry Goldsmith) for *Star Trek: The Motion Picture.*

Thus, he was more than happy to write music (for *Galaxy Quest*) that was intentionally influenced by *Star Trek.* Newman gave the producers two cues. One was reminiscent of Alexander Courage's music for the original series, the other inspired by what Jerry Goldsmith had written for *Star Trek: The Motion Picture.* "And they gravitated toward the Jerry Goldsmith," stated Newman. "I gave them a choice. Had they gone with the other one, we would have taken the movie probably in a completely different direction musically."[65] Newman's theme was original, but also effectively evoked the spirit of *Star Trek.* According to James Southall of Movie-Wave.Net, the theme is "[a] fluid, vaguely nautical melody, its appearances through the score are frequent but never to the point of it outstaying its welcome."[66]

Once the primary thematic music was agreed upon, Newman knew exactly how he would approach the rest of the movie:

> The thing was completely easy after that to figure out what to do because I have a lot of experience standing on a fence, moving a little this way and moving a little that way, but not too much. Allowing the humor, but not punching the humor. Making it heartfelt. Dealing with the slow burn of the characters coming together.[67]

The film was far more than a spoof of *Star Trek.* According to Newman,

> *Galaxy Quest* seems like a silly parody, but at its heart, it's not. It's a love letter—a romantic crew love story—with a lot of comedy in it. This is why I was hired to do *Serenity,* because it's nuanced. I just had a lot of practice doing that. Like all those Eddie Murphy movies that I did, *The Nutty Professor, Norbit* and *Daddy Day Care.* They all seem on the surface to be silly movies, but they're not. They're complicated.[68]

Newman had at his disposal an orchestra of 100 players as well as a chorus. But that many players were not always required. His main theme played a dual role in the film, both as the "motion picture" main theme and as the fictional TV series' title music. The original *Galaxy Quest* series would unquestionably have been on a tight budget; thus they would not have been able to afford a full orchestra. Newman recalled, "First we recorded the last cue, the big version of it, and then we just took out everybody except about 30 players, so it's the size of a regular TV orchestra of that time."[69] For example, they reduced the trumpet section from four trumpets to just one. Six horns would be reduced to just two, and 30 violins were replaced with just eight. "We just took everything and kind of pared it down. And also, John Kurlander, the engineer, miked it differently. He miked it more like it would have been miked for a TV show in the '60s."[70]

The music helps the story arc lift the jobless and depressed crew-cast members as well as the nerdy teenage "Questerians" (based on Trekkies) from the doldrums of their lives, to a place of victory. As director Parisot noted, "[T]here are a whole lot of themes playing in there. The movie needed to begin as a mockery and end as a celebration. That's a hard thing to do. Part of the mission for me was to make a great *Star Trek* episode."[71]

Galaxy Quest was only marginally successful at the box office. This may have been the result of a disconnect between the production and the studio. According to producer Mark Johnson, "I would maintain that the studio never quite understood the tone of the movie. They were expecting more of an out-and-out comedy, *à la Spaceballs*."[72] They also marketed the film as a children's movie rather the more sophisticated space comedy-drama for all audiences.

Largely through word of mouth, *Galaxy Quest* grew in popularity, particularly when it appeared on video. It became a cult classic that many *Trek* fans consider one of the best *Star Trek* movies.

Galaxy Quest is often cited as one of David Newman's most effective scores. According to the La La Land Records website, Newman

> pulls off an impressive musical feat, employing a comic touch while skillfully supporting the film's legitimate, considerable sci-fi action and well-drawn

Composer David Newman conducts a scoring session of the 1999 film *Galaxy Quest*.

character relationships. Newman continues in the rich tradition of the Newman family musical legacy, composing a score that employs big choral passages and wondrous melodic themes.[73]

Although *Galaxy Quest* was a "love letter" to *Star Trek*, the producers were very careful to differentiate the ship designs and other aspects of the show from *Star Trek* to avoid a lawsuit from Paramount. In the spirit of this fear of litigation, the registration number NTE-3120 is prominently painted on the hull of the ship. The "NTE" stands for "Not the *Enterprise*." Whether Paramount understood the joke is unknown.

*****

The 1990s had many other space-related films that explored a wide range of musical styles to portray space, aliens and adventure. The quality of these productions varied, but they all provided new perspectives in the space genre and sound.

Two of these films were scored by the former Oingo Boingo singer-songwriter Danny Elfman. Elfman had established himself as a successful and creative composer for motion pictures, starting with *Pee-wee's Big Adventure* in 1985, and went on to compose such major films as *Beetlejuice, Scrooged* and *Batman*.

Elfman worked with Tim Burton on *Edward Scissorhands, The Nightmare Before Christmas, Batman* and *Mars Attacks,* the latter a spoof of 1950s alien invasion films. "I just knew that it was going to be one of these movies that was just going to be fun," Elfman recalled.[74] The score has many retro throwbacks to 1950s science fiction films, including the "sound" of the theremin. According to Elfman, "The theremin is the classic spaceship sound. But in the end, we played the theremin parts on an instrument called an Ondes Martenot, which is a very unusual keyboard that has a theremin sound because we couldn't find a theremin player...."[75] The end product paid tribute to the theremin-laden 1950s scores, but also injected Elfman's signature big, driving (almost unrelenting) sound—bolstered by a chorus.

One day the following year, Elfman literally "wandered onto the set" of *Men in Black* and ended up with a job.[76] He had been on an adjacent set with Peter Jackson, but strolled over to the *Men in Black* set and thought it looked "cool."[77] *Men in Black*'s producers must have thought he was cool as well. As he drove home, his agent called to say he was hired to score *Men in Black*. Like *Mars Attacks*, the film enabled Elfman to experiment with different styles of music. "*Men in Black* has allowed me to visit this unique musical world where I'm combining retro and contemporary music in a playful way," said Elfman.[78]

In 1998, Elfman received his first two Oscar nominations for Best

Score, for *Good Will Hunting* and *Men in Black*. He did not win for either score.

That same year, a very different space film called *Starship Troopers* premiered. Based on a 1959 novel by Robert A. Heinlein, it was the over-the-top story of humanity battling a race of spacefaring insects. Composer Basil Poledouris was tasked with putting this story to music. Poledouris had scored some of the biggest action films of the 1980s, including *Conan the Barbarian*, *Iron Eagle* and *Red Dawn*, and was known to be able to produce a big and dramatic sound.

Director Paul Verhoeven gave Poledouris a copy of the script, providing extensive notes on the backs of the pages, giving his input on the music and other relevant aspects of the plot development. After providing these notes, Verhoeven simply suggested, "Read them. If you think any of it make sense, use it. If you don't, don't."[79] How much Poledouris followed the director's suggestions is unknown.

True to the over-the-top storyline and production, Poledouris produced a large and dramatic score using a 97-piece orchestra at the Sony Studios recording stage during the summer of 1997.[80]

The main theme music, which was used throughout the film, provided an effective vehicle for the large orchestra. According to James Southall of Movie-Wave.net, the most impressive moment of the *Starship Troopers* score was a scene called "Klendathu Drop." As the main theme emerges, "like a minor-key cousin to the Fed-Net March, the whole orchestra getting a workout—busy strings race along under the dynamic, driving horn theme, which goes through a thrilling set of variations over the cue's five minutes."[81]

Poledouris recalled that even though Verhoeven had offered numerous suggestions, the composer was given a significant amount of freedom on the film. "With Paul Verhoeven, there are never any expectations other than go as far as you can go with it, and bring as much to it as you possibly can ... which is really rather extraordinary."[82]

Japan has a strong appetite for space-related television. In 1998, what has been called a neo-noir science fiction anime premiered: *Cowboy Bebop*. Produced by Sunrise, the show follows the exploits of a group of bounty hunters aboard a spaceship called the *Bebop* in the year 2071.

To bring this show to musical life, composer Yoko Kanno was hired. Kanno had written music for numerous anime productions, including the TV shows *Brain Powerd* and *The Vision of Escaflowne*. For *Bebop*, she composed a diverse and energetic musical sound using jazz, soul, funk, pop music and other genres to depict this distant view of human civilization. According to Kanno, "I chose to create such music believing that people's emotions in their everyday life would be the same in the future, even in outer space."[83]

To find this sound, she drew from her days in middle and high school where she was a member of a brass band. But, according to Kanno, "part of me was always frustrated because I couldn't understand why everybody else was content playing the uncool music. I wanted to play brass music that shook your soul, made your blood boil, and made you lose it." She stated that this "yearning" was the inspiration for the jazzy theme song "Tank": "I wanted to make music which would light a fire in me when I played it."[84]

Twenty-six episodes of *Cowboy Bebop* aired in 1998 and 1999; it is often called one of the best animes ever produced, and Kanno's music remains highly acclaimed.

9

A New Century

The beginning of the twenty-first century was a time of new momentum for *real* space exploration endeavors. There were new calls for the United States to return to the Moon and then send humans to Mars. Commercial space entities like Space X, Blue Origin and Virgin Galactic rekindled the hope that ordinary citizens would be given the opportunity to voyage into space in the foreseeable future.

The turn of the century was also a time of transition within the entertainment industry. The influence and quality of television evolved in the latter half of the twentieth century, but it rarely achieved the prestige, production budgets or quality of major motion pictures. This balance of power began to shift as cable networks such as HBO began to mature in the 1980s and 1990s, producing new and innovative content. This balance shifted even more as streaming services (Netflix, Hulu, YouTube, Amazon, AppleTV+ *et al.*) emerged. The budgets for major TV shows grew substantially and series such as HBO's *Game of Thrones* demonstrated that TV could equal the budgets and quality of motion pictures, and often exceed them.

New sounds of space were emerging. Grand orchestral music was certainly not being displaced, but new sounds that reflected everyday life began to be used in space-based films and television more frequently.

Firefly

One of the first space-related TV series of the twenty-first century was Fox's *Firefly*, which premiered in 2002. Produced by Joss Whedon of *Buffy the Vampire Slayer* and *Angel* fame, the weekly space drama-adventure-Western took place 500 years in the future aboard a "Firefly-class" spacecraft named *Serenity*. Its crew: an oddball group of smugglers led by Captain Malcolm "Mal" Reynolds, a former soldier who fought on the losing side in a rebellion against "The Alliance." The show was modeled on post–Civil War America as settlers traveled westward and the country tried to reconcile the aftermath of the War Between the States. Whedon stated, "I wanted to tell the boring stories about Han Solo smuggling when he wasn't involved with the Rebellion."[1]

In contrast to many of the preceding space shows, *Firefly* was hard to define. Whedon called it "a science fiction westernoir action suspense drama."[2] To create the musical accompaniment for this plethora of genres, composer Greg Edmonson was hired. The protégé of prolific TV composer Mike Post, he had written music for such films as *Undercover Angel* and *Frog and Wombat*, and the TV series *Renegade*.

Edmonson probably did not appear on Whedon's original list of potential composers. According to Edmonson, "When *Firefly* was in pre-production, everyone in town wanted to do that gig because Joss Whedon had done so well with *Buffy* and with *Angel,* but he wasn't taking any calls from any agents, so they said, 'Send in a CD of what you think might be appropriate for this show and we'll get back to you.'"[3]

Edmonson submitted a CD, not expecting to hear back, but soon he received a call from Whedon's office asking if he would be interested in having a short meeting. When Edmonson hung up the phone, he said to himself, "I am so screwed! I've never seen an episode of *Buffy.* I've never seen an episode of *Angel.*" As it turned out, this would not be a problem. When Edmonson met with Whedon, "[w]e just started talking and were having fun—and our five-minute meeting turned into two hours." At the end of the meeting, Whedon said, "Call your agent and say you got the gig."[4]

Firefly did not rely on a classical sound to depict space. Since *Firefly* was essentially a Western in space, the music reflected that genre, using guitars and fiddles as well as ethnic instrumentation. According to Edmonson, Whedon requested a musical sound that "went in an opposite direction of the way most people go (for space shows). For example, on *Star Trek*, when you're in space, you hear French horns and really majestic music. [Whedon] said, 'We're going a completely different way'—and we did."[5] As Whedon explained it, "We live on the outer planets, where the entertainment you have, you make…. We make it with what we can carry. Working primarily, up: voice, drum, blowing air through wood, guitar."[6]

Edmonson envisioned the show as somewhere between a post-apocalyptic universe and the history of the United States. "Your resources determined your lifestyle," he stated. "For instance, if you were a Rockefeller, living in New York, your life was completely different than someone in the middle of the country trying to raise wheat. In his world, you could have laser guns, or you could have six-shooters—and it all made sense."[7] Within this context, it was a cultural melting pot requiring a wide range of ethnic and western instrumentation.[8]

Edmonson did not write themes for each character, believing that it was "self-defeating, because at some point, people just smell it coming." However, in some circumstances, he used specific instrumentation to help define characters, especially if they had a solo scene. For example, he would use piano for River, but mixed in other instruments depending on particular emotions and revelations of a scene.[9]

This was important to Edmonson. He loved the characters and felt an emotional connection to them. As the show neared its end, he expressed this connection, saying farewell to the characters musically in an unaired episode called "The Message," the final episode that was filmed. Edmonson recalled that there was a funeral at the end of this episode. "I wrote a piece of music that was me saying goodbye to those characters. It was the perfect opportunity since you had every one of those characters on screen…. It was just the perfect moment to be able to say an emotional goodbye to these people I had hoped to spend much longer with."[10]

The only major piece of original music that Edmonson did *not* write was the opening theme song. Whedon wrote "The Ballad of *Serenity*" and it was performed by blues singer Sonny Rhodes. Whedon's original vision for the opening montage featured a lone man sitting in a rocking chair on a porch, singing the song while playing a guitar, but Fox wanted an opening sequence that represented an action show. Thus, the montage was changed to action scenes and character images.

This disagreement over the opening sequence was just a symptom of a larger philosophical difference between Whedon and Fox, a difference that almost certainly was a factor in the show's cancellation after only one season. Edmonson recalled, "I think that's why Fox didn't like the show. Because they wanted an action show … with chases and shooting—and Joss was trying to write a show with human conundrums with complex, flawed people."[11]

Despite its early cancellation, *Firefly* established a tone, sound and feel that was mirrored by many other shows over the next 15 years.

While he was disappointed that the show was cancelled, Edmonson has fond memories of his time on *Firefly*. He recalled that after every episode he scored, he would say, "I am the luckiest guy on the planet."[12]

Serenity

The *Firefly* story did not end with its cancellation. After Fox dumped the series, Whedon pitched it to other networks. Universal eventually suggested the concept of a full-fledged motion picture rather than a TV series. According to Whedon,

> It's been the easiest process in terms of dealing with a studio that I've ever had. And they turned it into—not a blockbuster, which is not what I was trying to make, but not a low-budget movie either. They wanted to make a real movie out of it. They wanted to give us the scope that the show could never have had. So all I had to do was come up with a story that was worth that.[13]

Again, music was essential to establish the correct moods and depict different cultures. Whedon wanted music that would be "spare, intimate, mournful and indefatigable."[14] But Edmonson was not brought back; Universal wanted Whedon to hire a composer with more motion picture experience.

Eventually, David Newman was hired. He had already scored dozens of films including *Galaxy Quest, Anastasia* and *Bill and Ted's Excellent Adventure*. As mentioned earlier, Newman was a member of one of Hollywood's most legendary musical dynasties. In addition to his composition background, Newman also had experience from the vantage point of the orchestra, playing violin for two giants of motion picture composition. "I played on almost everything that John Williams did that was in L.A. from 1977 until 1983—same with Jerry [Goldsmith]," said Newman. "It was thrilling playing on *E.T.* I sat in the back of the first violins. I soaked it up, I listened—I was in my twenties. These guys were consistently great, but completely different personalities." He recalled that Williams was polite and gentlemanly, Goldsmith acerbic. "They influenced everything."[15]

According to Newman, Whedon called him over the 2004 holidays to discuss the prospect of scoring *Serenity*, but the composer believed (but was not certain) that the decision had already been "preordained" before they had even spoke because of internal politics that Newman was not privy to.[16]

Newman recalled that, initially, "Joss Whedon was struggling on how to score the film. Did he want to score it like the TV show ... or did he want it to be bigger?"[17] *Serenity* takes place in the future, but it feels like a tale that took place long ago. "This all derived from Western culture and Homer and Greek tragedy," said Newman. Just because it was a space-based film did not mean the music would be drawn from a single or even predictable genre. Newman added, "This is why I always tell film composers that the best thing that they can do is to be well read—and to know all these books and stories—as well as the history of film."[18]

The mixed-genre storyline was a musical challenge for Newman. Perhaps the most challenging part of the score was the main theme, which had to set the tone for the film. According to the composer, "The main title was very, very difficult. So difficult that I thought maybe I would get fired." He finally came up with a solution by reaching back over a century for inspiration. "What I hit on was a late nineteenth century Italian operatic procedure. I used a quartet of cellos to play the melody. There are four voices in a cello—high, middle, low and very low. When I hit on that, it worked."[19] Newman then transitioned into a faster section where he used ukuleles, mandolins and Appalachian instruments to play a two-step quirky melody. This transition between different types of music helped straddle the numerous cultures reflected in the film. Newman said, "When I look back at it, there's a lot of reference to opera, because of the big idea of what it was about. The drug that wrecked humanity—the danger of being extinct."[20]

Newman did not restrict himself to Italian opera references. His cue "Crash Landing" is a driving piece in which "there is an obsessive C major rhythmic passage that uses a little bit of River's theme—that's taken from a Leoš Janáček opera called *Jenůfa*, which is an early twentieth century modernist opera."[21]

Comedic moments were also an important element of the film. According to the composer, "Mal is kind of like an Indiana Jones character. He's quirky and there is a lot of implied humor in it that you could step on if you make it too dark in the wrong places." He referenced a scene where he wrote an abrupt stop in the music, like a record scratch.[22]

Serenity did not jumpstart a *Firefly* franchise. While it received numerous favorable reviews, *Serenity* was a box office disappointment. In his book Serenity: *The Official Visual Guide,* released just prior to the film, Whedon wrote, "If the film doesn't make any money at all, my guess is that *Serenity* is going back into my heart."[23] While the show and film may have gone back into Whedon's heart, they did inspire future TV and film storylines over the next couple of decades.

Battlestar Galactica: The Reboot

In 2003, shortly after the cancellation of *Firefly*, came the premiere of a miniseries based on the 1970s space series *Battlestar Galactica*. This was followed the next year by the launch of a successful TV series. Developed by producer Ronald D. Moore, the new *Battlestar* followed the same basic premise as the original series, but it updated for the twenty-first century. The special effects were far more advanced than the 1970s series and the mechanical villains, the Cylons, were redesigned. While the Centurions retained the same metallic look as they had in the original series (except they appeared to be on robotic steroids), the Cylon leadership was now an advanced race of cyborgs, indistinguishable from humans.

Another significant difference between the original show and the reboot was the music. The original series used an orchestral tradition like *Star Wars*, but the new series went in a new musical direction, beginning in the pilot miniseries. Composer Richard Gibbs, who had been the keyboard player for the band Oingo Boingo earlier in his career, made his transition to film scoring when composer Craig Safan took him under his wing on *The Last Starfighter*. Gibbs went on to score such films as *Say Anything* and *Fatal Instinct*, as well as over a dozen episodes of *The Simpsons*.

When Gibbs landed the scoring job on the new *Battlestar* miniseries, he assumed that he would be writing a big orchestral score similar to the original series. But the producers wanted a minimalist approach to the music. According to Gibbs,

> I did get in some orchestral scoring, but not in the big action scenes, where one would typically expect it. Those scenes were carried by the Taiko drums, mostly. I also threw in a few other ethnic elements—Persian and Bulgarian vocals, various ethnic flutes, Tuvan throat singing. No blazing trumpets, crashing guitars, drum kits.[24]

With several film commitments at the time the series was starting, Gibbs could not return to score the series. Instead, young composer Bear McCreary, who had worked as an assistant to Gibbs on the *Battlestar* miniseries, stepped in. But this did not mean that McCreary was slated to be the permanent composer. McCreary:

> I don't think the producers were interested in having a 24-year-old assistant score their show. So while they were looking for a real person to score their show, they let me do an episode ["33"]. I did a pretty good job on it … and at the end of that first episode, they asked me to come in and start working on the second one. Before you knew it, I scored between 75–80 hours of narrative over the [six or seven] years.[25]

Hiring such an inexperienced composer was a tremendous gamble for producer Ron Moore. *Battlestar* was McCreary's first real job out of college, but he had acquired some impressive accolades, including being apprenticed under legendary composer Elmer Bernstein.

Early on, McCreary was told that they did not want the show to sound like *Star Trek* or any of the other well-known space-related shows or films of the previous couple of decades. According to McCreary,

> The series began as a response to science fiction—television in particular—scoring and where that genre had arrived by the early 2000s—specifically *Star Trek*. At that time, *Enterprise* was just coming to the end of its run, and it felt like the end of an era. At that point in time, it was quite controversial to score any science fiction show with anything except orchestra.[26]

McCreary was trained in, and was a great proponent of, traditional orchestral music, but he saw a unique opportunity. Being told not to use the traditional orchestral sound "literally opened up a world of music. I suddenly had western classical music taken away as an influence ... instead I had to draw from world music."[27]

Under the musical stewardship of Richard Gibbs, *Battlestar* had used Taiko drums and ethnic woodwinds to establish a signature sound. When McCreary began scoring, the instrumentation was broadened even more with Middle Eastern drums and vocals, South American flutes, Celtic, Armenian and Turkish influences, and even popular and rock music.[28] Over time, more traditional orchestral music was integrated (including the use of the Stu Phillips original theme), but the show remained true to the initial musical doctrine, avoiding frequent use of traditional western classical orchestral music.

As the show became popular, McCreary grew concerned about his musical legacy. "I was responsible for the score that was a refutation of everything I loved about film music—big themes, big orchestra, big emotion. *Battlestar* is the opposite of that. I remember thinking, 'Am I killing film music?'"[29]

While the early seasons relied heavily on exotic styles and percussion, the scores tended to be subtle and modestly spotted throughout the episodes. There were significant stretches without music or with minimal scoring. Music played a more integrated role as the show reached the third and fourth seasons. An example of this occurred in the Season 3 episode "Crossroads, Part II." One of the show's writers, Ron Moore, and some of his writing colleagues had incorporated the famous Bob Dylan song "All Along the Watchtower" into the script, planning for it to play a central musical and symbolic role in the story. According to McCreary, when they handed him the script, they had provided no suggestions regarding what the song should sound like or what instruments would be used. "So I explored a version of the song using all the influences from the score," said McCreary. "[I used] a lot of world influences, Indian music and even heavy metal—rage against the machine kind of aesthetic."[30] The song does not reveal its secret until Starbuck discovers that a drawing that a child named Hera Agathon had given her reveals the musical notes to the song when it is held up to music (staff) paper.

McCreary provides exotic musical hints as certain crew members are unable to get the song out of their heads. Finally, in a scene when the fleet is coping with power disruptions, Saul Tigh, Samuel Anders, Tory Foster and Galen Tyrol assemble in an isolated room and come to the realization that they are Cylons. Tyrol says, "After all this time, a switch goes off, just like that." The group start humming McCreary's version of the Cylon song. Finally, a full rendition is sung as the Colonial fleet and the Cylons engage in battle.

The symbiosis of music and story evolved even more, to the point where McCreary played an unusually collaborative role with the writers. On one occasion, McCreary received a call from two of the show's writers, David Weddle and Bradley Thompson. They were working on the episode "Someone to Watch Over Me," in which Starbuck's husband is in a coma and she befriends a piano player in a bar. Starbuck reveals that her father, a piano player, had taught her to play before abandoning her and her mother. The piano player and Starbuck then collaborate on a song. However, the piano player is revealed to be a subconscious representation of her father.

Since music played such an integral role in this episode, McCreary was involved in the writing of the script.[31] It is highly unusual for a composer to take part on the formulation of a script, but McCreary was thrust even more deeply into the production when he was flown to the set to work with the actors. "I coached the actor who played Starbuck's dad," he revealed. "Many of [Starbuck's father's] comments about writing music were taken directly from interviews with me, talking about my creative struggles writing *Battlestar Galactica*."[32] Through her flashbacks, Starbuck's father teaches her a song on the piano, but the song may not entirely be a real memory. The song does not reveal its secrets to Starbuck until she discovers that a drawing that a child named Hera Agathon (the first human–Cylon hybrid) had given her revealed the song when held up to music

Starbuck and the piano player *Battlestar Galactica*.

paper. In fact, it was the same "music" that had revealed itself in Season 3's "All Along the Watchtower." The music played a critical role in the conclusion of the series.

Throughout the episode and remaining episodes, McCreary not only collaborated with the writers, but also with science adviser Kevin Grazier, "because in the finale, we needed to figure out how the song could be the clue that leads them to Earth—the real Earth."[33] This would be more easily suggested than accomplished. The composer was only given ten seconds of screen time to provide this musical clue and for Starbuck to solve the mystery that would lead them to *new* Earth. (In an earlier episode, they found the original Earth to be uninhabitable.)

McCreary worked closely with Grazer to determine how numerical digits could pinpoint a location in physical space. It required three sets of four digits, a total of 12. McCreary stated, "By happy accident, or by design, the melody that I'd composed, that is woven through 'All Along the Watchtower,' had 12 notes."[34] Each note in the scale was then assigned a number between one and seven and the story is told both visually and sonically as Kara (Starbuck) remembers the notes. During the final episode, as Galactica is being pulled toward a singularity, Starbuck says, "There must be some kind of way to get out of here" (a line from the song "All Along the Watchtower") and solves the musical puzzle. She enters the coordinates into the computer and Galactica jumps to Earth. They arrive at the planet 150,000 years before present time. In the final scene, the scene jumps ahead 150,000 years to a thriving New York City, and the Jimi Hendrix version of "All Along the Watchtower" is heard.

This use of music is reminiscent of the musical language devised by John Williams for *Close Encounters of the Third Kind*. Whereas in *Close Encounters*, the musical message is a "doorbell" or initial greeting for the people of Earth, in *Battlestar*, this musical message translates into a map to Earth. "I thought that was really cool," said McCreary. "Literally, music saves the human race."[35]

As the series progressed, *Battlestar Galactica* became a family project for Bear McCreary. His wife, noted vocalist Raya Yarbrough, sang for several cues in the show; and McCreary's brother Brendan sang "All Along the Watchtower."

Several productions were spun off from the successful new *Battlestar Galactica*. One was *Caprica*, which aired in 2010 for a single season. A prequel to *Battlestar*, it portrayed the height of Caprican society 58 years before the Cylons destroyed the 12 colonies. The show revealed how the Cylons were created and eventually turned against humanity.

McCreary scored the show with the full confidence of the production team from the first episode. *Caprica* took place in a wealthy and pretentious society, and the music reflected this. McCreary said he "pushed to the very distant background all the notion of tribal percussion,"[36] which was practically ubiquitous in the earlier series. Taking the opposite approach, he embraced the western orchestral tradition. "I started with strings and woodwinds and violin and oboe and sounds that you just didn't hear a lot during *Battlestar*. In many ways, it's the yin to the yang, because *Battlestar* was predominantly a world music score that ultimately had orchestral elements bleed into it to support the biggest moments."[37] However, as the story progresses and there are hints of the tragedy to come, more and more references to *Battlestar Galactica* were heard. According to McCreary, "You'd start hearing more of the tribal percussion and ethnic instruments."[38]

This musical progression was also reflected by budgetary reality. While McCreary was able to use a full orchestra in the *Caprica* pilot as well as some additional episodes, the rest of the series was performed by smaller ensembles.

Nonetheless, McCreary was committed to using live performers whenever possible in all his projects. He would pay orchestras out of his own pocket to guarantee maximum quality and impact. "I philosophically don't like using virtual instruments or samples to replicate something that's supposed to be emotional," McCreary commented. "If we're going for emotion, we need to hear a performance that actually evokes that emotion. I think of it like the difference between a really well-designed blueprint and the real thing."[39] *Battlestar* empowered him to convince later showrunners and producers (on other productions) of the need for real musicians. "It sort of spiraled into that they would hire me because they wanted that big orchestral sound."[40]

McCreary's experience with *Battlestar* enabled him to promote and compose orchestral music, and also have the freedom to experiment. In fact, McCreary looks to one of the great film composers for inspiration: "If I model myself after anyone's career, it's probably Jerry Goldsmith. He did every genre imaginable."[41]

Avatar

In 2009, the year that *Battlestar Galactica* was wrapping up, James Horner collaborated with James Cameron for a final time on the music for the film *Avatar*. In contrast to Horner's experience on *Aliens*, where he was only given two weeks to score the film, in the case of *Avatar* the composer worked on the film for over a year. According to Horner, "The bargain I made with James Cameron was, he wanted me to think about the movie a lot. He wanted me to be on set. He wanted me not to take on other films. He didn't want me to be diluted."[42]

Horner used this time to conceive of a score that had a substantially different sound than what he had composed in *Titanic* or his other films. He also did not want it to sound like music that had been written in the past to depict alien cultures. Cameron did not want to create a culture that was only slightly different than what we would find on Earth; it needed to be convincingly alien—convincingly indigenous. According to *Avatar* producer Jon Landau, their goal was to have *Avatar*'s score "resonate traditional film sensibilities, but also to introduce a new culture, the Na'vi of Pandora, and to make it part of the score."[43]

To achieve this, they needed a culture and a language that was as plausible as possible. But this could not be accomplished by relying on their own creativity. Professional help was needed.

They sought the help of an ethnomusicologist (a person who studies the music of different cultures), Wanda Bryant, to help Horner create a language and a culture, and develop a unique indigenous musical sound. "In our initial phone conversation, Horner asked me to find unusual musical sounds that 'no one has heard before,'" recalled Bryant. However, she clarified that what Horner really wanted were "sounds not readily recognizable by the average American moviegoer as belonging to a specific culture, time period or geographical location."

It could not be based on a single musical culture on Earth, no matter how obscure. Bryant revealed:

[W]e created a library of musical elements and performance techniques that would eventually be melded into a global mash-up, fusing musical elements from the numerous world cultures we had explored into one hybrid Na'vi style. Combining unrelated musical elements could evoke the "otherness" of the Na'vi without bringing to mind any specific Earth culture, time period or geographical location.[44]

Horner said that the sound world created for *Avatar*

had to be very different, really, than anything I ever created before. There is also three hours of music. I had to find a sound world that covered so much territory; it had to cover both the human side of the story and the indigenous side of the story and the tremendous, epic battles that take place as well as the love story that is at the core of the film.[45]

The creation of *Avatar* was also heavily dependent on CGI effects, creating some challenges for the composer. Horner explained:

In that world, actors are in black costumes with computer sensors on them. You're watching something that you have to totally take their storytelling, because you're watching people dodging things on gray boxes in black jumpsuits, with dots on them, that had nothing to do with what it's going to end up looking like. You have to make the magic in your head and rely on their storytelling—and that's, I guess, part of what my craft is.[46]

While Horner did create new sounds that effectively depicted the culture and feel of the Na'vi peoples, he also knew that the score could not be entirely "alien"-sounding. According to Cameron, Horner created "a unique sound that felt of another world, but at the same time, held on to the ways that music predictably, for a large number of people, encourages them to have an emotional response."[47]

Horner was not entirely successful in composing a score that was completely different than his previous music. Several cues were noticeably similar to music that he had written for *Glory* and *Titanic*. A female chorus piece ("Jake's First Flight") is quite reminiscent of the main chorus theme from Horner's *Glory* score.

Nonetheless, Horner once again produced an impactful and creative score that significantly elevated Cameron's film. *Avatar* went on to become the highest grossing film of all time ($2.789 billion) and Horner was nominated for a Best Original Score Oscar. (The award went to Michael Giacchino for his music to *Up*.)

On June 22, 2015, Horner died when the turboprop aircraft that he was piloting crashed in Los Padres National Forest. He was the only occupant of the airplane. He was 61 years old.

Gravity

The twenty-teens featured several films that did not follow the traditional approach of film scoring; for example, the space disaster adventure *Gravity* (2013), directed by Alfonso Cuaron. Sandra Bullock's character Ryan struggles to survive after a disaster aboard the International Space Station.

A late addition to the film, the score eventually evolved into an essential collaboration between composer and director, one that elevated the film's effectiveness. With only two weeks remaining until an early screening of *Gravity*, it still had no score. The screening could not take place without some form of musical underpinning, so they decided to hire someone to assemble a temp track. They approached British music editor–composer Steven Price, asking, "Can you help us do some musical stuff?"[48]

Price accepted the job to "do some musical stuff," but Cuaron requested that the composer use "no conventional music." Price began experimenting and inventing sounds that could be applied to the film. He then "started giving me notes back," recalled Price. "And I started doing a bit more. It kind of accelerated and, a few weeks in, he basically said, 'Would you like to come on as composer?'"[49]

Cuaron's "no conventional music" edict remained in place after Stevens accepted the job. "One of the first things Alfonso was really clear about was the fact that we were operating in a vacuum," said Price. "The stuff we're gonna be dealing with—vibrations and those sorts of sounds and low frequency kind of rumbles you might hear within a spacesuit—all of a sudden, this world opened up, and what could music be in that environment?"[50]

The music needed to match a mechanical environment, but also convey human emotion. Price explained, "[I]t was all very much led by the character of Ryan…. Some of it was melodic and some of it was intended to underscore a kind of emotional journey, and then there were a lot of sounds that were there to express real terror. It was those two extremes, really, expressing the beautiful nature of where they were but also absolutely a massively terrifying situation."[51]

To achieve this complex mix of sounds, Price relied primarily on a string section totaling 48 players. However, in most cases he used a much smaller grouping of strings to find the proper balance between a traditional orchestral approach and chaotic sound design. As a result of this eclectic mix of sounds, "*Gravity* is not a score which will appeal to the masses," according to Jonathan Broxton of MovieMusicUk.com:

> A large part of it is made up of challenging, uncompromising electronic dissonance, and if that sort of music leaves you running for the hills, then you can expect to be going there after listening to the first 15 minutes of this score. Similarly, anyone who immediately expects space music to be grand and symphonic, *á la* Holst, will also be disappointed.[52]

Interstellar

Focusing on the relationship between a father (Cooper) and his daughter (Murph), *Interstellar* (2014) takes place in the not-so-distant future when all life on Earth is dying off and the remaining humans struggle to survive. Cooper joins a crew of astronauts who will travel through a wormhole hoping to find a new home for humanity.

The film had an unusual origin. It was born out of a collaboration between writer-director Christopher Nolan and composer Hans Zimmer. Nolan, who had worked with the composer on several films, asked Zimmer, if Nolan was to write a page, would he take a day and write whatever came to mind in reaction to it?[53] Zimmer agreed, and soon thereafter, a

typewritten envelope appeared at his door containing a basic story premise. "It was this very personal fable about a father-son relationship. Now,
I have a son who wants to be a scientist. Chris knows him very well. I sat
down and wrote the tiniest, most intimate—really from the heart. I was
writing about my relationship with my son."[54] After playing it for Nolan,
Zimmer asked, "What do you think?" and Nolan replied, "I better make
the movie now!"[55] Of course, at that point, Zimmer had no inkling what
the movie would be about—and certainly did not know it was a space
drama. When Nolan told him what he had in mind, Zimmer reiterated
that he had written "this tiniest, intimate piece." How could it support a
space adventure? Nolan replied, "Yes, but I know what the heart of the
story is now!"[56] This intimate piece ends up being the primary theme,
interwoven throughout the film.

This process continued throughout production for two years. They
would discuss other elements of the plot and Zimmer would then produce
music to fit that scenario. "The whole score was written during the process
of making the movie." Thus, the day the film cut was completed, a synthesized score was already embedded in the movie.[57]

One of the score's central sounds of the was a pipe organ. Nolan and
Zimmer had just completed nine years of doing *Batman* films and both
agreed that a change in musical vocabulary was essential. Thus, the score
should have "none of the hyper-kinetic action strings. None of the crashing drums."[58] Nolan suggested, "What about a pipe organ?"[59]

Zimmer agreed—but he also did not want it to sound like a gothic
horror film. "Nobody is writing anything contemporary for the pipe
organ," stated Zimmer. "Part of the ambition became how can you write
something that is contemporary, but to avoid the gothic—all the horror
movie connotations?"[60] Zimmer was also drawn to the concept of using
a pipe organ because it had represented an extraordinary technology for
centuries: "By the 17th century, the pipe organ was the most complex
machine invented, and it held that number-one position until the telephone exchange. Think about the shape of it as well: Those pipes are like
the afterburners of spaceships."[61]

The choice of the organ also helped to emphasize the subtext of
"breathing, breath, air. This fundamental human thing, and the pipe
organ—you don't get a sound without the breath of the rush of air going
through it."[62]

There is also the religious aspect of a pipe organ. According to Nolan,
"I also made the case pretty strongly for some feeling of religiosity, even
though the film isn't religious, but the organ—the architectural cathedrals—they represent mankind's attempt to portray the mystical or the
metaphysical. What's beyond us, beyond the realm of the everyday."[63]

Harrison & Harrison organ in Temple Church, London used in Hans Zimmer's score to *Interstellar*.

To fulfill these abstract elements, they used the large 1926 four-manual Harrison and Harrison pipe organ at Temple Church in London. Church organist Roger Sayer performed all the organ pieces in the score. According to Sayer, "This organ has got body and bass. We have three 32-foot-length pipes [which play the deepest tones] and if you combine those with the 16-foot stops, it's amazing. It shakes the church, too, not just the cinema."[64] In short, it was precisely the style and scale of sound that Nolan and Zimmer were looking for. Jon Burlingame, who saw *Interstellar* at Grauman's Chinese Theater in Hollywood, recalled the power of the organ: "When the organ kicked in, the entire building shook. It was an extraordinary experience because this massive London pipe organ being used in a dramatic way for this outer space epic was simply wonderful. It was just a great, great choice."[65]

The organ music was supplemented by an unusual mix of instruments, including 34 strings, 24 woodwinds, four pianos and a 60-voice chorus. Zimmer also performed in the recording, playing the piano.[66] Together, this musical mix achieved Zimmer's vision:

> I wanted to hear the exhalation of 60 people, imagining the wind over the dunes in the Sahara. I got them to face away from the microphones, and used them as reverb for the pianos. The further we get away from Earth in the movie, the more the sound is generated by humans—but an alienation

of human sounds. Like the video messages in the movie, they're a little more corroded, a little more abstract.[67]

Despite the fact that the score had been written throughout the production of the film, it took 45 sessions with the orchestra to complete the recording of more than two hours of music—many more sessions than would be needed on most motion pictures. When asked why it took so long to complete the score, Zimmer replied, "Because we kept having ideas."[68]

Jupiter Ascending

Gravity and *Interstellar* were not the only films deviating from traditional film scoring norms.

On rare occasions, composers will be asked to write a score well before filming has been completed (such as Arthur Bliss' score for *Things to Come* in 1936). This was the case with the massive 2015 space opera *Jupiter Ascending*. Michael Giacchino was asked by the Wachowski siblings to write the entire score based largely on the script, without seeing the film. Composers will sometimes begin assembling their musical ideas after reviewing scripts, but final scores ordinarily are not completed until the composer has screened a version of the film. This is important since the final cut of a film will often deviate significantly from the script. However, the Wachowskis had successfully used this method on one of their earlier films, *Cloud Atlas*. They told Giacchino that they wanted to use the actual score to edit their film rather than a temp track. According to Giacchino, "Andy [Wachowski] said to me, 'Why would we want to use somebody else's music? We should use our own music to edit the movie.'"[69]

Giacchino was intrigued by this challenge: "It's much more freeing doing it that way. I'm not locked down to any specific timings and what the film is doing."[70] He also recalled, "I had no pictures. No bits of the movie to look at. What they gave me were these descriptions on cards, which described characters, described places, described situations. So, they basically wanted me to write a symphony for their story."[71]

This "symphony" (approximately 80 minutes) was recorded in London. Since the film had not been completed at the time, even in the best of circumstances the music would not fit cleanly into the film without significant editing. Eventually, roughly 55 percent of Giacchino's music was inserted into the film. According to music editor Paul Apelgren, "There's no way to predict what you're going to need at the script phase for any movie.... Michael got a lot right on the massive suites that he recorded for *Jupiter Ascending*, but there were two suites that ended up on the cutting room floor."[72] Giacchino viewed the film at a later date and wrote and recorded some additional music in a more traditional manner.

The score required a significant amount of music editing and reworking of various cues. While this approach may have given Giacchino more artistic freedom than he received on most films, it is unclear whether this method of film scoring was effective or practical. It may have ended up taking more time and more effort than the traditional film scoring approach.

Despite the high ambitions of the filmmakers, the movie was a box office failure and received poor reviews which often cited a confusing and unwieldy plot. *USA Today* film critic Claudia Puig called it "outlandish" as well as "loopy."[73]

Giacchino's music received many positive reviews. According to Jonathan Broxton of MovieMusicUK.com, the score "is full of life and energy, developing organically from within itself, like a concert piece, moving in a direction dictated by its own internal structure, rather than by edits within the picture, or the need to hit certain beat points within a scene."[74]

From Symphony to Film to Ballet

Despite the dismal critical and audience response to *Jupiter Ascending*, Michael Giacchino's music would live on and serve a new purpose. It was used to stage a ballet in 2018. Choreographer Kyle Davis asked Giacchino if he had any short concert works that could be choreographed for the Pacific Northwest Ballet (PNB). The composer suggested his *Jupiter Ascending* score. Since it had been written in the style of a symphony, it had the structure and musical unity of a concert piece.

Davis loved the music and instantly began work on a ballet that would be called "A Dark and Lonely Space." It featured 25 dancers representing the cosmos. "'A Dark and Lonely Space' conceptually began with the idea that the anthropomorphization of the birth of a planetary system could shed light on human behavior."[75] PNB musical director Emil de Cou described it as "sort of a sci fi ballet with a huge orchestra, double chorus (sung from the side balconies) and solo soprano on stage atop of something that looked like a huge planet."[76]

"A Dark and Lonely Space" was performed by the Pacific Northwest Ballet at the Seattle Opera House on November 2, 2018. According to journalist Gemma Alexander, the ballet was far from subtle, but that was a good thing. Alexander wrote,

> I can appreciate subtlety, but it's not really my native language. "A Dark and Lonely Space" speaks my language. It's not just the theme that's cosmic in scale. Everything about this ballet is big. There's a full cast of dancers and

125 musicians performing the music. Besides the full orchestra in the pit, the 60-some singers of the Pacific Lutheran University Choral Union fill the auditorium's box seats. Soloist soprano Christina Siemens hovers over the stage like a goddess or a sentient sun.[77]

The Martian

A more traditional film scoring process was embraced for another space film released that same year. Based on the bestselling novel by Andy Weir, director Ridley Scott's film adaptation of *The Martian* was released in October 2015. It told the story of American astronaut Mark Watney, accidentally stranded alone on the Martian surface. Through his tenacity and ingenuity, he survives by growing potatoes and eventually devises a plan that could return him to Earth.

To score this majestic film, Scott called upon Harry Gregson-Williams. Gregson-Williams had worked for years with Scott's brother Tony, but had also scored Ridley's *Kingdom of Heaven* (2005). Ten years later, the *Martian* script was left in his mailbox with a note from Ridley: "Read it! Love it! Do it! And don't fuck it up!"[78]

Gregson-Williams did read it and did love it and was determined not to "fuck it up." That summer, he visited Scott's home in the south of France. "He was in the process of cutting the film together and already it looked like a winner to me," recalled Gregson-Williams.

> It was clear that it was going to be a huge musical challenge. The film was in great shape, but at this point lacked the unique emotional beat that often a musical score can deliver. With Ridley Scott movies—as with his brother, Tony—there's something unique about how their movies flow and how they kind of suck up music. Almost begging for the score to bring things together.[79]

Scott had a reputation for having complicated relationships with some composers (most notably with Jerry Goldsmith during the production of *Alien*), but Gregson-Williams had a positive and constructive relationship with the director. Rather than providing specific musical ideas, according to Gregson Williams, "Ridley will flood you with his enthusiasm and joy for his characters and the story he wants to tell."[80] They watched a long cut of the film and discussed the fact that there was no human villain; the closest thing to a villain was the planet Mars itself. But they did not want a dark musical depiction of Mars. In fact, they wanted to highlight the grandeur and awe of the planet. "It was not to depict Mars as the big baddie, but more as the majestic, unflinching Red Planet that was capable of destroying their dreams and their lives."[81]

Scott provided a temp track to clarify his initial musical vision. According to Gregson-Williams, "Sometimes one is blessed with a serviceable temp track that does okay for the movie, and on this one I was quick to see it wasn't too damn good so that I couldn't beat it!"[82]

There were two essential characters in *The Martian* that Gregson-Williams needed to effectively capture musically. The first was the planet itself. The next challenge was finding the right sound for the character of Mark Watney, and how he interacted with Mars. Gregson-Williams:

> [Watney's] optimism for life, his love of science and problem-solving that he always seems to be able to handle with humor and charisma—all this should be reflected in the music. There's no reason for the music to be too dark for too long in this film. And that was quite a revelation, to begin with, because I had thought there would be a lot of darkness and despair. He's only hanging on to a tiny thread of belief that he could live. But for the most part, this is a guy who's up for the challenge.[83]

Nonetheless, it was still challenging finding the proper music to capture this. Scott pointed to a scene where Watney departs the relative safety of his habitat and travels hundreds of miles across the alien Martian landscape. With very little dialogue and featuring grand vistas on Mars, the scenes provided the composer with a magnificent musical canvas. Gregson-Williams recalled,

> In the middle of this big music moment was a very poignant and beautifully written monologue where [Watney] tells us that he is the only person to ever have been on a planet alone. There's a certain fear in his voice, but there is also joy and wonder. That was a critical kind of moment. If I could nail that

Mark Watney (Matt Damon) views the Martian landscape in the 2015 motion picture *The Martian.*

moment, it would inform the rest of the score that I would write around it. So that's where I started. That's where I created the main theme.[84]

Having decided upon the core of the sound, Gregson-Williams now wanted to ensure that the score conformed with another requirement: what it looks like on the manuscript paper. "I like to write music down on manuscript in order to be able to look at its contours—the way a melody moves, these leaps—the upward strokes"[85]—in this case, using open fourths and fifths. Since Watney remained optimistic and humorous through most of his adventure, his character's melody would always be "stepping up" and have a certain uplift to it. "Not be too heroic or too joyful, but literally, if one looks at the music one can see that there is plenty of upward movement depicting his hopeful and optimistic nature—the music is often giving you a certain levity."[86]

With the scene occurring midway through the film, Gregson-Williams had to determine: "How did we get to that point? We're not going to play this melody like that at the beginning of the film. It's something that had to evolve as the film unfolds."[87]

Throughout his composition process, Scott provided input, but not in the form of direct criticism or suggestions. "Ridley likes to talk about music conceptually," recalled Gregson-Williams. "He usually starts with a few questions—as opposed to dictating the path that we should go. He might say, 'Is it a little fast underneath Watney standing still on this hill? Is there a little too much movement?' Which basically means, 'There's too much movement, Harry!'"[88] Having been to art school, Scott phrased things utilizing visual arts terminology. "He will often describe to me something he's looking for in terms that mean something to him from the art world, so he might listen to a cue and say, 'I love the textures you're using. I think we could use a slightly darker shade here though.' He'll liken things to colors. He is clearly a visual thinker."[89]

To create these musical textures, colors and contours, Gregson-Williams needed more sounds than could be produced by a traditional orchestra. He integrated synthesized sounds, guitar, harp, keyboard and numerous other sounds to supplement the orchestra. "It's really a hybrid," he stated. To create variations with the Watney "upward strokes" theme, he used several instruments including piano, alto glockenspiel and an autoharp to create new colors. At one point, the piece gains more weight as a string ostinato begins and is interweaved with the theme. All combined, according to the composer, "There was a humungous orchestra we used in Abbey Road, Studio One—we probably used 90 pieces."[90]

There is a moment in the film where Watney says, "I'm going to science the shit out of it." In response, Gregson-Williams wrote a musical cue called "Science the Shit Out of It." "It seemed to me that what was needed within the sonic tapestry of his theme [was] a hybrid of synths and modern sounds combined with the gravitas that only an orchestra's classical sound can bring."[91]

As was the case with his previous score for the animated film *Shrek*, *The Martian* featured a significant number of pop songs. In *The Martian*, these songs played a more integral role in the plot than the ones in *Shrek*. As described in the original novel, the songs help Watney maintain his mental health during his time on Mars. The stranded astronaut listens to musical selections and television shows that his fellow crew members had brought with them. To Watney's dismay, the music was largely comprised of disco. In one scene, he passionately states, "I'm definitely going to die up here if I have to listen to any more god-awful disco music." According to Jonathan Broxton of MovieMusicUK,

> It may seem incongruous to see the broad, lush vistas of an alien world underscored with that type of music but, oddly, it works, and some of the songs—notably Donna Summer's "Hot Stuff," Thelma Houston's "Don't Leave Me This Way," David Bowie's "Starman," ABBA's "Waterloo" and Gloria Gaynor's "I Will Survive"—are on the nose in terms of the way the lyrics perfectly describe Mark's state of mind at the time.[92]

These songs had been integrated into the film's plot from the beginning of production, and therefore they presented no significant challenges to Gregson-Williams. In fact, the pop selections often informed Gregson-Williams' key selections or were echoed in the score itself.

In contrast to *Jupiter Ascending* (released eight months earlier), *The Martian* was a box office and critical success. Gregson-Williams' effective score both heightened the desolate grandeur of Mars and helped define Mark Watney's struggles, loneliness and never-failing optimism. Nevertheless, as strong as the composers' efforts were on *The Martian*, the film was musically dominated by disco.

***

Space Television in the Twenty-Teens

The twenty-teens saw the appearance of the space-based shows *The Expanse*, *Killjoys* and *Dark Matter*. These shows adhered to a musical mold with more similarity to *Firefly* and the new version of *Battlestar Galactica* than to *Star Wars* or *Star Trek*.

Premiering in 2015 on SyFy, *The Expanse* was one of that period's most successful space-related shows. Based on a series of novels by James

S.A. Corey, *The Expanse* was developed by Mark Furgus and Hawk Ostby, best-known for their screenplays for *Children of Men, Iron Man* and *Cowboys & Aliens*. Several hundred years in the future, human civilization has expanded throughout the solar system, but this was not to be the utopian society of *Star Trek*. In keeping with human history, tension, conflicts and suspicion pervade these new branches of humanity.

Clinton Shorter, who had written scores for *District 9, Pompeii* and *Gibraltar,* was hired to put this expansive human future to music. "This was a bit of a weird one," recalled Shorter. "I got hired without a phone call or meeting. They requested a demo and then I was told I was hired. When we talked about it one day mid-season, the producers thought that one of them had spoken to me and found it quite funny that I hadn't spoken to any of them."[93]

Shorter and showrunner Naren Shankar spoke extensively about how the show should be scored. *The Expanse* would feature high-end special effects and complex plots portraying these future distinct human cultures. Said Shorter:

> Originally when I was asked to demo they wanted a really ethnically diverse-sounding score, but as time went by as they produced the first episode they realized it would make more sense to have the source music [background music that is part of the scene] give it the world music sound and have my score use elements of world instruments but not be guided by them.[94]

Thus Shorter was able to score the episodes based on what he believed the scenes required; he did not need to create exclusively exotic or even alien sounds.

As usual, the opening theme music played a substantial role in setting the mood and expectations for the show. Shorter wrote a haunting and ethereal song for a female vocalist that was simultaneously uplifting and melancholy. Singer-songwriter Lisbeth Scott performed the song and also wrote the lyrics in what she called "future Norwegian." As explained by Scott in a Facebook post, "I wanted to reference the beautiful Norwegian language ... note the word reference! So below are the words I used and a very rough translation of their meaning! Clinton Shorter wrote a gorgeous and inspiring piece! ...All of you from Norway, feel free to laugh and cry at my lack of proper syntax and grammar, not to mention pronunciation!"[95]

Shorter and Shankar also determined that it might become too convoluted if the show featured too many character-driven themes. Instead, the main theme music serves as the basis for some of the major characters. Shorter said,

> I have a theme for Naomi and Holden (in my eyes they represent what we hope that universe will become). There's another theme from those same main titles

that I've used for Season 4 quite a bit. There is a theme for Miller, and the Martians; we settled on ethnic-sounding instruments for the Belters along with chimes and bells. I created some esoteric sounds for the protomolecule.[96]

As the show progressed from season to season, "the motifs got bigger," according to Shorter. "There are new ones that show up with the new characters, and you figure out how to combine them. You figure out how to make them larger and smaller. How to fracture them when a character breaks down. How to combine them when people team up."[97]

During the progression of the show, the role of music vs. the role of sound design became more clearly defined. According to Shankar, "In the formative episodes … we wanted big sounds in space. We didn't want to do the silent, Kubrick deal, because we wanted to convey big heavy ships, powerful rockets, impact hits from weapons." This was the case with both sound design and music. As the show evolved, they often let music take a more central role. According to Clinton Shorter, "the gold standard for me was the movie *Gravity*. They took the approach that you wouldn't ever hear sound design in space. Those elements would be scored."[98]

One of the most effective cues using this approach occurred in the Season 2 episode "Home," in which the asteroid Eros (which contains a base infested with the protomolecule) starts to inexplicably hurtle towards Earth. The Miller character searches the Eros base, trying to discover why Eros was now moving of its own accord. To his surprise, he finds Julie Mao at the center of the Eros base. Miller thought that she had died in an earlier episode, but now realizes that she has now become "one" with the protomolecule and is trying to go home to Earth; not understanding that if she (and Eros) reaches home, Earth will be destroyed. Miller removes his spacesuit, breathes in the protomolecule and convinces Julie to plunge Eros into Venus, presumably killing them both.

While the scene does not take place in the vacuum of space, Shorter's score compellingly carries the scene, driving the emotional content and standing in for sound design. Shorter composed a string quartet to accompany this scene and determined that he needed to hire real musicians. While they normally would not have the scoring budget for this type of live recording, Shorter recalled thinking, "If we're going to do this right, we're going to do this right in London at Air Studios." However, when he heard the final recording, he realized, "Oh my God! I did this in the wrong register. It's just too high a pitch for me…. I wanted it lower—to be deeper—to have more gravity to it."[99] The problem was, they had used the entire scoring budget (which was already much larger than a typical episode). Shorter decided to use his own money to re-record the piece, and he was pleased with the new recording. The register was much better and the string sounds "totally opened."[100] The end result was both expressive and somber, effectively elevating the visually stimulating and emotional scene. It was a good example of Shorter's ability to score the drama and emotional content rather than focus on the science fiction aspects of the series.

The two other 2015 premieres, *Killjoys* and *Dark Matter*, also deviated from the grand orchestral sound. As *Killjoys* series co-composer Jim McGrath noted, they were trying to achieve "an edgy, electronic, gritty vibe that supported the action and badass attitude of the main characters, as well as the quirky comic touches and emotional parts of the stories."[101] He added that this was achieved using "a lot of analog synth textures and aggressive, abstract percussion sounds"—but this was also combined with more traditional orchestral elements such as strings, low brass, choir effects and some orchestral percussion (snare drum, gongs, timpani).[102]

McGrath's co-composer, Tim Welch, preferred to create new sounds using guitar pedals and synth filters, but he would occasionally re-sample "these new sounds and [manipulate] them again during the composing process. I also have several unusual custom instruments from such builders as Folktek and Togaman GuitarViol, as well as some of my own creations thrown together from old instrument parts and trips to the hardware store."[103]

Benjamin Pinkerton's *Dark Matter* music was also striving for an edgier sound, with heavy use of electronic and rock sounds. These musical styles worked well within each show, supporting the plot and character development, but it is unlikely that the music from either show will be referred to as models of "space music" in years to come.

The Orville

An ambitious newcomer entered the space TV arena the same year that *Star Trek: Discovery* premiered (see "The Return of *Star Trek*"). In many respects, the Fox Network's *The Orville* reflected the look and feel of *Star Trek: The Next Generation* far more than *Discovery*.

In 2017, Seth MacFarlane launched *The Orville*, his homage to *Star Trek*. Initially advertised as a comedy in the style of *Galaxy Quest*, the show quickly revealed that it was something unique in science fiction television. While it contained some outrageously comical moments, the show was essentially a space-based drama that addressed complicated social issues. According to Will Harris of *The Verge*, "As early as its third episode, *The Orville*'s creators were offering allegorical, politically relevant plotlines."[104]

Over the previous decade, MacFarlane had written and produced the animated TV series *American Dad* and *Family Guy*. In 2014, his passion for space exploration inspired him to co–executive produce a reboot of the *Cosmos* series that had been hosted by Carl Sagan in the 1980s. MacFarlane partnered with the famous astronomer's wife and partner Ann Druyan to create *Cosmos: A Spacetime Odyssey*, hosted by Neil deGrasse Tyson (see "The Music of Real Space").

MacFarlane next wanted to produce a new space-based series that was not dystopian, but much more reminiscent of the optimism of the first two *Star Trek* TV series. According to MacFarlane, "What's missing is a utopian version of that—where's the blueprint for the way things could be?"[105] He wanted *The Orville* "to do big fun stuff, big sci-fi premises and action, and also be able to tell a story that takes place in a bottle, that's really about the human experience. Allegorical science fiction does play an important part in this show."[106]

This may have come as a surprise to Fox. Jonathan Frakes of *Star Trek* fame (who also directed some *Orville* episodes) called MacFarlane "a genius. He's quite a renaissance man and because of all the money he made from *American Dad* and *Family Guy*, Fox gave him this opportunity to make *The Orville*—and I don't think they knew that it was going to be as wonderful and dense and non-silly as it is."[107]

MacFarlane wrote and produced the show and also starred as Captain Ed Mercer. Mercer had let his life fall apart after finding his wife Kelly in bed with a blue alien. Out of guilt, and faith in his command ability, she arranges for Ed to take command of the *Orville*, with her as first officer. The show had a similar look and format as *Star Trek: The Next Generation*.

MacFarlane is also passionate about the music that accompanies his productions. He wanted to make certain that *The Orville* was supported by the best orchestral scoring possible. He said:

> With a lot of shows it tends to be wallpaper, but Spielberg showed us better than anybody that music can be a character in a show if you really embrace it and let it shine. I think a lot of directors tend to be scared of the score—either ignorant or scared. As a result, you see a lot of really boring music on television and in film....[108]

For MacFarlane, the proper music is as important as special effects and acting. According to Frakes:

> Seth's musical relationships and the scoring is a huge part of it, and he has his hands deep in that cement. His eyes light up when he's going to the scoring stage.... He knows exactly how he wants the show to be made so you don't roll on that show unless Seth's in the room. He knows the framing he wants—the timbre—the tone—camera placement.... It's the curse of his genius.[109]

MacFarlane described the power of music to transform a scene with an example from the original *Star Wars*:

> There's that scene in *Star Wars*, where Luke is looking out at the two suns, and it takes its time, and it's a really gorgeous piece of orchestral music. I always look to that scene as something that is woefully lacking in what directors are doing in the genre now. They just don't know to leave that space—and to have confidence in the fact that once the music is in there—you're going to be fine. You don't have to go at this kinetic pace. Just take a breath and let the composer do their thing.[110]

MacFarlane hired three accomplished composers to score his new series. The first was Bruce Broughton, who had been writing music for TV and film for over 40 years, including the original *Hawaii Five-O, Dallas* and *Young Sherlock Holmes*. Broughton had recently started working with MacFarlane on a Hollywood Bowl concert and on one of MacFarlane's studio albums.

Broughton was assigned to write the theme music and the score for the pilot episode, establishing the initial musical signature to the series. The theme would be a large and dramatic orchestral piece, that Broughton said was "a fitting way to do a sci fi theme."[111] A big opening theme was important to both Broughton and MacFarlane. Most modern television shows do not have the long opening music that was used in the past. Network shows often use just an opening musical riff or short musical statement. MacFarlane wanted a one-minute opening theme. According to Broughton, "The titles are one of the ways that you bring people back from the refrigerator.... You can go back to a TV show 20, 30, 40, 50 years ago and hear some of these themes and you know exactly what that's representing. The option to be able to do that again, now, was really great."[112]

As for the main score for the pilot, MacFarlane gave very specific instructions. According to Broughton, MacFarlane said, "Your job is *not* to play the comedy. Your job is just to play the drama. We'll let the comedy take care of itself."[113] MacFarlane provided a temp track to help guide Broughton, but told the composer, "You don't need to do any of this. I'm just putting it in as a guide for the tone of the scene...."[114] The temp track was comprised largely of Broughton's own cues for other projects as well as compositions by Jerry Goldsmith.

Using a 75-piece orchestra, Broughton produced an uplifting score, often using variations of his main theme, such as the grand moment when *The Orville* leaves the space dock. In many respects, this scene echoes the USS *Enterprise* leaving drydock in *Star Trek: The Motion Picture* to the accompaniment of Jerry Goldsmith's grand theme.

MacFarlane initially hired two additional composers, Joel McNeely and John Debney, for the weekly scoring of the show, then added composer

Andrew Cottee to help cover the musical load in Season 1. However, Debney and McNeely remained the primary composers for the show's first three seasons. Both had enjoyed long and successful film–TV careers. Debney's credits included *Iron Man 2, The Greatest Showman* and the TV series *American Odyssey.* McNeely had scored *Air Force One* and *The Young Indiana Jones Chronicles* and had worked with MacFarlane for over a decade, scoring *A Million Ways to Die in the West* and *American Dad* episodes. McNeely also assisted MacFarlane with his debut studio album "Music Is Better Than Words" in 2010 and helped produce five additional albums/

McNeely knew what he was getting into. MacFarlane is a highly accomplished musician with an awareness of the essential role of film and TV scores. When asked about MacFarlane's input on *The Orville*, McNeely stated, "It's all encompassing. He's very knowledgeable about film scores. He's kind of encyclopedic. He has very specific ideas about what he wanted. When I see it for the first time, it's already got his ideas about what he's looking for."[115] Extensive mockups follow, and MacFarlane typically provided detailed input on what he liked and did not like. This process continued throughout the recording sessions, with the *Orville* creator completely attuned to how the score integrated into each episode, and whether it was conveying the proper emotional content or musical motivations.

This type of musical oversight has the potential to cause friction between composers and creator, but in MacFarlane's case, the process appears to work well. Said McNeely, "It is unique—because of his extensive knowledge of scores—but I would say in the long run, it makes it easier, because the show is his vision from script, to direction, to shooting style. …So, when you're working with someone who has a very specific idea of what they're looking for, it does make things much easier."[116]

This clarity also helped the composers to deal with their substantial workload. Even with three composers and three to four weeks to compose each score (more than a typical TV series), it was a monumental task to complete the music for every episode. Each score is a complex symphonic composition of at least 30 minutes—often more. The show literally required a symphony-scale score for every episode with orchestras that ranged from 70 to 90 players.[117] "It's really unheard of in television," said McNeely. "That would be impossible if not for Seth's passion for scores. Even for *American Dad,* which is a half-hour animated series, we have a 35-piece orchestra—same with *Family Guy.*"[118]

Despite MacFarlane's input, McNeely needed time to establish confidence. "It took me a good portion of Season 1 to figure out what I wanted to do. By the time we got into Season 2, I felt much more comfortable with the musical narrative and felt like I had a vocabulary to draw on."[119] He added, "We started off stylistically referencing Jerry Goldsmith music—which was very intentional—and hopefully very respectful. Toward the end of the second season, we started incorporating more of a wide palette."[120] The plots and special effects became more sophisticated in Season 2 and this was reflected in the music, with heavy influences from John Williams (including references to the *Star Wars* trilogy and *Indiana Jones*), David Arnold and other composers. The overall musical production of the show was helped by the fact that an extra six to eight minutes were added to the overall episodes in Season 2. This was a result of how the commercial breaks were structured. According to MacFarlane, this extra time was *not* dedicated to expanding the plot but focused on "imagery that lets you take a breath and take in the set or the visual effects work and the music. …It was hugely transformative for the show."[121]

The production became even larger in scope in Season 3 when the Hulu streaming service picked up the series. Redubbed *The Orville: New Horizons,* the show was no longer subject to the tight show run limits of network television. Without these limits, the episodes were as long as they needed to be to tell the story. This included the opening theme.

In a time when many shows (particularly network shows) were phasing out long opening theme music, MacFarlane doubled down. Season 3 featured a more spectacular montage, with a revised version of Bruce Broughton's theme—this one lasting 90 seconds—expanded from the 60-second original theme.

Season 3 was also very challenging. The set had to close because of the COVID-19 pandemic. McNeely was ambivalent regarding how this unprecedented situation impacted the music production. They were accustomed to having 90-plus musicians crowded into a room—and even if they were able to do that, masks would be a substantial problem for wind and brass instruments. According to McNeely,

> For *American Dad,* I've been scoring it remotely where I have all the musicians playing their parts at home. The whole orchestra is playing their parts from home without hearing the other orchestra members. It works remarkably well, but it's not something we could do with *The Orville* because the music is much more complex—the cues are much longer.[122]

In the tradition of *Star Trek: The Next Generation, The Orville* occasionally featured musical performances by the crew members or other musicians. This included the youngest cast member. Dr. Claire Finn's youngest son Ty is a piano prodigy. During a Season 2 episode, "A Happy Refrain," Ty plays Chopin's Étude Op. 10, No. 3, in E major for the *Orville* crew. Later in that episode, the *Orville* hosts a concert by the Union Symphony in the cargo bay, with the stars in the background. This was not

The "Union Symphony" plays for the crew of the Orville in *The Orville*.

just a "make believe" orchestra: MacFarlane arranged for the Hollywood Chamber Orchestra to portray the futuristic musicians. As the romance between Dr. Finn and Isaac grows, they watch the concert as the orchestra plays the "MGM Jubilee Overture." The piece, written for the 30th anniversary of MGM in 1954, features a medley of well-known songs, most prominently "Singin' in the Rain."[123]

Lt. Gordon Malloy, the ship helmsman, sings and plays the guitar in several episodes, and performs a vocal duel with Ensign Charlie Burke in Season 3's "Twice in a Lifetime."

The series has also included excerpts from *The Sound of Music* and *The King and I*, and an episode where Billy Joel music becomes the soundtrack for Captain Mercer's emerging love affair with Lt. Janel Tyler (later discovered to be a Krill named Telaya). Perhaps most prominent was Dolly Parton's "Working 9 to 5," which becomes an anthem for the existence and liberation of Moclan women. MacFarlane was so passionate about this musical anthem and storyline that be began a quest to have Parton appear on *The Orville*. Show executive producer Jon Cassar recalled, "Seth was virtually a dog with a bone on this one, there was no way he was giving up on Dolly, no way at all. Finally, he got her to say yes and she was excited about doing it."[124] But tight COVID restrictions were then in place, and Parton did not want to get on an airplane. MacFarlane and his crew found a solution. According to a July 21, 2022, Tweet by MacFarlane, "Fun fact: Dolly and her side of the cabin were filmed in Nashville, while Heveena's side was filmed in L.A."[125]

The Orville's commitment to quality and power of music may exceed any other recent television show. This can be quantified by the fact that the show regularly retains three respected composers who are given the rare opportunity to write for an orchestra of 90-plus musicians. This commitment to music is attributable directly to Seth MacFarlane. As composer John Debney stated, "This is the best gig one can ever imagine as a composer because Seth is always saying, 'How high can we jump?' And he says, 'Jump higher!'"[126]

Cosmos

As mentioned earlier, MacFarlane was instrumental in rebooting *Cosmos*, the classic documentary series about the wonders of the universe. The original series aired in 1980, a 13-hour Public Broadcasting Service series with Carl Sagan providing a guided tour to the universe. That series featured the latest science and visual effects, and relied on music to help tell the epic story of the cosmos. The show was co-created by Sagan's wife and partner, Ann Druyan.

From the earliest conception of the show, music was going to play a major supporting role. "It began in 1978 when Carl Sagan, Steve Soter and I were conceiving the original *Cosmos* series," recalled Druyan. "Music was very important to us. Carl and I had just finished working on *Voyager*. We wanted [*Cosmos*] to be equally moving, affecting, persuasive to the brain, to the eye, the ear, the heart. Every story had to move you at all those different levels."[127] (See "The Music of Real Space" below.)

The series was accompanied by an album, and according to liner notes written by Sagan, Druyan and Steven Soter,

> The musical content of *Cosmos* seemed to create a message of its own—almost as though it were the collective intelligence of the universe pleasantly calling our attention to the lessons at hand…. Finding the music for *Cosmos* was in itself a voyage of discovery. We hope you will share in that experience, enjoy the music of this album and then sample the original works from which these pieces were excerpted. It was always our intention in *Cosmos* that the images and the music would be as important as the words, and that the series would speak to that part of us in which the heart and mind are one.[128]

Cosmos introduced most audiences to the music of the Greek composer Vangelis. Sound designer Kent Gibson had found Vangelis' distinctive song "Heaven and Hell" and it served as *Cosmos*' opening music. The series also featured other works by the composer, as well as a mix of classical and electronic music.[129]

In 2011, MacFarlane teamed with Druyan and Soter to produce a new version of *Cosmos*. Music was again an essential element of the series. "Seth McFarlane played a substantial role. There would be no *Cosmos: A Space-Time Odyssey* without him," stated Druyan.[130]

Unlike the 1980 series, the new series hired a composer to produce an original score for every episode: Alan Silvestri, who had scored such films as *Back to the Future, The Polar Express* and *The Avengers*. He had also written the score to *Contact*, based on the book by Sagan and Druyan. According to Druyan, "[W]e were very happy with the job that he did [on *Contact*]. Seth had become a friend of Alan's. Seth really wanted a lavish, lush musical score that would have that same transporting power that the original had—so he brought Alan on board."[131]

Regarding the score for the new *Cosmos*, Druyan stated,

> I didn't want it to be triumphalist as certain space operas can be—that sounds like we're conquering something. The music had to be imbued with humility. We're just finding our way. We're very young, very small, very ignorant in the face of the grandeur of the Cosmos. Science is a means to begin to understand where and when we are—and how the Cosmos came to be … the German word is Sehnsucht—"a longing"—a little bit of loneliness, but also a sense of the great beauty of searching.[132]

Dune

> "Wherever you have a goat, and you have a piece of wood—all I want to say is the goat better watch out, because he's probably going to end up being a bagpipe."—Hans Zimmer

In 1984, noted director David Lynch adapted the Frank Herbert novel *Dune* into a major motion picture—presumably to take advantage of the continuing interest in big space films in the post–*Star Wars* era. The film met with miserable reviews. Roger Ebert quoted a friend as saying, "It doesn't make any sense, and the special effects are straight from the dime store, but if you give up trying to understand it, and just sit back and let it wash around in your mind, it's not bad"—giving it one star.[133] The musical score did not fare much better. Composed by the rock band Toto, the music was given only mediocre reviews.

The public did not warm to the film either, resulting in a box office disaster. The movie had cost approximately $40 million to produce, and generated roughly $30 million in box office receipts.

Thirty-seven years later (2021), a new adaptation of *Dune* was released, this time with much better results. Denis Villeneuve, director of such films as *Arrival* and *Blade Runner 2049*, took on the challenge.

He was a huge fan of Herbert's book, a story about a human civilization 20,000 years in the future (long after humanity has left Earth). A young man named Paul Atreides and his family of the House Atreides are sent to the harsh and arid desert planet Arrakis. The planet is a source of "spice," which enables faster-than-light travel, but it's also a psychotropic drug. Within this backdrop, the Warner Brothers plot summary stated, "[M]alevolent forces explode into conflict over the planet's exclusive supply of the most precious resource in existence; a commodity capable of unlocking humanity's greatest potential; only those who can conquer their fear will survive."[134]

Villeneuve knew that the sound and music of the film would be as critical as the casting, acting and special effects. "When I decided to do *Dune*, I decided that I really wanted to create a new soundscape—and I was in need of a composer," he related. "I asked Hans Zimmer if he knew *Dune*, the book, and Hans answered that it was one of his favorite books of all times—and it was one of his biggest dreams to score *Dune*."[135]

Zimmer is one of the most successful film composers of the past several decades, having scored such films as *Gladiator, Pirates of the Caribbean* and Villeneuve's *Blade Runner 2049*. Zimmer knew the job of scoring the new *Dune* would come with a large amount of pressure and great expectations. Herbert's *Dune* was one of the most popular science fiction novels ever written and the previous motion picture adaptation had been a disaster. Zimmer had been so passionate about one day scoring *Dune* that he had never watched the 1984 film, listened to the Toto score or watched the television adaptation. He wanted to keep his ideas fresh in his mind.

To ensure the success of the film's musical elements, they began brainstorming new ways to interpret the novel musically, in a manner that was new and alien, but also emotionally effective. According to Zimmer, he and Villeneuve shared the same vision for the film. Zimmer noted, "As soon as we started, we were transported back in time ... and I did music with the recklessness and craziness that only a teenager has. Just whatever came to me. And one of the other things was that it's hard to explain musical concepts, but we'd finish each other's sentences, because we have both been making this movie in our heads for 40 years."[136]

Zimmer took an entirely different approach than the "John Williams" model of film scoring: He did not heavily rely on traditional western orchestral instruments. The core of his musical score revolved around female voices. "We're telling a story in multidimensional ways," he commented. "We're using voices and a language you don't understand; and at the same time somehow you understand emotionally ... The one thing we thought would be true through any culture would be the voice. The score is based on many female voices...."[137]

In a separate interview, Zimmer expanded on this: "One of the major themes of the book was the power of women. We were dealing with a culture that was extra-terrestrial. I felt that the only thing that should be pure—and even that shouldn't be quite pure—was the voice. I was trying to do the inner voices of the characters, without using words."[138]

The film begins with a non-female voice—a deep, guttural, presumably male chant. It does not sound entirely human. Zimmer revealed that vocalist Michael Geiger's voice was fed through a compressor "to reduce dynamic range—the span between the softest and the loudest sounds," to get the harsh, brutal and alien tone. "I had of course completely transformed his voice into something that was more like a cannonball hitting you in the head."[139]

According to Geiger,

> Just my opinion as a voice actor, but you might think of the [Sardaukar] throat singing sounds in *Dune* not as "language" but as an encoded military battle chant; a specific series of syllables with the consonants purposefully removed to render the remaining vowel sounds discernible only to the Sardaukar. The result of millennia of phonemic abbreviations meant to obfuscate a hidden message. Other examples of this might be huddle or line audibles from a football quarterback or a drill sergeant counting out a marching cadence. It sounds incomprehensible because it's meant to.[140]

The chant is translated on screen. Its meaning: "Dreams are messages from the deep."

In keeping with Zimmer's musical vision, a fanfare does *not* follow, as it would have in so many space dramas of the past. A high-pitched drumbeat and short burst of ethereal music sound in the opening sequence. Then a slow, pulsing rhythm begins, almost like a heartbeat, as a female voice says, "My planet Arrakis is so beautiful when the sun is low." According to Zimmer, "By putting that voice there as opposed to hearing the beautiful fanfare of a European orchestra, you instantly knew we were going to tell you a story that was dark and mysterious and different, and you couldn't quite work out was it human or was it beyond humanity?"[141] With this and other music in the film, he was also trying to evoke spirituality, but not in a traditionally religious manner—something that sounded alien.

To achieve the overall musical feel, they traveled the world collecting new and exotic sounds; inventing instruments and encouraging musicians to learn how to create new sounds from their existing instruments.[142] "I actually went into the desert," recalled Zimmer. "There was a moment when I disappeared into Monument Valley and the desert in Utah and Arizona to check the veracity of my ideas. How does the wind howl through the rocks? How does the sand grit [*sic*] in your teeth? It's just vastness and endlessness."[143]

The powerful main female vocal parts were performed by prominent rhythm vocalist Loire Cotler, who is able to produce remarkable rhythmic sounds with her voice. According to Zimmer, "*Dune* has its own rhythm. So, it's obvious that I would find a woman who should know everything about rhythm, and then give you the cry of a banshee.... There's a strength. There's a force that hits you."[144] Darryn King of the *New York Times* wrote that her voice "comes through like a war cry, all ancient, melismatic syllables in unsettled rhythms.... Stylistically, Cotler drew on everything from Jewish niggun (wordless song) to South Indian vocal percussion, Celtic lament to Tuvan overtone singing. Even the sound of John Coltrane's saxophone was an influence."[145]

Not all instruments were alien. The bagpipe was used to herald the arrival of House Atreides. According to Zimmer, bagpipes are not just "Scottish, Celtic, or Irish, but I know that there are Caledonian ones and Spanish ones and Middle Eastern ones. Wherever you have a goat, and you have a piece of wood—all I want to say is, the goat better watch out, because he's probably going to end up being a bagpipe."[146] However, the initial bagpipe does not sound exactly like the terrestrial instrument. The sound is created by an electric guitar, but then 30 bagpipes begin to play as well, producing an enormous sound. According to King of the *Times*, "Ear protection had to be worn: the volume reached 130 decibels, the equivalent of an air-raid siren."[147]

The final score was one of Zimmer's most unusual and innovative. "Even something that sounds like brass could be an electric guitar or electric cello, manipulated electronically," wrote Jon Burlingame. "Unusual woodwinds like the Armenian duduk or Scottish bagpipes occasionally peek through, but many sounds are from specially commissioned instruments and new synthesizer modules."[148]

A musician plays a bagpipe as the members of House Atreides arrive on Arrakis in the 2021 film *Dune*.

What makes the production more extraordinary is the fact that it was produced during the COVID-19 pandemic. As such, many of the musical performances were recorded from the singer's homes or even closets.

2020s and Beyond

The appetite for space-related content appears to be expanding, with new productions materializing frequently. These productions are too numerous to describe in detail, but the scope, production value and musical accompaniment continue to rise to new levels, particularly in television.

Apple TV is producing two ambitious space series. In 2019, the alternate history drama *For All Mankind* premiered, speculating what would have happened if the Russians had beaten the United States to the Moon in 1969. In short, the unexpected Soviet victory stimulates a decades-long extension to the space race resulting in the establishment of Moon bases and humas on Mars.

Jeff Russo and Paul Doucette score this series. Over the first three seasons, original music by Russo and Doucette features both intense and majestic cues, but the musical tone of the show is often driven by the popular songs from each time period, used effectively to convey the feel of the new decade. Combined, music elevates both the texture as well as the emotional and historical core of the series.

Another Apple TV offering is a TV adaptation of Isaac Asimov's *Foundation* series of novels. Bear McCreary did not get the job of composer through the usual process. He was offered the job at his daughter's birthday party. Showrunner David S. Goyer was attending that party and told McCreary that he had secured the rights to Asimov's story. According to McCreary, "My head exploded. My imagination went into overdrive at my kid's party."[149]

What he came up with was unlike his previous scores, approaching the musical underpinning of the story from two distinct perspectives. One is character-driven, emotional music. The other perspective is music based on mathematics to musically define psychohistory, a key element of the story. To achieve the mathematical portion of the score, he worked for over a year with composer–sound designer Jonathan Snipes to create software that would help bring the mathematics to life. According to McCreary, "I crafted an 'orchestra' of sampled instruments playing dazzling patterns of algorithmically generated musical notes that would be virtually impossible for human beings to play."[150] Nonetheless, a live orchestra remained the core musical ingredient, featuring big, sweeping cues.

This combination of the intellectual approach of composition intermingling with the emotional approach is a crucial element of the score. "One without the other wouldn't work in *Foundation*," said McCreary. "If it was just mathematics represented in music, it wouldn't resonate with you; and if it was just melodies and emotion, and didn't have a sense of mathematics, it wouldn't feel like *Foundation*."[151]

A popular video game has also been the inspiration for a space-related TV show: *Halo*, premiering in 2022 on Paramount+. Composer Sean Callery was hired and told by the producers that they were looking for new themes, textures and colors to expand the sound beyond the video game. Callery also needed to musically connect the show with the musical sound of the game. The show's main theme was a mix of the old and the new. Callery stated, "The very opening of the Main Title contains the first line from his iconic original theme (performed by solo cello and female vocalist Lisbeth Scott), and then segues into my Master Chief theme."[152]

The show features a significant amount of music, upwards of 35 to 40 minutes in an episode. These scores required a sizable orchestra, vocalists and chorus, plus some electronic sounds. While the show may have been inspired by a video game, the scope of the show and the music supporting it are substantial in scale.

✳✳✳

As the pace of real space activities accelerates, it is likely that space-related content will continue. However, the sound of space will also inevitably change as these stories become less and less the realm of science fiction, and reflect reality. Humans living and working in space will build their own, new musical sound that will almost certainly be reflected in film and television scoring. Nonetheless, the infinite scale of space and the expanding renaissance of space-related content will inevitably provide an extraordinary canvas for composers to express themselves and define the sound of space. Bear McCreary perhaps best described this phenomenon: "The science fiction genre in particular is special to me because I do think that it actively makes the world a better place by making people think about what could be."[153]

10

Star Wars Returns

With the turn of the twenty-first century came the return of a legendary franchise: *Star Wars*. Rumors had circulated since the end of the original trilogy regarding the prospect of prequel films. It was not until the 1990s, and the advancements in CGI technology, that George Lucas moved forward with a new trilogy. The world got a sneak peek at the impact of CGI and other new techniques within the *Star Wars* franchise in 1997, when a Special Edition of the original trilogy was theatrically released. Lucas had updated many of the scenes that had bothered him for 20 years because he lacked the technology in 1977 to fulfill his true vision.

Two years later, on May 19, 1999, after a 16-year hiatus following *Return of the Jedi*, *Star Wars: The Phantom Menace* was released. Directed by Lucas, the story takes place 32 years prior to the events of *Star Wars: A New Hope*. The prequel follows Anakin Skywalker's road to becoming a Jedi Knight, and eventually falling to the Dark Side of the Force—becoming Darth Vader. The plot primarily focuses on the relationships between Anakin and three other characters: his teacher Obi-Wan Kenobi; his love interest Padme, whom he secretly marries, resulting in the birth of Luke and Leia; and Chancellor-Emperor Palpatine, who lures Anakin to the Dark Side.

After the unprecedented success of the original trilogy, expectations were extremely high, including for the film's music. The original movies had literally transformed filmmaking and the expectations of what film scores could and should be. Thus, there was little doubt that John Williams would be invited back to score the new films. Williams was quite cognizant of the pressure, but calmly stated, "Rather than assume anything, I just have hope. I hope that they will enjoy it, that they will be moved by it...."[1]

The composer recalled that, after he and Lucas spotted the *Phantom Menace* music, "I went away, and four months later, I came back with two hours of orchestral music to accompany the film."[2] The score was not written in a linear manner, from beginning to end, however. He started the score in the middle of the film. "I wanted to find the human aspect of the story before going to action sequences," Williams said.[3]

Williams explained that about 90 percent of the music was new, the rest legacy music from the original trilogy. This ten percent was critical for the continuity of the films, and also as a tool to trigger an emotional and nostalgic response from the audience.

Once the *Phantom Menace* score was complete, Williams turned to the same orchestra with whom he had recorded the original trilogy, the London Symphony Orchestra. Rather than again recording at Anvil Studios, they recorded 120 minutes of music at the famed Abbey Road Studios. To Williams, the partnership with the London Symphony Orchestra was like uniting an old family, but also a reminder of how much time had elapsed. "I have had members of the London Symphony Orchestra say to me. 'We started studying music twenty years ago only because we heard *Star Wars* and then we wanted to play it in the London Symphony Orchestra when we grew up. And here we are playing on the soundtrack of the new film.'"[4]

The Phantom Menace, Attack of the Clones (2002) and *Revenge of the Sith* (2005) received mixed reviews from critics and fans, but Williams' music transcended the disappointing response. His new compositions received significant praise, enabling him to expand his impressive library of leitmotifs, motifs and other supporting music. As stated by Maurizio Caschetto of the John Williams Fan Network, "The glue that tied these new films to the old ones was essentially the music of John Williams. In fact, the composer returned to the film series virtually picking up the pencil from where he left it in 1983, aware of the quite singular occasion of further expanding his own musical glossary."[5]

Themes and Influences

As noted earlier, Williams drew on his legacy themes from the original trilogy to create continuity and to help develop characters and the plot(s) as they approached their outcomes. The most recognizable legacy music that Williams used was the opening fanfare ("Luke's Theme"). As it had in the original films, the big, brassy fanfare (preceded again by the 20th Century–Fox fanfare) served as both the opening music and began the initial portion of the closing music for all three prequel films. Luke Skywalker only appears as an infant in the final moments of *Revenge of the Sith*, but the music is also a reminder that *The Phantom Menace* is an essential part of Luke's backstory—and represents the ongoing struggle to defeat the Dark Side.

More integral legacy themes were woven throughout the film and overall prequel trilogy. The Force theme was essential to the progression of the prequel films. This music does not represent an individual or situation, but musically encapsulates the *Star Wars* theology. All nine films of the story arc center on the ongoing struggle between the light and dark side of the Force; thus the Force theme is heard in various forms in each film. One of the first examples occurs in *The Phantom Menace* as Qui-Gon explains to Anakin's mother Schmi that the Force "is unusually strong in him." A full but subdued expression of the well-known leitmotif plays as they discuss Anakin's special gifts. Many "story years" later, this musical signature was used during a far more dire scene, "Battle of the Heroes" in *Revenge of the Sith* (see below). With an ominous chorus singing in the background, its short treatment of the theme is heard on horns. This time, it is not subtle, but sounds strained as though the "light" side of the Force is under assault.

The Emperor's theme also returns in *Attack of the Clones* and *Revenge of the Sith*. This was a logical decision by Williams. As Palpatine slowly and carefully ascends to power and eventually becomes the Emperor, the theme (first heard in *Return of the Jedi*) emerges over these two films portraying the seductive, scheming and emotional path to power. For example, in *Attack of the Clones*, the Emperor's theme sounds as Anakin tells Padme that he killed every one of the Sand People responsible for his mother's death. Anakin is emotionally teetering between the dark and light side of the Force, and the music amplifies the growing influence of Palpatine in his life. Later in the film, a more potent rendition sounds, with a male chorus countered by a chilling siren-like female vocalist, as Lord Dooku meets with Darth Sidious. (The audience knows that Palpatine is Darth Sidious, but this is not known by the Jedi yet.)

Williams again demonstrates his mastery of subtle variations at the end of *The Phantom Menace*. During the final parade on Naboo, "Augie's Great Municipal Band," a seemingly joyful song, is sung as they celebrate defeating the Trade Federation. The song is based directly on the Emperor's theme, musically manipulating it to appear to be an expression of joy and triumph as Palpatine views the festive occasion. Mark Richards stated, "Although the song's cheerful tone expresses the jubilation of defeating the Federation, it is also an ironic statement that, through the subtle reference to the Emperor's theme, has sinister connotations."[6]

Williams slowly unveils "The Imperial March" as the plot unfolds through direct references and variations. For example, a short direct expression of "The Imperial March" sounds when Yoda tells Obi-Wan Kenobi, "Grave danger I see in [Anakin's] training." The brief expression provides a haunting reminder that there is danger and tragedy coming in the future. The grandest, most complete rendition of the theme occurs at the end of *Attack of the Clones* as Palpatine watches thousands of Clone Troopers board Star Cruisers as they go off toward battle. Even when Anakin becomes Darth Vader, the music is expressed in a more somber and subtle manner.

As noted earlier, the legacy themes only represented approximately ten percent of the music in *The Phantom Menace*. The rest was new, and Williams developed some memorable themes to support the new characters and circumstances. One of the most memorable of the new compositions was a powerful chorus piece, "Duel of the Fates." While Williams had used a male chorus in *Return of the Jedi* to amplify both the sinister and mysterious aspects of the Emperor, he uses a full chorus for the first time in the *Star Wars* franchise to powerful effect in "Duel of Fates." The piece is quite reminiscent of "O Fortuna" in the first movement of Carl Orf's 1936 cantata for chorus, orchestra and soloist, "Carmina Burana." Williams' visceral composition provides musical intensity as Qui-Gon and Obi-Wan Kenobi engage Darth Maul in a mesmerizing lightsaber battle. Williams wanted to capture a ritualistic-pagan sound to reflect the rise of the Dark Side of the Force. Unlike the wordless chorus he had used for the Emperor's theme, he believed text was needed to achieve the maximum impact. He turned to the epic Celtic poem by Cad Goddeu, "The Battle of the Trees," from Robert Graves' *White Goddess*, one of Williams' favorite books.

In an interview, Williams recalled the English translation of the poem: "Under the tongue root a fight most dread/While another raging, behind, in the head." Williams clarified that "for no conscious sensible reason, the idea of a fight, something raging and imagined in the head more than anywhere, seemed to be a good mystical cryptic piece of business."[7] These words were then translated into Sanskrit to serve as a mysterious alien language that would be sung by the large chorus. Richard Dyer of the *Boston Globe* wrote, "88 professional singers from London Voices arrive to record two episodes with chorus. One is funeral music for one of the film's emotional climaxes; the other is for the closing credits, a terrifying, primitive pagan rite that makes even Stravinsky's 'Les Noces' sound tame. Lucas loves this dark, driven music so much he shows off the recording for Spielberg when he arrives."[8]

The piece first appeared in *The Phantom Menace* and resurfaces in each of the prequel films; and Williams had anticipated the visceral chorus piece playing a role in the battle between good and evil. "Williams really composed an oratorio that captures the spiritual combat for the soul of Anakin Skywalker," stated film music reviewer Tim Greiving. "In fact, back in 1999, Lucas envisioned this piece reprising in a big way for the climactic clash between Anakin and Obi-Wan in *Revenge of the Sith*."[9] However, "Duel of the Fates" was not used in the final battle between Obi-Wan Kenobi and Anakin. A similar composition, "Battle of the Heroes," provided the emotional underpinning to that climax. But "Duel" does accompany another epic clash between good and evil: It is heard during the lightsaber conflict between Yoda and Palpatine in *Revenge of the Sith*.

Williams produces subliminal musical messaging in the young Anakin's leitmotif in *The Phantom Menace*. What appears on the surface to represent the innocence of youth is what might be called a musical anagram. According to Emilio Audissino, "It's the kind of theme you would have for a young boy, very innocent, lyrical, and idealistic. But it's made up of intervals from Darth Vader's 'Imperial March.'"[10] Only if you listen carefully does the more sinister melody reveal itself. Maurizio Caschetto expanded on this:

> The composer explored the DNA of his own musical creations and pushed them to a further level, taking elements written twenty years earlier and intermingling them with completely new material—the theme for Anakin Skywalker, for example, is one of Williams' most Wagnerian pieces, not much in terms of language or style, but in the way the composer deconstructs one of the signature themes of the series … into an innocent melody for strings in which the fate of the protagonist looms dark in the background.[11]

The trilogy executes a time shift of ten years between *Phantom Menace* and *Attack of the Clones*. Anakin has become a young man and a full-fledged romance develops between him and Padme. Williams introduces "Across the Stars," a grand "forbidden" love theme representing the burgeoning love affair. This theme largely replaces the young Anakin theme in the second film. It represents Anakin's obsessive love and the lengths he is willing to go to protect Padme. According to Williams, "[Lucas] wanted me to write a real old-fashioned love theme, and that is one of the hardest things to do—to write something that is melodic, accessible, and direct, able to take the lead but also able to be heard as an accompaniment to dialogue."[12] Lucas added, "Their love is complicated—pure yet forbidden, personal but with profound ramifications for an entire galaxy. Somehow, John has managed to convey all of that complexity in a simple, hauntingly beautiful theme."[13]

The symbolism goes deeper than merely the use of a minor key. While not an exact reference, the progression of the melody is reminiscent of "Dies Irae." It is also composed in a Dorian Mode (playing all white keys from D to D) in which "Dies Irae" was written, assuring that the theme always contains a hint of danger embedded within the love story. The theme is interwoven throughout the second and third films of the prequel trilogy, but perhaps the most emotional and impactful use of this cue comes at the end of *Attack of the Clones*. As mentioned earlier, "The Imperial March" sounds in all its glory as Palpatine watches legions of Clone Troopers head off to the Clone Wars; but the scene then shifts to a secret wedding between Anakin and Padme on Naboo as Williams seamlessly transitions to a full expression of the forbidden love theme. The music amplifies their intense love, but also heralds the doom that awaits them.

The final major theme of the prequels is "Battle of the Heroes." In this final battle between Anakin and Obi-Wan, the two former friends engage in a precarious lightsaber duel over molten lava as Anakin completes his descent to the Dark Side of the Force. This intense orchestral and choral piece is quite reminiscent of *Phantom Menace*'s "Duel of Fates" and references multiple cues from the prequel film as well as the original trilogy. Williams biographer Emilio Audissino stated, "It features violent wordless chorus bursts and interweaves 'The Force Theme'—associated throughout the saga with the Jedis and the good side of the Force—with an ominous horn motif based on the medieval sequence Dies Irae."[14] Again, Williams hints at the Gregorian "Day of Wrath" in this final battle between good and evil in the prequel trilogy.

While Williams' music for the *Star Wars* prequel films did not quite reach the level of public adoration that had been attained by the original films, he was able to add to his growing body of astonishing and often subtle leitmotifs. He wove variations and expressions of those themes throughout the trilogy to add complexity and subtext that would not be present otherwise. As Mark Richards pointed out, Williams uses methods similar to those used by Richard Wagner over a century earlier. "Like the leitmotifs of a Wagnerian opera, understanding more about how the particular themes of a work are interconnected only enriches its meaning and thus heightens its importance and renders it a more integral part of the entire score."[15]

Star Wars Animated Shows

Three years after *Revenge of the Sith*, *Star Wars* began a new chapter on television. Rather than grand live-action motion pictures, the new stories were animated productions, starting with a film called *Star Wars: The Clone Wars*. *Clone Wars* had a theatrical release; after poor critical and box office showings, it ran on the Cartoon Network as the pilot episode of a new series. The series ran from 2008 to 2014 (with a seventh season in 2020). Later in 2014, *Star Wars: Rebels* began a four-year run.

Co–executive produced by George Lucas and Dave Filoni, *Star Wars:*

The Clone Wars was set in the time period between *Attack of the Clones* and *Revenge of the Sith*, as Anakin Skywalker is drawn closer to the Dark Side of the Force. *Clone Wars* was not to be a typical child-oriented animated series; it featured many dark and mature themes.

Scoring a *Star Wars* series, even an animated one, would be no small task. There would be huge expectations after six iconic films scored by John Williams. George Lucas began an audition process to find a composer equal to the assignment. According to composer Kevin Kiner, "I think there were about five composers who were given the first 15 minutes of what became the *Clone Wars* feature film."[16] After they all presented their proposed scores, Lucas chose Kiner for the new series. Kiner said, "It was definitely daunting, but it was also a great challenge. I felt like I rose to the challenge."[17] For Kiner, it was a dream come true, one that he had worked toward for several decades. Since the early 1980s, he had studied John Williams' full score for *Star Wars*. As a result, when he got the call to do the audition, "I was fairly prepared. I knew that music inside out. I knew what the sound of *Star Wars* was."[18] Kiner was the first composer after Williams to score a major *Star Wars* production.

Once on the job, Kiner made frequent trips to Lucasfilm in San Francisco to meet with Lucas and discuss how each episode should be scored. "George Lucas really likes to experiment. He likes to throw things against the wall and hopefully find something brand new," Kiner revealed. "When you do that, you've got to be willing to do stuff that doesn't necessarily work."[19] According to Kiner, Lucas was also willing to concede when a concept did not work.

While Lucas played a substantial role in this process, executive producer Dave Filoni played a larger long-term role in the production of the show and input on the musical sound of the series. Kiner recalled, "Dave Filoni grew up going to the opera. Dave really understands music and he understands classical music but in the modern sense; kind of like John Williams has a modern take on classical music." As a result of this knowledge and passion for music, Filoni frequently suggested musical ideas for episodes. For example, when a theme for Grand Admiral Thrawn needed to be composed for a *Star Wars: Rebels* episode, Filoni suggested the use of a pipe organ. Kiner said, "That's not an instrument that's really ever used in *Star Wars*, but that cue, and that theme, turned out to be a fan favorite." However, they did not use a real pipe organ, instead using an organ-sampled synthesizer, because according to Kiner, "the sampled ones sound fantastic."[20]

There was a philosophical difference between how Kiner would score *Clone Wars* vs. his scoring of *Star Wars: Rebels*. *Clone Wars* avoided too many direct references to John Williams' legacy music, relying heavily on new Kiner themes. Kiner was particularly proud of the Ahsoka theme. While a simple melody, it conveys wonder and emotion, as well as melancholy. "That was the first theme I wrote. …I used a Japanese flute called a shakuhachi just trying to feel her femininity but her strength, there's this light and there's a Darkness to her and there's both of that in her theme, you know?"[21]

Variations of the theme are used throughout the series, using contrasting instrumentation. Perhaps the most emotional variations occur in a cue called "Ahsoka Leaves," as Ahsoka quits the Jedi Order at the end of Season 5 in the episode "The Wrong Jedi." In this case, Kiner does use a Williams legacy theme: A heavy, lush string rendition of the Force theme is heard, followed by lighter emotional strings as she turns down Anakin's final plea to stay. "I'm really proud of Ahsoka's theme," said Kiner. "When Ahsoka leaves the Jedi order, that's a really emotional moment."[22]

Kiner approached the show in the same ways that he would have if it had been a live-action film. This included retaining a big sound. The show usually utilized at least a 70-piece orchestra (very unusual for any TV series), often recording in Prague or Budapest. However, by the end of *Clone Wars*, Kiner had transitioned to almost entirely electronic scores.

As they moved on to *Star Wars: Rebels*, a revised musical direction was adopted. Kiner said that at the suggestion of Dave Filoni, "we did a complete reset for *Star Wars: Rebels*….. Initially, George Lucas wanted me not to use too many of John Williams' themes in *Clone Wars*. It wasn't that he didn't like the themes, but he wanted *Clone Wars* to go in its own direction and to take on a life of its own. He wanted to explore new things."

Kiner recalled that when they started *Rebels*, there was a big meeting at Lucas' Industrial Light and Magic:

> Dave said, "Let's go and watch *A New Hope*." What we found was that there was a lot less music in the first few *Star Wars* films than you think. You really do remember the music because the melodies are so tremendous and the big moments are scored so beautifully and so memorably, but there's a lot of that film where there's just fighting sounds or sound effects or spaceship sounds or lightsaber sounds and no music at all. We pulled back on *Rebels* to have less music…. Then we started going back to the source. We've done six years of *Star Wars* music that's new. Let's go back to John Williams and mine some of that great material.[23]

Roughly 30 percent of the music in *Rebels* was Williams' music or was derived from Williams' music.

Some of these themes were direct quotes, but others were variations to suit the needs of the show. According to Culture Slate reviewer Apinya Wong, "In using Williams' famous leitmotifs, he pays homage to the previous generation of *Star Wars*. By adding his own elements to those familiar themes, he essentially updates it for the new generation."[24]

For example, in a cue called "Glory to the Empire," Kiner turns "The Imperial March" on its head. It becomes an upbeat, major key marching band song in which the Empire celebrates their awesomeness. Wong wrote,

> Kiner hastens its tempo just a tad, bringing the celebratory music closer to the tempo of Sousa's march. The prominent snare drums and cymbals complete the image of the Imperial troops marching along. The trumpets round out the fanfare. Even though the Empire does not apologize for nor hide its ruthlessness and brutality, that does not mean that it cannot create an image of prosperity and joy with its victory parade.[25]

Despite the philosophical change, Kiner still wrote a substantial amount of new music and themes for the new series. One new theme was the mesmerizing "Journey into the Star Cluster," occurring in the second season episode "Legends of the Lasat." Driving yet brooding fugue-like strings magnify the swirling of the star cluster. Soon an erupting chorus is heard, backed by a full orchestra. The piece was inspired by a composition by minimalist American composer Philip Glass, "Prutt-Igoe," which appeared in *Koyaanisqatsi* (1982), a documentary about economic refugees being moved to the Prutt-Igoe housing project in St. Louis. According to *The Star Wars Report,* this cue "has an underlying, hidden message in Kevin Kiner's choice to use this Philip Glass composition as inspiration for the Lasat journey to their new home."[26]

Star Wars Returns to the Big Screen—Again

There was a disturbance in the Force in 2012. George Lucas sold Lucas Limited to Disney for over $4 billion. With the completion of this deal, Disney attained ownership of *Star Wars*. As Lucas stated in a Disney press release, "It's now time for me to pass *Star Wars* on to a new generation of filmmakers. I've always believed that *Star Wars* could live beyond me, and I thought it was important to set up the transition during my lifetime."[27]

Episodes 1–3

With the acquisition of Lucas Limited, Disney produced new *Star Wars* films, including episodes 7, 8, and 9—the sequels to the original films. They also made both live-action and animated television adaptations. J.J. Abrams, who had brought new life into the *Star Trek* film franchise several years earlier, directed the first of the new films, *The Force Awakens*. Taking place 30 years after *Return of the Jedi, The Force Awakens* premiered on December 18, 2015. In the years since the Empire was defeated, the First Order rose from the ashes of that evil organization. This new villainous organization is led by a mysterious Sith lord, Snoke. Meanwhile, General Leia Organa oversees the Resistance, fighting the advances of the First Order who are trying to topple the New Republic. This task is complicated by the fact that Han Solo and Leia's son Ben has turned to the Dark Side, taking on the Sith name Kylo Ren. Luke Skywalker, who had been Ben's Jedi teacher, was so overcome with guilt over his failure that he banished himself to an undisclosed location in the galaxy.

In additional to Kylo Ren, several other new characters are introduced. This included Rey, a young woman who accidentally becomes involved with the resistance and discovers that she is strong with the Force. Also introduced is Finn, a former First Order Storm Trooper who joins the resistance after becoming disillusioned.

John Williams once again provided the musical soul of the film, but moviemaking had changed dramatically since the completion of the earlier trilogies. In those past films, Williams had screened nearly final cuts of the films prior to scoring the films. This enabled him to deliver the entire film score at once. With modern films, this method is increasingly unviable. In the age of digital filmmaking, edits (sometimes significant edits) are conducted much closer to a film's release date than ever before. According to Emilio Audissino, "Williams never saw the whole film in a more or less stable rough cut, but was given the film piecemeal."[28] As a result, he needed to write sections of the score in a similarly piecemeal fashion.

Recording the score also deviated from the original trilogies. The new scores were not performed by the London Symphony Orchestra. They were recorded on the Sony Scoring Stage (formerly MGM) by freelance members of the Los Angeles branch of the American Federation of Musicians (AFM 47), unofficially known as the "Hollywood Studio Orchestra."[29] Rather than recording the score over a few days, which had been the norm for decades, the score was recorded over months to accommodate the fact that the film was in a constant state of flux.

Always mild-mannered and polite, Williams was not agitated by the elongated schedule. He stated, "It was a wonderful way to spend six or eight months. Each day I got up to work hard on difficult music. Yes, it was long, but I always had a sense of being grateful—having the energy and interest to do it and to work with the orchestra, which was especially lovely."[30] In fact, the relationship between Williams and J.J. Abrams appears to have been seamless. According to Abrams, his only instruction to the composer was to occasionally suggest the mood or emotion that he was trying to achieve. Abrams revealed,

> [Williams] watches the cuts, goes to his piano, writes his music, then goes to the recording sessions, and only John has really heard it in his head. All of a sudden, with a stroke of his baton, these masterful musicians are playing something that sounds like they've been rehearsing it forever. It's the most miraculous part of the process.[31]

Staying true to his approach from the earlier films, Williams relied heavily on leitmotifs associated with the characters or significant plot elements to advance the story both subtly and non-subtly. In fact, as outlined by Frank Lehman in his *Complete Catalogue of the Musical Themes of Star Wars*, Williams introduced 22 distinct themes (13 of which are in *The Force Awakens*) in the sequel trilogy and reprised several legacy themes. "There are several references to the older scores, which we felt were obligatory," noted Williams. "But we also felt that we should have new material that was an extension of the collection or glossary.... And my task and my challenge was to make it feel friendly and related, interrelated, to the other scores, so that it feels comfortably *Star Wars*-ian, if you can use that word."[32]

As expected, the most prominent themes are focused on the key characters and groups. Williams took particular care in constructing the Rey theme: "[It] has a musical grammar that is not heroic in the sense of a hero's theme. It's kind of an adventure theme that maybe promised more—resolving itself in the most major triumphant resolutions ... I felt a lot of empathy for that girl, and I think Rey's theme needed to illustrate that."[33] Like Luke Skywalker in *A New Hope*, Rey knows little about her parents and is unaware of her connection to the Force. However, at the time of the release of *The Force Awakens*, it was also unclear whether John Williams (or even J.J. Abrams) knew yet that Rey would eventually be revealed to be the granddaughter of Palpatine. The *Star Wars* fan community points out that Rey's theme bears many similarities to both Darth Vader's theme and Palpatine's theme.[34] This was more likely a result of Williams' thematic unity that the composer provided between characters and between each film. Many of Williams' cues are musically related, enabling him to transition and interweave various pieces of music.

Another major theme within the sequel trilogy was for Kylo Ren, the son of Han Solo and Princess Leia. Trained as a Jedi by Luke Skywalker, he turns to the Dark Side. He aspires to equal his famous grandfather Darth Vader, but his lack of confidence hobbles him. "Unlike Vader's mechanically resolute and seemingly unstoppable grand march, Kylo's music is characterized by a swinging mood," said Emilio Audissino. "The 'official' motif that we hear as he acts in public is an ostentatiously evil five-note motto played markedly by assertive horns…. Yet it is the music of someone who *wants* to play the villain more than someone who *is* the villain."[35]

Kylo's imposter complex is projected through Williams' music. According to Frank Lehman, "[Kylo is] announcing himself, or the music is announcing his presence in this big and bold way, which sometimes feels musically overcompensatory, because, yeah, he's not Darth Vader. He doesn't get this instantly memorable 'Imperial March' theme that's so famous from the older movies. It's kind of a wannabe theme."[36]

Williams also reintroduces many of the most prominent themes from the earlier films, particularly from the original trilogy. Some legacy themes were interwoven into the score either as standalone statements or musically interacting with the new material. Alex Ross wrote, "Williams manipulates his library of themes with extreme dexterity, often touching on a familiar motif for just a couple of bars."[37]

All combined, *Star Wars* sequels movies contained an unusually large amount of music. For example, in *The Last Jedi*, using a 101-piece orchestra and the 64-voice Los Angeles Master Chorale, Williams recorded 184 minutes of music, much more than the length of the film. This volume of music was made necessary by the arrival of digital films. Since these films could and would be edited and manipulated with ease much later in the production process than ever before, the musical score would therefore need to evolve along with the film.

With films in a constant state of flux, there is no way that Williams or any other composer can conceivably accommodate the significant number of changes. As a result, the role of music editors has expanded dramatically. Williams relied on editor Ramiro Belgardt to help produce the full score, but there were other editors playing critical roles, including Paul Apelgren. According to Apelgren, "Ramiro could just focus on score production and I could focus on proof of concept in house as they were still trying to figure things out at the last minute."[38] This process took months rather than the few days it took on the earlier films, but it allowed the production to spread the orchestra budget over time and to enable changes as the final cut of the film evolved through the editing process.

With the 2019 release of *The Rise of Skywalker*, Williams completed his 42-year reign as the franchise's primary composer (although he would later write the theme music for the TV series *Obi-Wan Kenobi* in 2022). Looking back on this extraordinary period, Williams often emphasized that in 1977, when the original Star Wars was released, he had no idea there would even be a second film, so he did not set out to create a decades-long glossary of leitmotifs. Nonetheless, his contribution to the *Star Wars* franchise is almost certainly unprecedented. According to Williams, "This is a unique opportunity, where a composer can keep working on the same body of work and continue to add to it. What a privilege is that!"[39] Over the course of the nine films, the composer wrote over 20 hours of music; more than Richard Wagner produced in his epic *Der Ring des Nibelungen* (*Ring Cycle*).

This achievement came into focus on the final day of recording for *Rise of Skywalker.* "The day was loaded with emotion," said an orchestra musician. "People were aware of the significance of the day, and how historic it was." At the end, the orchestra and members of the production gave Williams a prolonged standing ovation.[40] An extraordinary period in film scoring history was now complete. Nevertheless, upon completing his final Star Wars film, he stated, "I'd be quite happy for it to go on indefinitely."[41]

Rogue One

Meanwhile, in its role as the new caretakers of the franchise, Disney was actively expanding the *Star Wars* universe. They committed to developing both film and TV projects, telling side stories and back stories to enhance the *Star Wars* mythology.

The first of these films was *Rogue One* (2016). Directed by Gareth Edwards, it was the first *Star Wars* films not focused primarily on the characters of the nine-film story arc. While *Rogue One: A Star Wars Story* briefly featured Princess Leia and Darth Vader, it tells the backstory of the operatives who stole Death Star plans just prior to the events of the original *Star Wars* film, *A New Hope*.

Rogue One was also the first *Star Wars* film that did not employ John Williams as composer, as he had already committed to scoring *Star Wars: The Last Jedi* (and some unrelated projects). Selecting an appropriate composer would be challenging. Candidates needed to be capable of providing the quality of music that audiences expected in a *Star Wars* film, and also needed to work under substantial pressure; Williams is a hard act to follow.

Gareth Edwards hired Oscar-winning composer Alexandre Desplat, with whom he had worked on the 2014 *Godzilla*. But *Rogue One* required significant reshoots that delayed the scoring and recording schedule. Since Desplat wanted to score Luc Besson's *Valerian: City of a Thousand Planets*, he dropped out of *Rogue One*, stating, "When you work in the *Star Wars* movie you have the shadow of John Williams over your head. There's no doubt that you'd be under a lot of pressure, but I knew that pressure because of when I did the last two *Harry Potter* films."[42]

This put Edwards and the studio in an extremely challenging

position. They needed an A-list composer who could write and record a full orchestral score in a short period of time. They approached veteran science fiction composer Michael Giacchino, who had written the music for the reboot of the *Star Trek* motion picture series in 2009. In an interview with *Entertainment Weekly*, Giacchino recalled being offered the job. "We were literally planning a vacation when I got the call.... At the time, it left me with literally four and a half weeks to write."[43]

Giacchino loved the film immediately. Despite the substantial time constraint, "I concentrated on how cool it was to be scoring a *Star Wars* movie." Giacchino also recalls that any doubts were put to rest on whether to accept the gig after speaking to his brother. "When I told my younger brother Anthony that I had gotten the job but only had a limited time schedule, he laughed and said, 'But you have been scoring that movie since you were ten!'—which was basically true since the original film had been so influential in choosing my career path."[44] In an *Variety* interview, he said, "When I was nine, I saw *Star Wars* and it set me on a path to where I am today. There was this need inside of me to make sure that this film felt like what I loved as a kid, as a fan, somebody who grew up playing with the action figures."[45]

According to Giacchino's colleague Paul Apelgren, a film editor,

> That's one of his strengths. He's able to work very fast at building a blueprint, because really it's an architecture when you're talking about a good film score. He's able to sketch things out very quickly [and then hand off to orchestrators]. He really doesn't do a lot of ghost writing.... He writes everything and if he doesn't, he'll give credit.... I think what Michael's strength is—since he's a filmmaker himself—is the storytelling aspect. Not just the sound of the score that's important. You're actually trying to tell a story.[46]

As he did on *Star Trek*, Giacchino focused on the story's emotional core as he wrote the music. He also noticed that *Rogue One* had clear similarities to some of the great war films. "*Rogue One* is like a really great World War II film with a huge heart and tons of sacrifice at the center of it. I wanted to make sure that I emphasized that angle."[47]

There was another significant requirement: Giacchino paid homage to John Williams, carefully referencing the legacy themes:

> It was a chance to play in this world that I loved, but also do my own thing. I wasn't compelled to use what had come before to any great extent other than what I felt was appropriate. I wanted it to feel like a *Star Wars* movie, of course, because what John did with those films is absolutely amazing— he was able to take from the past the things that he grew up with and loved— Holst and Korngold—all those influences are part of the DNA that the music has.[48]

This homage to Williams included using both the Force theme and "Imperial March" when appropriate in the storyline. The end credits also begin with the traditional "Luke" theme. However, in the short amount of time in which Giacchino had to compose, he could not even attempt to produce the number or complexity of original themes as Williams tended to write in each film.

Nevertheless, Giacchino was able to construct an uplifting and effective orchestral score using a 110-piece orchestra and 80-voice chorus. "I'd say the score is 95 percent original but with little moments [of Williams' classic score] here or there to accent," he noted. "If I were sitting in that seat and I heard that, it would totally raise the hairs on my neck."[49]

In addition to variations of some Williams themes, there was another connection to the composer in this film. Don Williams, John's brother, played timpani on the score. Giacchino had worked with Don on several other films. Since Giacchino incorporated a lot of timpani into the score, he decided to reach out to Don. "I texted him about a week before the [scoring] sessions," recalled Giacchino. "I said, 'Don … there is an F-load of timpani in this movie! And it's complicated and it's hard.' And he was just like, 'Let me at it.' I don't know that I've written more timpani for a film than I have for this."[50]

Rogue One demonstrated that there was a substantial motion picture market for new *Star Wars* stories. The film was released to strong reviews and made over a billion dollars in worldwide box office receipts. Vann R. Newkirk II of *The Atlantic* wrote,

> From its opening flute solo, *Rogue One*'s music announces the film as a full member of the canon—one that shares its sense of nostalgia with *The Force Awakens*. But there are differences. Deviating occasionally from the slow buildup and royal fanfares of previous *Star Wars* scores, Giacchino uses thriller violins and thumping percussion in the film's more action-oriented scenes.[51]

Giacchino reflected on this unique experience: "Being able to carry that forward into something like *Rogue One* was a blast. Would I have liked to have more time to do it? Yes, but in the end, I was just thrilled to be a part of it."[52]

Solo: A Star Wars Story

Two years after the release of *Rogue One*, *Solo: A Star Wars Story* appeared in theaters. Directed by Ron Howard (*Apollo 13, A Beautiful Mind, Cocoon, The Da Vinci Code*), the film tells the story of Han Solo's life ten years prior to the events of *Star Wars: A New Hope*. It was scored by John Powell, who was best known for composing for *How to Train Your Dragon*, the *Kung Fu Panda* films and the Jason Bourne franchise.

Han Solo was one of the only lead characters in the original *Star Wars* who did not have an *individual* theme. (He did have the Han and Leia theme.) For *Solo*, John Williams wrote two themes for Han. One of them, "The Adventures of Han," was described by Jonathan Broxton of MovieMusicUk.com as "a rousing, energetic piece full of trumpet triplets and rampaging string figures, built around a long-lined central melody."[53] Williams' second Han piece was described by Powell as a "Han searching theme."

"John Williams' involvement was actually a huge factor in my wanting to take this gig," said Powell. He continued:

> I have such respect—perhaps awe is a better term—for the musical history of this series that being able to have the film-scoring equivalent of Yoda be part of it was a massive incentive, and an obvious advantage that I could not let pass. The actual experience of being allowed to see into John's process? I couldn't imagine a greater gift.[54]

Integrating these Williams themes with his own music, Powell produced an energetic score, with heavy use of percussion. This includes a piece called "The Marauders Arrive" that also uses a female chorus to great effect. According to Broxton,

> The "Marauders" theme is primal, rugged and exotic, with *Avatar*-like female ethnic vocals atop a bed of imposing brass and percussion hits. These sensational chanted, whooping vocal ideas add a brand new textural dimension to the *Star Wars* musical canon, and combine perfectly with the immense orchestral forces Powell employs to underscore the conflict as the two rival gangs face off.[55]

Powell wrote several other original themes, including a romantic theme for Han and his love interest Qi'ra, a Chewbacca theme, and a theme for L3 (a droid).[56] All of this music was written to integrate with Williams' themes (new and legacy). According to Powell, "I tried to keep in mind the DNA of how John writes, which is flow and polyphony and melody, and of course an incredibly interesting rhythmic use of the orchestra." He recalled visiting Williams and consulting with him via phone: "He was incredibly generous, and very trusting of me."[57]

Despite an effective and rousing Powell score and generally favorable reviews, *Solo* was a box office disappointment. The lackluster showing was likely one of the reasons that the studio did not move forward on any additional *Star Wars* motion picture side-stories, and focused instead on TV productions.

Star Wars on the Small Screen

As previously mentioned, motion pictures are not the only live-action *Star Wars* content being produced by Disney. An ambitious progression of television shows is currently in production: *The Mandalorian, The Book of Boba Fett, Obi-Wan Kenobi* and *Andor*. Well-funded and high-quality, these shows delve into untold stories within the *Star Wars* mythology. And like the *Rogue One* and *Solo* films, none of these productions was primarily scored by John Williams.

The Mandalorian

The Mandalorian premiered in November 2019 on Disney+. Created by Jon Favreau and Dave Filoni, the show is essentially a space Western taking place five years after the time of *Return of the Jedi*. It follows Din Djarin, a Mandalorian bounty hunter hired by remaining elements of the Empire to find a 50-year-old infant named Grogu, also known as "Baby Yoda." However, instead of handing Grogu over to the Empire, he protects the child and is pursued by a villain named Moff Gideon.

The series has a far grittier storyline than the original nine films, and so a new musical sound was needed. According to Jon Favreau, "The Empire has fallen and chaos is beginning to reign in the galaxy, so the romantic strains of John Williams' score would not sit well against the imagery that we have."[58]

Ludwig Göransson, who had just scored the Oscar- and Grammy-winning music for *Black Panther*, was hired to take on the challenge of setting the musical tone and expectations for *The Mandalorian*. He approaches the music unlike any previous *Star Wars* composer. According to Favreau, "Ludwig has one foot in traditional score and another foot in technology, creating sounds that feel very musical even though he's using non-traditional methods and instruments to achieve that."[59] While some of the legacy characters appear in the series (particularly in Season 2), no John Williams legacy music is used.

For roughly a month, Göransson cloistered himself in the studio, coming up with new and exotic themes. According to the composer, "I was closed off for ten hours a day, just coming up with music and sounds, going from instrument to instrument." He added, "There weren't a lot of computers involved. It was just me playing, so it felt timeless."[60] The final product required a much more hands-on approach than is ordinarily embraced by film and TV composers. Göransson plays an exotic array of percussion, guitars, woodwinds and piano, recording many segments of the score with an ensemble of one: himself.

Since *The Mandalorian* is modeled on the American wild west genre, one of the major musical influences was the legendary composer of spaghetti western scores, Ennio Morricone. In fact, the show's main theme is clearly influenced by Morricone's score to *The Good, the Bad, and the Ugly*. That film starts with the famous recorder trill; Göransson starts with a similar recorder trill, but in his version, the trill is slowed down and uses a bass recorder. The rest of the theme evokes a gunslinger walking into town. It is plodding yet unyielding, with a pulsating percussion rhythm and piano. This segment was performed and recorded almost entirely by Göransson in his studio. The piece eventually grew into a full orchestra fanfare. According to Göransson, to embody "the soul of *Star Wars*," he supplemented his recordings with a 70-piece orchestra.[61]

Another, lesser-known Morricone film, *El Humanoide* (*The Humanoid*), was another one of Göransson's primary inspirations. Göransson commented, "I found this movie [*The Humanoid*] that looks exactly like *Star Wars*. ...So, this is Morricone's take on *Star Wars*. It's awesome. It's like these weird '70s synthesizers and he found some way to combine that with a disco orchestra. It sounds European and a bit Japanese."[62]

In contrast to the *Star Wars* films, *The Mandalorian* (as well as the other shows) does not begin with a grand musical statement. Instead, it starts with a simple expression of the main theme that is judiciously wielded and manipulated throughout the series. Full concert renditions of these pieces are heard during the end credits.

Göransson also wrote the main themes for the next *Star Wars* series to appear in 2021,

The Book of Boba Fett

Göransson was not be the primary composer for the next *Star Wars* TV series, *The Book of Boba Fett*, but he would set the initial musical tone for the series. This time, he composed a driving, unrelenting and foreboding piece with heavy use of strings, percussion and an energetic male chorus. The piece may have been influenced by a 1984 Swedish film called *Ronia: The Robber's Daughter* (*Ronja Rövardotter*) which featured similar Nordic chorus and rhythmic elements. As notes *Zanobard Reviews*,

> This semi–Nordish, folk-like style actually works quite well, boosting the already fairly memorable motif to get it to stick in your head pretty much immediately, while also establishing a unique musical style that differs considerably from Göransson's other main Mandalorian motif. Dramatic drums

and bursts of heroic brass occupy the background for much of the piece, giving the music overall an orchestral boost while also taking a bit of a backseat in order to let the vocals take the forefront.[63]

The primary scoring for the series was composed by Joseph Shirley, who had worked with Göransson and provided additional music for *The Mandalorian*.

Obi-Wan Kenobi

In 2022, *Obi-Wan Kenobi* premiered. In contrast to the other live-action shows, it was not a side story. It reveals the events of Obi-Wan's life in the time period between *Revenge of the Sith* and *Star Wars: A New Hope*. At the end of *Revenge of the Sith*, Obi-Wan leaves the infant Luke with his (Luke's) aunt and uncle on Tatooine, and leaves Leia with Senator Organa and his wife on Alderaan. The new show takes place when Luke and Leia are ten years old. Obi-Wan is now a broken man after ten years of living in the Tatooine desert and monitoring young Luke from afar, unable to make direct contact with the child. He learns that Leia has been kidnapped, forcing him to rise to the challenge of rescuing her and enabling him to find new meaning in life. Unbeknownst to him, Leia's kidnapping was part of a plot to lure him out of hiding. As a result, he comes face to face with his old apprentice, Anakin Skywalker—now Darth Vader. The new miniseries was directed by Deborah Chow, a veteran of two episodes of *The Mandalorian* as well as episodes of *Reign* and *Murdoch Mysteries*.

To score this series, Chow selected an accomplished violinist and composer, Natalie Holt. Holt had scored the Marvel series *Loki* as well as the TV series *Beecham House* and *Knightfall*. She was the first female to score a live-action *Star Wars* production—and not just any *Star Wars* series, but one that expanded the main story arc. "The pressure was kind of intense,"[64] recalled Holt. This pressure was exacerbated by the fact that Holt was juggling many challenges, including being the single mother of a young child and the fact that her father suffered a heart attack as she was scoring the series. As a result, according to Holt, "I didn't have time to think about the gender aspect of it."[65]

After a period of uncertainty regarding whether he would contribute, John Williams joined the production in January 2022. He provided the main theme—the Obi-Wan Kenobi theme—as well as a suite of music that would be integrated into the series. His participation opened the door for using legacy music in the new series, but they would only be heard in the sixth and final episode. To help integrate these legacy themes, a long-time

222 The Music of Space

collaborator of Williams, conductor-arranger William Ross, also contributed musical cues.

Despite the potential complications in sharing scoring duties with two other composers, Holt was excited that Williams came on board. "Looking at all the trilogies, Obi-Wan was one of the few characters that he's never written a theme for. For me, *Star Wars* and John Williams—it wouldn't be the same without him. It's so inextricably tied and emotionally, it is Star Wars with John Williams."[66] She also acknowledged that Williams was one of the people who inspired her to pursue a career in film scoring. "This is why I'm doing what I'm doing since I've been such a fan of [Williams] for so long."[67]

Holt described Williams' main theme as "contemplative, soulful, quite lonely and slightly angst-y, but there's a sort of hope, which is exactly what Deborah [Chow] had instructed."[68]

This Obi-Wan theme has a similar feel to the original Force theme. Like many of Williams' *Star Wars* themes, it is derived from the DNA of other leitmotifs throughout the extended *Star Wars* franchise.

At the time Williams committed to contributing music, Holt had already composed a significant amount of music. She had been working under the assumption that no legacy music would be used. According to the composer, Chow did not provide specific musical instructions. Chow did explain "what the through lines were, and what the characters should be doing in each scene."[69]

With no access to the legacy music until episode 6, Holt found alternate musical approaches to develop the musical story. She recalled, "It was difficult to find the right balance between old and new." Perhaps the most notable challenge was Darth Vader. "The Imperial March" would not be used until the final episode. To justify this, the story shows a Darth Vader who is still in conflict. Vader has yet to fully emerge as the confident Sith lord that we see in the original trilogy. He is hobbled by self-doubts and a desire to prove himself to his old master, Obi-Wan Kenobi. "I use a kind of rhythmic 'Imperial March.' I use the rhythm of it and used these horrible, guttural, emotive sounds."[70]

However, as the story approaches its conclusion, Vader reassures the Emperor that he has no conflict, no allegiance to Obi-Wan. "The Imperial March" sounds, signaling that any hold that Obi-Wan may have had on him has now been released. This segment was composed and arranged by William Ross. ("The Imperial March" was used in the prequels, theoretically undermining the rationale that the theme could not be used until episode 6.)

Holt also had to avoid using the Leia theme from the original films. Since the Leia of the *Obi-Wan Kenobi* series was a ten-year-old, it provided the composer with flexibility to try new sounds. According to Holt, "The young Princess Leia theme is quite contemporary.... It's quite driving. It's quite a departure from the adult Leia theme. Everyone wanted young Leia's theme to be full of energy and tonal variation and not like a Disney princess."[71]

Another challenge was the diverse and broad landscapes. The show takes place on multiple planets with a variety of cultures as Obi-Wan tries to bring Leia back to Alderaan. Holt set out to create sounds that would both establish a musical continuity but would also reflect the ever-changing cultural backdrop. "You want to find a kind of 'other' foreignness," stated Holt. "You wanted it to sound like a foreign planet, so it's like using the world instruments with such a twist" (so that it did not sound like traditional music of countries and continents on Earth). Holt continued, "I'm just interested in the story and making sure that music is helping to tell the story. When I'm working on a project, I always feel like I'm living it. I think that means I'm doing a good job that I'm getting so into the music that I feel like I'm in the story."[72]

Holt composed an Obi-Wan theme, but it was set aside when Williams came aboard. But the music was not discarded: It was re-purposed in a cue called "Hold Hands" and heard at the end of episode 4, when Leia reaches out and holds Obi-Wan's hand. According to Jonathan Broxton of MovieMusicUk.com, Holt's original Obi-Wan theme "[has] some coincidental similarities to what Williams eventually wrote, and appears to also have some structural derivation from the Force theme."[73]

Even in the final episode, legacy music is used sparingly. In a scene where Obi-Wan and Vader meet for the last time before their famous duel in *Star Wars: A New Hope*, one might have expected that they would use "Battle of the Heroes" or even "Duel of the Fates" from the prequel films; but Ross wrote a new piece for orchestra and chorus that is reminiscent of the battle between Obi-Wan and Anakin in *Revenge of the Sith*. Broxton noted that the piece "features a choral version of the Obi-Wan theme, searching string writing filled with deeply tragic emotions, and some experimental harp textures that recall the haunting cave sequence from *The Empire Strikes Back*."[74] However, in a cue called "Saying Goodbye," he uses outward expressions of the adult Leia theme and the Force theme as Obi-Wan and Leia say goodbye.

11

Star Trek Returns—Again

After *Star Trek: Nemesis* faltered in 2002, it was unclear whether the *Star Trek* franchise would return to the big screen any time that decade. However, one of Hollywood's fastest rising producer-directors, J.J. Abrams, brought the franchise back to life with the release of *Star Trek* on May 8, 2009. Over the previous decade, Abrams had produced such shows as *Lost* and *Alias* and the motion picture *Cloverfield*.

Abrams' *Star Trek* was the first *Trek* picture to feature an entirely new cast of actors playing the original characters. In order to create new storylines that would not conflict with the original canon, Abrams opted to establish an alternate timeline in which Romulan miners from the future blame Spock for the destruction of Romulus and seek revenge. The angry Romulans overshoot their intended time-travel destination year, appearing over 20 years too early. As a result, they cause the death of George Kirk, Captain Kirk's father (on the day of James T. Kirk's birth) and alter James T. Kirk's timeline. The Romulans are then forced to wait for a couple decades until they can pursue Spock and force him to view the destruction of Vulcan. Both events change the timeline, erasing most of the original stories.

To score the new *Star Trek*, Michael Giacchino was an easy choice for Abrams. Abrams and Giacchino had worked together for years on the TV shows *Alias* and *Lost*, establishing a strong friendship and symbiotic relationship. Giacchino has the distinction of being the first composer to score a *Star Trek* film since Jerry Goldsmith and *Star Trek: Nemesis* in 2002.

During a 2011 public "conversation" between the two friends, Abrams explained to Giacchino why he had such strong faith in him not only as a composer, but also as a true partner in the filmmaking process. Abrams commented,

> You're not just an incredible composer, which you are, but you really are a storyteller, and you're a filmmaker, and a writer, and producer, and structuralist

as much as anyone I've worked with. It's one of the reasons why I give you the scripts so early on—I talk about stories as I'm writing them. I show you the earliest cuts, because your notes, your suggestions, which by the way, completely inform how you're able to write scores, to get inside a story and connect with characters. The notes you give are as powerful and important and valued as anyone's.[1]

As has been the case with John Williams' *Star Wars* score, much of Giacchino's work was clearly inspired by Hollywood classic film composers such as Korngold and more recent giants, including Jerry Goldsmith and James Horner. Jon Burlingame observed this influence when talking to Giacchino in 2009 and wrote, "The composer's affection for the traditions of Hollywood film music is obvious, as every conversation is laced with references to classic scores, from *Kings Row* and *Peter Pan* to *Planet of the Apes* and *Star Trek II: The Wrath of Khan*."[2]

Star Trek presented a technical and emotional challenge to Giacchino. A *Trek* fan all his life, he was aware of the extraordinary musical legacy that he had to live up to. Failing to compose an impressive and appropriate score for such a high-profile film could potentially set back his career. For this reason, he found the task of scoring *Star Trek* even more daunting and challenging than scoring *Star Wars: Rogue One* several years later—even though he was given only four and a half weeks to complete that score. The composer recalled:

> I think I would have to say that *Star Trek* was more challenging because with *Rogue One*, I didn't have the luxury of time to worry about it. I grew up watching the old *Star Trek* series, and was so excited when J.J. asked me to do the music for the new movie. I thought: Now I have the opportunity to write some great space music! I actually started composing a year ahead of the film's release, but was having trouble coming up with themes that satisfied me.[3]

Coming up with a new *Star Trek* sound was not easy, said Giacchino:

> My original cues were written in the style of a "space opera," and it just wasn't working. I finally sat down with Damon Lindelof, one of the film's producers. Damon said, "Let's forget about *Star Trek*. The *Star Trek* movie we want to do is not a space movie. It is basically the story of how two men become best friends." Suddenly it was clear to me. The next theme I wrote was "Enterprising Young Men." That was the first cue, and it finally felt true to the *Star Trek* story that we wanted to tell. But I think it took about 15 tries![4]

From the opening notes of music, as the studio logos appear on the screen, it was clear that Giacchino would not be opening the film like most of the previous production. Most noticeably, he does not use Alexander Courage's theme at the start of the film, as every *Star Trek* film had since *The Wrath of Khan*. The main title sequence did not come until after the initial scene where George Kirk dies. The theme music is big and bold, but is only a short sampling of the full piece that is revealed as the film progresses. The opening music does not directly quote legacy *Star Trek* music but, according to Jonathan Broxton of MovieMusicUK.com, Giacchino does subtly reference earlier films: "Beginning with soft horns and a cooing choir in the opening *Star Trek*, it owes a tonal debt to both the softer moments of James Horner's *Star Trek II* and to Alexander Courage's original TV show theme.... The theme is liberally applied throughout the score, often as an action motif."[5]

Giacchino's musical approach contrasted with that which had been embraced in *Star Trek: The Next Generation* (and subsequent series) two decades earlier. His music was allowed to be more assertive. Michael Quinn of the BBC wrote, "Bustle, bravura and sheer bombast are the defining elements of Michael Giacchino's brass-led, percussion-driven, drama-fueled score that successfully re-defines *Star Trek*'s musical landscape."[6]

For Giacchino, however, the purpose of an effective score is not to be intrusive. "I tend to think of the music as one of the characters," he related. "It's sort of that character that sits there and gently nudges you and says, 'You need to feel this' or 'You need to notice this.' It's sort of the subtext of everything that is going on."[7]

Giacchino effectively fuses the original Alexander Courage theme with his new music during the end credits sequence. Jonathan Broxton opined:

> Giacchino works several enormous orchestral re-statements of Alexander Courage's main theme into the fabric of his underscore. What's most impressive is how seamlessly the two themes merge together, as if both have flown from the same man's pen: the prancing, anticipatory string line which often precedes the bolder statements of Giacchino's theme brings Courage's theme to new life, and the way in which Giacchino intercuts between the two is a wonderful conceit, as if musically alluding to the two generations becoming the same.[8]

Giacchino had written some highly respected scores before his work on *Star Trek*, but 2009 was a transformative year for him. His *Star Trek* score showed that he could write powerful orchestral music for a blockbuster film, but he also demonstrated his musical range that year. He won an Academy Award for his subtle, emotional, and quirky music for the Pixar film *Up*.

Star Trek Returns to Television

Following *Star Trek: Enterprise* in 2005, the question of when or if *Star Trek* would return to TV was on the minds of fans. This was, after all, a mere three years after *Star Trek: Nemesis* had effectively driven the final nail into the *Next Generation* motion picture series. However, as had been the case in the wake of the release of *Star Trek: The Motion Picture* in 1979, after J.J. Abrams successfully brought *Star Trek* back to the big screen in 2009, anticipation grew regarding the prospect of a new *Star Trek* TV series. Finally, in September 2017, 51 years after the original *Star Trek* series, *Star Trek: Discovery* premiered on CBS All Access (a streaming service that later became Paramount+).

Created by Bryan Fuller and Alex Kurtzman, the series takes place ten years prior to the time of the original *Star Trek* series. Rather than being set on the *Enterprise*, this show follows the crew of another starship, the USS *Discovery*. The show begins when Commander Michael Burnham inadvertently starts a war with the Klingon Empire. For this serious *faux pas*, she is court-martialed and demoted, but is eventually sent to serve on *Discovery*, which has an experimental "spore drive" that can instantaneously transport the ship anywhere in the galaxy. (*Discovery* was the first live-action *Star Trek* series to feature a black female in the *lead* role.)

As with every manifestation of *Star Trek*, the music was an extremely important element. The fanbase was (and is) extremely sensitive to how a *Trek* show musically sounds. After several composers were considered, Jeff Russo was selected to take on this high-pressure assignment. His musical career started as a member of the rock bands Tonic and Low Stars; from there, he moved on to writing music for dozens of TV series, including *Extant*, *CSI: Cyber* and *Lucifer*.

According to Russo, when he met with the producers, "I had a musical idea and they agreed with my musical idea. Their ideas and my ideas were in lockstep. I think that was one of the reasons why I got the gig."[9]

As a result of this alignment of musical concepts, Russo did not receive much instruction from the producers:

> I put forth my own base idea of scoring. I like to score what a character is feeling rather than what a character is doing. Applying that to this particular type of music was and is very effective in how the narrative is propelled by a score. There are action scenes and swashbuckling adventure sequences that get a proper type of score, but I try never to be completely on the nose with it. That makes for something a little more subtle and a little more grounded.[10]

Russo was also cognizant of the musical legacy of the show. He stated, "*Star Trek* has a sound … and I utilize that. The brass and the horns." But he also wanted to introduce new elements to the *Star Trek* musical catalogue, such as using more electronic instrumentation, while always being very aware that he "inherited the *Star Trek* sound."[11] This was important to the composer, because he was a lifelong *Star Trek* fan. He revealed:

I was a late teenager when *The Next Generation* came on the air—and that was my introduction to *Star Trek* as a series. I'd seen the movies, but I hadn't watched the original series until after I watched *The Next Generation*. Music is important in the way we tell the story and the way we utilize the emotional context—especially in this new version of it—especially in this new version which I think is more grounded and emotionally contextual storytelling.[12]

One of his first tasks was the composition of theme music—music that would hearken back to the legacy *Star Trek* sound, but with a new spin. Russo brainstormed with the producers to find the correct balance between the harmony of the Federation, but also that reflected the conflict with the Klingons as well as internal conflicts with the crew. According to Russo, "Yes, people fight, but the overall theme is that we're all one. What could I do to embody that in music?"[13] Russo recalled that he used Alexander Courage's original theme as much as he could "because it's fantastic. It's an amazing piece of music. It's iconic and it gets you there. Immediately...."[14]

According to Jon Burlingame of *Variety*, Russo's theme "combines an air of mystery, a propulsive rhythm and a hopeful feeling while reminding viewers that it's all still *Star Trek*."[15]

As Russo approached the musical content, he focused on the characters. "I try to tell the story from a character perspective," he stated. "I end up with themes for different characters and different relationships between those characters."[16] This includes themes for the Klingons, for Michael Burnham (portrayed by Sonequa Martin-Green) and her relationship with Captain Philippa Georgiou (portrayed by actress Michelle Yeoh) and other cast members.

Russo also added to the cultural depth of alien cultures in the *Trek* franchise. In the episode "Vaulting Ambition," the composer imagined alien opera—specifically Kasseelian opera. Deep in a coma, Lt. Commander Stamets has a transcendent moment in his subconscious mind. Sitting with a projection of Dr. Culber, his husband and fellow crew member, who had been murdered in an earlier episode, Stamets reconciles his feelings, saying, "Computer, play Kasseelian opera. The aria he loves, the one I hate." Russo wrote a haunting aria that was sung by Ayana Haviv. The music becomes the soundtrack for the emotional reunification between Stamets and Culber. As the opera climaxes, they kiss and Culber says, "Follow the music, Paul. Look for the clearing in the forest. Open your eyes." Just then, Stamets awakens from his coma.

At the end of the Season 1 finale "Will You Take My Hand," *Discovery* receives a distress call from a Federation ship. Just as they realize which ship issued the distress call, the USS *Enterprise* comes into view and Season 1 ends with Alexander Courage's theme, supported by the vocal talents of Ayana Haviv. To assure maximum impact, and to show respect for this iconic piece of music, Russo used the original Courage score, but made it bigger, adding more strings and brass. According to the composer, it was an emotional experience. "That theme, that particular fanfare, when you hear the first note, you don't even have to hear the second note to know something about the sound of the trumpet playing that particular note. You just know what it is."[17]

Star Trek: Picard

Three years later came a new show that continued the story of one of the most popular characters of the franchise, Captain Jean-Luc Picard. Premiering on January 23, 2020, on CBS All Access (later Paramount+), *Star Trek: Picard* takes place 20 years after the events of *Star Trek: Nemesis*. Admiral Picard had retired from Starfleet years earlier in frustration after he rescued the Romulan people from annihilation by a planet-wide natural disaster, and in the wake of a violent uprising of synthetic lifeforms on Mars. Now residing at his family vineyard in France, Picard is visited by a young woman named Dahj. He soon discovers that the woman is not only an advanced android, but also the daughter of his former crewmate Data. After she is killed by Romulan agents, Picard learns that Dahj has a twin sister, Soji. The retired admiral then sets forth on a new adventure to find Soji.

Once again, Jeff Russo was called upon to score this series. As with his work on *Discovery*, Russo knew that blending heritage music with a new sound was essential, and it had to be executed perfectly. According to Russo, "I wrote the theme from the perspective of wanting to acknowledge what came before—and wanting to acknowledge how we'll move forward. Some of that is a nod to Goldsmith's theme at the very very end of it. A little nod to Chattaway music.... And the feeling of [Picard's] emotional growth ...."[18] This nod to Chattaway linked directly back to flute music that the earlier composer had written for Picard in the "Inner Light" episode. As mentioned earlier, Chattaway had written two flute themes. For *Picard*, Russo uses Chattaway's alternate theme as the basis for the *Picard* opening music.

In contrast to his *Discovery* theme music, Russo's *Picard* theme, as well as the music for the entire first season, was more individual and reflective. Russo said, "the show itself is a little more contemplative. I did approach it from that perspective. It's definitely a smaller score. ... A little more specific—as opposed to being generally broad and swashbuckling. I approached from Picard's perspective. His feelings. His emotional context."[19]

Russo's full-length opening theme music also helps to preserve a potentially dying art. Theme songs have been on the decline on network TV for years, many shows having dispensed with the classic musical introductions that were synonymous with weekly TV series for decades. Instead, many shows tend to have short riffs or motifs that last only a few seconds, displaying only the series logo. According to Russo, "I think networks are more concerned with how much time they spend, and how much time they can sell advertisers."[20] However, streaming services do not have the same restrictions, often not constrained by the exact episode lengths that the networks do. "They only really have the thought of how they can keep people watching," observed Russo. "I definitely think that theme music for shows is something that's very important to drawing lines between one part of a narrative and another, and keeping viewers engaged."[21]

While the *Picard* music is more subtle and reflective, the orchestra sizes of *Picard* and *Discovery* are comparable. Russo explained, "It's just a matter of how I utilized the instrumentation. There's a little more in the way of solo instrumentation in *Picard* than there is in *Discovery*."[22]

The main theme helps to thematically define *Picard*, but there are other characters and narratives that needed to be defined musically. In Season 1, the Romulans played a significant role and Russo reached back to the original series for his inspiration. "In the first episode, I tipped my hat to Fred Steiner's Romulan theme from the first time we see Romulans in the original series," recalled Russo. "Little things like that are extremely meaningful for people who are long-time fans."[23] The once unstoppable villains the Borg play a central role in Season 1. However, with these new Borg, resistance is definitely *not* futile. According to Jonathan Frakes, Russo helped to musically define these emasculated cybernetic beings: "The Borg under-theme has lost its power. The Romulans have taken them apart, physically, mechanically, and thematically."[24]

With Season 2 of *Picard*, Russo followed a similar character-based method of scoring episodes. One of the major differences was pacing. According to Russo, "I think we're on a bit more of a paced-up journey in Season 2, so I do tend to give it a little more get up and go."[25]

Between the release of Season 1 and 2, the world endured the major disruptions of the COVID pandemic. Fortunately, Russo's scoring of the second season was able to avoid most significant COVID challenges. As Russo stated, "It didn't impact *Picard*, but it did impact Season 3 of *Discovery*, which I recorded two-thirds of the score remotely—individual players at their own studios, and having to edit it all together, was quite complex in trying to put together a 45-piece orchestra."[26]

For both *Discovery* and *Picard*, Russo was able to blend his new spin on the series with the influence and musical quotes from the legacy series. There are even times when his scores seem to reference Michael Giacchino's music for the rebooted *Star Trek* films, but according to Russo, this was unintentional. He believes the similarity is more likely a result of the fact that *Star Trek* tends to elicit similar emotions in composers. "I think if there's any similarity it's probably in the fact that the world of *Star Trek* evokes a certain type of writing of music…. I'm inspired by all *Star Trek* music in general—the idea of what *Star Trek* music is and can be. I assume that's the same kind of thing that inspires Michael and anyone else who's written music for *Star Trek*."[27]

Even as new composers introduce their own sounds to the *Star Trek* franchise, there always has been a musical continuity. As Jon Burlingame stated, "I love the fact that *Star Trek* is moving in new directions—and it's employing new composers who I think respect and acknowledge the traditions of *Star Trek*, particularly in the use of an orchestra."[28] Each composer adds to the totality of the *Star Trek* sound, while also respecting the musical continuity that began in the 1960s. Burlingame observed, "What I love about these guys in the whole history of the *Trek* franchise is that over and over again, they have demonstrated that the traditional symphonic array—traditional orchestra—of strings and woodwinds and brass and percussion is still the best vehicle for creating and conveying emotion in drama."[29]

Star Trek: Prodigy

In October 2021, a new *Trek* series premiered. *Star Trek: Prodigy,* an animated series created by Kevin and Dan Hageman. It tells the story of a group of young aliens imprisoned in the Delta Quadrant. These prisoners find a Federation Starship called the *Protostar* and escape toward the Alpha Quadrant. The series takes place just a few years after *Voyager* (see *Star Trek: Voyager*) returned home from the Delta Quadrant. The show also features Kathryn Janeway, now a vice admiral. The series was produced in partnership with Nickelodeon to appeal to younger viewers.

Although the series is animated, the producers wanted to ensure that they produced a full *Star Trek* experience. This included the music, which meant an orchestral score. Up until this point in time, all the primary composers for the *Star Trek* franchise had been male. For *Prodigy,* they hired composer Nami Melumad. She had impressed the *Trek* producers with her score for the *Star Trek* short "Q & A," part of the *Star Trek: Short Treks* series in 2019. According to executive producer Alex Kurtzman,

She has a storytelling ability that truly great composers understand, which is to say that she knows intuitively when to play the text of a scene and when to do the opposite and let the music say all the things the characters aren't saying. On *Star Trek: Prodigy*, we asked her to give a children's animation show a score worthy of a live-action feature, and that's exactly what she did.[30]

Melumad had already established herself in TV, scoring shows such as *Absentia* and *Dead End*, and was mentored by composer Michael Giacchino. When it was time to score the Seth Rogan film *American Pickle*, Giacchino called upon Melumad to help because he did not have time to score the entire film. Giacchino wrote the film's primary themes, but Melumad produced the full score, and they shared credit. According to film editor Paul Apelgren, "He doesn't like the minions writing.... He writes his music. If he has to find a ghostwriter—it's not a ghostwriter, he gives at least an 'additional music by' credit."[31]

When Melumad was approached to score *Prodigy*, she was surprised. "I got the call to come on board. It was totally unexpected. There were no spoilers. It was 'Hey can you make it to a spotting session in the next day or so?' It completely took me by surprise. I was super-, super-excited."[32]

Melumad came to the production with an enormous amount of enthusiasm. A *Trek* fan all her life, she noted, "*Voyager* happens to be my favorite show."[33] That said, she also felt the pressure about taking the

Composer Nami Melumad in her studio (photography by Ray Costa).

reins of such a job: "I was excited, but also very nervous because it's a big responsibility. Especially with *Prodigy*, where you're introducing kids to *Star Trek*—you're telling what a replicator is—what beaming up is—what is a communicator—all these terms and Starfleet's values, you kind of want it to be exciting for kids, but also make it feel like *Star Trek*."[34] During the first season, there are very few recognizable *Star Trek*–type scenes. They slowly introduced elements of *Star Trek* and the existence of Star Fleet throughout the first season.

Alex Kurtzman and the showrunners wanted to be sure that there was musical continuity between previous *Star Trek* productions and this new series. They gave Melumad a list of musical references that they had listened to as they wrote the show. This included music by Giacchino, James Horner and Hans Zimmer as well as other big orchestral film score composers. But they were also flexible. Melumad recalled that they said, "We're totally open to what you want to do."[35] This was particularly the case during the first part of the season when there was little interaction with the Federation. Over time, however, as the Federation role grew within the storyline, Melumad needed to make sure that the scoring sounded more and more like the legacy music (without actually using legacy music). Since *Prodigy* was produced on Nickelodeon and not CBS, Melumad was not allowed to quote directly from legacy music. "What I did was use the same types of orchestrations...."[36] She composed music with a very similar feel to a *Star Trek* theme, but are not close enough to be considered plagiarism.

"We talked about having specific themes and motifs for each character," noted Melumad. "I'd identify them with a certain instrument or a certain melody.... We decided to do a theme for the USS *Protostar*, the ship—and Janeway has her theme, which at the beginning represents the Federation. Janeway is a representative of the Federation—her music aligns with that."[37]

Melumad's two biggest influences in creating the sound of *Prodigy* were Michael Giacchino and John Williams. She needed to be careful not to quote the latter composer too much. After all, Williams' music was written for *Star Wars*, not *Star Trek*. They have two distinct sounds, and the fans would notice if her score sounded too much like *Star Wars*. She conceded, "'Here you want to get closer to Jerry Goldsmith,'"[38] noting that there is more Goldsmith-influenced music in the second half of the season, as Janeway becomes a larger part of the plot.

Giacchino wrote the opening theme music for the *Prodigy* series. Since he and Melumad had such a good working relationship, he sent her an early version of the theme, asking what she thought. It was such a compelling and emotional theme that she integrated it into her scores. "I include the theme in the show whenever appropriate," stated Melumad. "It is such a strong theme—I use it whenever the team is successful—or a very emotional scene."[39] She also used portions of Giacchino's theme music that did not make the final cut into the opening credits. "The theme has an introduction that was not used in the opening credits—a slower part," Melumad revealed. "It's such great music, I use that for a lot of the emotional parts. I think our styles are very close to one another—we worked on a lot of other things together, so it works out really well."[40]

Melumad's score was recorded in Prague using a 55-piece orchestra to create the big sound she intended. The orchestra was supplemented with additional instrumentation. "I'm also using some synths, keyboard elements, some percussion and other things that are not entirely orchestral."[41] Melumad did not conduct the recording, preferring to listen from the recording booth. "I feel that composers need to be in the booth to hear the mix to say we need more of this or that—these are the changes that are important," said Melumad. "It allows you to remain a little more focused. You also often want to be where your directors or your showrunners are … You want to make sure that they're happy…"[42]

Throughout *Prodigy*'s first season, Melumad produced a substantial amount of rousing music to drive the storyline. In fact, the soundtrack contained 93 separate tracks of music. While the target audience for this *Star Trek* series was younger than previous productions in this franchise, they did not want to skimp or "dumb down" the music. Film reviewer Mike Poteet wrote, "Melumad turns in a score that's exactly the right amounts of exciting, tender, and humorous, as the action demands."[43]

Melumad remains honored not only to be able to expand the musical repertoire of the famed franchise, but also to play a role in introducing young audiences to the magic of *Star Trek*. "Our main audience is young, new Trekkies. They don't know *Voyager*, so they don't feel that nostalgic moment when we all see Janeway. For them, it's a cool and inspiring moment, but not nostalgic."[44]

Strange New Worlds

Premiering in May 2022, *Strange New Worlds* is the live-action *Star Trek* series depicting the *USS Enterprise* (NCC-1701) in the years prior to James T. Kirk taking the helm as captain.

Nami Melumad had just started scoring *Prodigy* when she was offered the *Strange New Worlds* job. After submitting her first full draft of the score for the *Prodigy* pilot, she received a request to join Alex Kurtzman, head of the franchise, on a Zoom call. This was highly unusual; Melumad worried that something was wrong—that they did not like her *Prodigy* pilot music. Kurtzman gave her a lot of notes, and then informed her to drop off the call, and that the showrunners would provide any additional input.

Soon after this, Kurtzman's assistant emailed Melumad, saying that Kurtzman never got around to saying what he had intended to say during the original meeting. They got on another Zoom call, and according to Melumad, Kurtzman said, "Oh, I want to talk to you about *Strange New Worlds*. We think you should do it. Do you want to do it?" After believing that Kurtzman and the showrunners were not happy with her *Prodigy* score, Melumad recalled, "It was a very welcome surprise."[45]

Since this new series was produced by CBS/Paramount, there was no restriction on using *Star Trek* legacy music. Melumad enthused, "I am allowed to quote Alexander Courage's theme from the original series. I get to do all sorts of variations and really go for an older feel."[46] At times, they would refer to some of the original scores of Fred Steiner and other composers, particularly if there were scenes and/or characters that had appeared in the 1960s series.

There are some differences in musical philosophy between *Prodigy* and *Strange New Worlds*. According to Melumad, "With *Prodigy*, [the music] is so present. It's like one of the characters. It's very dominant. In *Strange New Worlds*, it's not as dominant. It's still very much moving the story forward, and doing everything that we should be doing, but there are so many other components of the storyline...." This does not mean that music plays less of a role than in other *Star Trek* productions. Melumad observed, "I think the score for *Strange New Worlds* is more present—much more active—than many of the other *Trek* scores that have been released in the last few years...."[47]

While Melumad had as many as 55 players while recording *Prodigy* in Prague, she had to make do with an orchestra of roughly 37 players *for Strange New Worlds*, recording on the Warner Brothers stage in Hollywood. She convinced the producers to increase the size of the orchestra for Season 2.

As had been the case with *Prodigy*, Melumad did not write the opening theme music. This time Jeff Russo, who had written the scores for *Star Trek: Discovery* and *Picard*, wrote the opening credit sequence music. He starts with the initial notes of Alexander Courage's famous theme and transitions into a driving score that is also at times reminiscent of Courage's music, but with a more foreboding feel. According to Russo, he hoped to "evoke the same things as the original show evokes. So, I took a little of Alexander Courage's original theme and then sort of tried to come up with melodies and harmonic content that would really evoke the same kind of thing, but with a sort of deconstruction of what will come in the next series."[48]

Nonetheless, Melumad composed the scores for every episodes, and her music has the greatest impact on the sound of the show. She musically referenced the original *Star Trek* music, but also provides her own interpretation of this spacefaring vision of humanity in the future.

The first music she wrote for the series was for the second episode, "Children of the Comet," in which they find a comet that contains sentient life that communicates through music. Since they needed the music to help drive the story, Melumad wrote portions of the music for this episode before it was shot. The story required a very specific sound. "[The producers] wanted something that would feel really alien, really weird, and also unrecognizable, but it will have roots in a melody in Kenya where Uhura grew up,"[49] stated Melumad. The composer wrote a folk song that Uhura would hum at the beginning of the episode, "so my variation of that later on would be a super-alien variation. That's what the comet is playing. That's how the computer on the *Enterprise* recognizes that this is rooted in that melody, and it's not a coincidence that the comet chose that specific song."[50] The actors learned all the variations to communicate with the comet. Both Spock (played by Ethan Peck) and Uhura (played by Celia Rose Gooding) sing in this episode. Gooding had the advantage of being an award-winning vocalist. She came to *Strange New Worlds* from a successful time on Broadway, where she had become one of the youngest nominees for a Best Actress Tony Award.

Reminiscent conceptually of the role of music in *Close Encounters* and in an episode called "Someone to Watch Over Me" in *Battlestar Galactica*, it conveyed the possibility that music could link all sentient beings in the universe. According to Melumad, "I like the message of that—music is the universal language that even the comet can understand."[51]

12

Music in "Real" Space

"I believe music is a universal language for all humans
and even for a lot of other living creatures on our
planet. Music trespasses physical, ideological, genera-
tional, language, etc., frontiers, and it's certainly a universal way of communication. So, I think it's natural to
use music or sound (traveling frequencies) as a way of
communication to outer space."—Felipe Santiago[1]

Music in space has been discussed for centuries. Well before humanity had any hopes of leaving our home planet, music in space was an area
of scientific and metaphysical study. The Music of the Spheres (also known
as *musica universalis*) was conceived of in ancient Greece. According to
the Merriam-Webster Dictionary, the music of the spheres is "an ethereal harmony thought by the Pythagoreans to be produced by the vibra-
tion of the celestial spheres."[2] Proponents of this theory believed that
celestial bodies emitted tones that were inaudible to the human ear. However, starting in the twentieth century, the music of humanity would journey into space. For a century, Hollywood has defined the soundtrack of
space, but reality is swiftly catching up with the entertainment industry.
As mentioned in earlier chapters, humanity has been transporting music
into "real" space for decades. While musicianship has not been an official
requirement of national space programs, music *is* an essential ingredient
to being human—and is critical for astronaut health, happiness and the
advancement of civilization as we live, work and recreate away from our
home planet.

Musical instruments such as harmonicas, guitars, keyboard, flutes,
saxophones, a didgeridoo, as well as the human voice, have produced the
music of many nations off-planet since the early days of human space
flight. Music of all varieties has been broadcast into space. For example, to commemorate the fiftieth anniversary of NASA, the Beatles' song
"Across the Universe" was broadcast toward Polaris, a star 431 light years

from Earth; the message will take 431 years to reach that star system. Upon hearing about this transmission, Paul McCartney exclaimed, "Amazing! Well done, NASA! Send my love to the aliens. All the best, Paul."[3]

Music has also been sent to much closer destinations in space to serve as wakeup calls for crews in orbit, as well as for the NASA rovers on the surface of Mars. Broadcasting music to Mars raised the morale of mission engineers and scientists back on Earth. According to the team that managed the Spirit and Opportunity rovers that landed on the Martian surface in 2004,

> The Mars rover engineering team works on Mars time. A Martian day, also called a "sol," is 40 minutes longer than an Earth day. Each Martian morning as the rover wakes up, they play a song related to the events of the upcoming sol. Occasionally a second or third song is played during the sol in addition to the wakeup song. This is a tradition from the manned space program. Unfortunately, robotic probes are not yet capable of feeling inspiration from music, but Mission Control is.[4]

The first time a song broadcast from Mars was on August 28, 2012. The song "Reach for the Stars," by performer Will.i.am, was broadcast from the Curiosity Rover.

The first known song (or any other musical performance) to have been performed in space occurred on August 12, 1962, during the *Vostok 3 and 4* mission. Soviet-Ukrainian cosmonaut Pavlo Popovych sang a nineteenth-century Ukrainian song called "Watching the Sky and Thinking a Thought." His performance was requested by Soviet space engineer (and chief designer) Serhiy Korolyov, who was also Ukrainian. In December 1965, the first documented off-world American musicianship took place to celebrate the holiday season during the first rendezvous between two spacecraft. The *Gemini 6A* mission, crewed by Walter M. "Wally" Schirra and Thomas P. Stafford, and the *Gemini 7* mission, crewed by Frank Borman and James A. Lovell, had just completed their microgravity ballet and rendezvous when the crew of *Gemini 6A* (Wally Schirra and Thomas P. Stafford) called out on the radio, "We have an object. It looks like a satellite going from north to south, up in a polar orbit. He's in a very low trajectory, traveling from north to south. It has a very high [fineness] ratio. It looks like it might be [inaudible]. It's very low; it looks like he might be going to re-enter soon. Stand by, One. It looks like he's trying to signal us." Schirra and Stafford then played "Jingle Bells" on harmonica and bells. The *Gemini 7* crew (Frank Borman and Jim Lovell) also replied that they had also shared the Santa Claus sighting.[5] During this same mission, Beethoven's 6th Symphony as well as the popular holiday song "I Saw Mommy Kissing Santa Claus" were broadcast into space to the crew. The latter was reportedly requested by Jim Lovell's daughter Barbara.

Seven years later, on the surface of the Moon during the *Apollo 17* mission, astronauts Harrison Schmitt and Gene Cernan performed the first duet (impromptu) on another planetary body, and probably the first duet in space. The two moonwalkers were hopping along on the lunar surface when Schmitt began singing, "I was strolling on the Moon one day…" Cernan then joined in, and they both sang, "in the merry, merry month of," but then had the first lyrical disagreement in space: Cernan said "May," Schmitt said, "December"—since it was, in fact, December.

Harmonicas and bells were just the beginning. Larger musical instruments eventually traveled into space, including guitars. The first guitar to travel into space was played by Soviet cosmonaut Aleksandr Ivanchenkov aboard the *Salyut-6* space station in 1978. The Russians understood the value of music in space. According to John Uri at NASA Johnson Space Center,

> Russian space psychologists realized that playing music in orbit improved the well-being of cosmonauts on long-duration missions and ensured that an acoustic guitar made it aboard Mir as early as possible. Cosmonauts Yuri Romanenko and Aleksandr Laveykin enjoyed strumming the strings during Mir's second expedition in 1987, as did many cosmonauts throughout the space station's lifetime.[6]

The Russians were not the only spacefaring humans to play larger instruments in space. American Ronald McNair, the second African American astronaut, carried a saxophone aboard the Space Shuttle (STS 41-B) in 1984. His performance was not recorded. McNair hoped to remedy this on his next mission. He arranged for French composer Jean-Michel Jarre to write a saxophone piece that would be played on Space Shuttle mission STS-51L on *Challenger* in 1986. He had arranged a live feed to the concert that Jarre was conducting back to Earth. Tragically, this space-based performance was never to happen; McNair and his fellow crew members perished when *Challenger* exploded a few minutes after liftoff.

After much anguish and consideration, Jarre decided to move forward with the concert as a memorial to McNair. He asked Kirk Whalum, a young saxophonist, to play the piece. "I was just blown away, I mean, I was just 24 years old, I was so honored," recalls Whalum.[7] As for the song, Jarre reflected that he never would have guessed how poignant his song would be. "I found out from talking to people that in the total silence of space, what you can hear the most is your own heartbeat. And then I got the idea to use Ron's heartbeat to create the loop and the beat of the track. Obviously now, looking back, it has such a meaning given what happened later on."[8]

In more recent years, there have been numerous performances in space, many of them well-planned collaborations with partners on the ground and receiving hundreds of millions of online views. Perhaps the most famous space-based performance was Canadian astronaut Chris Hadfield's rendition of David Bowie's "Space Oddity" in 2013. Hadfield revealed how this came about: "When I was on Mir on my first flight in 1995, there was an old guitar made in St. Petersburg—and I had brought an American-made guitar up with me as a gift (STS 74) to a German guitar player on board, Thomas Reiter." The guitar that Hadfield presented to Reiter was a Soloette guitar made by Wright Guitars in Eugene, Oregon. That guitar returned to Earth on the last shuttle flight to and from Mir and now resides in the Museum of Aviation and Space in Ottawa, Canada.[9]

As the International Space Station (ISS) became the primary destination in Low Earth Orbit, musical instruments followed. As Hadfield planned his trip to the ISS in 2013, he knew that two guitars resided on the orbital facility. With this in mind, he and his songwriter brother Dave began to brainstorm songs that could performed in space. "I had no idea how I was going to [record],"[10] Hadfield admitted. He also had to meticulously plan *when* he would be able to play and record his musical pieces. Astronauts get seven or eight hours of scheduled sleep and according to Hadfield, their time is planned down to five-minute increments. As a result, "I would steal the first couple hours of my sleep, if I had the energy, and do the things I wanted to do.... If I had enough creative energy left, I'd work on the music."[11]

In advance of the mission, Hadfield's son Evan had suggested that he perform "Space Oddity," but the astronaut was initially resistant. One reason for his hesitancy was that he did not feel equal to the song, and he did not want to record a poor version of the Bowie classic. Perhaps more concerning was when he read the lyrics and exclaimed, "Holy crap! The astronaut dies!"[12] Whether he did not want to tempt fate or merely did not want to sing a depressing song in space is unclear.

Evan, not dissuaded by his father's concerns, told him, "If you don't do it, you'll regret it."[13] To alleviate his father's concern that the musical astronaut dies, Evan revised the lyrics. After this change, Hadfield agreed to record the song during his stay on ISS and began to develop a plan to record it.

One of the biggest challenges was finding a place to practice, perform and record and not disturb the other crew members. His sleeping area proved to be one of the best options. Roughly the size of a coffin, it was the quietest and most private location on ISS, allowing him to write and record (using Garage Band) music late at night. Another consideration was physics. Playing the guitar and singing in a microgravity environment was quite challenging. As observed in Sir Isaac Newton's Third Law of Motion,

"For every action, there is an equal and opposite reaction"; and when one plays a guitar and sings in microgravity, there are significant equal and opposite reactions with one's body, the instrument and the microphone. Hadfield revealed that after numerous experiments, "it turns out the best quality sound was just floating one of the mics weightlessly in front of me; and recorded directly into Garage Band."[14]

The physics of space had also impacted Hadfield's performance physiologically. In the microgravity environment, the human diaphragm is not pushed down into the bottom of your thorax as it would be in the 1 g (1 gravitational force) on the Earth's surface. In addition to this, most astronauts (including Hadfield) have reported that their sinuses never drain in this environment because of the absence of gravity. As a result, high notes are easier, but deep resonant notes much more difficult. However, this physiological change to his voice benefited his performance of "Space Oddity" with the lighter, higher tonality of his voice. Hadfield recalled, "When I listened to my clean vocal track, it was really nice."[15]

With the vocal recording complete, his son recommended that a music video be filmed to accompany the performance. Otherwise, nobody would believe it was recorded in space. Hadfield continued, "One afternoon, I grabbed a camera and floated around, singing along with myself to the audio track we'd made."[16] He artistically filmed in multiple locations around the station, including the cupola with its spectacular views of Earth. In one shot, just prior to the first chorus of "This is ground control to Major Tom," the guitar is seen floating away from the camara within the station.

Once the music video was complete, they received permission from David Bowie's attorneys to release the song with the modified lyrics, and it instantly went viral. By the time Hadfield had landed back on Earth, the video had already been viewed by over seven million people; ultimately it was viewed by hundreds of millions of people around the world. This included Bowie, who reportedly loved Hadfield's version. Hadfield said, "I got to know Bowie a little bit, which was great. He thought it was a great version of the song and he always wanted to fly in space."[17] Hadfield's recording of "Space Oddity" and several other songs were included in an album that he called *Space Sessions: Songs from a Tin Can*.

The flute also become a popular choice of instruments in space, having the benefit of being extremely transportable. NASA astronauts Ellen Ochoa and Cady Coleman both played flutes (on separate missions). Ochoa's orbital flute performances took place aboard the Space Shuttle at a time when there was a NASA rule limiting musical instruments flying into space. Nevertheless, she was able get approval to carry a flute on her mission as a prop in a STEM video in space comparing a day in the life of

Top: Chris Hadfield playing a guitar on the International Space Station in 2013 (NASA). *Bottom:* Cady Coleman playing her flute on the International Space Station in 2011 (NASA).

astronauts with that of students around the world. This included playing music.

By the time Cady Coleman performed flute duets from space in 2011, the musical instrument limitation had (apparently) been lifted. Like Hadfield, Coleman prepared extensively for her performances, arranging multiple duets with collaborators on Earth. First and foremost on her list was Ian Anderson, founder of the rock band Jethro Tull. Anderson had the distinction of introducing the flute to rock music, and she wanted to honor this achievement by bringing his rock'n'roll flute to space. Coleman asked prominent Houston deejay Dayna Steele (wife of a NASA pilot) if she had any "interfaces" with Anderson. Dayna replied, "I'm on it!"[18]

Not long after this discussion, Coleman received a letter from Anderson that said (paraphrased by Coleman), "Well, I have heard that I myself am quite a reliable interface and I'd like to be that person. I'm responsive to email … and I take a shower almost every day."[19] They began a conversation resulting in Anderson sending Coleman one of his flutes to carry into space.

The two flute players quickly became pen pals and began brainstorming flute pieces that she could play on her mission. According to Coleman, Anderson said, "I think you could do two things. I think we could figure out something we could play together—and I think you could play things that beginning or intermediate flute players could play—that kids could play along with you."[20] They agreed to play "Bourée," which Tull had played on his concert tour in 1969 as Neil Armstrong and Buzz Aldrin walked on the Moon. "Bourée" was a jazzy arrangement of a French folk dance dating from no later than the early seventeenth century. The most famous arrangement of the piece was by Johann Sebastian Bach.

Coleman launched from Baikonur, Russia, as part of Expedition 26 to the International Space Station on December 16, 2010. She stayed on the orbital laboratory for the next 159 days, which meant that she was in space on the fiftieth anniversary of Yuri Gagarin's 1961 flight into space aboard Vostok-1.

Serendipitously, Anderson was also scheduled to perform in Russia on April 12, 2011. This was a perfect occasion for their duet to air. But they needed to figure out how to record the duet in space and on the ground. Anderson recorded his part of the duet first. From this recording, wearing earbuds, Coleman was able to record her part aboard the ISS. The video starts in an airlock on ISS with international flags adorning the wall. Then from above the frameline, a flute seemingly descends from the ceiling, followed by Coleman who states, "Tonight, Ian Anderson and I would like to honor Yuri Gagarin for his brave journey 50 years ago. And we would like to celebrate the role that humans play in the exploration of our universe, past, present and future, by sharing some music between Earth and space."[21]

While her performance looked seamless and natural, it took a lot of preparation. First, she needed to determine where to record. The sound of the flute varied significantly depending on which part of the station she played in. The Japanese logistics module "Kibō" has an acoustically dead sound because of cloth bags and other materials lining the walls. By comparison, playing in the cupola, an observation dome with window panes, produced a "nice, bright kind of ringing sound"; and playing in the airlock produced deep and echoey sound. Based on this, Coleman chose to play in the cupola.

The microgravity environment also posed some physical challenges. "The flute kind of bobbles a little bit in your hands," stated Coleman. "A flute has three points of contact. (1) Under your lip, (2) the edge of your pointing finger (left hand) and (3) your thumb on your other hand. But there is force number (4), which is gravity. Without that, it does bobble."[22]

Coleman also played a duet with Matt Molloy from the traditional Irish band The Chieftains. Molloy lent Coleman an antique Irish E flat flute that he had played on his first solo album, made with Dónal Lunny in 1976.[23] According to Coleman, the flute was a "treasure of Ireland." This type of flute is shorter than a standard flute and more suitable for small hands. According to Coleman, "At the time, I didn't play the Irish flute yet, so I bought one and was taking it around the world with me trying to learn...."[24]

When Molloy's flute arrived (wrapped in a piece of cardboard with no padding) Coleman could not get it to play. "I ended up calling the local coffee shop where there is a local Irish group that plays every week. 'I have an Irish flute from Matt Molloy. I'm bringing it to space. It needs to be at NASA within a week. He sent it to me, and I think it's damaged.'"[25] Fortunately, one of the members of the local band was an antique flute repairman and he was able to repair it before she flew.

Musical performances on the ISS have also served solemn purposes. Perhaps the most poignant performance occurred in the wake of the September 11, 2001, terrorist attacks on the United States. NASA astronaut Frank Culbertson, Jr., commander of the ISS, was the only American in space on that date (his two crewmates were from Russia). As details of the terrorist attacks emerged, Culbertson learned that the pilot of American Flight 77, the plane that struck the Pentagon, was his Naval Academy classmate Charles "Chic" Burlingame. As fate would have it, Culbertson had brought his trumpet with him to space so that could join the elite group of amateur musicians who had played in orbit. To honor his friend and all the other people who had died, Culbertson addressed his fellow Naval Academy graduates and said,

I would like to send a message from the station, in memory of "Chic," and all of our graduates who perished, and all of the victims of this tragedy, something that has never been done before from space. I'd like all of you to rise for a moment of silence as we play something from the International Space Station Alpha.

He then played on his trumpet a solemn rendition of "Taps."[26]

Astronaut Soundtracks

Playing and performing music in space is not restricted to private performances in remote parts of the ISS. Music is a part of the culture in space, and critical to the mental health, happiness and bonding of crew members. Chris Hadfield explained, "Music is there all the time on a spaceship. On my first flight on Mir, there was always music playing.... Because we're so isolated from everybody, music is doubly important because it's a link with everybody's traditions." As international crews sit around the dinner table, they listen to music and talk about the music they heard while growing up. "It was a really important part of the celebrations we had on board—and still is."[27]

Cady Coleman insists "It's huge!" for long periods in space. Loud music can create an atmosphere of "hard work and industry, and passion."[28] The music can serve as a tool to close cultural divides between crew members. She adds, "Music and songs are storytelling ... When you're sharing a song, you're sharing a story; telling them something about yourself. It's hard to find something that six people from two, three different countries and several different languages can all enjoy together."[29]

As logical and seemingly non-controversial as this concept appears to be, Coleman had to defend the role of music to NASA. She was called into a meeting and asked, "Someone wants to send a second guitar up to the ISS. Why in the world would we need two guitars up there?"[30]

Coleman replied, "So that people can play together ... Music makes people relatable."[31] This is critical. It helps to build camaraderie, bridge language and cultural gaps, and improve quality of life in space—something that engineers and mission planners have often undervalued or not appreciated. It is part of being human, part of moving human culture off-world. Even if instruments were still discouraged in space, astronauts would certainly find a way. For example, in 2012, American astronaut Don Pettit made a didgeridoo out of vacuum cleaner parts on the station. It shows that humans will find a way to create music for personal pleasure and to strengthen bonds with each other.

This musical tradition has continued as commercial human space flight has accelerated. In September 2021, the Inspiration4 mission was the first all-private expedition to orbit the Earth. Its four crew members put significant thought into the music soundtrack that would be played on the historic journey. Each one selected several pieces that they thought would best express their emotions and signify the grandeur of their extraordinary experience. According to crew member Dr. Sian Proctor, "Music captures the moment and the playlist, for me, encapsulates it. I also downloaded John Williams' greatest hits. I had that cued up for funny moments." For example, while in orbit on the last day, Jared Isaacman said that "the splashdown party was going to be 'awesome' … and we're going to have the 'Cantina' from Mos Isley's in *Star Wars*," at which point Sian was able to instantly play 'Cantina.'"[32] (The post-landing splashdown party in Orlando had a re-creation of the Cantina bar.)

Perhaps the most dramatic musical moment of that mission occurred when they opened the outer door of the cupola, a dome with awe-inspiring views of Earth. As the door slowly opened, Strauss' "Also sprach Zarathustra" thundered in the Dragon capsule and the crew's eyes widened as they saw the full view of Earth for the first time.

Musical Analogs

The therapeutic role of music in long-term space missions has been observed on the ISS and other vehicles, but few of these musical experiences in space have been part of a formal study. However, it has been studied at a Mars analog facility on Earth. Analog Mars missions are facilities-missions designed to simulate the physical, psychological and geological environment, as well as the isolation, that might be encountered by the first astronauts on the Martian surface.

In 2001, the first crew of the Mars Society's Flashline Mars Arctic Research Station on Devon Island in the Canadian Arctic quickly learned that music would play a central role in the lives and culture on future Mars missions and settlements. The eclectic crew included NASA flight surgeon Rainer Effenhauser; Darlene Lim, a research scientist from NASA Ames Research Center; Steve Braham, quantum cosmologist; Charlie Cockell from the British Antarctica Survey; Frank Schubert, architect (and occasional guitarist for the rock band Devo), and Sam Burbank, a documentary filmmaker.

Shortly after they closed the hatch to begin the simulation, Burbank, Schubert and Braham "proceeded to perform 'Stairway to Heaven' using the guitar that Frank Schubert had brought with him."[33] Each of them demonstrated their own interpretations. Burbank said, "Nobody plays 'Stairway to Heaven' the same way. It's one of the weird anomalies in the universe. After about ten minutes into this musical session, it hit me that this was a great way for people to have a more humanizing experience in space."[34] Music became one of the primary leisure activities during that mission. "We decided that if we did another simulation, let's try to record a song or two to see if this would be a good way to spend down time in space," recalls Burbank. "There are activities that you can do in which you disappear from your environment and music is one of them."[35]

In 2003, Schubert, Burbank, NASA exobiologist Penny Boston and Kelly Snook were among the crew members selected to participate in Crew 6 of the Mars Desert Research Station (MDRS), an analog facility operated by the Mars Society near Hanksville, Utah. In addition to a series of planned science experiments, the crew also wrote and recorded music during their stay at the facility. They called this project the Interplanetary Collaborative Music Project.

The team had planned to write and record a couple of original songs and possibly record some cover songs as well, but according to Burbank, "The strangest thing happened where these songs just started pouring out."[36] Schubert, Snook and Burbank generated songs, and Boston wrote lyrics. Not only were they able to relax and enjoy themselves, but these activities were a highly effective way to build camaraderie and collaboration between crew members—not always an easy task when a group of people are confined to a small space for an extended period of time.

But they also encountered a potential risk: They found themselves spending too much time on music composition, at the expense of their science and extra-vehicular activity (EVAs) objectives. As a result, they had to cut back on sleep to complete all these projects. "I suspect on a multiyear mission to Mars, it would become a more balanced part of their down time activity," noted Burbank. "We proved that it could be done in a spaceship-size space; and we recorded an album that ended up being very successful for an independent band."[37]

This process was not restricted to the crew members in the habitat. According to their final report, they collaborated with musicians of all levels around the world to produce their recordings. The paper stated,

A low-mass but high-performance recording infrastructure was required for deployment in the field (MDRS). The system had to fit on a desk and support multi-track recording and playback, and interface with the various instruments brought by the participants of the MDRS. This computer also had to be capable of communicating with the satellite dish on the MDRS and subsequently with the computers in studios on Earth.[38]

In fact, Burbank considers collaboration with the outside world (Earth) the "secret sauce" of the project:

We are now collaborating with people not in the habitat (on Earth) including a couple guys from Devo—and had studios in Portland, Los Angeles, San Francisco, and multiple other cities. We'd send out a track and while we were sleeping, people would be working on this stuff. …Through this kind of collaboration, you could have a bigger friend group—and even grow your friends—even if you are on your way to Mars; or on Mars.[39]

This lesson has been solidified even more by the COVID-19 pandemic years. The world was thrown into isolation, forcing musicians to collaborate remotely, utilizing new processes that could be directly applied to musical and other collaborations between people in space and people on Earth.

Music in Deep Space—The Golden Record

Music has been broadcast to the far reaches of space since the invention of radio. If there are advanced civilizations on planets orbiting nearby stars, they theoretically may have already heard music, news and content of all varieties from Earth.

Perhaps the most renowned collection of pre-recorded music traveling through space was not sent by radio waves or some other form of wireless communication, but on a record—a golden one. Conceived of by astronomer Carl Sagan, the Golden Record was an audio documentation of life on Earth launched aboard the *Voyager* spacecrafts in 1977. According to the NASA JPL website, the record includes "a variety of natural sounds, such as those made by surf, wind and thunder, birds, whales, and other animals. To this they added musical selections from different cultures and eras, and spoken greetings from Earth-people in 55 languages, and printed messages from President Carter and U.N. Secretary General Waldheim."[40] Sagan hoped that the spacecraft "will be encountered and the record played only if there are advanced spacefaring civilizations in interstellar space."[41]

Sagan asked Ann Druyan to lead this project as creative director of NASA's *Voyager* Interstellar Message Project. Selecting the musical portion of the record, music that would represent all of humanity, was not an easy job. According to Druyan, "Even though we had so much more space on a phonograph record than any other medium at that moment, it wasn't an infinite amount of space."[42] Druyan and her team believed that it was critical that the record should reflect all the world's musical traditions, "not just the immediate traditions of the people who built the spacecraft. We did not want it to be an imperialistic statement…."[43]

While most of the world was listening to American popular music or

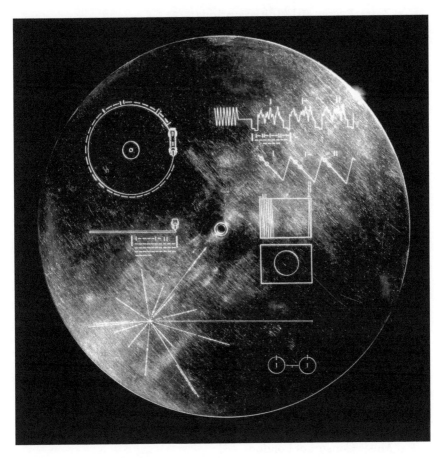

Image of The Golden Record, launched aboard the Voyager missions in 1977 (NASA).

European music, Druyan wanted to ensure the selections on the record truly represented a significant cross-section of human culture, even if the music of some other cultures had much less penetration into the global consciousness. To add to this challenge, they only had six weeks to assemble these representatives of the music of Earth.

The final record included greetings in 55 languages and 90 minutes of music from various cultures that Druyan calls "Earth's Greatest Hits."[44] According to the Jet Propulsion Laboratory, the Golden Record contained such pieces as:

- Bach, Brandenburg Concerto No. 2 in F
- Java, court gamelan, "Kinds of Flowers"
- Senegal, percussion

- Zaire, Pygmy girls' Initiation Song
- Australia, Aborigine songs "Morning Star" and "Devil Bird"
- Mexico, "El Cascabel," performed by Lorenzo Barcelata and the Mariachi México
- "Johnny B. Goode," written and performed by Chuck Berry
- New Guinea, men's house song, recorded by Robert MacLennan
- Japan, shakuhachi, "Tsuru No Sugomori" ("Crane's Nest"), performed by Goro Yamaguchi
- Bach, "Gavotte en rondeaux" from the Partita No. 3 in E major for Violin, performed by Arthur Grumiaux
- Mozart, "The Magic Flute," "Queen of the Night" aria, no. 14
- Georgian S.S.R., chorus, "Tchakrulo," collected by Radio Moscow
- Peru, panpipes and drum, collected by Casa de la Cultura, Lima
- "Melancholy Blues," performed by Louis Armstrong and his Hot Seven
- Azerbaijan S.S.R., bagpipes, recorded by Radio Moscow
- Stravinsky, "Rite of Spring," "Sacrificial Dance," Columbia Symphony Orchestra, Igor Stravinsky, conductor
- Bach, "The Well-Tempered Clavier," Book 2, Prelude and Fugue in C, No.1. Glenn Gould, piano
- Beethoven, Fifth Symphony, First Movement, the Philharmonia Orchestra, Otto Klemperer, conductor
- Bulgaria, "Izlel je Delyo Hagdutin," sung by Valya Balkanska
- Navajo Indians, Night Chant, recorded by Willard Rhodes
- Holborne, Paueans, Galliards, Almains and Other Short Aeirs, "The Fairie Round," performed by David Munrow and the Early Music Consort of London
- Solomon Islands, panpipes, collected by the Solomon Islands Broadcasting Service
- Peru, wedding song, recorded by John Cohen
- China, ch'in, "Flowing Streams," performed by Kuan P'ing-hu
- India, raga, "Jaat Kahan Ho," sung by Surshri Kesar Bai Kerkar
- "Dark Was the Night," written and performed by Blind Willie Johnson
- Beethoven, String Quartet No. 13 in B flat, Opus 130, Cavatina, performed by Budapest String Quartet[45]

As brilliant and diverse as this list was, Druyan also understood that, to an alien civilization, humanity's great musical works may not be distinguishable from the sounds of birds, the ocean or the sounds of the city. But she hopes that they will recognize the organized structure and rhythms:

I'm not saying that we're expecting these putative extra-terrestrials to completely rock out to "Johnny B. Goode" but I am saying that the rhythm in that message, if you will, suggests something of an intelligence maker, rather than something random. So there are patterns to be found in the record itself. The Golden Record cover is inscribed with scientific hieroglyphics, which any self-respecting space-farer will know is a pulsar map. The idea is that we'll have something in common with them, no matter who they are.[46]

Since its launch in 1977, *Voyager 1* and the Golden Record have flown over 13.2 billion miles (over 21 billion kilometers) from Earth, but it is still at the very beginning of its journey. "It has a shelf life of five billion years," notes Druyan. "So, it promises to outlive our tenure on Earth…. As long as it is not intercepted by aliens, it will circumnavigate the Milky Way Galaxy 12 times."[47]

If the mission were to be launched today, Druyan conceded that it would not be as difficult to choose because of technologies that can compress and store information. It would be possible to send every piece of music ever recorded. Nonetheless, Druyan remains extraordinarily proud of what she, Sagan and the *Voyager* team accomplished. "Our choices were made without prejudice—without bias—with a completely open heart."[48]

Music in Deep Space—The Earthling Project

A new project has been created by the SETI: the Earthling Project, which hopes to take advantage of technological advances that were not available at the time of *Voyager*. It will "collect songs from people worldwide to create musical compositions and send them into space." The project is led by Mexican composer-conductor Felipe Pérez Santiago.

Santiago has always been interested in space exploration and has followed the mission of SETI for years. "A series of fortunate coincidences"[49] led to his partnership with SETI and the creation of the Earthling Project. It began when Santiago read that the Icelandic rock band Sigur Rós was visiting Mexico City on tour, and that they were collaborating with the International Space Orchestra, an orchestra made up of scientists from NASA Ames Research Center, SETI and Singularity University. Given the fact that the orchestra was comprised of mostly scientists and not professional musicians, Santiago knew that their quality of music was probably vastly inferior to a professional orchestra. Nonetheless, he thought it was "such a cool idea"[50] that he wanted to work with that orchestra. He hoped to write a piece of music or conduct the orchestra. It would be a great way for him to team his musical talents with his love of space exploration. The problem was, he did not know anyone with SETI or with Sigur Rós.

He began researching online and found the SETI Artist-in-Residence program website. This program intrigued him, but there was very little information available on the site, forcing him to reach out via a phone call and leaving a voicemail. A few days later, he was invited to come to a SETI party celebrating Earth Day. Santiago attended the event and met numerous remarkable people, including celebrated astronomer Jill Tarter, the inspiration for the Ellie Arroway character in Carl Sagan's novel *Contact*.

Dr. Tarter requested that he sit at her table, and invited him to collaborate on a project that "represented humanity." She suggested calling it "Earthling." Tarter wanted to collect the sounds of ordinary people singing from around the world; no matter what their level of training. Santiago loved the idea and began creating "mashups" of the various voices interacting together. Tarter wanted something more ambitious. She asked Santiago to write a symphony that could be combined with the pre-recorded voice mashups.

On December 17, 2020, in the middle of the COVID pandemic, the Earthling Project was officially announced. According to a SETI Institute press release:

> The project will collect 10,000 voices from people who will submit songs through the Earthling Project app. Pérez Santiago will use the submitted pieces to create a composition representing the sounds of humanity. ...Unlike the Golden Record, which curated sounds and images representing Earth's diversity to send to space, the Earthling Project will be an original creation intended to be from all humanity.[51]

The recordings launched with the Peregrine Lander from Kennedy Space Center aboard a United Launch Alliance's Vulcan Centaur rocket in 2024. Peregrine failed soon after launch and was unable to land on the lunar surface.

✳✳✳

Music has been an indispensable aspect of human cultures from the earliest moments of civilization. It has been used and innovated in support of entertainment, religion, ceremonies, communication, social interactions, and diplomacy for thousands of years. Over multiple millennia, it has evolved in innumerable ways from major population areas to remote and isolated portions of the planet. This is likely to occur when humanity truly establishes civilization in space. As astronaut Chris Hadfield observed, "Music evolved as you got to a new cultural and physical location, like how bagpipe music became bluegrass, and how the mix of people in New Orleans created jazz that never would had evolved the way that it did if you didn't bring in the whole cultural mix, but put them in a physically different location."[52] Hadfield is firmly of the opinion that this evolution will continue as humanity leaves Earth, reflecting new cultures as well as the unique environments that space settlers will endure:

> We'll begin to start living on the Moon relatively soon. When we have the first makeshift bar on the Moon and they start playing music there, it's going to be the nascent evolution of what music will be like on another planet. That's what I was thinking of when I was writing music on the spaceship; this is like the start of sea shanties, but in this case; space shanties.[53]

In the short term, however, music plays an unheralded role in uniting space explorers from around the world. They may speak different languages and their countries may have radically contrasting ideological beliefs, but music has the power to transcend these differences.

As more musicians, composers, artists and ordinary people move beyond our home planet, the "sound" of space will no longer be defined by Hollywood, but by the people living, working and performing in space.

Conclusion

"If movies are like lightning, then the musical score for me is like thunder. It can shake things up for years and it can even remain in our memories a lot longer than the films they accompany.... There is no better marriage of mediums than music and movies."—Steven Spielberg[1]

Music has the capacity to capture and articulate the human experience and emotions more than can be expressed in words. In reference to filmmaking, composer Bernard Herrmann explained, "I feel that music on the screen can seek out and intensify the inner thoughts of the characters. It can invest a scene with terror, grandeur, gaiety or misery."[2] Herrmann's statement is supported by innumerable scientific studies regarding the psychology of film music. Annabel J. Cohen, director of the Auditory Perception and Music Cognition laboratory, notes,

> The capacity of music to accomplish the emotional task, arguably far better than the screen itself ... may be based on the ability of music to simultaneously carry many kinds of emotional information in its harmony, rhythm, melody, timbre and tonality. Real life entails multiple emotions, simultaneously and in succession.[3]

The power of these musical works also can transcend filmmaking; to inspire the public and symbolize the exploration of space nearly as much as the spectacular images and footage of our space exploration activities.

This symbiotic relationship between film and music is not unique to space-based films, but the vastness and the majesty of well-produced space epics enable composers to utilize a much larger musical palette and emotional range than most other subject matters (much like the historical, epic, often religious films of the 1950s). As Tim Greiving of the *Los Angeles Times* stated,

> There's something mystical and almost religious about space and the cosmos and the search for the divine. There's mysticism and grandeur and a sense of

awe that lends itself to really great music. It's such a great canvas for a composer. Unrestricted and unlimited because it's often dealing with things that we have never seen or experienced.[4]

According to composer Craig Safan:

> You involuntarily respond to music. It changes your heartbeat. It changes your conductivity of your skin. You can't stop it. You can be cynical and say this is "bullshit," but the music will go beyond that. Your brain immediately responds to music, and you immediately get a dopamine rush from music ... it goes right to the pleasure center of your brain.... Ultimately what it's really doing [in film] is bypassing the part of your brain that's trying to be critical ... that's why there's music in film.[5]

This is true whether the music is attached to a film or television show or played by travelers in space. While ominous and creepy music in a film can manipulate an audience to believe something scary will happen, an uplifting piece of music or a song that is associated with a happy memory can transform the mood and expectations of a film. The same can be said for music in "real" space. The right collection of music has the capacity to elevate the morale and psychological wellbeing of a group of astronauts to great effect. The European Space Agency stated that, "Music can help release a cocktail of hormones that have a positive effect on us: oxytocin, endorphin, serotonin and dopamine. Besides the pleasure we get from it, music can be used to prolong efficiency and reduce anxiety."[6] As such, music may be the most cost-effective remedy to ensure that the women and men on deep space exploration missions remain happy and motivated.

Within motion pictures and television, a well-crafted score can provide subtle and non-subtle insights regarding the plot, characters or other aspects of the production that are not outlined in the film or even the script. According to composer Harry Gregson-Williams, this abstract element is

> something that we wouldn't know otherwise. Perhaps something concerning the unsaid and unseen elements of someone's story or of their location or the environment we see—or maybe an emotion that isn't necessarily evident but that could deepen the richness of a character or place. Music can work in many different ways. Yes, it can reflect what's on screen simply supporting what we see, but it can also work on a more subliminal level. And often that's not noticeable to the viewer, yet it can be a very productive asset and contribution to telling the story at hand.[7]

Musical scores have faced some significant challenges over the past decade, constantly adapting to align with modern films that are in a constant state of flux. Music is in a competition with sound design for aural supremacy more than ever before. The sound of space has also evolved in recent years. While the grand orchestral sounds of John Williams and Jerry Goldsmith have not been discarded, new musical styles—styles to capture the exotic, the alien and even the environment of space—have been on the rise. These new musical interpretations of space have not caused the type of tectonic shift in scoring that occurred when *Star Wars* was released in 1977, but in many cases they are creating a positive evolution. They are expanding the palette from which composers draw, but the traditional orchestra remains at the center of the musical sound of space in film and television.

Despite the challenges of new technologies and changes in how people consume their entertainment, musical scores will almost certainly play a major role in filmmaking and TV as long as these art forms are produced. As Jonathan Frakes explained, this is true for obvious as well as more abstract reasons:

> I think [film music] gets into your soul and I think it's one of the most magical parts of the entire process. To me, it's the most mysterious. I understand everything else about how TV and film are made, but I don't understand how the brilliance of a composer finds what instruments to use, what phrases and melodies. We all know that the power and the emotion that can be created by music is just immeasurable.[8]

Film and television music is one of the most potent ingredients in achieving cinematic and programmatic greatness, but it is also one of the most mysterious elements. Adding the proper musical accompaniment can elevate a flawed movie to heights that would not be conceivable otherwise. It can also raise a good film to the realm of greatness.

Chapter Notes

Introduction

1. "George Lucas Toasts John Williams," *YouTube*, American Film Institute, August 5, 2016.
2. Siu-Lan Tan, "Music and the Moving Image Keynote Address 2015: 'The Psychology of Film Music: Framing Intuition,'" *Music and the Moving Image*, vol. 9, no. 2 (Summer 2016): 23–38.
3. Maurizio Caschetto, "John Williams and the Music of STAR WARS—A Further Step into a Larger Musical World," *John Williams Fan Network*, April 28, 2018.
4. *Score: A Film Music Documentary*, directed by Matt Schrader (Los Angeles: Epicleff Media, 2017).
5. Craig L. Byrd. "John Williams: The Star Wars Interview," *Film Score Monthly*, vol. 2, no. 1 (January/February 1997): 20.
6. *Score: A Film Music Documentary*.
7. Stuart Fischoff, "The Evolution of Music in Film and Its Psychological Impact on Audiences," June 24, 2005.
8. Alex Ross, "The Spooky Fill," *The New Yorker*, May 10, 2010.

Chapter 1

1. Edward Ross Dickinson, *The World in the Long Twentieth Century: An Interpretive History* (2018), 3.
2. Marc Hartzman, *The Big Book of Mars* (2020), 22.
3. *Ibid.*, 23.
4. Marc Hartzman, interview with the author, July 2022.
5. Jon Burlingame, interview with the author, July 2020.

6. Paul Cuff, "Encountering Sound: The Musical Dimensions of Silent Cinema," *Journal of Aesthetics & Culture*, vol. 10, no. 1 (2018).
7. Alissa Wilkinson, "How Georges Méliès' Films Are Still Influencing Cinema, More Than 100 Years Later," *Vox*, May 3, 2018.
8. *Ibid.*
9. Martin Marks, "*Music for a Trip to the Moon*: An Obscure English Score for a Famous French Fantasy," *AMS-NE: New England Chapter of the AMS*, February 4, 2012.
10. Ben Erickson, "L'ASSASSINAT DU DUC DE GUISE—Camille Saint-Saëns," *Movie Music UK*, May 13, 2019.
11. *Ibid.*
12. *Ibid.*
13. Ruth Barton and Simon Trezise, *Music and Sound in Silent Film: From Nickelodeon to The Artist* (2019), 15.
14. Hartzman, *The Big Book of Mars*, 168.
15. "Ashley Miller (director)," *Wikipedia*.
16. Barton and Trezise, *Music and Sound in Silent Film*, 10.
17. Amy Nelson, *Music for the Revolution* (2004), 98.
18. Philip Hayward, ed., *Off the Planet: Music, Sound and Science Fiction Cinema* (2004), 4.
19. "Our Heavenly Bodies," *Wikipedia*.
20. Michael Cowan, "In Depth: Wunder der Schöpfung," *DCA: Dundee Contemporary Arts*, September 1, 2016.
21. David Green, interview with the author, December 2021.
22. *Ibid.*
23. *Ibid.*

24. *Ibid.*

25. *Ibid.*

26. "Ignatz Waghalter," *Wikipedia.*

27. Mitch Waldrop, "Inside Einstein's Love Affair with 'Lina'—His Cherished Violin," *National Geographic*, February 3, 2017.

28. Craig Lysy, "METROPOLIS—Gottfried Huppertz," *Movie Music UK*, May 20, 2019.

29. Emilio Audissino, "Gottfried Huppertz's *Metropolis*: The Acme of 'Cinema Music,'" in *Today's Sounds for Yesterday's Films* (2016), 47.

30. Audissino, "Gottfried Huppertz's *Metropolis*," 49.

31. Hayward, *Off the Planet*, 4.

32. Craig Lysy, "METROPOLIS—Gottfriend Huppertz."

33. *Ibid.*

34. Audissino, "Gottfried Huppertz's *Metropolis*," 53.

35. *Der Film, Berlin*, vol. 12, no. 1, January 15, 1927, 5–6.

36. Bob McQuiston, "Classical Lost and Found: Remaking 'Metropolis,'" *NPR*, July 26, 2011.

37. Audissino, "Gottfried Huppertz's *Metropolis*," 56.

38. Emilio Audissino, interview with the author, September 2021.

39. Ransom Wilson, "A Brief History of Film Music," *Redlands Symphony*, October 24, 2016.

40. Chloé Huvet, "From Europe to Hollywood, and Back. The Classic Hollywood Film Score," *Transatlantic Cultures*, April 2022.

41. Stacia Kissick Jones, "Just Imagine (1930)," *She Blogged by Night*, November 26, 2007.

42. Mathew J. Bartkowiak, ed., *Sounds of the Future: Essays on Music in Science Fiction Film* (2010), 68.

43. Jones, "Just Imagine (1930)."

44. Craig Lysy, "KING KONG—Max Steiner," *Movie Music UK*, October 12, 2015.

45. Steven C. Smith, *The Music of Max Steiner: The Epic Life of Hollywood's Most Influential Composer* (2020), 100.

46. Chris Willman, "Max Steiner Biographer Breaks Down How the 'King Kong' Composer 'Established the Grammar of Film Music,'" *Variety*, June 4, 2020.

47. Smith, *The Music of Max Steiner*, 110.

48. "Steiner King Kong (1933 Filmscore)," *Gramophone.*

49. Craig Lysy, "KING KONG—Max Steiner."

50. Audissino, interview with the author, September 2021.

51. Roger Ebert, "King Kong," *Roger Ebert.com*, February 3, 2002.

52. Hector DeJean, "The Flash Gordon Serials of the 1930s Changed the Face of Sci-Fi," *Tor.com*, August 21, 2019.

53. Stephen Lloyd, "The Film Music of Sir Arthur Bliss," *Classical Music on the Web*, June 2001.

54. *Ibid.*

55. H[erbert]. G[eorge]. Wells, The King Who Was a King: *The Book of a Film* (2017), 90.

56. Craig Lysy, "THINGS TO COME—Arthur Bliss," *Movie Music UK*, August 19, 2015.

57. Hayward, *Off the Planet*, 6.

58. Lloyd, "The Film Music of Sir Arthur Bliss."

59. *Ibid.*

60. Robert Rider, "LSO and Film Music," *London Symphony Orchestra*, 2004.

61. Matthew Riley, 'Music for the Machines of the Future: H.G. Wells, Arthur Bliss and Things to Come (1936),' in *British Music and Modernism, 1895–1960* (2010), 82.

62. *Ibid.*

63. Craig Lysy, "THINGS TO COME—Arthur Bliss."

64. Lloyd, "The Film Music of Sir Arthur Bliss."

65. *Ibid.*

66. Byron Adams, "Sir Arthur Bliss, Things to Come, Suite," *American Symphony Orchestra*, January 31, 2014.

Chapter 2

1. Rebecca Saunders, "Nuclear and Social Anxiety in 1950s Horror Films," *Horror Obsessive*, 2020.

2. William H. Rosar, "Music for Martians: Schillar's Two Tonics and Harmony of Fourths in Leith Stevens' Score for *War of the Worlds*," *The Journal of Film and Music*, vol. 1, no. 4 (2006): 396.

3. Laura Boyes, "The Day the Earth Stood Still," *Movie Diva*, January 2007.

4. Anthony J. Bushard, "Waging the

Peace: Bernard Hermann and *The Day the Earth Stood Still*," *College Music Symposium*, vol. 49/50 (2009–2010): 314–326.

5. Bushard, "Waging the Peace," 314.

6. Anthony D. Collins, "Bernard Hermann's Sonic Influence on Robert Wise's 'The Day the Earth Stood Still' (1951)," *HopkinsCinemAddicts*, September 24, 2012.

7. Craig Lysy, "THE DAY THE EARTH STOOD STILL—Bernard Hermann," *Movie Music UK*, March 20, 2017.

8. Bartkowiak, *The Sounds of the Future*, 116.

9. Jon Burlingame, interview with the author, June 2022.

10. Burlingame, interview with the author, June 2022.

11. James Wierzbicki, *Louis and Bebe Barron's* Forbidden Planet (2005), 7.

12. *Ibid.*

13. *Ibid.*, 27.

14. Donald John Long, "Forbidden Film Score: The Life, Death, and Rebirth for Music for a '50s Sci-Fi Classic," *Film Score Monthly*, vol. 9, no. 4 (April/May 2004): 24.

15. Susan Stone, "The Barrons: Forgotten Pioneers of Electronic Music," *NPR*, February 7, 2005.

16. *Ibid.*

17. Craig Lysy, "FORBIDDEN PLANET—Louis Barron and Bebe Barron," *Movie Music UK*, June 15, 2020.

18. Rebecca Leydon, "*Forbidden Planet*: Effects and Affects in the Electro AvantGarde," in *Off the Planet: Music, Sound and Science Fiction Cinema* (2004), 61–76.

19. David Cooper, "James Wierzbicki: Louis and Bebe Barron's Forbidden Planet: A Film Score Guide," *Journal of Film Music*, vol. 2, no. 1 (Fall 2007): 80.

20. *Ibid.*

21. Leydon, "*Forbidden Planet*, 66.

22. *Ibid.*, 67.

23. Lysy, "FORBIDDEN PLANET—Louis Barron and Bebe Barron."

24. Ian Olney, "Forbidden Planet," Library of Congress.

25. Jeff Bond, interview with the author, December 2021.

26. Thomas Kent Miller, *Mars in the Movies: A History* (2016), 43.

27. *Ibid.*

28. Rosar, "Music for Martians," 400.

29. *Ibid.*

30. Leith Stevens, "Destination Moon [Original Motion Picture Score]," *All Music*.

31. Burlingame, interview with the author, June 2022.

32. Rosar, "Music for Martians," 407–408.

33. *Ibid.*, 409.

34. Steve Rubin, "War of the Worlds," *Cinefantastique*, vol. 5, no. 4 (Spring 1977): 16.

35. Rosar, "Music for Martians," 396.

36. *Ibid.*, 397.

37. Rubin, "War of the Worlds," 9.

38. *Ibid.*, 42.

39. *Ibid.*, 42.

40. Bond, interview with the author, December 2021.

41. Bond, interview with the author, December 2021.

42. "The War of the Worlds," *Variety*, December 31, 1952.

43. "The War of the Worlds (1953 Film)," *Wikipedia*.

44. Audissino, interview with the author, September 2021.

45. *Ibid.*

46. *Ibid.*

47. Bond, interview with the author, December 2021.

48. Burlingame, interview with the author, June 2022.

Chapter 3

1. John F. Kennedy, "Address at Rice University on the Nation's Space Efforts," Rice University, September 12, 1962.

2. Jessica Leah Getman, "Music, Race, and Gender in the Original Star Trek (1966–1969)," University of Michigan, doctoral dissertation, 2015.

3. Lee Thacker, "Fireball XL5: Original Television Soundtrack—Barry Gray—Review," *Set the Tape*, January 20, 2021.

4. John Fordham, "Paul Horn Obituary," *The Guardian*, July 7, 2014.

5. Jon Burlingame, *TV's Biggest Hits* (1996), 247.

6. *Ibid.*, 249.

7. *Ibid.*

8. *Ibid.*

9. David Wharton, "'Jetsons' Revival Brings Limelight to Composer," *Los Angeles Times*, August 26, 1986.

10. Mark Ayres, "Making of the

Doctor Who Theme Music," *Effectrode Thermionic.*

11. "Musique Concrete," *Encyclopaedia Britannica.*

12. David Butler, "Women of the Workshop: The Women Who Shaped the Pioneering Sound of the BBC Radiophonic Workshop," *BBC-The History of the BBC.*

13. Ayres, "Making of the Doctor Who Theme Music."

14. *Ibid.*

15. *Ibid.*

16. "Delia Derbyshire Interview with BBC Radio Scotland, (1997)," *YouTube,* Emma, May 13, 2019.

17. *Ibid.*

18. Amy Mulligan, "Who Really Created the Doctor Who Theme Song?" Spark Museum of Electrical Invention.

19. David Butler, "Delia Derbyshire," *BBC-History of the BBC,* https://www.bbc.com/historyofthebbc/100-voices/pioneering-women/women-of-the-workshop/delia-derbyshire.

20. Adam Blackshaw, "Ron Grainer and Doctor Who: Australian Composer of Iconic Theme Music," *National Film and Sound Archive of Australia.*

21. Ian Jones and Graham Kibble-White, "The Key to Time," *BBC Special Edition: Doctor Who Magazine* (2015), 31.

22. Alexander Walls, "From Electronic Beginnings to Orchestral Splendour: A Comparison of Doctor Who's 'The Daleks' (1963–64) and 'Heaven Sent' (2015)," *Sonic Scope,* October 27, 2021.

23. *Ibid.*

24. Ethan Iverson, "The Music of 'Doctor Who' Makes a Glorious Return to Form," *The New Yorker,* October 24, 2018.

25. Mark Ayers, "Notes from Long Island," *Doctor Who Magazine: The Music of Doctor Who,* BCC (2015), 44.

26. *Ibid.,* 46.

27. "Dudley Simpson (1985)," Doctor Who Interview Archive, September 29, 2009.

28. Iverson, "The Music of 'Doctor Who.'"

29. Walls, "From Electronic Beginnings to Orchestral Spendour."

30. Ron Rodman, "John Williams's Music to Lost in Space: The Monumental, the Profound, the Hyperbolic," in *Music in Science Fiction Television: Tuned to the Future* (2013), 35.

31. *Ibid.*

32. *Ibid.,* 38.

33. *Ibid.,* 39.

34. Burlingame, *TV's Biggest Hits,* 113.

35. Rodman, "John Williams's Music," 39.

36. *Ibid.*

37. Burlingame, *TV's Biggest Hits,* 114.

38. Rodman, "John Williams's Music," 35.

39. Burlingame, *TV's Biggest Hits,* 114.

40. Rodman, "John Williams's Music," 40.

41. Neil Learner, "Hearing the Boldly Goings: Tracking the Title Themes of the *Star Trek* Television Franchise, 1966–2005," in *Music in Science Fiction Television* (2013), 55.

42. Nicholas Meyer, interview with the author, May 2020.

43. Stefan Rabitsch, "Space-Age Hornblowers, or Why Kirk and Co. Are *Not* Space Cowboys," *Networking Knowledge,* vol. 5, issue 2 (September 2012).

44. "Alexander Courage on Writing the 'Star Trek' Theme Song—EmmyTVLegends.org," *YouTube,* FoundationINTERVIEWS, May 5, 2009.

45. "Alexander Courage Pt 4 of 4," *YouTube,* GentleGim, August 18, 2006.

46. *Ibid.*

47. Jeff Bond, *The Music of Star Trek: Profiles in Style* (1999), 66.

48. *Ibid.*

49. *Ibid.*

50. Learner, "Hearing the Boldly Goings," 57.

51. Eddie Deezen, "The Star Trek Theme Song Has Lyrics," *Mental Floss,* July 20, 2018.

52. *Ibid.*

53. David Alexander, Star Trek *Creator: The Authorized Bio of Gene Roddenberry* (1994), 235.

54. Herbert F. Solow and Bob Justman, Star Trek: *The Inside Story* (1996), 185.

55. Jeff Bond, interview with the author, June 2020.

56. Bond, interview with the author, June 2020.

57. Bond, *The Music of Star Trek,* 16.

58. *Ibid.,* 57.

59. "Fred Steiner Interview," *Television Academy Foundation: The Interviews—25 Years,* June 25, 2003.

60. Bond, interview with the author, June 2020.

61. Bond, *The Music of* Star Trek, 35.

62. Mekado Murphy, "Remembering Apollo 11: What to Watch and Listen To," *New York Times*, July 3, 2019.

63. Michael Benson, *Space Odyssey: Stanley Kubrick, Arthur C. Clarke, and the Making of a Masterpiece* (2018), 21.

64. *Ibid.*, 27.

65. *Ibid.*

66. *Ibid.*, 3.

67. Boston Symphony Orchestra Programme, Pierre Monteux Conductor.

68. "Apollo 11 Lift-Off," *BBC Teach*, School Radio.

69. Emil de Cou, interview with the author, January 2021.

70. "What Is It About the Music in Kubrick's 2001: A Space Odyssey That's So Tantalizing?" *WRTI*, May 21, 2018.

71. "Gyorgy Ligeti," *Britannica*.

72. Audissino, interview with the author, September 2021.

73. Christine Lee Gengaro, *Listening to Stanley Kubrick: The Music in His Films* (2012), 93.

74. Alex Ross, "Space Is the Place," *The New Yorker*, September 16, 2013.

75. Gengaro, *Listening to Stanley Kubrick*, 92.

76. Julia Heimerdinger, "'I have been compromised. I am now fighting against it': Ligeti vs. Kubrick and the Music for 2001: A Space Odyssey," *Journal of Film Music*, vol. 3, no. 2 (September 2011).

77. Russell Platt, "Clarke, Kubrick, and Ligeti: A Tale," *The New Yorker*, August 12, 2008.

78. Gengaro, *Listening to Stanley Kubrick*, 76.

79. Eric Norton, "Playboy Interview: Stanley Kubrick (1968)," *Scraps from the Loft*, October 2, 2016.

80. Dan Chiasson, "2001: A Space Odyssey: What It Means, and How It Was Made," *The New Yorker*, April 16, 2018.

81. Ethan Alter, "Why You'll Never See the Missing 17 Minutes from '2001: A Space Odyssey,'" *Yahoo! Entertainment*, May 11, 2018.

82. Jerry Goldsmith interview with Tony Thomas, in *Film Score: The View from the Podium* (1970), 228.

83. Gengaro, *Listening to Stanley Kubrick*, 71.

84. Jon Burlingame, "Liner Notes," *Music for 2001: A Space Odyssey: The Original Score by Alex North* (2009).

85. Benson, *Space Odyssey*, 392.

86. Gengaro, *Listening to Stanley Kubrick*, 78.

87. Benson, *Space Odyssey*, 394.

88. Burlingame, interview with the author, July 2020.

89. Burlingame, "Liner Notes," 1.

90. Gengaro, *Listening to Stanley Kubrick*, 78.

91. "*2001: A Space Odyssey*—Alex North's Unused Soundtrack," *mfiles*.

92. Burlingame, interview with the author, July 2020.

93. Dale Winogur, "Apes, Apes, and More Apes," *Cinefantastique* (1972), 37.

94. Craig Lysy, "PLANET OF THE APES—Jerry Goldsmith," *Movie Music UK*, February 26, 2018.

95. *Ibid.*

96. Burlingame, interview with the author, July 2020.

97. "The Planet of the Apes and Escape from the Planet of the Apes," *Jerry Goldsmith Online*.

98. Winogur, "Apes, Apes, and More Apes," 37.

99. "Planet of the Apes (Soundtrack Album)," *Planet of the Apes Wiki*.

100. Josh Robertson, "Barbarella, Jane Fonda's Horny Sci-Fi Sex Kitten," *Groovy History*, October 11, 2020.

101. *Ibid.*

102. "Barbarella," Roger Vadim (director), Maurice Jarre (composer), 1967.

103. Dan Goldwasser, "Review: Barbarella," *Soundtrack.net*, October 4, 2002.

104. Frank J. Oteri, "Charles Fox: Ready to Take a Chance," *NewMusicUSA*, May 27, 2011.

105. Austin Trunick, "Reissued and Revisited: Eduard Artemiev's Solaris 'Original' Soundtrack," *Under the Radar*, November 13, 2013.

106. Trace Reddell, *The Sound of Things to Come: An Audible History of the Science Fiction Film* (2018).

107. *Ibid.*

108. *Ibid.*

109. Roger Ebert, "Solaris," *Chicago Sun-Times*, December 23, 1976.

110. Perry Fulkerson, "Space: 1999 Worth the Cost?" *Evening Telegraph of St. Petersburg* (Florida), September 5, 1975.

111. Ian Fryer, *The Worlds of Gerry and Sylvia Anderson* (2016).

112. Fryer, *The Worlds of Gerry and Sylvia Anderson*.

113. "*SPACE: 1999*—YEAR ONE: Limited," *The Sound of Vinyl*.
114. Fryer, *The Worlds of Gerry and Sylvia Anderson*.
115. Gary S. Dalkin, "Space 1999 Year 1," *Music Web International*.
116. K.J. Donnelly, "Television's Musical Imagination," in *Music in Science Fiction Television* (2013), 118.
117. "Derek Wadsworth Interview," *Catacombs Reference Library*, December 18, 1997.
118. *Ibid.*
119. Donnelly, "Television's Musical Imagination," 117.
120. *Ibid.*, 116.
121. *Ibid.*, 119.

Chapter 4

1. Emilio Audissino, "John Williams, Star Wars and the Canonization of Hollywood Film Music," in *Il Canone Cinematografico/The Film Canon* (2011), 273–278.
2. "The Mythology of 'Star Wars' with George Lucas," *Moyers*, June 18, 1999.
3. *Ibid.*
4. Emilio Audissino, interview with the author, April 2021.
5. Michael Heilemann, "The Origins and Inspiration of John William's [sic] Star Wars Score," *Kitbashed*.
6. *Ibid.*
7. Alex Ross, "The Force Is Still Strong with John Williams," *The New Yorker*, July 21, 2020.
8. Emilio Audissino, *John Williams's Film Music* (2014), 71.
9. Byrd, "The Star Wars Interview," 18.
10. "George Lucas 1995 Interview with Leonard Maltin—Star Wars Trilogy Bonus Content-HD." *YouTube*, CLK's Music Vault, November 28, 2021.
11. Byrd, "The Star Wars Interview," 19.
12. Chris Malone, "Recording the Star Wars Saga."
13. Alex Ross, "Listening to 'Star Wars,'" *The New Yorker*, January 1, 2016.
14. *Ibid.*
15. *Ibid.*
16. Nicholas Meyer, interview with the author, May 2020.
17. Chris Malone, "Recording the *Star Wars* Saga," 6.
18. Byrd, "The Star Wars Interview," 18.

19. Richard Dyer, "In London John Williams Puts Sound to Lucas's Next Adventure," *Film Score Monthly*, vol. 4, no. 5 (June 1999).
20. Mark Richards, "John Williams Themes, Part 2 of 6: Star Wars, Main Title," *Film Music Notes*, March 9, 2013.
21. Byrd, "The Star Wars Interview," 20.
22. Charles Lippincott, "*Star Wars*—Liner Notes," (1977).
23. Byrd, "The Star Wars Interview," 20.
24. Lippincott, "*Star Wars*—Liner Notes."
25. Caschetto, "John Williams and the Music of STAR WARS."
26. Alex Ross, "A Field Guide to the Musical Leitmotifs of 'Star Wars,'" *The New Yorker*, January 3, 2018.
27. Mark Richards, "John Williams Themes, Part 1 of 6: The Force Theme," *Film Music Notes*, March 2, 2013.
28. Daniel Rosen, "Out of Tune #3: Figrin D'an and the Modal Nodes," *Mic Drop Music*, February 22, 2022.
29. Malone, "Recording the *Star Wars* Saga," 7.
30. Jesse Kinos-Goodin, "5 Things You Didn't Know About the Star Wars Cantina Band (Unless You Are a Total Star Wars Nerd)," *CBC*, December 18, 2015.
31. J.W. Rinzler, *The Making of Star Wars: The Definitive Story Behind the Original Film* (2008), 429.
32. Robert Rowat, "Princess Leia's Theme: A Detailed Analysis," *CBC*, May 25, 2017.
33. Rinzler, *The Making of Star Wars*, 429.
34. "George Lucas Toasts John Williams," *YouTube*, American Film Institute, August 5, 2016.
35. Michael Matessino, Star Wars *Special Edition: The Original Motion Picture Soundtracks*, liner notes.
36. Jeff Russo, interview with the author, September 2019.
37. Burlingame, interview with the author, July 2020.
38. Byrd, "The Star Wars Interview," 19.
39. Paul Scanlon, "George Lucas Wants to Play Guitar as 'Star Wars' Takes a Vacation," *Rolling Stone*, July 21, 1983.
40. Malone, "Recording the *Star Wars* Saga," 7
41. *Ibid.*
42. *Ibid.*
43. Gary Arnold, "Darth Vader's

Surprise Attack," *The Washington Post*, May 18, 1980.

44. Juanjo Molina, "The Music of Star Wars—The Leitmotif and Its Use in 'The Empire Strikes Back,'" *SoundTrackFest*, November 17, 2018.

45. Doug Adams, "Sounds of the Empire," *Film Score Monthly*, vol. 4, no. 5 (June 1999): 24.

46. Andrew Filmer, Sanjiv Indran, and Tan Mei Ying, "Imagery and the Interpretive Canonic Power of the Audience in the Music of Star Wars," December 2018.

47. Doug Adams, "Sounds of the Empire," 22.

48. Charlie Brigden, "How John Williams Struck Back," *Film School Rejects* (FSR), May 21, 2020.

49. Byrd, "The Star Wars Interview," 20.

50. Scanlon, "George Lucas Wants to Play Guitar as 'Star Wars' Takes a Vacation."

51. *Ibid.*

52. Frank Lehman, "How John Williams's Star Wars Score Pulls Us to the Dark Side," *The Washington Post*, December 13, 2019.

53. Adams, "Sounds of the Empire," 24.

54. Lehman, "How John Williams's Star Wars Score Pulls Us to the Dark Side."

55. Lehman, "How John Williams's Star Wars Score Pulls Us to the Dark Side."

56. Charlie Brigden, "The Emperor's New Score," *Film School Rejects* (FSR), August 3, 2020.

57. "Star Wars Oxygen #10: *RETURN OF THE JEDI* Part One," *Rebel Force Radio*, September 16, 2014.

58. Scanlon, "George Lucas Wants to Play Guitar as 'Star Wars' Takes a Vacation."

59. Jonathan Frakes, interview with the author, May 2020.

60. Burlingame, interview with the author, July 2020.

61. Jason Zumwalt, "'Star Wars': How John Williams Helped Created an Epic," *udiscovermusic*, May 4, 2023.

62. Ron Jones, interview with the author, May 2020.

63. Tim Greiving, "'Solo' Hits the Big Screen Minus One Classic 'Star Wars' Moment: The Fox Fanfare," *Los Angeles Times*, May 25, 2018.

64. "Why Do Star Wars Fans Care So Much About that 20th Century-Fox Fanfare?" *Episode Nothing*, April 22, 2015.

65. David Newman, interview with the author, June 2020.

66. Greiving, "'Solo' Hits the Big Screen."

67. Malone, "Recording the *Star Wars* Saga."

68. Emilio Audissino, *The Film Music of John Williams: Reviving Hollywood's Classical Style* (2021), 79.

69. Newman, interview with the author, June 2020.

70. *Ibid.*

71. Tim Greiving, interview with the author, September 2019.

72. *Spielberg*, directed by Susan Lacy (HBO Documentary Films, 2017).

73. *Ibid.*

74. Ray Morton, Close Encounters of the Third Kind: *The Making of Steven Spielberg's Classic Film* (2007), 147.

75. Craig Lysy, "CLOSE ENCOUNTERS OF THE THIRD KIND—John Williams," *Movie Music UK*, May 28, 2018.

76. Morton, Close Encounters of the Third Kind, 82.

77. *Ibid.*

78. *Spielberg* documentary.

79. Morton, Close Encounters of the Third Kind, 147.

80. "Steven Spielberg Talking About the Music of Close Encounters of the Third Kind," *YouTube*, Rob Wainfur, August 18, 2019.

81. Felipe Pérez Santiago, interview with the author, January 2021.

82. Joshua Barone, "'Psycho' and 'Close Encounters' Roll at the Philharmonic," *New York Times*, September 10, 2019.

83. Audissino, interview with the author, April 2021.

84. *Ibid.*

85. Tom Schneller, "Sweet Fulfillment: Allusion and Teleological Genesis in John Williams's *Close Encounters of the Third Kind*," *The Musical Quarterly*, vol. 97, issue 1 (Spring 2014).

86. Schneller, "Sweet Fulfillment," 12–13.

87. Schneller, "Sweet Fulfillment," 12.

88. Lysy, "CLOSE ENCOUNTERS OF THE THIRD KIND."

89. Morton, Close Encounters of the Third Kind, 288.

90. Schneller, "Sweet Fulfillment," 11.

91. *Ibid.*

92. *Ibid.*

93. Timothy Judd, "John Williams'

'Close Encounters of the Third Kind': A Cinematic Tone Poem," *The Listeners' Club*, January 3, 2020.

Chapter 5

1. Stu Phillips, interview with the author, January 2021.
2. *Ibid.*
3. *Ibid.*
4. *Ibid.*
5. *Ibid.*
6. Bear McCreary, interview with the author, September 2019.
7. Phillips, interview with the author, January 2021.
8. *Ibid.*
9. "Battlestar Galactica," editorial review, *Filmtracks*, September 10, 1999.
10. Jonathan Bailey, "The Lawsuit That Set Star Wars Against Battlestar Galactica," *Plagiarism Today*, April 21, 2022.
11. Emmalee Boekweg, "Star Wars V. Battlestar Galactic [*sic*]: Saga of a Fact Question," *Utah Law Student Land*, February 23, 2015.
12. Phillips, interview with the author, January 2021.
13. "When John Williams Visited the Battlestar Galactica Recording Sessions," *John Williams Fan Network*, forum, February 2011.
14. Burlingame, interview with the author, July 2020.
15. Phillips, interview with the author, January 2021.
16. Phillips, interview with the author, January 2021.
17. David Weiner, "'We Never Had an Ending': How Disney's 'Black Hole' Tried to Match 'Star Wars'" *The Hollywood Reporter*, December 13, 2019.
18. *Ibid.*
19. *Ibid.*
20. Craig Lysy, "THE BLACK HOLE—John Barry," *Movie Music UK*, September 11, 2011.
21. Joe Marchese, "Review: John Barry, 'The Black Hole: Original Motion Picture Soundtrack,'" *The Second Disc*, September 6, 2011.
22. Lysy, "THE BLACK HOLE."
23. Ibid.

Chapter 6

1. *The Beast Within: The Making of Alien*, 20th Century Fox Home Entertainment Video, 2003.
2. *Ibid.*
3. *Ibid.*
4. *Ibid.*
5. Charlie Brigden, "The Great Unknown: The Story Behind Jerry Goldsmith's Score for *Alien*," *RogerEbert.com*, May 17, 2017.
6. Mauricio Dupuis, *Jerry Goldsmith: Music Scoring for American Movies* (2014), 48.
7. *Ibid.*
8. *The Beast Within: The Making of Alien*.
9. *Ibid.*
10. Brigden, "The Great Unknown."
11. *The Beast Within: The Making of Alien*.
12. *Ibid.*
13. David Alexander, *Star Trek Creator* (1994), 414.
14. Alexander, *Star Trek Creator*, 413.
15. Craig Lysy, "STAR TREK: THE MOTION PICTURE—Jerry Goldsmith," *Movie Music UK*, June 11, 2018.
16. Dupuis, *Jerry Goldsmith*, 121.
17. "Star Trek The Motion Picture: 20th Anniversary Edition Review," *Jerry Goldsmith Online*.
18. Dupuis, *Jerry Goldsmith*, 125.
19. *Ibid.*, 122.
20. Charlie Brigden, "Looking Back at the Music of 'The Motion Picture,'" *Star Trek*, December 6, 2019.
21. Lysy, "STAR TREK: THE MOTION PICTURE."
22. Jeff Bond, *The Music of* Star Trek: *Profiles in Style* (1999), 88.
23. James Southall, "Star Trek: The Motion Picture," review, *Movie Wave Classics*, 2003.
24. Dupuis, *Jerry Goldsmith*, 122.
25. Bond, *The Music of* Star Trek, 89.
26. *Ibid.*
27. Lysy, "STAR TREK: THE MOTION PICTURE."
28. Southall, "Star Trek: The Motion Picture," review.
29. Dupuis, *Jerry Goldsmith*, 124.
30. Peter T. Chattaway, "Music for Klingons, Part One: Jerry Goldsmith," *Patheos*, May 7, 2013.

31. "Star Trek the Motion Picture," *Jerry Goldsmith Online.*

32. Lysy, "STAR TREK: THE MOTION PICTURE."

33. Nicholas Meyer, *The View from the Bridge: Memories of* Star Trek *and a Life in Hollywood* (2009), 76.

34. Nicholas Meyer, interview with the author, May 2020.

35. Meyer, interview with the author, May 2020.

36. *Ibid.*

37. Meyer, *The View from the Bridge,* 101.

38. Meyer, interview with the author, May 2020.

39. "James Horner Talks STAR TREK II Score," *YouTube,* Pete Saville, May 13, 2009.

40. Bond, *The Music of Star Trek,* 105–106.

41. "James Horner Talks STAR TREK II Score," *YouTube.*

42. Bond, *The Music of Star Trek,* 106.

43. "James Horner Talks STAR TREK II Score," *YouTube.*

44. *Ibid.*

45. Kelly Konda, "Appreciating James Horner's Musical Score for Star Trek II: The Wrath of Khan," *We Minored in Film,* June 23, 2015.

46. Meyer, interview with the author, May 2020.

47. Bond, *The Music of* Star Trek, 108.

48. Meyer, *The View from the Bridge,* 157.

49. Craig Lysy, "STAR TREK III: THE SEARCH FOR SPOCK—James Horner," *Movie Music UK,* August 19, 2015.

50. Randall Larson, "Leonard Rosenman on Scoring Star Trek IV," *Soundtrack! The CinemaScore and Soundtrack Archives,* June 18, 2013.

51. Bond, *The Music of* Star Trek, 119.

52. Larson, "Leonard Rosenman on Scoring Star Trek IV."

53. Bond, *The Music of* Star Trek, 131.

54. James Southall, "Star Trek IV: The Voyage Home," *Movie Wave Classics,* January 29, 2012.

55. *Ibid.*

56. Bond, *The Music of* Star Trek, 131.

57. *Ibid.,* 133.

58. Dupuis, *Jerry Goldsmith,* 125.

59. "Star Trek V: The Final Frontier," album review, *Jerry Goldsmith Online.*

60. Francis Fukuyama, "The End of History?" *The National Interest,* no. 16 (Summer 1989): 3–18.

61. Meyer, interview with the author, May 2020.

62. Cliff Eidelman, interview with the author, December 2021.

63. Meyer, *The View from the Bridge,* 220.

64. Eidelman, interview with the author, December 2021.

65. *Ibid.*

66. Craig Lysy, "STAR TREK VI: THE UNDISCOVERED COUNTRY—Cliff Eidelman," *Movie Music UK,* May 4, 2012.

67. Eidelman, interview with the author, December 2021.

68. *Ibid.*

69. Meyer, *The View from the Bridge,* 225.

70. Eidelman, interview with the author, December 2021.

71. Bond, *The Music of* Star Trek, 141.

Chapter 7

1. Jeff Giles, "When Queen Sailed the Seas of Sci-Fi Cheese with 'Flash Gordon,'" *Ultimate Classic Rock,* December 8, 2015.

2. Brian May's tweets, *Brain News.*

3. Giles, "When Queen Sailed the Seas of Sci-Fi Cheese with 'Flash Gordon.'"

4. Max Bell, "'Flash Gordon': How Queen Soundtracked the High Camp Classic," *udiscovermusic,* December 8, 2022.

5. *Ibid.*

6. Daniel Ross, "Flash Gordon, Queen and the Art of the Rock OST," *The Quietus,* April 27, 2009.

7. *Ibid.*

8. Gary S. Dalkin, "Flash Gordon," Review from *Film Music Web,* January 7, 2000, shared on *HowardBlake.com.*

9. Howard Blake, interview with the author, January 2022.

10. Blake, interview with the author, January 2022.

11. Dalkin, "Flash Gordon," review.

12. Blake, interview with the author, January 2022.

13. Ross, "Flash Gordon, Queen and the Art of the Rock OST."

14. Audissino, interview with the author, April 2021.

15. "The Music of ET, a discussion with John Williams," *YouTube,* Maestro-Sanaboti, March 9, 2012.

16. *Ibid.*

17. Audissino, interview with the author, April 2021.

18. Chris Heckmann, "What Is a Leitmotif? Definition and Examples in Film," Studiobinder, January 30, 2022.

19. Jeff Cummings, "E.T.—The Extra Terrestrial (1982)—Album Reviews (2002 Expanded Edition)," *John Williams Fan Network*, January 28, 2003.

20. Jon Burlingame, "E.T. Turns 30: Williams' Score Soars on New Blu-Ray Release," *The Film Music Society*, October 10, 2012.

21. *Score: A Film Music Documentary.*

22. Craig Lysy, "E.T. THE EXTRA-TERRESTRIAL—John Williams," *Movie Music UK*, July 30, 2018.

23. Burlingame, "E.T. Turns 30."

24. "The Music of ET, a Discussion with John Williams," *YouTube.*

25. *Ibid.*

26. *Score: A Film Music Documentary.*

27. Patricia Read Russell, "Parallel Romantic Fantasies: Barrie's *Peter Pan* and Spielberg's *E.T.: The Extraterrestrial*," *Children's Literature Association Quarterly* (Winter 1983): 28–30.

28. Lysy, "E.T. THE EXTRATERRESTRIAL—John Williams."

29. "The Music of ET, a Discussion with John Williams," *YouTube.*

30. *Ibid.*

31. "The Right Stuff," *Music By John Barry*, February 18, 2015.

32. "Directing Last Starfighter & Writing Escape from New York with Nick Castle// Indie Film Hustle Talks," *YouTube*, Indie Film Hustle Podcast, July 13, 2021.

33. Craig Safan, interview with the author, November 2020.

34. Safan, interview with the author, November 2020.

35. *Ibid.*

36. *Ibid.*

37. *Ibid.*

38. Lawrence Van Gelder, "More Wars in 'Last Starfighter,'" *The New York Times*, July 13, 1984.

39. Safan, interview with the author, November 2020.

40. *Ibid.*

41. *Ibid.*

42. Adam B. Vary, "'Star Trek: The Next Generation': An Oral History," *Entertainment Weekly*, September 25, 2007.

43. Lacey Rose, "The Time Is Now to 'Make People Uncomfortable': Patrick Stewart, Yahya Abdul-Mateen II and The Hollywood Reporter Drama Actor Roundtable," *The Hollywood Reporter*, June 10, 2020.

44. Rick Berman, interview with the author, May 2020.

45. Jeff Bond, *The Music of* Star Trek (1999), 167.

46. Frakes, interview with the author, May 2020.

47. "Rick Berman Interview Part 1 of 7," *The Television Academy Foundation: The Interviews–25 Years*, May 31, 2006.

48. Berman, interview with the author, May 2020.

49. Jay Chattaway, interview with the author, October 2021.

50. Peter Lauritson, interview with the author, May 2020.

51. Lauritson, interview with the author, May 2020.

52. Berman, interview with the author, May 2020.

53. Ron Jones, interview with the author, May 2020.

54. Berman, interview with the author, May 2020.

55. *Ibid.*

56. Jones, interview with the author, May 2020.

57. Chattaway, interview with the author, October 2021.

58. *Ibid.*

59. *Ibid.*

60. *Ibid.*

61. Lauritson, interview with the author, May 2020.

62. Bond, *The Music of* Star Trek, 170.

63. Jones, interview with the author, May 2020.

64. *Ibid.*

65. Chris Hadfield, interview with the author, October 2020.

66. Jones, interview with the author, May 2020.

67. Chattaway, interview with the author, October 2021.

68. Jones, interview with the author, May 2020.

69. *Ibid.*

70. "Star Trek: The Next Generation—The Best of Both Worlds—Parts 1 and 2," Screen Archives Entertainment.

71. Frakes, interview with the author, May 2020.

72. Chattaway, interview with the author, October 2021.

73. *Ibid.*
74. *Ibid.*
75. Jon Burlingame, "'Star Trek: The Ultimate Voyage' Goes Where Few Have Gone Before: The Music of the Sci-Fi Franchise," *Los Angeles Times*, March 25, 2016.
76. Chattaway, interview with the author, October 2021.
77. "40 Years of Star Trek: The Collection—Picard's Ressikan Flute," Christie's, auction closed October 7, 2006, https://www.christies.com/en/lot/lot-4780101.
78. Chattaway, interview with the author, October 2021.
79. Graeme McMillan, "How *Star Trek: The Next Generation* Changed Pop Culture Forever," *Time*, September 26, 2012.
80. Bond, *The Music of Star Trek*, 173.
81. Lauritson, interview with the author, May 2020.
82. Bond, *The Music of Star Trek*, 171 and 173.
83. Chattaway, interview with the author, October 2021.
84. *Ibid.*
85. *Ibid.*
86. Adam Dean, "Star Trek Voyager (Theme)," *Jerry Goldsmith Online*.
87. Robert Picardo, interview with the author, January 2021.
88. *Ibid.*
89. *Ibid.*
90. Berman, interview with the author, May 2020.
91. *Ibid.*
92. *Ibid.*
93. Kevin Kiner, interview with the author, May 2020.
94. *Ibid.*
95. Frakes, interview with the author, May 2020.
96. Berman, interview with the author, May 2020.
97. Craig Lysy, "STAR TREK: GENERATIONS—Dennis McCarthy," *Movie Music UK*, July 3, 2013.
98. Berman, interview with the author, May 2020.
99. Frakes, interview with the author, May 2020.
100. Berman, interview with the author, May 2020.
101. Frakes, interview with the author, May 2020.
102. "Star Trek Tribute to Jerry Goldsmith," *YouTube*, Ulrich Krause, July 18, 2014.
103. Adam Dean, "Star Trek First Contact," *Jerry Goldsmith Online*.
104. Dean, "Star Trek First Contact."
105. Frakes, interview with the author, May 2020.
106. "Star Trek Tribute to Jerry Goldsmith," *YouTube*.
107. Craig Lysy, "STAR TREK: INSURRECTION—Jerry Goldsmith," *Movie Music UK*, September 5, 2013.
108. *Ibid.*
109. Chris Swanson and Jason Needs, "Star Trek Insurrection," *Jerry Goldsmith Online*.
110. Lauritson, interview with the author, May 2020.
111. James Southall, "Star Trek: Insurrection," *Movie Wave*, August 28, 2013.
112. Bond, interview with the author, January 2020.

Chapter 8

1. "082: David Arnold, Composer, 'Stargate' the Movie (Interview)," *YouTube*, Dial the Gate, May 2, 2021.
2. "Babylon 5: 25 Years Later—Is It Still Worth Watching?" *YouTube*, MetaStatistical, December 16, 2021.
3. J. Michael Straczynski, "Music Change from Gathering to," *JMS News*, February 8, 1994.
4. Rudy Koppl, "Christopher Franke: Babylon 5: Messages from Earth—The Interview," EarthTone/Sonic Images Records, December 17, 1992.
5. "Christopher Franke," The Music of Babylon 5.
6. Straczynski, "Music Change from Gathering to."
7. "Christopher Franke," The Music of Babylon 5.
8. *Ibid.*
9. Koppl, "Christopher Franke: Babylon 5."
10. "Christopher Franke," The Music of Babylon 5.
11. Koppl, "Christopher Franke: Babylon 5."
12. "Christopher Franke," The Music of Babylon 5.
13. Koppl, "Christopher Franke: Babylon 5."
14. *Ibid.*
15. Jeff Bond, "More Babylon 5 CDs

Than You Will Ever Need," *Film Score Monthly*, March 3, 1998.

16. *Ibid.*

17. David Arnold, interview with the author, August 2022.

18. *Ibid.*

19. *Ibid.*

20. *Ibid.*

21. *Ibid.*

22. Daniel Schweiger, "Independence Day: An Interview with David Arnold," *Film Score Monthly*, no. 71 (July 1996): 12–14.

23. Arnold, interview with the author, August 2022.

24. *Ibid.*

25. *Ibid.*

26. Schweiger, "Independence Day: An Interview with David Arnold."

27. Arnold, interview with the author, August 2022.

28. *Ibid.*

29. *Ibid.*

30. "082: David Arnold, Composer, 'Stargate' the Movie (Interview)," *YouTube*.

31. Arnold, interview with the author, August 2022.

32. Jeff Bond, "Score: Soundtrack CD Reviews," *Film Score Monthly*, no. 52 (December 1994): 15.

33. Arnold, interview with the author, August 2022.

34. *Ibid.*

35. *Ibid.*

36. Schweiger, "Independence Day: An Interview with David Arnold," 13.

37. "Independence Day: Editorial Review," *Film Tracks*, September 24, 1996.

38. *Ibid.*

39. "David Arnold Wrote Independence Day Theme in a Dream," *YouTube*, Epicleff Media, May 14, 2020.

40. Schweiger, "Independence Day: An Interview with David Arnold," 13.

41. "Independence Day," *Film Tracks*.

42. Arnold, interview with the author, August 2022.

43. *Ibid.*

44. David Read, "Gate Harmonics (Part 1): An Interview with Joel Goldsmith," *Gate World*, November 23, 2006.

45. David Read, "Revelations: An Interview with Jonathan Glassner," *Gate World*, September 10, 2009.

46. Giles Nuytens, "Interview with Joel Goldsmith—Music Composer of Stargate SG1 and Atlantis," *The SciFi World*, March 16, 2006.

47. Glen Morgan, interview with the author, February 2022.

48. *Ibid.*

49. *Ibid.*

50. *Ibid.*

51. Randall D. Larson, "An Interview with Shirley Walker," *Soundtrack Magazine*, vol. 17, no. 66 (1998).

52. Morgan, interview with the author, February 2022.

53. *Ibid.*

54. *Ibid.*

55. *Ibid.*

56. Mark R. Hasan, "3CDs: Space—Above and Beyond (1995)" *KQEK*, February 16, 2012.

57. Larson, "An Interview with Shirley Walker."

58. Morgan, interview with the author, February 2022.

59. *Ibid.*

60. Bear McCreary, interview with the author, May 2022.

61. *Ibid.*

62. *Ibid.*

63. Morgan, interview with the author, February 2022.

64. *Ibid.*

65. David Newman, interview with the author, June 2020.

66. James Southall, "Galaxy Quest," *Movie Wave Classics*, April 28, 2012.

67. Newman, interview with the author, June 2020.

68. *Ibid.*

69. Ford A. Thaxton, "An Interview with David Newman: David Newman on Scoring Galaxy Quest," *Soundtrack Magazine*, vol. 19, no. 73 (2000).

70. *Ibid.*

71. Jordan Hoffman, "'Galaxy Quest': The Oral History," *MTV*, July 23, 2014.

72. *Never Surrender: A* Galaxy Quest *Documentary*, directed by Jack Bennett (2019).

73. *Galaxy Quest: Limited Edition*, soundtrack, La-La Land Records, 2012.

74. Ralph Jones, "The Oral History of *Mars Attacks*, Tim Burton's Misunderstood Sci-Fi Masterpiece," *Inverse*, December 13, 2021.

75. *Ibid.*

76. "Composer Danny Elfman Tells All: Beetlejuice, Batman, The Simpsons

& More | People TV," *YouTube, People,*
November 23, 2017.
77. *Ibid.*
78. Gil Kaufman, "Danny Elfman on
Composing Score for 'Men in Black: International': 'I Get to Visit a World I Love,'"
Billboard, June 6, 2019.
79. "Basil Poledouris: About Starship
Troopers," *YouTube,* Film Music Composer, August 19, 2021.
80. "*Starship Troopers* (film),"
Wikipedia.
81. James Southall, "Starship Troopers," *Movie Wave,* October 17, 2016.
82. "Basil Poledouris: About Starship
Troopers," *YouTube.*
83. Günseli Yalcinkaya, "Cowboy
Bebop Composer Yoko Kanno Reinvented
What Anime Scores Could Be," *Dazed,*
December 3, 2020.
84. Akihiro Tomita, "Interview with
Composer Yoko Kanno," *The Cowboy
Bebop Attic,* November 2014.

Chapter 9

1. Joss Whedon, Serenity: *The Official
Visual Companion* (2005), 10.
2. Whedon, *Serenity,* 30.
3. Craig Edmonson, interview with
the author, October 2019.
4. *Ibid.*
5. *Ibid.*
6. Whedon, Serenity, 30.
7. Edmonson, interview with the
author, October 2019.
8. *Ibid.*
9. *Ibid.*
10. *Ibid.*
11. *Ibid.*
12. *Ibid.*
13. Whedon, Serenity, 17.
14. *Ibid.,* 30.
15. David Newman, interview with the
author, June 2020.
16. *Ibid.*
17. *Ibid.*
18. *Ibid.*
19. *Ibid.*
20. *Ibid.*
21. *Ibid.*
22. *Ibid.*
23. Whedon, Serenity, 38.
24. Ted Gorospe, "Sources: Interview
with Richard Gibbs," *Battlestar Wiki,*
November 25, 2003.

25. Bear McCreary, interview with the
author, September 2019.
26. *Ibid.*
27. *Ibid.*
28. *Ibid.*
29. *Ibid.*
30. *Ibid.*
31. *Ibid.*
32. *Ibid.*
33. *Ibid.*
34. *Ibid.*
35. *Ibid.*
36. *Ibid.*
37. *Ibid.*
38. *Ibid.*
39. *Ibid.*
40. *Ibid.*
41. *Ibid.*
42. James Horner, "Avatar Interview,"
Trailer Addict, 2009.
43. Wanda Bryant, "Creating the
Music of the Na'vi in James Cameron's
Avatar: An Ethnomusicologist's Role,"
Ethnomusicology Review, vol. 17 (2012).
44. *Ibid.*
45. Geoff Boucher, "From the Archives:
James Horner on Creating a 'Sound
World,'" *Los Angeles Times,* June 23, 2015.
46. "Composer James Horner Exclusive Interview-Titanic Live/Avatar Sequels,"
YouTube, HeyUGuys, April 28, 2015.
47. "Behind the Score: James Cameron
on James Horner & Avatar/Score: The Podcast," *YouTube,* Epicleff Media, April 10,
2018.
48. Jon Burlingame, "Steven Price's
Immersive Music for Gravity," *The Film
Music Society,* February 25, 2014.
49. *Ibid.*
50. Mike Ayers, "Secrets of the 'Gravity' Soundtrack," *Rolling Stone,* October 9,
2013.
51. *Ibid.*
52. Jonathan Broxton, "GRAVITY—
Steven Price," *Movie Music UK,* October
8, 2013.
53. "Hans Zimmer—Interstellar Interview," *YouTube,* Elegyscores, February 19,
2015.
54. *Ibid.*
55. *Ibid.*
56. *Ibid.*
57. "DP/30 Interstellar, Hans Zimmer,"
YouTube, DP/30: The Oral History of Hollywood, February 12, 2015.
58. *Ibid.*
59. *Ibid.*

60. *Ibid.*

61. Jon Burlingame, "Hans Zimmer's Interstellar Adventure," *The Film Music Society*, November 6, 2014.

62. "DP/30 Interstellar, Hans Zimmer," *YouTube.*

63. "Hans Zimmer & Christopher Nolan—Interstellar Interview," *YouTube*, Elegyscores, April 6, 2015.

64. Jon Burlingame, "Pipe Organ Has Starring Role in *Interstellar*," *The Film Music Society*, November 14, 2014.

65. Burlingame, interview with the author, June 2022.

66. Maddy Shaw Roberts, "Church organ playing Hans Zimmer's epic '*Interstellar*' theme makes out world feel tiny," *Classic fm*, September 24, 2020.

67. Burlingame, "Hans Zimmer's Interstellar Adventure."

68. "DP/30 Interstellar, Hans Zimmer," *YouTube.*

69. "Interview Michael Giacchino JUPITER ASCENDING," *YouTube*, kinowetter, February 6, 2015.

70. Jonathan Broxton, "JUPITER ASCENDING—Michael Giacchino," *Movie Music UK*, February 13, 2015.

71. "Interview Michael Giacchino JUPITER ASCENDING," *YouTube.*

72. Paul Apelgren, interview with the author, March 2022.

73. Tim Greiving, "Panned by Critics, Sci-Fi Film 'Jupiter Ascending' Reborn as Ballet," WBUR, *Here and Now*, November 2, 2018.

74. Broxton, "JUPITER ASCENDING—Michael Giacchino."

75. "A Dark and Lonely Space," *Pacific Northwest Ballet.*

76. Emil de Cou, interview with the author, January 2021.

77. Gemma D. Alexander, "A Dark and Lonely Space at Pacific Northwest Ballet," *gemma D. alexander*, November 6, 2018.

78. Harry Gregson-Williams, interview with the author, April 2022.

79. *Ibid.*

80. *Ibid.*

81. *Ibid.*

82. *Ibid.*

83. "The Music Of 'The Martian,' Deconstructed," *NPR: All Things Considered*, October 30, 2015.

84. Gregson-Williams, interview with the author, April 2022.

85. *Ibid.*

86. *Ibid.*

87. *Ibid.*

88. *Ibid.*

89. *Ibid.*

90. *Ibid.*

91. *Ibid.*

92. Jonathan Broxton, "THE MARTIAN—Harry Gregson-Williams," *Movie Music UK*, October 9, 2015.

93. Clinton Shorter, interview with the author, October 2019.

94. *Ibid.*

95. Lisbeth Scott, Facebook post, April 19, 2017.

96. Shorter, interview with the author, October 2019.

97. "Music of The Expanse w/Clinton Shorter & Naren Shankar," *YouTube*, TY & That Guy, November 9, 2022.

98. *Ibid.*

99. Shorter, interview with the author, October 2019.

100. *Ibid.*

101. Jim McGrath, interview with the author, November 2019.

102. *Ibid.*

103. Tim Welch, interview with the author, November 2019.

104. Will Harris, "With the Two-Part Episode Identity, The Orville Has Matured into Serious Science Fiction," *The Verge*, May 7, 2019.

105. Jeff Bond, *The World of the Orville* (2018), 11.

106. *Ibid.*

107. Frakes, interview with the author, May 2020.

108. "La-La Land Records Presents: The Music of 'The Orville,'" *YouTube*, La-La Land Entertainment, May 9, 2019.

109. Frakes, interview with the author, May 2020.

110. "La-La Land Records Presents: The Music of 'The Orville,'" *YouTube.*

111. Bruce Broughton, interview with the author, September 2019.

112. "La-La Land Records Presents: The Music of 'The Orville,'" *YouTube.*

113. Broughton, interview with the author, September 2019.

114. *Ibid.*

115. Joel McNeely, interview with the author, April 2020.

116. *Ibid.*

117. *Ibid.*

118. *Ibid.*

119. *Ibid.*

120. *Ibid.*
121. "La-La Land Records Presents: The Music of 'The Orville,'" *YouTube.*
122. McNeely, interview with the author, April 2020.
123. Brian Drew, "Review: 'The Orville' Delivers A Glorious Feeling in 'A Happy Refrain,'" *Trekmovie.com*, February 4, 2019.
124. Gina Levine, "How Dolly Parton's The Orville Season 3 Cameo Happened," *Screen Rant*, August 5, 2022.
125. Seth MacFarlane, Twitter, July 21, 2022.
126. "La-La Land Records Presents: The Music of 'The Orville,'" *YouTube.*
127. Ann Druyan, interview with the author, January 2021.
128. Jacob Shelton, "1980: With 'Cosmos,' Carl Sagan Makes A PBS Blockbuster," *Groovy History*, September 28, 2020.
129. "The Music of Cosmos," *Connolly & Company, LLC.*
130. Druyan, interview with the author, January 2021.
131. *Ibid.*
132. *Ibid.*
133. Roger Ebert, "Dune," *RogerEbert.com*, January 1, 1984.
134. "Dune (1984)," plot summary, *IMDb.*
135. "Dune Score / Hans Zimmer & Denis Villeneuve," *YouTube*, DuneInfo, September 17, 2021.
136. Bill Desowitz, "'Dune': How Composer Hans Zimmer Invented a Retro-Future Musical Sound for the Arrakis Desert Planet," *Indiewire*, October 20, 2021.
137. "Dune Score / Hans Zimmer & Denis Villeneuve," *YouTube.*
138. Jon Burlingame, "Hans Zimmer on 'Dune' Score's Electronic Textures and Made-Up Choral Language ... and His Head Start on Part 2," *Variety*, October 21, 2021.
139. "How 'Dune' Composer Hans Zimmer Created the Oscar-Winning Score," *YouTube, Vanity Fair*, March 17, 2022.
140. "Michael Geiger Voice," geigervoice.com.
141. "How 'Dune' Composer Hans Zimmer Created the Oscar-Winning Score," *YouTube.*
142. "Dune Score / Hans Zimmer & Denis Villeneuve," *YouTube.*
143. Burlingame, "Hans Zimmer on 'Dune' Score's Electronic Textures and Made-Up Choral Language."
144. "How 'Dune' Composer Hans Zimmer Created the Oscar-Winning Score," *YouTube.*
145. Darryn King, "How Hans Zimmer Conjured the Otherworldly Sounds of 'Dune,'" *New York Times*, October 22, 2021.
146. "How 'Dune' Composer Hans Zimmer Created the Oscar-Winning Score," *YouTube.*
147. King, "How Hans Zimmer Conjured the Otherworldly Sounds of 'Dune.'"
148. Burlingame, "Hans Zimmer on 'Dune' Score's Electronic Textures and Made-Up Choral Language."
149. Bear McCreary, Interview with the author, May 2022.
150. Vanessa Armstrong, "Foundation: Bear McCreary Reveals Apple Series' Title Theme," *SyFy*, September 21, 2021.
151. McCreary, interview with the author, May 2022.
152. Jeff Ames, "Halo Interview: Composer Sean Callery Discusses His Score," Comingsoon.net, April 16, 2022.
153. McCreary, interview with the author, May 2022.

Chapter 10

1. "STAR WARS Episode 1—The Phantom Menace: Interview with John Williams," *Film Music on the Web* (UK), April 9, 1999.
2. Laurent Bouzereau and Jody Duncan, "The Making of The Phantom Menace (1999)," *John Williams Fan Network*, June 4, 1999.
3. *Ibid.*
4. "STAR WARS Episode 1—The Phantom Menace: Interview with John Williams."
5. Caschetto, "John Williams and the Music of STAR WARS."
6. Mark Richards, "Celebrating Star Wars Themes, Part 3 of 6: The Emperor's Theme," *Film Music Notes*, November 22, 2015.
7. Audissino, *John Williams's Film Music*, 79.
8. Doug Adams, "Sounds of the Empire," *Film Score Monthly* 4, no. 5 (June 1999): 22–25.

9. Tim Greiving, "Here's Why 'Duel of the Fates' Transcends the *Star Wars* Prequels," *Vulture*, December 13, 2017.

10. Audissino, *John Williams's Film Music*, 79.

11. Caschetto, "John Williams and the Music of STAR WARS."

12. Emilio Audissino, *The Film Music of John Williams: Reviving Hollywood's Classical Style* (2021), 86.

13. "Across the Stars," *Wookieepedia*.

14. Audissino, *The Film Music of John Williams*, 80.

15. Mark Richards, "Celebrating Star Wars Themes, Part 6 of 6: Battle of the Heroes," *Film Music Notes*, December 23, 2015.

16. Kiner, interview with the author, May 2020.

17. *Ibid.*

18. *Ibid.*

19. *Ibid.*

20. *Ibid.*

21. "Kevin Kiner: An Interview with the Star Wars Legend," CineConcerts, April 19, 2021.

22. Kiner, interview with the author, May 2020.

23. *Ibid.*

24. Apinya Wong, "Kevin Kiner's Music Is One of the Best Parts of 'Star Wars Rebels,' and Here's Why," *Cultureslate*, April 10, 2022.

25. *Ibid.*

26. Shazbazzar, "Rebels: Legends of the Lasat and Other Alliterations," *The Star Wars Report*, February 9, 2016.

27. "Disney to Acquire Lucasfilm Ltd.," Press Release, The Walt Disney Company, October 30, 2012.

28. Audissino, *The Film Music of John Williams*, 252.

29. Linda A. Rapka, "STAR WARS: The Orchestra Awakens," *Pull My Daizy*, January 4, 2016.

30. Jon Burlingame, "With 'Rise of Skywalker,' Composer John Williams Puts His Coda on 'Star Wars'" *Variety*, December 18, 2019.

31. *Ibid.*

32. Caschetto, "John Williams and the Music of STAR WARS."

33. "The Sound of a Galaxy: Inside the Star Wars: The Force Awakens Soundtrack," *YouTube*, Star Wars, February 22, 2016.

34. Jake Kleinman, "'Force Awakens' Music Teased a Huge Palpatine Twist in 'Rise of Skywalker,'" *Inverse*, December 26, 2019.

35. Audissino, *The Film Music of John Williams*, 88.

36. Alexandra Svokos, "There Are Major Clues About Kylo Ren Hidden in 'The Last Jedi' Music," *Elite Daily*, December 21, 2017.

37. Alex Ross, "A Field Guide to the Musical Leitmotifs of 'Star Wars,'" *The New Yorker*, January 3, 2018.

38. Apelgren, interview with the author, March 2022.

39. "John Williams—The Maestro's Finale—The Rise of Skywalker," *YouTube*, Z3TO, March 19, 2020.

40. Burlingame, "With 'Rise of Skywalker.'"

41. "John Williams—The Maestro's Finale—The Rise of Skywalker," *YouTube*.

42. Dominic Jones, "Alexandre Desplat Explains Why He Dropped Out of Scoring 'Rogue One,'" StarWarsUnderworld.com, November 21, 2017.

43. Hannah Shaw-Williams, "Star Wars: Rogue One's Composer Given 4 Weeks to Write Score," *Screen Rant*, November 27, 2016.

44. Michael Giacchino, interview with the author, January 2022.

45. Jon Burlingame, "Michael Giacchino Caps Busy Year with 'Rogue One' Score," *Variety*, January 4, 2017.

46. Apelgren, interview with the author, March 2022.

47. Giacchino, interview with the author, January 2022.

48. *Ibid.*

49. Anthony Breznican, "Rogue One: First Listen to Michael Giacchino's Score," *Entertainment Weekly*, December 9, 2016.

50. Anthony Breznican, "Rogue One Composer Michael Giacchino Reveals New Star Wars Music," *Entertainment Weekly*, November 23, 2016.

51. Vann R. Newkirk, II, "What's a *Star Wars* Film Without John Williams?" *The Atlantic*, December 26, 2016.

52. Giacchino, interview with the author, January 2022.

53. Jonathan Broxton, "SOLO—John Powell," *Movie Music UK*, May 29, 2018.

54. Jon. Burlingame, "'Solo' Composer John Powell Reveals His Process for

Tackling a 'Star Wars' Movie," *Variety*, May 24, 2018.

55. Broxton, "SOLO—John Powell."

56. Burlingame, "'Solo' Composer John Powell."

57. *Ibid.*

58. Jon Burlingame, "Composer Takes Music for the 'Star Wars' Series 'The Mandalorian' to a New Universe," *Variety*, November 13, 2019.

59. *Ibid.*

60. *Ibid.*

61. *Ibid.*

62. Ryan Britt, "How an Obscure *Star Wars* Knockoff Inspired the Music of *The Mandalorian*," *Inverse*, October 28, 2020.

63. Zanobard, "The Book of Boba Fett—Soundtrack Review," *Zanobard Reviews*, April 23, 2022.

64. Natalie Holt, interview with the author, June 2022.

65. *Ibid.*

66. Jon Burlingame, "'Obi-Wan Kenobi' Score Has 'Loki' Composer Natalie Holt Balancing 'Star Wars' Heritage with Fresh Touches," *Variety*, May 26, 2022.

67. Holt, interview with the author, June 2022.

68. *Ibid.*

69. *Ibid.*

70. *Ibid.*

71. *Ibid.*

72. *Ibid.*

73. Jonathan Broxton, "OBI-WAN KENOBI—Natalie Holt, William Ross, John Williams," *Movie Music UK*, July 1, 2022.

74. *Ibid.*

Chapter 11

1. "JJ Abrams and Composer Michael Giacchino in Conversation and Q&A (2011)," *YouTube*, Manufacturing Intellect, July 12, 2016.

2. Jon Burlingame, "Composer Michael Giacchino's Summer Crescendo," *Los Angeles Times*, June 4, 2009.

3. Giacchino, interview with the author, January 2022.

4. *Ibid.*

5. Johathan Broxton, "STAR TREK—Michael Giacchino," *Movie Music UK*, May 8, 2009.

6. Michael Quinn, "Michael Giacchino Star Trek Review," *BBC*, May 5, 2009.

7. "Michael Giacchino Talks Scoring Star Trek," StarTrek.com, September 17, 2013.

8. Broxton, "STAR TREK—Michael Giacchino."

9. Russo, interview with the author, September 2019.

10. *Ibid.*

11. *Ibid.*

12. *Ibid.*

13. Jon Burlingame, "Composer Jeff Russo Boldly Takes 'Star Trek: Discovery' into New Musical Territory," *Variety*, September 21, 2017.

14. Russo, interview with the author, September 2019.

15. Burlingame, "Composer Jeff Russo."

16. "Interview: 'Star Trek: Discovery' Composer Jeff Russo," TrekCore, December 8, 2017.

17. "Discovery Composer Russo Talks TOS Theme in Season Finale," StarTrek.com, March 28, 2018.

18. Russo, interview with the author, September 2019.

19. *Ibid.*

20. *Ibid.*

21. *Ibid.*

22. *Ibid.*

23. *Ibid.*

24. Frakes, interview with the author, May 2020.

25. Russo, interview with the author, September 2019.

26. *Ibid.*

27. *Ibid.*

28. Burlingame, interview with the author, July 2020.

29. *Ibid.*

30. Jon Burlingame, "'Star Trek' Franchise Gets Its First Female Composer as Nami Melumad Visits 'Strange New Worlds,'" *Variety*, May 17, 2022.

31. Apelgren, interview with the author, March 2022.

32. Diana Keng, "Star Trek: Prodigy's Nami Melumad Composes the Score for the Future of Which She Dreams," *TV Fanatic*, November 11, 2021.

33. Nami Melumad, interview with the author, March 2022.

34. *Ibid.*

35. *Ibid.*

36. *Ibid.*
37. *Ibid.*
38. *Ibid.*
39. *Ibid.*
40. *Ibid.*
41. *Ibid.*
42. *Ibid.*
43. Mike Poteet, "Star Trek Prodigy Pilot Episode Review: 'Lost and Found,'" Fansided, October 29, 2021.
44. Melumad, interview with the author, March 2022.
45. *Ibid.*
46. *Ibid.*
47. *Ibid.*
48. "Watch Opening Titles for 'Star Trek: Strange New Worlds,'" Trekmovie. com, April 29, 2022.
49. Melumad, interview with the author, March 2022.
50. *Ibid.*
51. *Ibid.*

Chapter 12

1. Santiago, interview with the author, January 2021.
2. "Music of the Spheres," *Merriam-Webster*.
3. "NASA Beam Beatles' 'Across the Universe' into Space," NASA, January 31, 2008.
4. John Carr, "Mars Rover Soundtrack," MIT, January 2004.
5. John Uri, "Space Station 20th: Music on ISS," NASA, May 12, 2020.
6. *Ibid.*
7. Jonathan Hawkins, "The Tragic Triumph of the World's Largest Concert," *New York Amsterdam News*, April 5, 2016.
8. *Ibid.*
9. Hadfield, interview with the author, October 2020.
10. *Ibid.*
11. *Ibid.*
12. *Ibid.*
13. *Ibid.*
14. *Ibid.*
15. *Ibid.*
16. *Ibid.*
17. *Ibid.*
18. Cady Coleman, interview with the author, October 2020.
19. *Ibid.*
20. *Ibid.*
21. "Ian Anderson and Cady Coleman Flute Duet in Space," *YouTube*, Jethro Tull & Ian Anderson, April 8, 2011.
22. Coleman, interview with the author, October 2020.
23. Diarmaid Fleming, "Molloy's Flute to Help Irish Music Breach the Final Frontier," *The Irish Times*, December 15, 2010.
24. Coleman, interview with the author, October 2020.
25. *Ibid.*
26. Frank Culbertson, "Sept. 11, 2001 Video from the International Space Station," *YouTube*, NASA, September 7, 2011.
27. Hadfield, interview with the author, October 2020.
28. Coleman, interview with the author, October 2020.
29. *Ibid.*
30. *Ibid.*
31. *Ibid.*
32. Sian Proctor, interview with the author, November 2022.
33. Sam Burbank, interview with the author, October 2020.
34. *Ibid.*
35. *Ibid.*
36. *Ibid.*
37. *Ibid.*
38. Sam Burbank, Kelly Snook, and Frank Schubert, "Interplanetary Collaborative Music Project," May 6, 2002.
39. Burbank, interview with the author, October 2020.
40. "What Are the Contents of the Golden Record?" Jet Propulsion Laboratory, California Institute of Technology.
41. *Ibid.*
42. Druyan, interview with the author, January 2021.
43. *Ibid.*
44. *Ibid.*
45. "What Are the Contents of the Golden Record?"
46. Michael Haskoor, "A Space Jam, Literally: Meet the Creative Director Behind NASA's 'Golden Record,' an Interstellar Mixtape," *Vice*, April 15, 2014.
47. Druyan, interview with the author, January 2021.
48. *Ibid.*
49. Santiago, interview with the author, January 2021.
50. *Ibid.*
51. "Earthling Project Launches," SETI Institute, December 17, 2020.

52. Hadfield, interview with the author, October 2020.

53. *Ibid.*

Conclusion

1. "Steven Spielberg on Film and John Williams," Facebook post, Seattle Symphony, February 2022.

2. Fischoff, "The Evolution of Music in Film and Its Psychological Impact on Audiences."

3. Annabel Cohen, "Music as a Source of Emotion in Film," in *Handbook of Music and Emotion: Theory, Research, Applications* (2011).

4. Greiving, interview with the author, September 2019.

5. Safan, interview with the author, November 2020.

6. "Music for Space," European Space Agency, May 4, 2019.

7. Gregson-Williams, interview with the author, April 2022.

8. Frakes, interview with the author, May 2020.

Bibliography

Abel, Richard, Rick Altman, and International Domitor Conference. *The Sounds of Early Cinema*. Bloomington, IN: Indiana University Press, 2001.

"Across the Stars." *Wookieepedia*. https://starwars.fandom.com/wiki/Across_the_Stars.

Adams, Bryan. "Sir Arthur Bliss, Things to Come, Suite." *American Symphony Orchestra*, January 31, 2014. https://americansymphony.org/concert-notes/sir-arthur-bliss-things-to-come-suite/.

Adams, Doug. "Sounds of the Empire." *Film Score Monthly*, vol. 4, no. 5 (June 1999): 22–25. https://www.filmscoremonthly.com/.

"Alexander Courage on Writing the 'Star Trek' Theme Song—EmmyTVLegends.org," *YouTube*, FoundationINTERVIEWS, May 5, 2009. https://www.youtube.com/watch?v=BvftpMe97_0.

"Alexander Courage Pt 4 of 4." *YouTube*, GentleGim, August 18, 2006. https://www.youtube.com/watch?v=9oppn9BT6XM.

Alexander, David. *Star Trek Creator*. New York: A Roc Book, 1994.

Alexander, Gemma D. "A Dark and Lonely Space at Pacific Northwest Ballet." *gemma D. alexander*, November 6, 2018. https://gemmadeealexander.com/a-dark-and-lonely-space-at-pacific-northwest-ballet/.

Alter, Ethan. "Why You'll Never See the Missing 17 Minutes from '2001: A Space Odyssey.'" *Yahoo Entertainment*, May 11. 2018. https://www.yahoo.com/entertainment/youll-never-see-missing-17-minutes-2001-space-odyssey-135044817.html.

Ames, Jeff. "Halo Interview: Composer Sean Callery Discusses His Score." Comingsoon.net, April 16, 2022.

"Apollo 11 Lift-Off." *BBC Teach*, School Radio. https://www.bbc.co.uk/.

Armstrong, Vanessa. "Foundation: Bear McCreary Reveals Apple Series' Title Theme." *SyFy*, September 21, 2021. https://www.syfy.com/.

Arnold, Gary. "Darth Vader's Surprise Attack." *The Washington Post*, May 18, 1980. https://www.washingtonpost.com/.

"Ashley Miller (director)." *Wikipedia*. https://en.wikipedia.org/wiki/Ashley_Miller_(director).

Audissino, Emilio. *The Film Music of John Williams: Reviving Hollywood's Classical Style*. Madison: University of Wisconsin Press, 2021.

Audissino, Emilio. "Gottfried Huppertz's *Metropolis*: The Acme of 'Cinema Music.'" In *Today's Sounds for Yesterday's Films*, K.J. Donnelly and Ann-Kirsten Wallengren, eds., 45–63. New York: Palgrave Macmillan, 2016.

Audissino, Emilio. "John Williams, Star Wars, and the Canonization of Hollywood Film Music." In *Il Canone Cinematografico/The Film Canon*, Pietro Bianchi, Giulio Bursi, and Simone Venturini, eds. Udine, Italy: Forum, 2011.

Audissino, Emilio. *John Williams's Film Music: Jaws, Star Wars, Raiders of the Lost Ark and the Return of the Classical Hollywood Music Style* (Wisconsin Film Studies). Madison: University of Wisconsin Press, 2014.

"Avatar Interview—James Horner (2009)." *Trailer Addict*. https://www.traileraddict.com/avatar/interview-james-horner.

Ayres, Mark. *Doctor Who Magazine: The Music of* Doctor Who: *Special Edition*. BBC, 2015.

Ayres, Mark. "Making of the Doctor Who Theme Music." *Effectrode Thermionic*. https://www.effectrode.com/knowledge-base/making-of-the-doctor-who-theme-music/.

Ayers, Mike. "Secrets of the 'Gravity' Soundtrack." *Rolling Stone*, October 9, 2013. https://www.rollingstone.com/.

"Babylon 5: 25 Years Later—Is It Still Worth Watching?" *YouTube*, MetaStatistical, December 16, 2021. https://www.youtube.com/watch?v=ONyf4kcO8Zw.

Bailey, Jonathan. "The Lawsuit That Set Star Wars Against Battlestar Galactica." *Plagiarism Today*, April 21, 2022. https://www.plagiarismtoday.com/.

Baker, Joanne. "The Doctor Who Theme and Beyond: Female Pioneers of Electronic Music." *Nature*, November 16, 2018. https://www.nature.com/.

Ball, Barbara. "Astronaut Formerly of Ridgeway Captured This 9/11 Photo from Space." *The Voice*, September 9, 2021. https://www.blythewoodonline.com/2021/09/astronaut-formerly-of-ridgeway-captured-this-9-11-photo-from-space/.

Barbarella. Roger Vadim (director), Maurice Jarre (composer), 1967. Library of Congress. https://www.loc.gov/item/jots.200013632/.

Barber, Nicholas. "The Film Star Wars Stole from." *BBC*, January 4, 2016. https://www.bbc.com/.

Barone, Joshua. "'Psycho' and 'Close Encounters' Roll at the Philharmonic." *New York Times*, September 10, 2019.

Bartkowiak, Mathew J., ed. *The Sounds of the Future: Essays on Music in Science Fiction Film*. Jefferson, NC: McFarland, 2010.

Barton, Ruth, and Simon Trezise, eds. *Music and Sound in Silent Film: From the Nickelodeon to* The Artist. New York: Routledge, 2019.

"Battlestar Galactica." Editorial review. *Film Tracks*, September 10, 1999. https://www.filmtracks.com/titles/battlestar_galactica.html.

The Beast Within: The Making of Alien. 20th Century Fox Home Video Entertainment, 2003. https://www.youtube.com/watch?v=GUXvJVZzOLk&t=7848s.

"Behind the Score: James Cameron on James Horner & Avatar/Score: The Podcast." *YouTube*, Epicleff Media, April 10, 2018. https://www.youtube.com/.

Bell, Max. "'Flash Gordon': How Queen Soundtracked the High Camp Classic." *udiscovermusic*, December 8, 2022. https://www.udiscovermusic.com/behind-the-albums/queen-flash-gordon/.

Bellis, Richard. *The Emerging Film Composer: An Introduction to the People, Problems, and Psychology of the Film Music Business*. Richard Bellis, 2007.

Benson, Michael. *Space Odyssey: Stanley Kubrick, Arthur C. Clarke, and the Making of a Masterpiece*. New York: Simon & Schuster Paperbacks, 2018.

"Bernard Herrmann's Sonic Influence on Robert Wise's 'The Day the Earth Stood Still.'" *HopkinsCinemAddicts*, September 24, 2012. https://hopkinscinemaddicts.typepad.com/.

"The Best of Both Worlds (expanded soundtrack)." https://memory-alpha.fandom.com/wiki/The_Best_of_Both_Worlds_(expanded_soundtrack).

Blackshaw, Adam. "Ron Grainer and Doctor Who: Australian Composer of Iconic Theme Music." *National Film and Sound Archive of Australia*. https://www.nfsa.gov.au/latest/ron-grainer-australian-doctor-who-theme-composer.

Bliss, Arthur. "Those Damned Films!" *Musical News and Herald*, February 18, 1922.

Boekweg, Emmalee. "Star Wars V. Battlestar Galactic [*sic*]: Saga of a Fact Question." *Utah Law Student Land*, February 23, 2015. https://ut.lawstudentland.com/post/112081931892/star-wars-v-battlestar-galactic-saga-of-a-fact.

Bond, Jeff. "More Babylon 5 CDs Than You Will Ever Need." *Film Score Monthly*, March 3, 1998. https://www.filmscoremonthly.com/daily/article.cfm?articleID=2383.

Bond, Jeff. *The Music of* Star Trek: *Profiles in Style*. Los Angeles: Ione Eagle, 1999.

Bond, Jeff. "Voyage to Utopia." The Orville: *Original Television Soundtrack*. Season 1 Liner Notes, LaLa Records, 2017, 2019.

Bond, Jeff. *The World of the Orville*. London: Titan Books, 2018.

Boston Symphony Orchestra. "Programme: With Historical and Descriptive Notes by Phillip Dale." 1922. http://worldcat.org/.

Boucher, Geoff. "From the Archives: James Horner on Creating a 'Sound World.'" *Los Angeles Times*, June 23, 2015. https://www.latimes.com/.

Bouzereau, Laurent, and Jody Duncan. "The Making of The Phantom Menace (1999)." *John Williams Fan Network*, June 4, 1999. https://www.jwfan.com/?p=4565.

Boyes, Laura. "The Day the Earth Stood Still." *Movie Diva*, January 2007. http://www.moviediva.com/MD_root/reviewpages/MDDayEarthStoodStill.htm.

Brennan, Pat. "To Boldly Go: How 'Star Trek' Inspired NASA's Planet Hunters." NASA, September 5, 2016. https://exoplanets.nasa.gov/news/1385/to-boldly-go-how-star-trek-inspired-nasas-planet-hunters/.

Breznican, Anthony. "Rogue One Composer Michael Giacchino Reveals New Star Wars Music." *Entertainment Weekly*, November 23, 2016. https://ew.com/.

Breznican, Anthony. "Rogue One: First Listen to Michael Giacchino's Score." *Entertainment Weekly*, December 9, 2016. https://ew.com/.

Bribitzer-Stull, Matthew. *Understanding the Leitmotif: From Wagner to Hollywood Film Music.* Cambridge: Cambridge University Press, 2015.

Brigden, Charlie. "The Emperor's New Score." *Film School Rejects* (*FSR*), August 3, 2020. https://filmschoolrejects.com/john-williams-return-of-the-jedi-score/.

Brigden, Charlie. "The Great Unknown: The Story Behind Jerry Goldsmith's Score for *Alien.*" *RogerEbert.com*, May 17, 2017. https://www.rogerebert.com/.

Brigden, Charlie. "How John Williams Struck Back." *Film School Rejects* (*FSR*), May 21, 2020. https://filmschoolrejects.com/john-williams-empire-strikes-back-score/.

Brigden, Charlie. "Looking Back at the Music of 'The Motion Picture.'" *Star Trek*, December 6, 2019. https://www.startrek.com/news/looking-back-at-the-music-of-the-motion-picture.

Broxton, Jonathan. "GRAVITY- Steven Price." *Movie Music UK*, October 8, 2013. https://moviemusicuk.us/.

Broxton, Jonathan. "JUPITER ASCENDING—Michael Giacchino." *Movie Music UK*, February 13, 2015. https://moviemusicuk.us/.

Broxton, Jonathan. "THE MARTIAN—Harry Gregson-Williams." *Film Music UK*, October 9, 2015. https://moviemusicuk.us/.

Broxton, Jonathan. "OBI-WAN KENOBI—Natalie Holt, William Ross, John Williams." *Movie Music UK*, July 1, 2022. https://moviemusicuk.us/2022/07/01/obi-wan-kenobi-natalie-holt-william-ross-john-williams/.

Broxron, Jonathan. "SOLO—John Powell," *Movie Music UK*, May 29, 2018. https://moviemusicuk.us/2018/05/29/solo-john-powell/.

Broxton, Jonathan. "STAR TREK—Michael Giacchino," *Film Music UK*, May 8, 2009. https://moviemusicuk.us/2009/05/08/star-trek-michael-giacchino/.

Bryant, Wanda. "Creating the Music of the Na'vi in James Cameron's Avatar: An Ethnomusicologist's Role." *Ethnomusicology Review*, vol. 17 (2012).

Burbank, Sam, Kelly Snook, and Frank Schubert. "Interplanetary Collaborative Music Project (ICoMP)." May 6, 2002.

Burlingame, Jon. "Composer Jeff Russo Boldly Takes 'Star Trek: Discovery' into New Musical Territory." *Variety*, September 21, 2017. https://variety.com/.

Burlingame, Jon. "Composer Michael Giacchino's Summer Crescendo." *Los Angeles Times*, June 4, 2009. https://www.latimes.com/.

Burlingame, Jon. "E.T. Turns 30: Williams' Score Soars on New Blu-Ray Release." *The Film Music Society*, October 10, 2012. http://www.filmmusicsociety.org/news_events/features/2012/101012.html.

Burlingame, Jon. "Film Composer Michael Giacchino to Premiere Ballet in Seattle." *Variety*, October 22, 2018. https://variety.com/.

Burlingame, Jon. "Hans Zimmer's Interstellar Adventure." *The Film Music Society*, November 6, 2014. http://www.filmmusicsociety.org/news_events/features/2014/110614.html.

Burlingame, Jon. "Liner Notes." *Music for* 2001: A Space Odyssey: *The Original Score by Alex North*. Intrada, 2009.

Burlingame, Jon. "Michael Giacchino Caps a Busy Year with 'Rogue One' Score." *Variety*, January 4, 2017. https://variety.com/.

Burlingame, Jon. "'Solo' Composer John Powell Reveals His Process for Tackling a 'Star Wars' Movie," *Variety*, May 24, 2018. https://variety.com/.

Burlingame, Jon. "'Star Trek' Franchise Gets Its First Female Composer as Nami Melumad Visits 'Strange New Worlds.'" *Variety*, May 17, 2022. https://variety.com/2022/artisans/news/star-trek-first-female-composer-strange-new-worlds-nami-melumad-1235268386/.

Burlingame, Jon. "'Star Trek: The Ultimate Voyage' Goes Where Few Have Gone Before: The Music of the Sci-Fi Franchise." *Los Angeles Times*, March 25, 2016. https://www.latimes.com/.

Burlingame, Jon. "Steven Price's Immersive Music for Gravity." *The Film Music Society*, February 25, 2014. http://www.filmmusicsociety.org/news_events/features/2014/022514.html?isArchive=022514.

Burlingame, Jon. *TV's Biggest Hits*. New York: Schirmer Books, 1996.

Burlingame, Jon. "With 'Rise of Skywalker,' Composer John Williams Puts His Coda on 'Star Wars.'" *Variety*, December 18, 2019. https://variety.com/.

Bushard, Anthony J. "Waging the Peace: Bernard Herrmann and *The Day the Earth Stood Still*." *College Music Symposium*. College Music Society, vol. 49/50 (2009–2010): 314–326.

Butler, David. "Women of the Workshop: The Women Who Shaped the Pioneering Sound of the BBC Radiophonic Workshop." *BBC-History of the BBC*. https://www.bbc.com/historyofthebbc/100-voices/pioneering-women/women-of-the-workshop/.

Byrd, Craig L. "John Williams: The Star Wars Interview." *Film Score Monthly*, vol. 2, no. 1 (January/February 1997): 18–21. https://www.filmscoremonthly.com/.

Caschetto, Maurizio. "John Williams and the Music of STAR WARS—A Further Step into a Larger Musical World." *John Williams Fan Network*, April 28, 2018. https://www.jwfan.com/.

Chattaway, Peter T. "Music for Klingons, Part One: Jerry Goldsmith." *Patheos*, May 7, 2013. https://www.patheos.com/blogs/filmchat/2013/05/music-for-klingons-part-one-jerry-goldsmith.html.

Chiasson, Dan. "'2001: A Space Odyssey': What It Means, and How It Was Made." *The New Yorker*, April 16, 2018. https://www.newyorker.com/.

"Christopher Franke." The Music of Babylon 5. https://musicofbabylon5.com/christopher-franke/.

"Classic FM Partner Orchestras Week: London Symphony Orchestra." *Classic fm*. https://www.classicfm.com/radio/shows-presenters/full-works-concert/london-symphony-orchestra/.

"Close Encounters of the Third Kind." FilmScoreClickTrack, October 2, 2009. https://filmscoreclicktrack.com/close-encounters-of-the-third-kind/.

Cohen, Annabel. "Music as a Source of Emotion in Film." In *Handbook of Music and Emotion: Theory, Research, Applications*, Patrick N. Juslin, ed. (Oxford: Oxford University Press, 2011).

Collins, Anthony D. "Bernard Herrmann's Sonic Influence on Robert Wise's 'The Day the Earth Stood Still' (1951)." *HopkinsCinemAddicts: Blog of the JHU Film and Media Studies Program*, September 24, 2012. https://hopkinscinemaddicts.typepad.com/hopkinscinemaddicts/2012/09/bernard-herrmann-and-the-day-the-earth-stood-still.html.

"Composer James Horner Exclusive Interview-Titanic Live/Avatar Sequels." *YouTube*, HeyUGuys, April 28, 2015. https://www.youtube.com/.

Cooper, David. "James Wierzbicki: Louis and Bebe Barron's *Forbidden Planet*: A Film Score Guide." *The Journal of Film Music*, vol. 2, no. 1 (Fall 2007): 79–81.

Cowan, Michael. "In Depth: Wunder der Schöpfung." *DCA: Dundee Contemporary Arts*, September 1, 2016. https://www.dca.org.uk/stories/article/in-depth-wunder-der-schoepfung.

Cuff, Paul. "Encountering Sound: The Musical Dimensions of Silent Cinema." *Journal of Aesthetics & Culture*, vol. 10, no. 1 (2018).

Culbertson, Frank. "Sept. 11, 2001 Video from the International Space Station." *YouTube*, NASA, September 7, 2011. https://www.youtube.com/watch?v=bxtlzby4YjM.

Cummings, Jeff. "E.T.—The Extra-Terrestrial (1982)—Album Reviews (2002 Expanded Edition)." *John Williams Fan Network*, January 28, 2003. https://www.jwfan.com/.

Dalkin, Gary S. "Space 1999 Year 1." *Music Web International*. http://www.musicweb-international.com/film/2004/sep04/space_1999.html.

"A Dark and Lonely Space." *Pacific Northwest Ballet*. https://www.pnb.org/repertory/dark-lonely-space/.

Davis, Grant. "Disney Plus: Star Wars Movies in 4K and Come with Changes; Han and Greedo's Encounter and the Fox Fanfare Restored," *Star Wars News Net*, November 12, 2019. https://www.starwarsnewsnet.com/2019/11/star-wars-fox-fanfare-disney-plus.html.

Day, Debbie. "Composer Jeff Russo Shares How the Music for That Big *Star Trek: Discovery* Finale Moment Came Together." *Rotten Tomatoes*, February 11, 2018. https://editorial.rottentomatoes.com/.

Dean, Adam. "Star Trek First Contact." *Jerry Goldsmith Online*. http://www.jerrygoldsmith online.com/.

Dean, Adam. "Star Trek Voyager (Theme)." *Jerry Goldsmith Online*. http://www.jerry goldsmithonline.com/s.

Deezen, Edie. "The Star Trek Theme Song Has Lyrics." *Mental Floss*, July 20, 2018. https://www.mentalfloss.com/.

DeJean, Hector. "The Flash Gordon Serials of the 1930s Changed the Face of Sci-Fi." *Tor.com*, August 21, 2019. https://www.tor.com/.

"Delia Derbyshire Interview with BBC Radio Scotland (1997)." *YouTube*, Emma, May 13, 2019. https://www.youtube.com/watch?v=2-Fw5aTz_2I.

"DELIA DERBYSHIRE: On Our Wavelength." Delia Devonshire: Electronic Music Pioneer. http://www.delia-derbyshire.com/interview_boa.php.

Der Film, Berlin, vol. 12, no. 1, January 15, 1927.

"Derek Wadsworth Interview." *Catacombs Reference Library*, December 18, 1997. https://catacombs.space1999.net/main/pguide/wrefidw1.html

Desowitz, Bill. "'Dune': How Composer Hans Zimmer Invented a Retro-Future Musical Sound for the Arrakis Desert Planet," *IndieWire*, October 20, 2021. https://www.indiewire.com/2021/10/dune-hans-zimmer-score-1234673017/.

Dickinson, Edward Ross. *The World in the Long Twentieth Century: An Interpretive History*. Oakland: University of California Press, 2018.

"Directing Last Starfighter & Writing Escape from New York with Nick Castle//Indie Film Hustle Talks." *YouTube*, Indie Film Hustle Podcast, July 13, 2021. https://www.youtube.com/watch?v=B2Qzmt72I70.

"Discovery Composer Russo Talks TOS Theme in Season Finale." *StarTrek.com*, March 28, 2018. https://www.startrek.com/news/discovery-composer-russo-talks-tos-theme-in-season-finale.

"Disney to Acquire Lucasfilm Ltd." Press Release, The Walt Disney Company, October 30, 2012. https://thewaltdisneycompany.com/disney-to-acquire-lucasfilm-ltd/.

Donnelly, K.J., and Philip Hayward, eds. *Music in Science Fiction Television: Tuned to the Future*. New York: Routledge, 2013.

"DP/30 Interstellar, Hans Zimmer." *YouTube*, DP/30: The Oral History of Hollywood, February 12, 2015. https://www.youtube.com/watch?v=jU5rfokh4vw.

Drew, Brian. "Review: 'The Orville' Delivers a Glorious Feeling in 'A Happy Refrain.'" *Trekmovie.com*, February 4, 2019. https://trekmovie.com/.

"Dudley Simpson (1985)." Doctor Who Interview Archive, September 29, 2009. https://drwhointerviews.wordpress.com/category/dudley-simpson/.

Dupuis, Mauricio. *Jerry Goldsmith: Music Scoring for American Movies*. DMG, 2014.

Durwood, Thomas, ed. *Close Encounters of the Third Kind: A Document of the Film*. New York: Ballantine Books, 1979.

Dyer, Richard. "In London, John Williams Puts Sound to Lucas's Next Adventure." *Film Score Monthly*, vol. 4, no. 5 (June 1999). https://www.filmscoremonthly.com/.

Ebert, Roger. "The Black Hole." *RogerEbert.com*, January 1. 1979. https://www.rogerebert.com/.

Ebert, Roger. "Dune." *RogerEbert.com*, January 1, 1984. https://www.rogerebert.com/.

Ebert, Roger. "King Kong." *RogerEbert.com*, February 3, 2002. https://www.rogerebert.com/.

Ebert, Roger. "Solaris." *Chicago Sun-Times*, December 23, 1976. https://www.rogerebert.com/.

Edar, Bruce. "Destination Moon [Original Motion Picture Score]." *All Music*. https://www.allmusic.com/.

"Editorial Review: Star Trek: First Contact." Film Tracks. https://www.filmtracks.com/.

Erickson, Ben. "L'ASSASSINAT DU DUC DE GUISE—Camille Saint-Saëns." *Music Music UK*, May 13, 2019. https://moviemusicuk.us/.

Evans, Charles. "Star Trek: The Next Generation Theme Song Review." Fansides, 2017. https://redshirtsalwaysdie.com/2016/09/29/star-trek-next-generation-theme-song-review/.

Filmer, Andrew, Sanjiv Indran, and Tan Mei Ying. "Imagery and the Interpretive Canonic Power of the Audience in the Music of Star Wars." International Research Symposium 2018, University of the Visual & Performing Arts, Colombo, Sri Lanka, December 2018. https://static.s123-cdn-static-c.com/uploads/3167268/normal_5e70f6c64842e.pdf.

Fischoff, Stuart. "The Evolution of Music in Film and Its Psychological Impact on Audiences." June 24, 2005. https://sscdigitalstorytelling.pbworks.com/f/music_film.pdf.

"Flash Gordon." Howardblake.com. https://www.howardblake.com/music/Film-TV-Scores/524/FLASH-GORDON.htm.

Fleming, Diarmaid. "Molloy's Flute to Help Irish Music Breach the Final Frontier." *The Irish Times*, December 15, 2010. https://www.irishtimes.com/.

Fordham, John. "Paul Horn Obituary." *The Guardian*, July 7, 2014. https://www.theguardian.com/music/2014/jul/07/paul-horn.

"40 Years of Star Trek: The Collection—Picard's Ressikan Flute." Christie's, auction closed October 7, 2006. https://www.christies.com/lot/lot-picards-ressikan-flute-4780101/.

"Fred Steiner Interview." *Television Academy Foundation: The Interviews—25 Years*, June 25, 2003. https://interviews.televisionacademy.com/interviews/fred-steiner?clip=chapter1#interview-clips.

Fryer, Ian. *The Worlds of Gerry and Sylvia Anderson: The Story Behind International Rescue*. Stroud, UK: Fonthill Media, 2016.

Fukuyama, Francis. "The End of History?" *The National Interest*, no. 16 (Summer 1989): 3–18. https://www.jstor.org/stable/24027184.

Fulkerson, Perry. "Space: 1999 Worth the Cost?" *Evening Telegraph of St. Petersburg* (Florida), September 5, 1975. https://catacombs.space1999.net/press/wrefp75cost.html.

Galaxy Quest: Limited Edition. Soundtrack. La La Land Records, 2012. https://lalalandrecords.com/galaxy-quest-limited-edition/.

Gengaro, Christine Lee. *Listening to Stanley Kubrick: The Music in His Films*. London: Rowman & Littlefield, 2012.

"George Lucas 1995 Interview with Leonard Maltin—Star Wars Trilogy Bonus Content-HD." *YouTube*, CLK's Music Vault, November 28, 2021. https://www.youtube.com/watch?v=MviHyksdytk.

"George Lucas Toasts John Williams." *YouTube*, American Film Institute, August 5, 2016. https://www.youtube.com/watch?v=wMWzkYgfiUA.

Getman, Jessica Leah. "Music, Race, and Gender in the Original Star Trek (1966–1969)." University of Michigan, doctoral dissertation, 2015.

Giles, Jeff. "When Queen Sailed the Seas of Sci-Fi Cheese with 'Flash Gordon.'" *Ultimate Classic Rock*, December 8, 2015. https://ultimateclassicrock.com/queen-flash-gordon/.

Giuffre, Liz. "The Australians Who Created the Sonic World of Doctor Who." *The Conversation*, November 19, 2013. https://theconversation.com/the-australians-who-created-the-sonic-world-of-doctor-who-20096.

Goldwasser, Dan. "Review: Barbarella." *Soundtrack.net*, October 4, 2002. https://www.soundtrack.net/album/barbarella/.

Good, Owen S. "If Disney Buys Fox, Does Star Wars Get Its Opening Music Back?" *Polygon*, November 6, 2017. https://www.polygon.com/2017/11/6/16614664/disney-fox-star-wars-music.

Greiving, Tim. "Here's Why 'Duel of the Fates' Transcends the *Star Wars* Prequels."

Vulture, December 13, 2017. https://www.vulture.com/2017/12/heres-why-duel-of-the-fates-transcends-star-wars.html.

Greiving, Tim. "Panned by Critics, Sci-Fi Film 'Jupiter Ascending' Reborn as Ballet." WBUR, *Here and Now*, November 2, 2018. https://www.wbur.org/hereandnow/2018/11/02/jupiter-ascending-ballet.

Greiving, Tim. "'Solo' Hits the Big Screen Minus One Classic 'Star Wars' Moment: The Fox Fanfare." *Los Angeles Times*, May 25, 2018. https://www.latimes.com/entertainment/arts/la-et-cm-fox-fanfare-solo-movie-20180525-story.html.

"Gyorgy Lieti." *Britannica*. https://www.britannica.com/biography/Gyorgy-Ligeti.

Hall, Roger. "Destination Moon (1950)." *American Music Preservation*, November 30, 2012. http://www.americanmusicpreservation.com/DestinationMoon.htm.

"Hans Zimmer—Interstellar Interview." *YouTube*, Elegyscores, February 19, 2015. https://www.youtube.com/watch?v=lyW3WfOW3tM.

"Hans Zimmer & Christopher Nolan—Interstellar Interview." *YouTube*, Elegyscores, April 6, 2015. https://www.youtube.com/watch?v=K7JoiyPvfRI.

Harris, Will. "With the Two-Part Episode Identity, The Orville Has Matured into Serious Science Fiction." *The Verge*, May 7, 2019. https://www.theverge.com/.

Hartzman, Marc. *The Big Book of Mars*. Philadelphia: Quirk Books, 2020.

Hasan, Mark. "3CDs: Space—Above and Beyond (1995)." KQED, February 16, 2012. https://kqek.com/mobile/?p=4301.

Haskoor, Michael. "A Space Jam, Literally: Meet the Creative Director Behind NASA's 'Golden Record,' an Interstellar Mixtape." *Vice*, April 15, 2014. https://www.vice.com/da/article/rgpj5j/the-golden-record-ann-druyan-interview.

Hawkins, Jonathan. "The Tragic Triumph of the World's Largest Concert." *New York Amsterdam News*, April 5, 2016. https://amsterdamnews.com/.

Hayward, Philip, ed. *Off the Planet: Music, Sound, and Science Fiction Cinema*. Bloomington, IN: John Libby Publishing, 2004.

Heckman, Chris. "What Is a Leitmotif? Definition and Examples in Film." Studiobinder, January 30, 2022. https://www.studiobinder.com/blog/what-is-a-leitmotif-definition/.

Heilemann, Michael. "The Origins and Inspirations of John William's [*sic*] Star Wars Score." Kitbashed. https://kitbashed.com/blog/the-score.

Heimerdinger, Julia. "'I have been compromised. I am now fighting against it': Ligeti vs. Kubrick and the Music for 2001: A Space Odyssey." *Journal of Film Music*, vol. 3, no. 2 (September 2011). https://www.academia.edu/.

Hill, Andy. *Scoring the Screen: The Secret Language of Film Music*. Milwaukee, WI: Hal Leonard Books, 2017.

Hoberman, J. "The Cold War Sci-Fi Parable That Fell to Earth." *New York Times*, October 31, 2008. https://www.nytimes.com/.

"hocket." *Britannica*. https://www.britannica.com/art/hocket.

Hume, Paul. "Close Encounters with the Music of the Spheres." *The Washington Post*, December 18, 1977.

Huvet, Chloé. "From Europe to Hollywood, and Back. The Classic Hollywood Film Score." *Transatlantic Cultures*, April 2022 (translated by Larry Kuiper). https://www.transatlantic-cultures.org/.

"Ignatz Waghalter," *Wikipedia*. https://en.wikipedia.org/wiki/Ignatz_Waghalter.

"Independence Day: Editorial Review." *Film Tracks*, September 24, 1996. https://www.filmtracks.com/titles/id4.html.

"Interview Michael Giacchino JUPITER ASCENDING." *YouTube*, kinowetter, February 6, 2015. https://www.youtube.com/watch?v=DjSV1z7qVfE.

"Interview: 'Star Trek: Discovery' Composer Jeff Russo." TrekCore, December 8, 2017. https://blog.trekcore.com/2017/12/interview-star-trek-discovery-composer-jeff-russo/.

"An Interview with Jay Chattaway." *Drinks with Explore Mars*, October 20, 2020.

Iverson, Ethan. "The Music of 'Doctor Who' Makes a Glorious Return to Form." *The New Yorker*, October 24, 2018. https://www.newyorker.com/.

"James Horner Talks STAR TREK II Score." *YouTube*, Pete Saville, May 13, 2009. https://www.youtube.com/watch?v=g-8D6j5LPho.

"Jerry Goldsmith: Composer Apes 1 and 3." *Cinefantastique*, Summer 1972, 37. https://pota.goatley.com/magazines/cinefantastique-summer-1972.pdf.

Jerry Goldsmith interview with Tony Thomas. In Tony Thomas, *Film Score: A View from the Podium* (South Brunswick, NJ: A.S. Barnes, 1970).

"JJ Abrams and Composer Michael Giacchino in Conversation and Q&A (2011)." *You-Tube*, Manufacturing Intellect, July 12, 2016. https://www.youtube.com/watch?v=VRvQOQ1Xp8U.

John Williams Fan Network - https://www.jwfan.com/

Jones, Dominic. "Alexendre Desplat Explains Why He Dropped Out of Scoring 'Rogue One.'" StarWarsUnderground.com, November 21, 2017. https://www.starwarsunderworld.com/.

Jones, Stacia Kissick. "Just Imagine (1930)." *She Blogged by Night*, November 26, 2007. https://shebloggedbynight.com/2007/just-imagine-1930/.

Judd, Timothy. "John Williams' 'Close Encounters of the Third Kind': A Cinematic Tone Poem." *The Listeners Club*, January 3, 2020. https://thelistenersclub.com/.

Kaku, Michio. *The God Equation: The Quest for a Theory of Everything*. New York: Doubleday, 2021.

Kehr, Dave. "'Things to Come' Is a Trip Back to the Retro-Future." *New York Times*, June 28, 2013. https://www.nytimes.com/.

King, Darryn. "How Hans Zimmer Conjured the Otherworldly Sounds of 'Dune.'" *New York Times*, October 22, 2021. http://www.nytimes.com.

"King Kong (1933 film)." *Wikipedia*. https://en.wikipedia.org/wiki/King_Kong_(1933_film).

Kinos-Goodin, Jesse. "5 Things You Didn't Know About the Star Wars Cantina Band (Unless You Are a Total Star Wars Nerd)." *CBC*, December 18, 2015. https://www.cbc.ca/.

Kit, Borys. "Alexandre Desplat Was Originally Slated to Compose the Music for the New Movie. Then the Reshoots Happened." *The Hollywood Reporter*, September 15, 2016. https://www.hollywoodreporter.com/.

Kleinman, Jake. "'Force Awakens' Music Teased a Huge Palpatine Twin in 'Rise of Skywalker.'" *Inverse*, December 26, 2019. https://www.inverse.com/.

Konda, Kelly. "Appreciating James Horner's Musical Score for Star Trek II: The Wrath of Khan." *We Minored in Film*, June 23, 2015. https://weminoredinfilm.com/.

Koppl, Rudy. "Christopher Franke: Babylon 5: Messages from Earth—The Interview." EarthTone/Sonic Images Records, December 17, 1992. http://www.sonicimages.com/Sub/SIR/b5/misc/interview.html.

Larson, Randall D. "An Interview with Shirley Walker." *Soundtrack Magazine*, vol. 17, no. 66 (1998). https://cnmsarchive.wordpress.com/2013/09/13/shirley-walker/.

Lehman, Frank. "How John Williams's Star Wars Score Pulls Us to the Dark Side." *The Washington Post*, December 13, 2019. https://www.washingtonpost.com/.

"Leonard Rosenman on Scoring Star Trek IV: An Interview with Leonard Rosenman by Randall D. Larson." *The Cinemascore & Soundtrack Archives*, 1987. https://cnmsarchive.wordpress.com/.

Levine, Gina. "How Dolly Parton's The Orville Season 3 Cameo Happened." *Screen Rant*, August 5, 2022. https://screenrant.com/orville-season-3-dolly-parton-cameo-scene-explained/.

Leydon, Rebecca. "Forbidden Planet: Effects and Affects in the Electro Avant Garde." In *Off the Planet: Music, Sound and Science Fiction Cinema*, Philip Hayward, ed. (Indianapolis: Indiana University Press, 2004) 61–76.

Lloyd, Stephen. "The Film Music." In *Arthur Bliss: Music and Literature*, Stewart R. Craggs, ed. London: Routledge, Taylor, & Francis Group, 2002.

Lloyd, Stephen. "The Film Music of Sir Arthur Bliss." *Classical Music on the Web*, June 2001. http://www.musicweb-international.com/classrev/2001/June01/BlissFilm.htm.

Long, Donald John. "Forbidden Film Score: The Life, Death and Rebirth of Music for a '50s Sci-Fi Classic." *Film Score Monthly*, vol. 9, no. 4 (April/May 2004): 23–25. https://www.filmscoremonthly.com/.

Lysy, Craig. "The Black Hole." *Movie Music UK*, September 11, 2011. https://moviemusicuk.us/.

Lysy, Craig. "CLOSE ENCOUNTERS OF THE THIRD KIND—John Williams." *Movie Music UK*, May 28, 2018. https://moviemusicuk.us/.

Lysy, Craig. "THE DAY THE EARTH STOOD STILL—Bernard Herrmann." *Film Music UK*, March 20, 2017. https://moviemusicuk.us/.

Lysy, Craig. "DESTINATION MOON—Leith Stevens." *Film Music UK*, October 8, 2014. https://moviemusicuk.us/.

Lysy, Craig. "E.T. THE EXTRA-TERRESTRIAL—John Williams." *Move Music UK*, July 30, 2018. https://moviemusicuk.us/.

Lysy, Craig, "FORBIDDEN PLANET—Louis Barron and Bebe Barron." *Movie Music UK*, June 15, 2020. https://moviemusicuk.us/.

Lysy, Craig. "KING KONG—Max Steiner." *Movie Music UK*, October 12, 2015. https://moviemusicuk.us/.

Lysy, Craig. "METROPOLIS—Gottfried Huppertz." *Movie Music UK*, May 20, 2019. https://moviemusicuk.us/.

Lysy, Craig. "PLANET OF THE APES—Jerry Goldsmith." *Film Music UK*, February 26, 2018. https://moviemusicuk.us/.

Lysy, Craig. "STAR TREK: GENERATIONS—Dennis McCarthy." *Film Music UK*, July 3, 2013. https://moviemusicuk.us/.

Lysy, Craig. "STAR TREK: INSURRECTION—Jerry Goldsmith." *Film Music UK*, September 5, 2013.

Lysy, Craig. "STAR TREK VI: THE UNDISCOVERED COUNTRY—Cliff Eidelman." *Film Music UK*, May 4, 2012. https://moviemusicuk.us/.

Lysy, Craig. "STAR TREK: THE MOTION PICTURE—Jerry Goldsmith." *Film Music UK*, June 11, 2018. https://moviemusicuk.us/.

Lysy, Craig. "STAR TREK III: THE SEARCH FOR SPOCK—James Horner." *Film Music UK*, August 19, 2015. https://moviemusicuk.us/.

Lysy, Craig. "THINGS TO COME—Arthur Bliss." *Movie Music UK*, August 19, 2015. https://moviemusicuk.us/.

MacFarlane, Seth. Twitter post. July 21, 2022, 3:24 p.m. https://twitter.com/SethMacFarlane/status/1550199935844229120.

Malone, Chris. "Recording the *Star Wars* Saga." 2005. https://www.malonedigital.com/starwars.pdf.

Marks, Martin. "*Music for a Trip to the Moon*: An Obscure English Score for a Famous French Fantasy." *AMS-NE: New England Chapter of the AMS*, February 4, 2012. http://ams-ne.blogspot.com/2012/02/winter-chapter-meeting-february-4-2012.html.

Marks, Martin Miller. *Music and the Silent Film: Contexts and Case Studies, 1895–1924.* New York: Oxford University Press, 1997.

"Mars Rover Soundtrack." MIT. http://www.mit.edu/~jfc/MER%20Soundtrack.html.

Matessino, Michael. "A New Hope for Film Music"; "John Williams Strikes Back"; "Return of the Composer." *Star Wars Special Edition: The Original Motion Picture Soundtracks*, liner notes. New York: BMG Entertainment. http://pop-sheet-music.com/.

McClintock, Pamela. "'Star Wars' Flashback: When No Theater Wanted to Show the Movie in 1977." *The Hollywood Reporter*, December 9, 2015. https://www.hollywoodreporter.com/.

McMillan, Graeme. "How *Star Trek: The Next Generation* Changed Pop Culture Forever." *Time*, September 26, 2012. https://entertainment.time.com/.

McQuiston, Bob. "Classical Lost and Found: Remaking 'Metropolis.'" *NPR*, May 26, 2011. https://www.npr.org/.

Meyer, Nicholas. *The View from the Bridge: Memories of* Star Trek *and a Life in Hollywood.* New York: Viking, 2009.

"Michael Giacchino Talks Scoring Star Trek," StarTrek.com, September 17, 2013. https://www.startrek.com/news/michael-giacchino-talks-scoring-star-trek.

Miller, Thomas Kent. *Mars in the Movies: A History.* Jefferson, NC: McFarland, 2016.

Molina, Juanjo. "The Music of Star Wars—The Leitmotif and Its Use in 'The Empire Strikes Back.'" *SoundTrackFest*, November 17, 2018. https://soundtrackfest.com/.

Morton, Ray. Close Encounters of the Third Kind: *The Making of Steven Spielberg's Classic Film.* Montclair, NJ: Applause, 2007.

Mulligan, Amy. "Who Really Created the Doctor Who Theme Song?" Spark Museum of Musical Invention. https://www.sparkmuseum.org/who-really-created-the-doctor-who-theme-song/.

Murphy, Mekado. "Remembering Apollo 11: What to Watch and Listen To." *New York Times,* July 3, 2019. https://www.nytimes.com/.

"Music for Space." European Space Agency, May 4, 2019. https://www.esa.int/Science_Exploration/Human_and_Robotic_Exploration/Music_for_space.

"The Music of ET, a Discussion with John Williams." *YouTube,* MaestroSanaboti, March 9, 2021. https://www.youtube.com/watch?v=OQ5WxSh9Amo.

"Music of The Expanse w/Clinton Shorter & Naren Shankar." *YouTube,* TY & That Guy, November 9, 2022.

"The Music of 'The Martian,' Deconstructed." *NPR: All Things Considered,* October 30, 2015. https://www.npr.org/.

"musique concrète" *Britannica.* https://www.britannica.com/art/musique-concrete.

"The Mythology of 'Star Wars' with George Lucas." *Moyers,* June 18, 1999. https://billmoyers.com/content/mythology-of-star-wars-george-lucas/.

"NASA Beams Beatles' 'Across the Universe' into Space." NASA, January 31, 2008. https://www.nasa.gov/topics/universe/features/across_universe.html.

Nelson, Amy. *Music for the Revolution: Musicians and Power in Early Soviet Russia.* University Park, PA: Pennsylvania State University Press, 2004.

Never Surrender: A Galaxy Quest *Documentary.* Directed by Jack Bennett. Journeyman Pictures, 2019.

Newkirk, Vann R., II. "What's a *Star Wars* Film Without John Williams?" *The Atlantic,* December 26, 2016. https://www.theatlantic.com/entertainment/archive/2016/12/whats-a-star-wars-film-without-john-williams/511631/.

Norton, Eric. "Stanley Kubrick: Playboy Interview (1968)." *Scraps from the Loft,* October 2, 2016. https://scrapsfromtheloft.com/movies/playboy-interview-stanley-kubrick/.

Nuytens, Giles. "Interview with Joel Goldsmith—Music Composer of Stargate SG-1 and Atlantis." *The SciFi World,* March 16, 2006. http://www.thescifiworld.net/interviews/joel_goldsmith_01.htm.

Olney, Ian. "Forbidden Planet." Library of Congress. https://www.loc.gov/.

Oteri, Frank J. "Charles Fox: Ready to Take a Chance." *NewMusicUSA,* May 27, 2011. https://newmusicusa.org/nmbx/charles-fox-ready-to-take-a-chance/.

"Our Heavenly Bodies." *Wikipedia.* https://en.wikipedia.org/wiki/Our_Heavenly_Bodies.

Parker, D.C. "Camille Saint-Saëns: A Critical Estimate," *The Musical Quarterly,* vol. 5, no. 4 (October 1919): 561–577. https://www.jstor.org/stable/738128?seq=15#metadata_info_tab_contents

"The Planet of the Apes and Escape from the Planet of the Apes." *Jerry Goldsmith Online.* http://www.jerrygoldsmithonline.com/.

"Planet of the Apes (Soundtrack Album)." *Planet of the Apes Wiki.* https://planetoftheapes.fandom.com/wiki/Planet_of_the_Apes_(Soundtrack_Album)#cite_note-interview-2.

Platt, Russell. "Clarke, Kubrick, and Ligeti: A Tale." *The New Yorker,* August 12, 2008. https://www.newyorker.com/.

Poteet, Mike. "Star Trek Prodigy Pilot Episode Review: 'Lost and Found.'" Fansided, October 29, 2021. https://redshirtsalwaysdie.com/2021/10/29/star-trek-prodigy-pilot-episode-review-lost-found/.

Quinn, Michael. "Michael Giacchino Star Trek Review," BBC, May 5, 2009. https://www.bbc.co.uk/music/reviews/rfzf/.

Rabitsch, Stefan. "Space-Age Hornblowers, or Why Kirk and Co. Are *Not* Space Cowboys: The Enlightenment Mariners and Transatlanticism of Star Trek." *Networking Knowledge,* vol. 5, issue 2 (September 2012): 27–54. https://ojs.meccsa.org.uk/index.php/netknow/article/view/268/120.

Rapka, Linda A. "STAR WARS: The Orchestra Awakens." *Pull My Daizy,* January 4, 2016. https://pullmydaizy.wordpress.com/2016/01/04/star-wars-the-orchestra-awakens/.

Read, David. "Gate Harmonics (Part 1): An Interview with Joel Goldsmith." *Gate World,* November 23, 2006. https://www.gateworld.net/.

Read, David. "Revelations: An Interview with Jonathan Glassner." *Gate World*, September 10, 2009. https://www.gateworld.net/news/2009/09/revelations/.

Reddell, Trace. *The Sounds of Things to Come: An Audible History of the Science Fiction Film.* Minneapolis: University of Minnesota Press, 2018.

Richards, Mark. "Celebrating Star Wars Themes, Part 3 of 6: The Emperor's Theme." *Film Music Notes*, November 22, 2015. https://filmmusicnotes.com/.

Richards, Mark. "Celebrating Star Wars Themes, Part 4 of 6: Duel of the Fates." *Film Music Notes*, November 30, 2015. https://filmmusicnotes.com/.

Richards, Mark. "Celebrating Star Wars Themes, Part 6 of 6: Battle of the Heroes." *Music Film Notes*, December 23, 2015. https://filmmusicnotes.com/.

Richards, Mark. "John Williams Themes, Part 1 of 6: The Force Theme." *Film Music Notes*, March 2, 2013. https://filmmusicnotes.com/.

Richards, Mark. "John Williams Themes, Part 2 of 6: Star Wars, Main Title." *Film Music Notes*, March 9, 2013. https://filmmusicnotes.com/.

"Rick Berman Interview Part 1 of 7." *The Television Academy Foundation: The Interviews–25 Years*, May 31, 2006. https://interviews.televisionacademy.com/interviews/rick-berman.

Rider, Robert. "LSO and Film Music." *London Symphony Orchestra*, 2004. https://lso.co.uk/orchestra/history/lso-and-film-music.html.

"The Right Stuff." *The Music of John Barry*, February 18, 2015. https://johnbarry.org.uk/index.php/jb7/missing-music/item/78-the-right-stuff.

Riley, Matthew, ed. *British Music and Modernism, 1895–1960.* Burlington, VT: Ashgate Publishing, 2010.

Riley, Matthew. "Music for the Machines of the Future: H.G. Wells, Arthur Bliss and *Things to Come* (1936)." In *British Music and Modernism, 1895–1960*, Matthew Riley, ed. Burlington, VT: Ashgate Publishing, 2010.

Rinzler, J.W., *The Making of* Star Wars: *The Definitive Story Behind the Original Film.* London: Ebury Press, 2008.

Roberts, Maddy Shaw. "Church Organ Playing Hans Zimmer's Epic 'Interstellar' Theme Makes Our World Feel Tiny." *Classic fm*, September 24, 2020. https://www.classicfm.com/.

Robertson, Josh. "Barbarella, Jane Fonda's Horny Sci-Fi Sex Kitten: Facts and Trivia." *Groovy History*, October 11, 2020. https://groovyhistory.com/barbarella-jane-fonda-facts-trivia/10.

Robinson, Kim Stanley. *Antarctica*. New York: Bantam Books, 1997.

Rosar, William H. "Music for Martians: Schillar's Two Tonics and Harmony of Fourths in Leith Stevens' Score for *War of the Worlds*." *The Journal of Film Music*, vol. 1, no. 4 (2006): 395–438.

Rose, Lacey. "The Time Is Now to 'Make People Uncomfortable': Patrick Stewart, Yahya Abdul-Mateen II and The Hollywood Reporter Drama Actor Roundtable." *The Hollywood Reporter*, June 10, 2020. https://www.hollywoodreporter.com/.

Rosen, Daniel. "Out of Tine #3: Figrin D'An and the Modal Nodes." *Mic Drop Music*, February 22, 2022. https://micdropmusic.com/out-of-tune-3-figrin-dan-and-the-modal-nodes/.

Ross, Alex. "A Field Guide to the Musical Leitmotifs of 'Star Wars.'" *The New Yorker*, January 3, 2018. https://www.newyorker.com/.

Ross, Alex. "The Force Is Still Strong with John Williams." *The New Yorker*, July 21, 2020. https://www.newyorker.com/.

Ross, Alex. "Listening to 'Star Wars.'" *The New Yorker*, January 1, 2016. https://www.newyorker.com/.

Ross, Alex. "Space Is the Place." *The New Yorker*, September 16, 2013. https://www.newyorker.com/.

Ross, Alex. "The Spooky Fill." *The New Yorker*, May 10, 2010. https://www.newyorker.com/.

Ross, Daniel. "Flash Gordon, Queen and the Art of the Rock OST." *The Quietus*, April 27, 2009. https://thequietus.com/.

Rowat, Robert. "Princess Leia's Theme: A Detailed Analysis." *CBC*, May 25, 2017. https://www.cbc.ca/music/read/princess-leia-s-theme-a-detailed-analysis-1.5063899.

Rubin, Steve. "War of the Worlds." *Cinefantastique*, vol. 5, no. 4 (Spring 1977): 4–17, 34–46. https://archive.org/details/cinefantastique-v-5-n-4-spring-1977/page/n3/mode/2up.

Russell, Patricia Read. "Parallel Romantic Fantasies: Barrie's *Peter Pan* and Spielberg's *E.T.: The Extraterrestrial*." *Children's Literature Association Quarterly*, vol. 8, no. 4 (Winter 1983): 28–30. https://muse.jhu.edu/article/248258/summary.

Sammon, Paul M. *The Making of* Starship Troopers. New York: Boulevard Books, 1997.

Saunders, Rebecca. "Nuclear and Social Anxiety in 1950s Horror Films." *Horror Obsessive*, 2020. https://horrorobsessive.com/2020/05/15/anxiety-in-1950s-horror-films/.

Scanlon, Paul. "George Lucas Wants to Play Guitar as 'Star Wars' Takes a Vacation." *Rolling Stone*, July 21, 1983. https://www.rollingstone.com/.

Schneller, Tom. "Sweet Fulfillment: Allusion and Teleological Genesis in John Williams's *Close Encounters of the Third Kind*." *The Musical Quarterly*, vol. 97, issue 1 (Spring 2014): 98–131.

Schweiger, Daniel. "Independence Day: An Interview with David Arnold." *Film Score Monthly*, no. 71 (July 1996): 12–14. https://www.filmscoremonthly.com/.

Score: A Film Music Documentary. Directed by Matt Schrader. Los Angeles: Epicleff Media, 2017.

Shaw-Williams, Hannah. "Star Wars: Rogue One's Composer Given 4 Weeks to Write Score." Screen Rant, November 27, 2016. https://screenrant.com/.

Shelton, Jacob. "1980: With 'Cosmos,' Carl Sagan Makes A PBS Blockbuster." *Groovy History*, September 28, 2020. https://groovyhistory.com/carl-sagan-cosmos-pbs-1980/6.

Smith, Steven C. *The Music of Max Steiner: The Epic Life of Hollywood's Most Influential Composer*. New York: Oxford University Press, 2020.

Solow, Herbert F., and Robert H. Justman. *Inside* Star Trek: *The Real Story*. New York: Pocket Books, 1996.

"The Sound of a Galaxy: Inside the Star Wars: The Force Awakens Soundtrack." *YouTube*, Star Wars, February 22, 2016. https://www.youtube.com/watch?v=5cPvY17ZdFM.

Southall, James. "Galaxy Quest." *Movie Wave Classics*, April 28, 2012. http://www.movie-wave.net/.

Southall, James. "The Right Stuff: Spectacular, Heroic, Oscar-Winning Adventure Score." *Movie Wave Classics*. http://www.movie-wave.net/

Southall, James. "Star Trek: Insurrection." *Movie Wave*, August 28, 2013. http://www.movie-wave.net/.

Southall, James. "Star Trek: The Motion Picture." *Movie Wave Classics*, 2003. http://www.movie-wave.net/.

Southall, James. "Star Trek IV: The Voyage Home." *Movie Wave Classics*, January 29, 2012. http://www.movie-wave.net/.

"SPACE: 1999—YEAR ONE: Limited Edition Luna." The Sound of Vinyl, 2021. https://thesoundofvinyl.com/*/New-Vinyl-Today/SPACE-1999-YEAR-ONE-Limited-Edition-Luna-White-Vinyl-2LP/71EL146P000.

"Space Station 20th: Music on ISS." NASA, May 12, 2020. https://www.nasa.gov/feature/space-station-20th-music-on-iss.

Spielberg. Directed by Susan Lacy. HBO Documentary Films, 2017.

"Steven Spielberg Talking About the Music of Close Encounters of the Third Kind." *YouTube*, Rob Wainfur, August 18, 2019. https://www.youtube.com/watch?v=tW5CnwnRisE.

"Star Trek: The Motion Picture: 20th Anniversary Edition Review." *Jerry Goldsmith Online*. http://www.jerrygoldsmithonline.com/.

"Star Trek V: The Final Frontier," album review. *Jerry Goldsmith Online*. http://www.jerrygoldsmithonline.com/.

"Star Trek Tribute to Jerry Goldsmith." *YouTube*, Ulrich Krause, July 18, 2014. https://www.youtube.com/watch?v=1pKdXAU-Y_0.

"Star Trek's Four Composers on Scoring 26 Seasons of Trek Television." SyFy.com. https://www.syfy.com/.

"STAR WARS Episode 1—The Phantom Menace: Interview with John Williams." *Film Music on the Web* (UK), April 9, 1999. http://www.musicweb-international.com/.

"Star Wars Oxygen #10: RETURN OF THE JEDI Part One." *Rebel Force Radio*, September 16, 2014. https://www.rebelforceradio.com/shows/2015/10/1/star-wars-oxygen-vol-10.

"Steiner King Kong (1933 Flimscore)." *Gramophone*. https://www.gramophone.co.uk/.
Stone, Susan. "The Barrons: Forgotten Pioneers of Electronic Music." *NPR*, February 7, 2005. https://www.npr.org/.
Straczynski, J. Michael. "Music Change from Gathering to." *JMS News*, February 8, 1994. https://web.archive.org/web/20201028174040/http://jmsnews.com/messages/message?id=19189.
Svejda, Jim. "Interview with John Williams." *KUSC*, February 16, 2018. https://media.kusc.org/.
Svokos, Alexandra. "There Are Major Clues About Kylo Ren Hidden in 'The Last Jedi' Music." *Elite Daily*, December 21, 2017. https://www.elitedaily.com/.
Swanson, Chris, and Jason Needs. "Star Trek Insurrection." *Jerry Goldsmith Online*. http://www.jerrygoldsmithonline.com/star_trek_insurrection_review.htm.
Tan, Siu-Lan. "Music and the Moving Image Keynote Address 2015: 'The Psychology of Film Music: Framing Intuition.'" *Music and the Moving Image*, vol. 9, no. 2 (Summer 2016): 23–38.
Thacker, Lee. "Fireball XL5: Original Television Soundtrack—Barry Gray—Review." *Set the Tape*, January 20, 2021. https://setthetape.com/.
Thaxton, Ford. A. "An Interview with David Newman: David Newman on Scoring Galaxy Quest." *Soundtrack Magazine* vol. 19, no. 73 (2000). https://cnmsarchive.wordpress.com/2013/06/23/david-newman-on-scoring-galaxy-quest/.
Thornton, Daniel. "Star Wars Soundtracks: The Worship Music of John Williams." *The Journal of Religion and Popular Culture*, vol. 31, no. 1 (Spring 2019).
Tomita, Akihiro. "Interview with Composer Yoko Kanno." *The Cowboy Bebop Attic*, November 2014. http://bebopattic.weebly.com/.
"Transcript: Brian 'Flash Gordon' Interview for the The Web Show Pt 1 and 2." *Brianmay.com*, September 1, 2020. https://brianmay.com/brian-news/2020/09/transcript-brian-flash-gordon-interview-for-the-web-show-pt-1/.
Trunick, Austin. "Reissued and Revisited: Eduard Artemiev's Solaris 'Original' Soundtrack." November 13, 2013. https://undertheradarmag.com//
Turner, Stephen Davis. "Of Sharks and Spaceships: The Role of the Tuba in John Williams's Film Scores for *Jaws* and *Close Encounters of the Third Kind*." PhD Dissertation, University of Nevada, Las Vegas, May 2017.
"2001: A Space Odyssey—Alex North's Unused Soundtrack." *mfiles*. https://www.mfiles.co.uk/reviews/alex-norths-2001-a-space-odyssey.htm.
Vanderbilt, Mike. "Read This: In 1977, 20th Century Fox Had a Disturbing Lack of Faith in *Star Wars*." *AV Club*, December 10, 2015. https://www.avclub.com/.
Van Gelder, Lawrence. "More Wars in 'Last Starfighter.'" *The New York Times*, July 13, 1984. https://www.nytimes.com/.
Vary, Adam B. "'Star Trek: The Next Generation': An Oral History." *Entertainment Weekly*, September 25, 2007. https://ew.com/.
Waldrop, Mitch. "Inside Einstein's Love Affair with 'Lina'—His Cherished Violin." *National Geographic*, February 3, 2017. https://www.nationalgeographic.com/.
Walls, Alexander. "From Electronic Beginnings to Orchestral Splendour: A Comparison of Doctor Who's 'The Daleks' (1963–64) and 'Heaven Sent' (2015)." *Sonic Scope*, October 27, 2021. https://www.sonicscope.org/pub/lsyp62wj/release/3.
"Watch Opening Titles for 'Star Trek: Strange New Worlds.'" Trekmovie.com, April 29, 2022. https://trekmovie.com/2022/04/29/watch-opening-titles-for-star-trek-strange-new-worlds/.
Weiner, David. "'We Never Had an Ending': How Disney's 'Black Hole' Tried to Match 'Star Wars,' *The Hollywood Reporter*, December 13, 2019. https://www.hollywoodreporter.com/.
Wells, H[erbert]. G[eorge]. *The King Who Was a King: The Book of a Film*. Warsaw: Ventigo Media, 2017.
Westfahl, Gary. *The Spacesuit Film; A History, 1918–1969*. Jefferson, NC: McFarland, 2012.
Wharton, David. "'Jetsons' Revival Brings Limelight to Composer." *Los Angeles Times*, August 26, 1986. https://www.latimes.com/.
"What Are the Contents of the Golden Record?" Jet Propulsion Laboratory,

California Institute of Technology. https://voyager.jpl.nasa.gov/golden-record/whats-on-the-record/.

"What Is It About the Music in Kubrick's 2001: A Space Odyssey That's So Tantalizing?" *WRTI*, May 21, 2018. https://www.wrti.org/.

Whedon, Joss. Serenity: *The Official Visual Companion*. London: Titan Books, 2005.

"When John Williams Visited the Battlestar Galactica Recording Sessions." *John Williams Fan Network*: Forum, February 2011. https://www.jwfan.com/.

"Why Do Star Wars Fans Care So Much About that 20th Century-Fox Fanfare?" *Episode Nothing*, April 22, 2015. http://episodenothing.blogspot.com/2015/04/why-do-star-wars-fans-care-so-much.html.

Wierzbicki, James. *Louis and Bebe Barron's Forbidden Planet: A Film Score Guide*. Lanham, MD: Scarecrow Press, 2005.

Wilkinson, Alisson. "How Georges Méliès' Films Are Still Influencing Cinema, More Than 100 Years Later." *Vox*, May 3, 2018. https://www.vox.com/.

Willman, Chris. "Max Steiner Biographer Breaks Down How the 'King Kong' Composer 'Established the Grammar of Film Music.'" *Variety*, January 4, 2020. https://variety.com/.

Wilson, Ransom. "A Brief History of Film Music." *Redlands Symphony*, October 24, 2016. https://www.redlandssymphony.com/articles/a-brief-history-of-film-music.

Wong, Apinya. "Kevin Kiner's Music Is One of the Best Parts of 'Star Wars Rebels' and Here's Why." *Cultureslate*, April 10, 2022. https://www.cultureslate.com/.

Yalcinkaya, Günseli. "Cowboy Bebop Composer Yoko Kanno Reinvented What Anime Scores Could Be." *Dazed*, December 3, 2020. https://www.dazeddigital.com/.

Zanobard. "The Book of Boba Fett—Soundtrack Review." *Zanobard Reviews*, April 23, 2022. https://zanobardreviews.com/2022/01/23/the-book-of-boba-fett-soundtrack-review/.

"082: David Arnold, Composer, 'Stargate' the Movie (Interview)." *YouTube*, Dial the Gate, May 2, 2021. https://www.youtube.com/watch?v=FBz3qfeM9Pk.

Zumwalt, Jason. "'Star Wars': How John Williams Helped Created an Epic." *udiscovermusic*, May 4, 2023. https://www.udiscovermusic.com/.

Interviews

Paul Apelgren (music editor)
David Arnold (composer)
Emilio Audissino (film music expert)
Rick Berman (producer)
Howard Blake (composer)
Jeff Bond (author)
Bruce Broughton (composer)
Sam Burbank (documentary filmmaker)
Jon Burlingame (journalist)
Jay Chattaway (composer)
Cady Coleman (American astronaut)
Emil de Cou (conductor)
Ann Druyan (writer, producer, director)
Greg Edmonson (composer)
Cliff Eidelman (composer)
Jonathan Frakes (actor-director)
Justin Freer (producer-conductor)
Michael Giacchino (composer)
David Green (grandson and archivist of composer Ignatz Waghalter)
Harry Gregson-Williams (composer)
Tim Greiving (journalist)

Chris Hadfield (Canadian astronaut)
Natalie Holt (composer)
Ron Jones (composer)
Kevin Kiner (composer)
Peter Lauritson (producer)
Dennis McCarthy (composer)
Bear McCreary (composer)
Jim McGrath (composer)
Joel McNeely (composer)
Nami Melumad (composer)
Nicholas Meyer (director, author, screenwriter)
Glen Morgan (producer)
David Newman (composer)
Robert Picardo (actor)
Stu Phillips (composer)
Jeff Russo (composer)
Craig Safan (composer)
Felipe Pérez Santiago (composer-conductor)
Clinton Shorter (composer)
Neil deGrasse Tyson (astrophysicist)
Tim Welch (composer)

Index

Numbers in **bold italics** indicate pages with illustrations